Negotiating the Industrial Metaverse

Negotiating the Industrial Metaverse

A Legal Guide to Industry 4.0

Jacqueline Watts

Contributors
Gordon Brebner
Omer Guy
Colin Paterson
Paul Schwartfeger

BLOOMSBURY PROFESSIONAL
Bloomsbury Publishing Plc
50 Bedford Square, London, WC1B 3DP, UK
1385 Broadway, New York, 10018, USA
Bloomsbury Publishing Ireland Ltd
29 Earlsfort Terrace, Dublin 2, D02 AY28, Ireland

First published in Great Britain 2026

1

British Library Cataloguing-in-Publication Data

A catalogue record for this book is available from the British Library.

ISBN:	PB:	978-1-52653-292-3
	Epdf:	978-1-52653-294-7
	Epub:	978-1-52653-293-0

Typeset by Evolution Design and Digital (Kent)
Printed and bound by TJ Books, Padstow

FSC www.fsc.org MIX Paper | Supporting responsible forestry FSC® C013056

For product safety related questions contact productsafety@bloomsbury.com

To find out more about our authors and books visit www.bloomsburyprofessional.com. Here you will find extracts, author information, details of forthcoming events and the option to sign up for our newsletters

Dedication

This book is dedicated to my wonderful family. Thank you to my son, Matthew, whose wonder and curiosity reminds me every day why this work matters and what an amazing world we live in; To my amazing husband, Danny, who stands by my side, always giving me the love and support to make this all possible; To my mum and dad, for your unwavering belief in me; and to my nephews, Carter and Cian, and niece, Caila, who will all grow up in this brave new digital world.

This book is dedicated to you all, with love and gratitude, and is also in loving memory of Jean Halliday, my devoted grandmother, who passed peacefully during the writing of this book at 95 years old.

Preface

> *'This is only a foretaste of what is to come and only the shadow of what is going to be'*[1]
>
> *Alan Turing*

The digital revolution is already upon us and it is imperative that lawyers keep pace with these changes and the impacts of the same.

This book looks at some of the key legal topics impacting the digital revolution of Industry 4.0 and its regulation. It is impossible for a book of this nature to keep pace with the evolving legal changes we are already witnessing in this space. Instead, it sets the scene, and lays the foundations to be able to successfully navigate a new time, with its new opportunities and risks.

Over the last decade my work has increasingly focused on helping innovators understand the risks, make informed decisions and build technology responsibly. I hope that this book encourages its readers to critically examine these new frontier technologies which are redefining industry; to consider how these technologies should be regulated; where we can lean into the already established fundamental principles which underpin our legal and justice system, and where this is simply impossible or undesirable to do so.

My aim is to encourage the readers to question how legal concepts should apply in this new age; to examine whether these new technologies fundamentally alter the underlying rationale behind the law thus requiring legislative change, or whether it is just merely a sophisticated tool that should not obliterate established legal precedent.

Law is fundamentally rooted in society, and its protection of people, whether that is harm to their body, their property, their enjoyment, or their finances. As we rapidly embark on this exciting industrial revolution, we must not forget the importance of humans, being human and governing humans; but still be aware that these harms may just look different and manifest in different forms as the world around us changes.

The English common law has served us well with its remarkable evolutionary capabilities, and it has already adapted through significant industrial revolutions before. We must however be alive to the challenges of these new technologies on both national and international laws and not just be blinkered by this.

Jacqueline Watts

July 2026

1 https://www.turing.ac.uk/blog/alan-turing-quotes-separating-fact-fiction.

Contributors

GENERAL EDITOR AND CONTRIBUTOR

Jacqueline Watts

Jacqueline is an experienced solicitor who specialises in acting for clients with cutting-edge innovations in the emerging technologies space. She is the director of a boutique law firm in the City of London and heads up its busy Corporate and Commercial Team.

Jacqueline advises a range of innovative clients across a multitude of sectors and disciplines, each at varying stages of funding, expansion and exits. She is an expert in emerging technologies and has a busy practice supporting pioneering clients in artificial intelligence, blockchain, cryptoassets, Web3, quantum computing, Internet of Things (IoT) and autonomous vehicles.

She has a keen eye for emerging trends, is the Vice Chair of the IEEE Spatial Computing for Metaverse Initiative, an active member of the Innovate UK immersive Tech Network Ethics Group and sits on working groups for the global UN collaboration United for Smart Sustainable Cities (U4SSC) initiatives on Agentic AI for Cities and the Digital Transformation for people-centred cities. Jacqueline was shortlisted in the Women Leaders in Tech Law for the Women, Influence & Power in Law UK Awards 2024 and Women Leaders in Tech Law 2025, regularly speaks at industry events including Tech Summit London, Zebu Live and the Global Intellectual Property ConfEx in London.

Jacqueline completed her law degree and Masters in Law at King's College, London. She started her legal career focusing on criminal and international criminal law, having interned at the Special Court for Sierra Leone in the Charles Taylor Defence Team, then working at a specialist criminal law, criminal appeals and prison law firm in Mayfair, London before moving into corporate and commercial law in the City of London.

CONTRIBUTORS

Colin Paterson

Colin is a UK and European patent attorney, and a partner at Keltie LLP, a boutique firm of patent and trade mark attorneys. He specialises in complex and emerging technology areas, and his practice spans a broad range of industries, including drug discovery, renewable energy, space technology, consumer electronics and gaming.

Colin advises on the best approaches for subject matter on the borderline of patentability, having been instructed on a number of matters related to machine learning and other software innovation. He has a PhD in Mathematics, which makes him particularly suitable for representing clients operating at the forefront of the AI revolution, and he is a member of the AI, Data and New Emerging Technologies committee of the Intellectual Property Owners trade association.

Colin is recognised for his thorough and solution-focused approach, and he provides advice that reflects the commercial environment in which his clients operate. He has extensive experience in drafting and prosecuting patent applications across many jurisdictions. He has represented clients on contentious matters – including oppositions at the European Patent Office – and provides infringement and freedom-to-operate opinions. Colin has also spent time inhouse on secondment at different multinational corporations, managing global patent portfolios and conducting invention harvesting and inventor-liaison activities. Colin is consistently recognised in the IP STARS directory published by Managing IP.

Omer Guy

Omer Guy is the General Counsel for the Digital Container Shipping Association (DCSA), a non-profit organisation supported by the 10 largest global container carriers to address a clear industry need: common ground for digitalisation. Today, DCSA's members represent 75% of global container trade. DCSA's mission is to shape the digital future of container shipping by being the industry's collective voice, working towards alignment and standardisation. By setting frameworks for effective, universally adoptable solutions and innovating, the industry can enable transparent, reliable, easy to use, secure and environmentally-friendly transportation services.

Omer is a maritime lawyer. Prior to joining DCSA, he spent almost 10 years as a practising attorney, handling a broad range of both contentious and non-contentious matters, acting on behalf of insurance companies, carriers, ship owners and operators, cargo owners, as well as airlines. Before that, Omer worked in the aviation industry in various operations positions for several years. With more than two decades of experience in supply chain, transport, and logistics, Omer brings his expertise and experience from both the business and legal perspectives into practice, contributing to the transformation of the container shipping industry through the work of DCSA. Omer is educated in business, international relations, and law (BA, LL.B, LL.M).

Gordon Brebner

Gordon Brebner, BSc, ChCSP, is an incident response and digital forensics specialist with extensive experience in government and defence security. He currently leads technical teams at Orange Cyberdefense, advising large enterprise organisations on containment and recovery during complex incident response engagements, including active network intrusions and post-ransomware forensic investigations.

With nearly 20 years of experience across multiple sectors, his background includes eight years in the Royal Marines specialising in electronic warfare and signals intelligence, followed by a leadership role at the UK Civil Aviation Authority, where he was responsible for cybersecurity oversight, risk management, and resilience across critical national infrastructure.

Paul Schwartfeger

Paul Schwartfeger is a barrister practising in commercial disputes, with a focus on matters involving technology, digital and physical infrastructure and complex systems. He is instructed in cases that are often technically dense, factually demanding and cross-border in nature, including those involving software, data, cyber incidents and fraud.

Before coming to the Bar, Paul worked in technology and business consulting across Europe and the United States. He brings that practical experience to disputes involving the design, deployment and failure of technical systems. His work frequently centres on matters where technical architecture and data flows are central to the issues in the case.

Paul acts both as sole counsel and as part of larger teams in high-value and complex matters. He is known for his ability to engage quickly with highly technical material and large volumes of evidence and for providing advice that is both analytically rigorous and commercially grounded, translating technical detail into clear, persuasive legal argument.

Alongside his court practice, Paul acts in arbitration and is a member of the Chartered Institute of Arbitrators. He has a strong interest in the use of arbitration and other dispute resolution mechanisms in international commercial disputes involving technology.

His contribution to this volume reflects that interest, examining how questions of jurisdiction and dispute resolution arise in increasingly digital and interconnected systems. He also writes widely on emerging issues in technology law.

Contents

Table of statutes

Table of statutory instruments

Table of international material

Table of cases

Chapter 1

Introduction

'The industrial metaverse will reshape the economy. Just as the internet has, it will also fundamentally transform the day-to-day experience of people all over the world. Expect the industrial metaverse to significantly impact how we experience the physical environment, how we work, and how our activities impact the planet.'[1]

MIT Technology Review Insight Report sponsored by Siemens

AN INDUSTRIAL REVOLUTION

1.1 We stand at the precipice of the next industrial revolution. The changes brought about in industry in the last five years by artificial intelligence (AI) are just the tip of the iceberg. Changes with the move to Industry 4.0 will be far and wide, impacting all aspects of industry, the workplace and society. The World Economic Forum has cautioned that the fourth industrial revolution 'is unprecedented in its speed, depth and breadth, offering both promise and peril as it changes nearly every industry in every country.'[2] Lawyers need to keep abreast of these seismic changes, and the legal challenges and risks brought about as a result of the same.

1.2 We are already seeing the disruption that is being brought about by the use of AI in industry; businesses are having to incorporate strategies at pace to try and deal with its use, all the while the technologies continue to outpace them. AI is just one piece of the Industry 4.0 puzzle. When we consider the potential for the AI technologies, being combined with some of the other key emerging technologies which are also synonymous with Industry 4.0, such as virtual reality and robotics, we can expect nothing other than the radical changes that are being predicted in the way we work, coexist, and produce and sell goods.

1.3 The move to Industry 4.0 is akin to the previous industrial revolution of the 1700 and 1800s, and has in fact been referred to as 're-industrialisation' and the advent of 'Industrial Intelligence'.[3] Siemens has already declared that they think that Industry 4.0 will radically change everything[4] and that the industrial

1 https://assets.new.siemens.com/siemens/assets/api/uuid:e36f2de7-f3c4-481f-bb20-9791dc12bbec/the-emergent-industrial-metaverse-update-2024.pdf.

2 https://www3.weforum.org/docs/WEF_Agile_Regulation_for_the_Fourth_Industrial_Revolution_2020.pdf.

3 Atik and Ünlü (2020), 'Industry 4.0 – Related Digital Divide in Enterprises: An Analysis for the European Union-28' Sosyoekonomi Journal, 28(45): 225–244.

4 https://assets.new.siemens.com/siemens/assets/api/uuid:e36f2de7-f3c4-481f-bb20-9791dc12bbec/the-emergent-industrial-metaverse-update-2024.pdf.

metaverse will revolutionise all industries.[5] In fact, going further still the World Economic Forum has said that:

> 'We stand on the brink of a technological revolution that will fundamentally alter the way we live, work, and relate to one another. In its scale, scope, and complexity, the transformation will be unlike anything humankind has experienced before. We do not yet know just how it will unfold, but one thing is clear: the response to it must be integrated and comprehensive, involving all stakeholders of the global polity, from the public and private sectors to academia and civil society.'[6]

WHAT IS INDUSTRY 4.0?

1.4 Industry 4.0, or the fourth industrial revolution, is a term that has been coined[7] to describe rapid digitalisation, predominately within the manufacturing sectors and heavy industries. It is the blending of real-life industry with emerging digital frontier technologies. Industry 4.0 is a true coming together of many of the 'new' emerging technologies of the last 10–15 years, and in more recent years this digital revolution has been combined with a desire for change spurred on by the Covid-19 pandemic and its repercussions across industry and throughout the supply chain.[8]

1.5 As with any industrial revolution it is hard to define the exact point in time that Industry 4.0 starts, and such eras are typically defined retrospectively in the history books as opposed to in real-time. Accordingly, we may already be said to be in the digital revolution, or we may still be in the transition period; what is true is that these are fundamental industrial changes that we are living through, with AI and automation already permeating all aspects of life from the workplace to warfare.

1.6 This book focuses on the use of emerging technologies within the industrial space. It goes further than the concept of an immersive industrial metaverse alone, and instead focuses on the preparatory steps needed by all legal professionals as we all start to encounter and embrace the industrial revolution that is Industry 4.0 and beyond. This book explores some of the key legal considerations for this new world, from navigating the legal implications of smart factories, smart supply chains and smart cities; exploring the range of digital twins from those of physical infrastructure for whole cities and individual buildings to personalised medicine replicating patients hearts and circulatory systems; and contemplating the revolution in logistics from last-mile autonomous freight vehicles to distributed ledger technology in international shipping.

5 Ibid.

6 https://www.weforum.org/stories/2016/01/the-fourth-industrial-revolution-what-it-means-and-how-to-respond/.

7 Originally in German manufacturing as part of its 2011 economic policy. See https://www.europarl.europa.eu/RegData/etudes/BRIE/2015/568337/EPRS_BRI(2015)568337_EN.pdf.

8 https://www.weforum.org/publications/navigating-the-industrial-metaverse-a-blueprint-for-future-innovations/.

THE EMERGING TECHNOLOGIES

1.7 Industry 4.0 expands a number of deep tech innovations. To understand Industry 4.0 therefore you first have to understand the main underlying Industry 4.0 technologies. These are discussed further throughout the book, but include:

1. robotics;
2. artificial intelligence;
3. virtual reality (augmented and extended reality (XR));
4. drones;
5. 5G;
6. 3D printing or additive manufacturing;
7. Internet of Things devices/sensors (IoT) – these are sensors which enable objects to communicate with computers and their introduction can be dated to around 2008/2009.[9] IIoT, or the Industrial Internet of Things has been used to define their use within the industrial sector.
8. blockchain;
9. cloud computing;
10. edge computing;
11. Big Data;
12. cyber-physical systems;
13. holographic technology;
14. biotechnology;
15. nanotechnology; and
16. neurotechnology.

Industry 4.0 has been fuelled by the significant advancements in these digital technologies over the last decade, and we expect to see quantum computing added to the above list of technologies being actively deployed in the near future as well.

WHAT IS THE INDUSTRIAL METAVERSE?

1.8 There is no universally accepted definition of the 'industrial metaverse', however, in its 2023 briefing paper the World Economic Forum in collaboration with the University of Cambridge categorised it as:

9 Krzysztof Witkowski, 'Internet of Things, Big Data, Industry 4.0 – Innovative Solutions in Logistics and Supply Chains Management', https://doi.org/10.1016/j.proeng.2017.03.197.

> 'A persistent 3D platform that is implemented across an organization, value chain and product life cycle, serving as a digital reflection of an entire organization in its operational environment. In its combinatory nature, it integrates processes, materials, machines and people in a bi- directional flow between real and virtual worlds. It builds on enabling technologies, including extended reality (XR), robotics, sensors and actuators as part of the internet of things (IoT), artificial intelligence (AI), development tools, blockchain, computing and connectivity.'[10]

1.9 The industrial metaverse is made up of multiple different technologies and multiple different layers of technologies. It will typically sit on-top of IoT devices as part of an industrial network.[11] At the core of the industrial metaverse is the creation of highly sophisticated immersive real-time simulations which enables a seamless transition between the real-life and the digital. There is typically some form of immersive technology that is utilised; however, augmented reality and mixed reality is preferred over full virtual reality in the industrial space.[12]

MULTI-LAYERS OF TECHNOLOGY

1.10 For the industrial metaverse to work there is a 'multi-stack' of different technologies in play, from the underlying hardware and software, right through to interactive interfaces, holographics, robotics and digital twins. The true value of the industrial metaverse comes from the combined use of these different emerging technologies. This may, for example, be the design of an autonomous vehicle powered by AI, which is designed virtually, stress tested in a digital twin environment, then manufactured in a smart factory. The vehicle is then test driven virtually within an immersive environment and then once the real-life product leaves the showroom it can be continually monitored via its built-in sensors, the data obtained from them are fed back into its digital twin system to extract learnings on improvements and to make maintenance decisions. The digital and real-life seamlessly intertwined to improve not only the product but the user's experience as well.

1.11 There are widely considered to be five different layers of technology within the industrial metaverse, each of which are built upon each other to create an industrial metaverse. These are:[13]

1. the hardware infrastructure level, which typically includes cloud computing infrastructure or edge technology systems;
2. the software infrastructure level, which may be the AI systems, or developer tools or the distributed ledger technology or blockchain infrastructure;
3. the industrial systems level, which includes the robotics and IoT sensors;

10 https://www3.weforum.org/docs/WEF_Industrial_Metaverse_2023.pdf.
11 https://ieeexplore.ieee.org/document/10596039.
12 Ibid.
13 https://www3.weforum.org/docs/WEF_Industrial_Metaverse_2023.pdf.

4. the platform layer, which integrates the other technologies and brings them together to enable the operation of the system. This is effectively the interface aspect of the system; and
5. the interaction layer, which includes devices where input and outputs can take place, such as an XR headset, wearable devices or even via mobile telephone applications.

THE INDUSTRIAL METAVERSE AS THE ENTIRE SUPPLY CHAIN

1.12 The industrial metaverse encompasses the entire supply chain, from production to post-sales, in a coming together of the real and virtual, or the '*phygital*'.[14] The industrial metaverse heralds the birth of concepts such as 'digital twins', 'smart factories', 'factoryverse',[15] 'digital industry',[16] 'smart enterprise'[17] and Industrial Virtual Worlds.[18] It is expected that the industrial metaverse will see users seamlessly flit between virtual and digital interactions to real-life interactions, and back again, especially where machinery requires real-life monitoring and checks.[19]

1.13 The industrial metaverse is intrinsically linked to Industry 4.0 and sits fairly within the concept of Industry 4.0 and the digital revolution, with some even considering that the industrial metaverse will be the driver which pushes Industry 4.0 to Industry 5.0.[20]

1.14 For the purpose of this book, the idea of the industrial metaverse and Industry 4.0 have been used largely interchangeably, each see the emergence of, and adoption of frontier technologies such as robotics and cyber physical systems, AI, XR (such as virtual reality and augmented reality) and the opportunities and challenges this brings.

14 'Industrial Metaverse – what is it? How to get started into the future of digitalization', T-Mobile, https://www.t-systems.com/resource/blob/657992/8f0df20456be8f86c20293fae0e9e375/GC-Industrial-Metaverse-T-Systems-EN-12-2023-data.pdf.
15 Ibid.
16 Gromova, E.A., Koneva, N.S., and Titova, E.V. (2022) 'Legal barriers to the implementation of digital industry (Industry 4.0) components and the ways to overcome them', The Journal of World Intellectual Property, 25: 186–205, http://doi.org/10.1111/jwip.12215.
17 Ibid.
18 https://digital-strategy.ec.europa.eu/en/policies/internet-things-policy.
19 https://ieeexplore.ieee.org/document/10596039.
20 Martínez-Gutiérrez et al (2024), 'Towards industry 5.0 through metaverse', Robotics and Computer-Integrated Manufacturing, 89: 102764, https://www.sciencedirect.com/science/article/pii/S0736584524000504.

THE INDUSTRIAL METAVERSE IS HERE AND NOW

1.15 The industrial world is changing, and is set to continue to change as the industrial metaverse picks up pace. Industry 4.0 has started to have the biggest impact on the automotive industry, the energy sector, agriculture, and the construction industry.

1.16 In its 2024 report 'Navigating the Industrial Metaverse: A Blueprint for Future Innovations' the World Economic Forum and Accenture predict that the metaverse will be a $100 billion market by 2030, and consider that it will be the industrial metaverse that will have the most scale and influence.[21] In fact they reported that 92% of US manufacturers in 2023 were already using some form of metaverse technology within their business.[22]

1.17 Nvidia has sought to cement itself as the main architect of the industrial metaverse infrastructure with its Omniverse product. As of July 2025, Nvidia was valued at over $3.85 trillion, making it the most valuable company by market cap at that time.[23] This demonstrates clearly the size, scale and importance of the industrial metaverse and Industry 4.0.

MODERN STRATEGY

1.18 The UK Government is starting to take Industry 4.0 seriously. The Government has prioritised the use of technology within manufacturing as part of its 2025 Modern Industrial Strategy, and has tasked the Industrial Strategy Advisory Council, which is made up of different industry leaders, with monitoring and advising the Government on this strategy.[24] The Government has confirmed that it will also be looking at reforming the regulatory framework to support innovation in this space.[25]

1.19 The EU is similar in its feeling that the transition to Industry 4.0 should be used to boost manufacturing for European businesses.[26] In its Digital Decade Policy, the EU calls for at least 75% of EU businesses to be transformed by using some form of the Industry 4.0 technologies by 2030[27] and since 2019 it

21 https://www.weforum.org/publications/navigating-the-industrial-metaverse-a-blueprint-for-future-innovations/.

22 Ibid.

23 https://companiesmarketcap.com/gbp/nvidia/marketcap/.

24 https://assets.publishing.service.gov.uk/media/68595e56db8e139f95652dc6/industrial_strategy_policy_paper.pdf.

25 https://assets.publishing.service.gov.uk/media/68920a3366bdd4490c61098f/industrial_strategy_advanced_manufacturing_sector_plan_accessible.pdf.

26 Which had historically pre-2015 been in decline due to the rise of manufacturing in countries such as China, https://www.europarl.europa.eu/RegData/etudes/BRIE/2015/568337/EPRS_BRI(2015)568337_EN.pdf.

27 https://commission.europa.eu/strategy-and-policy/priorities-2019-2024/europe-fit-digital-age/europes-digital-decade-digital-targets-2030_en.

has expanded its 5G and fibre optic infrastructure, and introduced regulations such as the provision for Digital Identity Wallets,[28] the Artificial Intelligence Act, the Data Act, the Cyber Resilience Act, the European Chips Act and the Digital Skills and Jobs Platform.[29]

LEGAL ISSUES IN INDUSTRY 4.0

1.20 In the same way that the Industrial Revolution of the 1700s and 1800s necessitated fundamental changes in the law to reflect the changes in the ways of work,[30] we expect to see the same need for changes as a result of the digital revolution. Industry is fundamentally changing again. This technological revolution will require legal reform, and it will change the nature of both clients and their issues.[31] Law firms and legal education will also change as a result.[32] We are already starting to see the start of this evolution with the rise of legal technology and new roles such as legal operations and 'AI lawyers'[33] within law firms.

1.21 Changes brought about by the first and second industrial revolutions resulted in the need for changes in factory laws, company laws, intellectual property laws, employment law, human rights laws and environmental laws.[34] We should all expect the need for new laws, and changes in existing laws, as we navigate this industrial revolution.

1.22 Just as the first Industrial Revolution was powered by steam, the fourth industrial revolution will be powered by data. In the industrial metaverse data is key. With the advent of the fourth Industrial Revolution, we have already seen a significant shift in the commoditisation of data. In all sectors there has been a seismic shift, with a focus on the extraction and use of data.

1.23 There are many legal barriers that need to be overcome to enable the proper adoption of Industry 4.0, and fundamental to this is the need of legislators to balance the promotion of innovation against protection from harms, and human rights. Gromova et al[35] consider that the underlying issues with the regulation of Industry 4.0 comes from the above competing interests which underpin most

28 The framework establishing the European Digital Identity Framework regulation 2024/1183.

29 https://commission.europa.eu/strategy-and-policy/priorities-2019-2024/europe-fit-digital-age_en.

30 Steven R. Smith (2023), 'The Fourth Industrial Revolution and Legal Education', 39 GA ST UL Rev. 337, available at http://readingroom.law.gsu.edu/gsulr/vol39/iss2/9.

31 Ibid.

32 Ibid.

33 https://www.linklaters.com/en/about-us/news-and-deals/news/2025/november/linklaters-launches-20-strong-global-team-of-specialist-ai-lawyers.

34 Dr Md. Nayem Alimul Hyder (2021), 'Impact of Fourth Industrial Revolution on Law', BILD Law Magazine, 4(2): 15–18, https://www.researchgate.net/publication/357660920_Impact_of_4th_Industrial_Revolution_on_Law.

35 Gromova, Koneva, and Titova (n 16).

legislative policies and the desire to protect digital sovereignty. They believe that to address the technological advances of Industry 4.0 there will be the need for changes in the way that these technologies are regulated. It is not that existing laws can just be adapted, but for the proper integration of Industry 4.0 there needs to be a fundamental shift in laws and regulation. We have seen this with the work done by the Law Commission over the last few years, whether recommending changes through statute or by providing firm direction on the interpretation of existing common law to address some of the numerous different legal challenges created by these emerging technologies. One of the issues that Gromova et al[36] identify is that when there is a lack of law and regulation covering a particular technology or its impact, then there is a lack of certainty for industry to innovate.

1.24 The overriding theme of regulators and legislators in both the UK and EU is the challenge of trying to balance the risks of emerging technologies as against a desire not to stifle innovation. Industry 4.0 brings new risks, which legislators will have to address and there will be changing norms, which society and the state will need to address. When debated in The House of Lords in 2017, Baroness Lane-Fox of Soho said:

> 'arguably the biggest challenge facing Governments globally at the moment is the disconnection between policy, legislation and the pace of technological change.'[37]

1.25 The way of working is set to evolve as a result of the industrial metaverse and an 'enterprise metaverse',[38] with greater opportunities for engagement, learning and upskilling. Industry 4.0 will also see multiple different industries coming together, such as data scientists, software developers, engineers, mathematicians, economists, biochemists, biologists and more, moving more into more traditional heavy industries. This all in turn will have an impact on employment law considerations, and health and safety laws. As we see a revolution in the way of working, we expect in turn to see an evolution in laws designed to safeguard employees in the workplace. In many cases, a focus on advancements in safety testing via an immersive industrial metaverse can have a positive impact, reduce safety concerns and identify perilous hazards early.

1.26 We now see a complex web of new technologies woven seamlessly between the real and the digital. Accordingly, fundamental legal considerations of Industry 4.0 include those relating to the divisions of legal liability, as well as those relating to intellectual property rights, product liability concerns and new data protection issues, especially as data becomes a consumable commodity of significant value in the changing landscape. Academics also consider that there is a need for a strong focus on human rights laws in the digital revolution, as well

36 Ibid.

37 https://hansard.parliament.uk/Lords/2017-11-15/debates/47509D26-EC9B-479C-9A2B-58900F1C19FD/FourthIndustrialRevolution.

38 https://www.weforum.org/publications/navigating-the-industrial-metaverse-a-blueprint-for-future-innovations/.

as controls on the weaponisation of these technologies.[39] In addition, with the expected impact on employment, and employment rates, it is likely we will see an impact on crime fuelled by the fourth revolution.[40]

ETHICS IN THE INDUSTRIAL METAVERSE

1.27 There are many ethical issues presented by Industry 4.0. These include a number of questions, such as:

- Should technology be developed just because it is now possible?
- Where should the lines be drawn?
- How should the technology be used?
- Should it be used for good purposes only, or can it also be permitted for bad purposes?
- Who should determine this and on what parameters?
- How should the technology be governed and controlled and by who?
- How should the technology deal with the digital divide?[41]

A NEW WORLD

1.28 For the industrial metaverse to work there is the need for suitable human resources, suitable organisation structures, suitable governance to deal with the responsible use of the industrial metaverse and an appropriate culture to adopt the systems.[42] It is fundamental that the industrial metaverse is designed to be safe, with privacy and security by design; and that there are suitable financial resources invested to properly create it and fulfil these objectives.[43]

1.29 In order to achieve Industry 4.0's potential there is the acute need to create trust in the new technology, otherwise these new innovations are unlikely to be fully and properly adopted.[44] Part of the issue with these new frontier technologies is what is often termed as the 'black box' effect. This is where the inner workings of a technology is so complex that there is a lack of knowledge and understanding on how it works, which in turn creates a lack of trust in it.

39 Dr Md. Nayem Alimul Hyder (n 34).
40 Ibid.
41 https://www.weforum.org/stories/2016/10/how-can-we-enjoy-the-benefits-of-the-fourth-industrial-revolution-while-minimizing-its-risks/.
42 https://www3.weforum.org/docs/WEF_Industrial_Metaverse_2023.pdf.
43 Ibid.
44 https://www.turing.ac.uk/sites/default/files/2023-05/turing_asg_whitepaper_digitaltwins.pdf.

1.30 It is important that as part of the development of these technologies, and the move towards Industry 4.0 generally, proper effort is made to raise public awareness as to how the technologies themselves work, how fundamental concerns such as safety and privacy are being addressed, and the individual and public benefits of these technological developments. Part of the concern around the mistrust in these technologies can be addressed through effective regulation, to show the public how these technologies either fit into existing legislative frameworks or how the law can be used effectively to encourage responsible innovation, and to still protect society. The World Economic Forum calls for the focus to be on promoting a 'principles-based approach to innovation'[45] with an emphasis on collaboration, sustainability, resiliency, human-centricity, transparency, accessibility, efficiency and scalability.

1.31 Collaboration is key in the industrial metaverse.[46] An industrial metaverse requires regulation with a legal framework which is fair, ethical and coordinated.[47]

1.32 Industry 4.0 is not country-specific and involves a significant amount of cross-border transactions, often in real-time and involving complex exchange of data and involving multiple different organisations. The changes required will also all need to fit within the cross-border nature of industry and trade. The European Parliament, for example, feels that it is essential for clear international standards on Industry 4.0, rather than country-specific standards, given the nature of the technological changes impact everyone and transcends jurisdictional borders.[48]

1.33 Finally in this new world there is the need for courts to be able to adapt to accommodate these new technologies, especially when dealing with the level and extent of the type of disclosure anticipated from these technological advances. We are already now seeing the need for changes to civil court procedures rules brought about by some of these technological changes, especially the widespread use of AI within court documents. The Civil Justice Council has been specifically tasked with considering what changes are needed to the Civil Procedure Rules,[49] and judicial guidance has already had to be issued on the use of AI by judicial office holders, reflecting some of the wide-reaching ramifications of this new technology on the law and judicial process generally.[50]

45 https://reports.weforum.org/docs/WEF_Shaping_Tomorrow_Responsible_Innovation_for_a_Brighter_Future_2025.pdf.

46 https://www3.weforum.org/docs/WEF_Navigating_the_Industrial_Metaverse_A_Blueprint_2024.pdf.

47 https://www3.weforum.org/docs/WEF_Industrial_Metaverse_2023.pdf.

48 https://www.europarl.europa.eu/RegData/etudes/BRIE/2015/568337/EPRS_BRI(2015)568337_EN.pdf.

49 https://www.judiciary.uk/related-offices-and-bodies/advisory-bodies/cjc/current-work/use-of-ai-in-preparing-court-documents/.

50 https://www.judiciary.uk/wp-content/uploads/2025/10/Artificial-Intelligence-AI-Guidance-for-Judicial-Office-Holders-2.pdf.

KEY TAKEAWAY POINTS

1.34 The key takeaway points in respect of the introduction are:

- We are currently in the midst of an industrial revolution; a digital revolution. As a result, we are experiencing seismic changes in society, and the law needs to react.
- Industry 4.0 technologies include the emerging frontier technologies of: robotics; artificial intelligence; virtual reality (augmented and extended reality (XR)); drones; 5G; 3D printing or additive manufacturing; IoT devices/sensors (Industrial Internet of Things, IIoT); blockchain; cloud computing; edge computing; Big Data; cyber-physical systems; holographic technology; biotechnology; nanotechnology; and neurotechnology.
- The industrial metaverse is made up of multiple layers of technologies. Industry 4.0 and the industrial metaverse is the coming together of multiple different emerging technologies.
- Despite a lack of specific laws and regulations most governments are now taking Industry 4.0 and the digital revolution seriously. This is reflected in the UK Government's 2025 Modern Industrial Strategy and the EU's Digital Decade Policy.
- Data is fuelling the digital revolution.
- Policymakers have been trying to balance mitigating the risk of new technologies against promoting innovation.

Chapter 2

Legal considerations in Industry 4.0 and its technologies

'We must develop a comprehensive and globally shared view of how technology is affecting our lives and reshaping our economic, social, cultural, and human environments. There has never been a time of greater promise, or greater peril.'[1]

Klaus Schwab, World Economic Forum Chairman

2.1 The underlying technologies which make up Industry 4.0 each present significant legal challenges. These challenges are due to a lack of legal certainty, a lack of case law and legal writing on the topic, which in turn leads to business uncertainty and puts those working and operating within the sector at risk.[2] Different technologies which make up Industry 4.0 have different levels of risk; academics consider that the Internet of Things (IoTs) and cyber-physical systems present a high risk in respect of legal challenges, and cloud computing and Big Data each present a medium risk.[3]

2.2 Many of the risks associated with these technologies share similar legal themes. The main areas of legal risks in Industry 4.0 are around issues concerning personal injury, product damage, contractual risks, data protection considerations, employment law and intellectual property law.[4] These risks are present in a regulatory climate where law makers are making a concerted efforts to not stifle innovation by onerous regulations, especially where technological developments outpace any ability to update laws and regulations fast enough to keep ahead of the new and emerging risks as they arise.

2.3 Being able to properly address the different legal issues presented by Industry 4.0 remains further constrained by the fact that legislation and regulation is on the whole still territorially-based, yet the technology is global and has cross-border implications.[5] Industry 4.0 is multidisciplinary. One of the main features of Industry 4.0 is the integration of traditional heavy industry with

1 https://www.weforum.org/stories/2016/01/9-quotes-that-sum-up-the-fourth-industrial-revolution/.

2 Habrat (2020), 'Legal challenges of digitalization and automation in the context of Industry 4.0', Elsevier Ltd, Procedia Manufacturing 51: 938–942.

3 Ibid.

4 Ibid.

5 Ibid.

digital technologies.[6] It sees the merging of digital sciences, with other forms of physical science and engineering.

2.4 This chapter focuses on some of the common legal themes for consideration in respect of Industry 4.0 and the industrial metaverse generally, such as privacy, human rights, liability and sustainability, and then goes on to consider some of the key specific legal considerations in the emerging frontier technologies most associated with Industry 4.0 today of artificial intelligence (AI), cyber-physical systems, edge computing and semiconductors.

INDUSTRY 4.0

2.5 In 2013 a group of experts prepared a report on behalf of the German Federal Ministry of Education and Research titled 'Securing the future of German manufacturing industry – recommendations for implementing the strategic initiative Industrie 4.0'.[7] This is an important early paper given that for many people the concept of Industry 4.0 itself originated from Germany and this report.

2.6 The German Federal Ministry highlights the following as the main legal issues to consider in respect of Industry 4.0:

1. Corporate data – Industry 4.0 sees the mixing of sensitive information from multiple different parties. They suggest that this in itself is likely to result in new forms of technology to try and safeguard against this risk as well as needing to have sufficient contractual provisions in place dealing with the same. They did not feel that at the time trade secret regulation went far enough and felt that contracts needed updating to reflect the increased risks in this emerging market. Trade secret regulations have been updated since this report, which now at least go some way towards protecting trade secrets generally, albeit not necessarily with a distinct focus on the specific challenges of Industry 4.0 where there are technologies with many different interrelated parties and technologies collaborating together.[8] It still remains essential to have sufficient processes in place for each organisation to protect their secrets, limit unnecessary access to the same, and to ensure that there are effective contractual protection in place;

6 Gromova, E.A., Koneva, N.S., and Titova, E.V. (2022) 'Legal barriers to the implementation of digital industry (Industry 4.0) components and the ways to overcome them', The Journal of World Intellectual Property, 25: 186–205, http://doi.org/10.1111/jwip.12215.

7 https://www.din.de/resource/blob/76902/e8cac883f42bf28536e7e8165993f1fd/recommendations-for-implementing-industry-4-0-data.pdf.

8 Which in the UK is under the Trade Secrets (Enforcement, etc) Regulations 2018 and in the EU under Directive (EU) 2016/943 of the European Parliament and of the Council of 8 June 2016 on the protection of undisclosed know-how and business information (trade secrets) against their unlawful acquisition, use and disclosure.

2. Liability – The report highlighted the liability risks where systems sit within a wider network of systems. They felt that contracts could go some way in dealing with some of the risks with the differing liabilities, but that these would need updating to reflect the changes in the technology. They suggest clearly spelling out who is responsible for what within the contracts and where liability sits, especially in circumstances where there are other forms of liability, such as tortious liability. Whereas this may work for parties who have a contractual relationship, where this is not the case this will present more of a significant legal concern. In some cases, collateral warranties may provide a solution where there is a technology stack, but this is often an imperfect solution.
3. Personal data – The report flags concerns in respect of the volume of personal data which will be generated in Industry 4.0. The report, however, pre-dates GDPR regulations. Whilst these regulations have updated data protection generally, they are not able to keep pace with the technological advances, which still present challenges.
4. Trade restrictions – The report highlights that issues may arise from trade restrictions, such as specific licences needed for certain types of technology and its application. Whilst this is without doubt an important consideration, the world has changed considerably since 2013, especially with the imposition of tariffs by the USA under President Trump from 2025 onwards. International tariffs and trade restrictions will now arguably be an even more important consideration than that in 2013. Whilst not a trade restriction per se, the export trade restrictions imposed on Anthropic in June 2026 by the US Government prohibiting foreign access to Fable 5 and Mythos 5[9] are a clear example of the ongoing risk of restrictions being imposed on frontier technology by states, and intensify calls for sovereign AI systems to be developed and maintained.

HUMAN-CENTRIC VALUES

2.7 The EU's 'Digital Decade' policy puts the protection of humans at the centre of its digitalisation policy.[10] This includes creating an inclusive system, which is safe, and gives citizens control of their own data. The 2022 Joint Declaration of the European Parliament, European Council and European Commission on Digital Rights and Principles for the Digital Decade and for digital transformation,[11] considers that:

1. Digital transformation must reflect and uphold the European values of democracy, equality and human rights.

9 http://www.anthropic.com/news/fable-mythos-access.

10 https://commission.europa.eu/strategy-and-policy/priorities-2019-2024/europe-fit-digital-age/europes-digital-decade-digital-targets-2030_en.

11 https://digital-strategy.ec.europa.eu/en/policies/digital-principles#tab_1.

2. Digital transformation must respect the key fundamental principles of consumer protection, data protection, privacy rights and equality.
3. Any digital transformation must be balanced with the rights of workers, including the right to disconnect from work for periods of time, so to ensure that there is a suitable work home-life balance.
4. Environmental sustainability must be a central consideration in respect of digital transformation.
5. Digitisation must always be human centric and designed with humans in mind.
6. Digitalisation must foster an inclusive society and benefit all citizens.
7. There is a need for a framework to be put in place to ensure that digitalisation creates a fair society.
8. Attempts must be made to bridge the digital divide (as discussed below at para **2.14**), and there should be suitable access to high-speed internet for all EU citizens. The internet should be accessible and not be blocked or access be denied, there should also be suitable digital education, training and up-skilling.
9. Safeguards must be put in place to protect the workplace and working conditions with regards to any form of digitalisation. This includes being transparent about the use of AI and safeguarding human involvement within industry and the workplace.
10. Everyone should have the right to access public services, even if these are digital.
11. AI should aid wellbeing and it should benefit people. AI should be transparent, ethical and trustworthy. It should not be based on discriminatory data sets and should have sufficient safeguards in place.
12. The right to freedom of expression must be retained, which should include the large tech platforms.
13. All technology must be designed as privacy by design, with suitable cybersecurity protections.
14. Children and young people must always be protected.
15. Digital technologies must not damage the environment and should be sustainable.

INTELLECTUAL PROPERTY LAW

2.8 The protection of intellectual property rights is vital in Industry 4.0. This is due to the nature of the technologies in Industry 4.0, which are described by the World Intellectual Property Office as being 'frontier technologies'.[12] Cutting edge advances need suitable intellectual property right protection to encourage investment and growth. In 2016 the House of Commons Hon. Member of Parliament for Havant Mr Mak said that *'A strong legal regime, especially in respect of intellectual property, is certainly key to making Britain a world leader in the 4IR'*.[13]

PRODUCT LIABILITY

2.9 Another central legal consideration in Industry 4.0 is where, and with whom, the legal liability should sit when you merge together traditional industry with emerging technologies.

2.10 Most product liability imposes some form of strict liability because of the issues posed by traditional products which, until now have lacked an ability to think independently; however, with advances in AI this may now be changing, and as a result consideration has to be had as to the impact AI and emerging technologies have on product liability laws and offences.[14] This is an area which the Law Commission has identified as requiring a detailed consideration, having announced on 31 July 2025 that it was reviewing product liability rules and the changes brought about by these frontier technologies.[15]

2.11 The EU adopted the Product Liability Directive[16] on 8 December 2024 which is due to come into force from December 2026. This Directive now treats software as a product for the purpose of product liability, and deals with it in the same way as physical goods. This is the first time in the EU that software will be treated in this way. It covers both software generally as well as the Internet of Things (IoT), operating systems and AI systems. This Directive enables compensation claims to be brought against software developers as 'manufacturers' where there is a defective software product. This will cover both software developers and online platforms.[17] Whilst the Directive covers only individuals as victims, this is already being extended to businesses in some EU states. This Directive clearly aligns the software and AI systems with other parts of a system. This move is an important step in updating product liability in the context of Industry 4.0.

12 https://www.wipo.int/en/web/frontier-technologies.

13 https://hansard.parliament.uk/commons/2016-09-08/debates/5C9878D9-EC7E-4713-A573-D8B0A9771402/FourthIndustrialRevolution.

14 Louisa McDonald, (2023), 'AI Systems and Liability: An Assessment of the Applicability of Strict Liability & A Case for Limited Legal Personhood for A', St Andrews Law Journal, 3(1): 5–21.

15 https://lawcom.gov.uk/news/law-commission-to-review-the-law-relating-to-product-liability/.

16 Directive (EU) 2024/2853 of the European Parliament and of the Council of 23 October 2024 on liability for defective products and repealing Council Directive 85/374/EEC.

17 https://single-market-economy.ec.europa.eu/single-market/goods/free-movement-sectors/liability-defective-products_en.

PRIVACY

2.12 Privacy and data protection are also important considerations in the context of Industry 4.0. There is an abundance of data generated, and moving around, in the industrial metaverse. This includes the real-time collection of multiple different types of data, some of which will be personal data.

2.13 There are privacy concerns in the industrial metaverse and Industry 4.0 space. Innovative systems are often vulnerable to data breaches, cyberattack and data theft. This is partly as a result of these systems often utilising different integrated third-party software which are exposed to cyber-threats.[18]

THE DIGITAL DIVIDE

2.14 The digital divide refers to an inequality caused as a result of poor digital infrastructure and access to online materials. Academics have highlighted the presence of a digital divide in the EU between states such as the UK and Germany, compared with Bulgaria and Cyprus, and that one of the key desires of the EU is to bridge this gap.[19] The lack of access to digital infrastructure, whether this is because of poor internet infrastructure, or widespread poverty, means a lack of access to accessible digital products.

HUMAN RIGHTS

2.15 The impact of Industry 4.0 and mass digitalisation on human rights is one of the drivers behind a shift towards what some consider is Industry 5.0, which is said by some to have more of a focus on human rights and sustainability than Industry 4.0. Whether Industry 4.0 has yet been achieved is much more difficult to determine, and often shifts in Industrial Revolutions are identified retrospectively in history as distinct eras of change. What is important for now, however, is the identification of a need to focus on human rights in respect of the digital revolution rather than focusing on arbitrary labels like Industry 4.0 or Industry 5.0 or otherwise.

2.16 The Guiding Principles on Business and Human Rights: Implementing the United Nations 'Protect, Respect and Remedy' Framework[20] calls for all businesses to respect human rights, and also requires that states ensure that this is fulfilled by setting clear expectations and providing suitable training and guidance

18 Tanisha et al (2024), 'Privacy and Data Protection Challenges in Industry 4.0: An AI-driven perspective', World Journal of Advanced Engineering Technology and Sciences, 12(02): 064-089, https://doi.org/10.30574/wjaets.2024.12.2.0287.

19 Atik and Ünlü (2020), 'Industry 4.0 – Related Digital Divide in Enterprises: An Analysis for the European Union-28', Sosyoekonomi Journal, 28(45): 225–244.

20 https://www.ohchr.org/sites/default/files/documents/publications/guidingprinciples businesshr_en.pdf.

for businesses. It is important that as we embrace Industry 4.0, all businesses design their frontier technology with the protection of human rights in mind, especially given the changing relationship between humans and machines as a result of advancing technologies. Risks of the adverse impact on human rights caused by these technologies should be mitigated by suitable impact assessments being prepared by all organisations specifically identifying the impact and steps taken to counteract the same.

2.17 It is important that the Human Rights Act 1998 and European Convention on Human Rights are considered in the context of Industry 4.0 and amendments made where necessary to bring these up to date to cover relevant changes. For example, academics[21] consider the right to life in respect of the impact of cyber-attacks, and rights to privacy in the context of workplace surveillance need to be properly protected. As we see an uptake throughout industry in advancing AI, wearable devices and smart glasses, it is fundamental that we do not lose sight of the underpinning fundamental protections enshrined in human rights principles. These may need to be adapted as the technology continues to advance, but given the involvement of humans in all processes, inputs and outputs, it is vital that this is continually monitored and sight is not lost of these enshrined principles.

2.18 Gender inequality is a key concern in Industry 4.0.[22] UNESCO stresses the need for Industry 4.0 to be inclusive and ensure that women make up a fair percentage of digital jobs, especially since they have been traditionally under-represented in these fields.[23]

ENVIRONMENTAL CONSIDERATIONS

2.19 Sustainability is an important topic in Industry 4.0 and the industrial metaverse. Countries are trying to balance innovation, and a global race to emerge as a leading power in the new technological landscape, against the climate change implications of emerging technology[24] and their environmental commitments.[25] The environmental impact of Industry 4.0 is explored further in **Chapter 10**.

COMPETITION LAW

2.20 Concerns around monopoly are beginning to be raised in the industrial metaverse. It is anticipated that Nvidia is involved in around 88% of the graphics

21 Emanuilov et al (2022), 'Business and human rights in Industry 4.0: a blueprint for collaborative human rights due diligence in the Factories of the Future', Journal of Responsible Technology, 10 (July 2022): 100028, https://doi.org/10.1016/j.jrt.2022.100028.

22 https://www.unesco.org/en/articles/women-minority-industry-40-fields.

23 Ibid.

24 Such as the extensive energy and resources used by emerging technologies.

25 Amongst others the legally binding commitments made under the Paris Agreement in December 2015 at COP21 including meeting various 2030 targets.

processing units (GPU) market, the chips used to effectively power AI and the industrial metaverse.[26] Given its market stake, it decided not to purchase a UK semiconductor manufacturer called Arm Limited in 2022. The merger was investigated by the Competition and Markets Authority under section 45(4) of the Enterprise Act 2002 from November 2021 until the merger was abandoned by Nvidia, and the investigation was accordingly cancelled in February 2022.[27] In the matter of Nvidia/Arm[28] a Federal Trade Commission antitrust claim was filed against Nvidia in America in respect of the proposed merger with Arm, which was dismissed in February 2022 following Nvidia's termination of the proposed merger.[29]

2.21 Concerns around competition can be addressed through interoperability, being the ability of a technology to work across different platforms with other providers and environments, as demonstrated in the *Microsoft v Commission* case.[30] Interoperability itself being a fundamental concern and an often cited weakness of the current state of the Industrial Metaverse and in Industry 4.0 generally.

2.22 The Law Commission raised specific concerns in its 2025 discussion paper on 'AI and the Law' that autonomous agents may autonomously and without human oversight flout competition law principles and laws for example by colluding on price.[31]

CRIME AND INDUSTRY 4.0

2.23 Concerns have been expressed by experts that with the advent of Industry 4.0 there is also the need to change the way in which crime and compliance is dealt with, especially at an enterprise level.[32] They consider that one of the key changes is the need to move away from businesses taking a siloed approach to compliance and risk. Instead, with a move towards Industry 4.0, we see multidisciplinary roles and technologies converging. Effective governance of staff, especially those with access to pioneering technology with tremendous capabilities is also now a key consideration with the introduction of section 250 of the Crime and Policing Act 2026, which came into force on 29 June 2026, and expands how corporates themselves can be held criminally liable for offences which are committed by senior managers acting within the scope of their authority.

26 Harrison Smith (2025), 'The metaverse-industrial complex', Information, Communication & Society, 28(5): 797–814, DOI: 10.1080/1369118X.2024.2423346.
27 https://www.gov.uk/cma-cases/nvidia-slash-arm-merger-inquiry.
28 FTC Matter 2110015, docket 9404.
29 https://www.ftc.gov/legal-library/browse/cases-proceedings/2110015-nvidiaarm-matter.
30 Case T-201/04.
31 https://cdn.websitebuilder.service.justice.gov.uk/uploads/sites/54/2025/07/AI-paper-PDF.pdf.
32 https://www.financierworldwide.com/crime-and-corruption-in-the-4th-industrial-revolution.

2.24 We now see the increased digitalisation in areas which were traditionally the realms of physical science and engineering, areas which previously were low risk targets to fraud are now more accessible and a more attractive target, especially to cyber criminals. Experts[33] call on enterprises to adopt digital strategies to mitigate the risks and to assist with compliance.

LIABILITY

2.25 Some consider, and are advocating, that certain smart autonomous robots should have their own distinct legal personality, meaning in the future we could see robots being sued as distinct entities.[34] This would be much in the same way as how the limited liability of corporate entities has evolved as being distinct from its human owners and controllers.

CONTRACTS

2.26 Especially whilst there is still uncertainty in the way that the law treats some of the different legal implications surrounding emerging technologies, contracts are vital. Contracts can go some way to offer some legal certainty for contracting parties. The different parties can contractually agree upon expectations, ownership rights, the division of liability, and any limitations of liability. It is important that insurance providers are brought into contractual discussions early with new technologies and new use cases, to ensure that liability is properly covered and that there are no liability gaps or risks that are not adequately covered.

FORCE MAJEURE

2.27 Considerations must be had to the concept of force majeure in the Industry 4.0 context. In the new technological landscape, issues present themselves which are outside of the reasonable control of a party such as power outages, cyber attacks, a lack of connectivity or cloud computer outages such as the issues experienced by AWS in October 2025 and Cloudflare in November 2025. It is important that contracts are carefully drafted to reflect suitable force majeure clauses given the uncertainty in this area and the developing law.

33 https://www.financierworldwide.com/crime-and-corruption-in-the-4th-industrial-revolution.
34 Habrat (n 2).

CROSS-BORDER CONSIDERATIONS

2.28 The emerging technologies associated with Industry 4.0 typically cross through traditional jurisdictional borders. This makes traditional enforcement complex. This is discussed further in **Chapter 3**.

ETHICS

2.29 With the change in society brought about by the seismic changes in the technology, it is inevitable that new and emerging ethical issues will arise. UNESCO have taken the reins in trying to establish international ethical guidelines.[35] In 2021 it released its ethical standards on AI, which applies to its 194 member states, puts human rights, the protection of the environment, and inclusiveness at its core, and identifies the need for agile standards which evolve with the technology.[36] UNESCO identifies 11 key areas that needed policy action, including on data, education, and ethics.

REGULATION OF IOTS

2.30 Smart devices for consumer use are governed in the UK under the Product Security and Telecommunications Infrastructure (Product Security) regime.

2.31 The Product Security and Telecommunications Infrastructure Act 2022 mandates that certain security requirements must be implemented for connectable products which are made available to consumers in the UK. This applies to manufacturers, importers and distributors. The penalties for breach under the Act are significant and must be appropriate and proportionate.[37] Fines can reach up to a maximum[38] of £10,000,000 or 4% of global revenue[39] (whichever is higher), plus a daily penalty of £20,000 for each day that the breach remains after the date the penalty is due.[40]

2.32 The specific regulations are currently contained in the Product Security and Telecommunications Infrastructure (Security Requirements for Relevant Connectable Products) Regulations 2023. The regulations deal with multiple manufacturers, which is likely to be the case in digital twins, and confirm that each manufacturer is required to meet the security requirements or deemed

35 https://www.unesco.org/en/artificial-intelligence/recommendation-ethics.
36 Ibid.
37 Section 37(1).
38 Section 36(4).
39 Section 38(1).
40 Section 36(5).

compliance conditions.[41] The Office for Product Safety and Standards (OPSS) regulates compliance with the 2023 Regulations.

2.33 The European Telecommunications Standards Institute (ETSI)[42] has established a number of international standards for IoT devices, including ETSI EN 303 645 and ETSI TS 103 701.

2.34 In the EU, the IoT falls under the Data Governance Act[43] and the Data Act[44] which deals with the regulation of access and use of data.

A FOCUS ON THE LEGAL CONSIDERATIONS OF AI IN INDUSTRY 4.0

What is artificial intelligence?

2.35 Artificial intelligence (AI) is a broad term which is typically used to refer to machines which are capable of human-like intelligence. The EU Commission helpfully sought to define artificial intelligence in 2018 as:

> 'systems that display intelligent behaviour by analysing their environment and taking actions – with some degree of autonomy – to achieve specific goals. AI-based systems can be purely software-based, acting in the virtual world (e.g. voice assistants, image analysis software, search engines, speech and face recognition systems) or AI can be embedded in hardware devices (e.g. advanced robots, autonomous cars, drones or Internet of Things applications).'[45]

2.36 There are numerous subsets of AI, all of which are at varying degrees of maturity and development, both in general and within the industrial metaverse. These include:

1. generative AI – which uses AI to learn patterns from data;
2. machine learning – this is a type of AI which trains itself and evolves without being programmed;
3. computer vision – which is AI that reviews visual representations and images;
4. natural language – this is AI which deals with human language; and
5. predictive AI – which is AI which predicts outcome;

41 Regulation 5 of the Product Security and Telecommunications Infrastructure (Security Requirements for Relevant Connectable Products) Regulations 2023.

42 https://www.etsi.org/technologies/consumer-iot-security.

43 Regulation (EU) 2022/868 of the European Parliament and of the Council of 30 May 2022 on European data governance and amending Regulation (EU) 2018/1724 (Data Governance Act).

44 Regulation (EU) 2023/2854 of the European Parliament and of the Council of 13 December 2023 on harmonised rules on fair access to and use of data and amending Regulation (EU) 2017/2394 and Directive (EU) 2020/1828 (Data Act).

45 https://digital-strategy.ec.europa.eu/en/library/definition-artificial-intelligence-main-capabilities-and-scientific-disciplines.

2.37 AI is now one of the main Industry 4.0 technologies, and its mass adoption and scale is what is now accelerating our rapid approach towards Industry 4.0 and changing the landscape of industry generally.

THE UK APPROACH

2.38 There is currently no one piece of legislation covering the regulation of AI in the UK. Despite calls for a specific AI law from some Parliamentarians such as Lord Holmes of Richmond MBE,[46] and the recommendations for reform by the House of Lords select committee report of 6 March 2026 on Communications and Digital Committee AI, Copyright and the Creative Industries,[47] this has not yet happened and the UK Government appear to still remain reluctant to over regulate this technology despite its mass adoption, which is discussed further in **Chapter 3**.

2.39 The UK Parliament highlights that many existing regulations do already cover the use of AI, such as the UK General Data Protection Regulation (UK GDPR), the Equality Act 2010 and consumer protection regulation.[48] Furthermore, its use in specific sectors, such as finance, healthcare and legal services, also sees further regulations from regulators such the Financial Conduct Authority, Solicitors Regulation Authority and Medicines and Healthcare Products Regulatory Agency to name a few.

2.40 In its 2024 Horizon scanning paper, the UK Government highlights some of the issues that regulating AI causes for regulators.[49] The Digital Regulation Cooperation Forum (DRCF) is a multi-regulator taskforce in the UK whose mission is to consider the specific impact of different emerging technologies on the different regulatory landscapes, noting that many of these technologies impact various different regulators in an unprecedented manner, and therefore a multi-regulatory approach is necessary as a result. The DRCF has considered the different applications of AI, and established the Thematic Innovation Hub in October 2025 which will look at agentic AI as its first theme.[50]

2.41 The 2023 House of Commons Science, Innovation and Technology Committee report on the governance of AI identifies 12 issues with AI that it felt that effective governance needs to address:[51]

46 https://lordchrisholmes.com/ai-regulation-report/ and his private members bill Artificial Intelligence (Regulation) Bill.

47 https://publications.parliament.uk/pa/ld5901/ldselect/ldcomm/267/26702.htm.

48 https://post.parliament.uk/artificial-intelligence-ethics-governance-and-regulation/#_edn1.

49 https://post.parliament.uk/artificial-intelligence-ethics-governance-and-regulation/#_edn8.

50 https://www.drcf.org.uk/news-and-events/news/drcf-launches-thematic-innovation-hub-for-innovators-with-first-focus-on-agentic-ai.

51 https://committees.parliament.uk/publications/41130/documents/205611/default/.

1. the issue of bias – which the Government raises the concern that it may increase inequalities in society;[52]
2. issues of privacy;
3. issues around data causing the misrepresentation of someone;
4. the need for significant volumes of data;
5. the need for sophisticated systems;
6. the 'black box' nature of the technology, meaning that many do not understand how the technology works so it in turn forms distrust;
7. the need for the underlying codes to be open-source and readily available for all;
8. concerns with intellectual property rights;
9. issues of where liability should lie when harm is suffered;
10. the impact of AI on jobs and employment;
11. the cross-border nature of the technology; and
12. the risk of ai on national security.

THE AI FRAMEWORK

2.42 In 2023, the UK Government published its policy paper 'A pro-innovation approach to AI regulation'.[53] In its paper, which was based on a significant amount of industry and regulator feedback, the Government highlighted the need for appropriate regulations to balance innovation against the risks of AI. It considers that any regulation needs to be dynamic, flexible and based on a clear set of principles as a framework. The policy paper supported the introduction of the regulatory AI sandbox and confirmed that the reason why the UK was looking to avoid legislating on AI in a similar vein to the EU was to avoid it becoming an unnecessary burden to businesses in the UK. The legislators have sent a clear message that in the race to try and establish itself as an AI superpower, sacrifices have had to be made around legislation and regulation which they felt may have otherwise become a disproportionate barrier to adoption and use.

2.43 Whilst the UK has taken the approach at this juncture not to specifically legislate on AI as a stand-alone piece of legislation, the 2023 'pro-innovation' framework seeks to try and provide some certainty to businesses as to the underlying regulatory framework, which may not be immediately obvious. Whilst the beauty of the common law is its ability to react to evolutions in technologies, this does often come with some initial uncertainties. With identified risks around

52 https://post.parliament.uk/artificial-intelligence-ethics-governance-and-regulation/#_edn8.
53 https://www.gov.uk/government/publications/ai-regulation-a-pro-innovation-approach/white-paper.

issues such as safety, fairness and security, the framework[54] is intended to guide regulators and identifies five guiding principles for AI use:

1. it must be safe;
2. it must be transparent;
3. it must be fair;
4. it must have suitable governance; and
5. it must have a right of redress.

2.44 The Framework is designed to provide the principles to guide the regulation of AI by the different regulators, which should be based on the specific context, focusing on the use of the AI and not the AI per se itself. In a move similar to many different modern forms of regulations, the idea is to focus on outcomes rather than create a prescriptive set of rules. The idea is to empower regulators to guide the regulations themselves in respect of AI within their relevant context, based on a set of underlying guiding principles. The policy paper states that the Government should, however, keep a close eye on this and step in should the law start to make perverse decisions concerning liability in the context of AI.

THE EU APPROACH

The EU Artificial Intelligence Act

2.45 The EU was perhaps, unsurprisingly, the first to regulate AI. This was done under the EU Artificial Intelligence Act (the AI Act).[55]

2.46 The AI Act establishes different levels of risks for different AI systems, and then implements different rules based on these levels. Certain risks, known as unacceptable risks, such as real-time biometric ID systems, are effectively banned unless they fall under a law enforcement exception. Certain uses of AI are categorised as high risk, and will need to be assessed prior to being deployed. Depending on the area in which the AI system fits it will need to be registered. There are also transparency requirements for high impact systems. Even in the EU, however, the AI Act itself has not been without challenges in its adoption. On 19 November 2025, the European Commission published its Digital Omnibus on AI[56] which called for changes to the AI Act given the detrimental impact on

54 https://www.gov.uk/government/publications/ai-regulation-a-pro-innovation-approach/white-paper.

55 Regulation (EU) 2024/1689 of the European Parliament and of the Council of 13 June 2024 laying down harmonised rules on artificial intelligence and amending Regulations (EC) No 300/2008, (EU) No 167/2013, (EU) No 168/2013, (EU) 2018/858, (EU) 2018/1139 and (EU) 2019/2144 and Directives 2014/90/EU, (EU) 2016/797 and (EU) 2020/1828 (Artificial Intelligence Act).

56 COM(2025) 836 final at https://eur-lex.europa.eu/legal-content/EN/TXT/?uri=CELEX:52025PC0836.

innovation, including amongst other items a delay in the commencement of those obligations required for high-risk systems given a lack of standards, guidance, guidelines and tools. The postponement of the commencement of these obligations implementation from August 2026 to now being between December 2027 and August 2028 was provisionally agreed between the European Commission, the European Parliament and European Council on 7 May 2026.[57]

2.47 The European AI Office was implemented by the decision of the European Commission of 24 January 2024[58] and oversees and enforces the implementation of the provisions of the AI Act. There are six units within the AI office including the 'excellence in AI and Robotics' and 'AI in Health and Life Science'.[59]

Framework on artificial intelligence and human rights, democracy and the rule of law

2.48 The Council of Europe adopted its Framework Convention on 17 May 2024 concerning AI and human rights under Treaty 225. As of March 2026, it has 19 signatories including the UK, the EU and the USA. The framework calls for a global legal framework to ensure that there is 'responsible innovation'.[60]

2.49 The framework is designed as a starting point, which can evolve as the technology advances. The Council of Europe cautions that it has serious concerns around discrimination, and the violations of human rights in respect of the widespread adoption of AI, and highlights that there is the need for AI to respect the following:[61]

1. 1948 Universal Declaration of Human Rights;
2. 1950 Convention for Protection of Human Rights and Fundamental Freedoms;
3. 1966 International Covenant on Civil and Political Rights;
4. 1966 International Covenant on Economic, Social and Cultural Rights;
5. 1961 European Social Charter and 1996 European Social Charter (Revised);
6. 1989 United Nations Convention on the Rights of the Child;
7. 2006 United Nations Convention on the Rights of Persons with Disabilities; and
8. 1981 Convention for the Protection of Individuals with regards to Automatic Processing of Personal Data.

57 https://www.europarl.europa.eu/news/en/press-room/20260427IPR42011/ai-act-deal-on-simplification-measures-ban-on-nudifier-apps.
58 C(2024) 390.
59 https://digital-strategy.ec.europa.eu/en/policies/ai-office.
60 https://rm.coe.int/1680afae3c.
61 Ibid.

2.50 The framework requires that AI systems are built with human rights by design.

2.51 Article 4 states:

> 'Each Party shall adopt or maintain measures to ensure that the activities within the lifecycle of artificial intelligence systems are consistent with obligations to protect human rights, as enshrined in applicable international law and in its domestic law'.

2.52 Article 5 requires that systems are designed to respect the rule of law and democratic principles. Article 7 enshrines the principles of human dignity and autonomy as paramount, whilst Article 8 protects principles of transparency and Article 9 highlights the need for accountable and responsible systems. Article 10 highlights the need for equality and measures to ensure that risks of discrimination are minimised.

Industrial policy on AI and robotics

2.53 In the EU even before the regulation of AI with the EU AI Act in 2024, the European Parliament passed a resolution on a comprehensive Industrial policy on AI and robotics (2018/2088 (INI)) on 12 February 2019. This regulation highlights many of the key considerations around the regulation of AI and robots, many of which come up time and again when considering the governance of AI which includes:

1. The need to balance the risk to jobs against innovation. Considerations as to what can be done to upskill workers include comprehensive training and rigorous education opportunities. This is discussed in more detail in **Chapter 13**.
2. Concerns around the malicious use of AI which have a significant impact on the public, especially if there are coordinated widespread cyber-attacks on key infrastructure. The policy considers both intentional attacks and negligent adoption of AI which exposes structures and systems to risks.
3. The need for continual monitoring of systems and the setting of suitable standards for the technology.
4. Concerns around privacy, security and transparency, which need to be recognised and acknowledged.
5. The need for rules around data protection being respected.
6. The need for rules around non-personal data being respected, to ensure that there is integrity in the data, and that it is not bias.
7. The need to focus on cloud computing and high-performing computing systems.
8. The need for any regulation to have flexibility baked within it to allow for future advances in the technologies.

9. Recommendation in using public-private partnerships, which are as discussed in more detail in **Chapter 3**.
10. A focus must be made on the key areas of:
    a. the public sector;
    b. health;
    c. energy;
    d. transport; and
    e. agriculture.
11. The need for the technology to remain focused on a human-centric approach which should be 'ethical-by-design'.

THE AI SAFETY SUMMIT

2.54 On 1 and 2 November 2023, 29 countries agreed to adhere to the Bletchley Declaration, with New Zealand committing later to this international commitment on 23 October 2024.[62] The Declaration recognises that international efforts are required to deal with AI, which is why a series of high-level strategic state level commitments were made including that:

> 'AI should be designed, developed, deployed, and used, in a manner that is safe, in such a way as to be human-centric, trustworthy and responsible.'[63]

INTERNATIONAL APPROACH

2.55 In the effort to build international trust in AI, the World Economic Forum[64] calls for a comprehensive global framework and international protocols on AI. Different national and supranational organisations are approaching the regulation of AI from different perspectives. For example, the US is approaching this from a largely laissez-faire approach driven predominantly by innovation and with a desire for limited regulatory 'red tape', compared with the EU's strict regulation and adoption of a detailed regulatory framework. The significant divergence between states does not facilitate international cohesion or certainty for businesses who want a framework with common principles, that is underpinned with trust and enables interoperability. It is considered that a framework of this

62 https://www.gov.uk/government/publications/ai-safety-summit-2023-the-bletchley-declaration/the-bletchley-declaration-by-countries-attending-the-ai-safety-summit-1-2-november-2023.

63 https://www.gov.uk/government/publications/ai-safety-summit-2023-the-bletchley-declaration/the-bletchley-declaration-by-countries-attending-the-ai-safety-summit-1-2-november-2023.

64 https://www.weforum.org/stories/2025/11/trust-ai-global-governance/.

nature could balance the different competing attitudes of regulators and countries, to the regulation of AI, with the need for a suitable benchmark.

2.56 Multiple different international organisations have sought over the last 10 years to establish different frameworks and policies to try and help guide policy makers on the ethical adoption and use of AI. The UN has looked at the idea of the development of international standards on AI adoption and praised the joint ISO (International Organization for Standardization) and IEC (International Electrotechnical Commission) committee on AI.[65] Whilst the standards are voluntary, they do go some way to reflect global views on AI adoption.

UNESCO AI ETHICS STANDARDS

2.57 UNESCO produced its own AI ethics standards in 2021,[66] which apply to its 194 members. The standards recognise that AI can create significant opportunities, but there are also significant ethical concerns, which includes discrimination, bias and the digital divide. UNESCO seeks, in a similar vein to the Council of Europe's Framework and the UK's general regulatory approach to AI, to try and balance innovation against the harms of AI. They identify that these harms are likely to impact certain countries more than others, and therefore the benefits of global standards are such that they can be used to then guide an individual countries policies and regulations.

2.58 In its 2021 standards, UNESCO recognises numerous UN Conventions as being relevant to the ethical use of AI, including: the 1986 UN Declaration on the Right to Development; the 1997 Declaration on the Responsibilities of the Present Generations Toward Future Generations; the United Nations General Assembly Resolution on Transforming our World: the 2030 Agenda for Sustainable Development; and the Human Rights Council's resolutions on 'The right to privacy in the digital age' and on 'New and emerging digital technologies and human rights'.[67]

2.59 The UNESCO standards reflect the unique challenges posed by AI given its impact on almost all aspects of life, including those in industry and employment. The standards promote the idea of the 'do no harm' principle[68] and that the safety risks of AI should be overcome.[69] The standards stipulate that there is a clear need to ensure that AI systems have effective human oversight[70] and that key decisions of 'life and death'[71] should not be delegated to AI. Finally,

65 https://www.unesco.org/en/articles/how-iso-and-iec-are-developing-international-standards-responsible-adoption-ai.
66 https://unesdoc.unesco.org/ark:/48223/pf0000381137.
67 Ibid.
68 Standard 25 – https://unesdoc.unesco.org/ark:/48223/pf0000381137.
69 Standard 27 – https://unesdoc.unesco.org/ark:/48223/pf0000381137.
70 Standard 35- https://unesdoc.unesco.org/ark:/48223/pf0000381137.
71 Standard 36 – https://unesdoc.unesco.org/ark:/48223/pf0000381137.

the UNESCO standards promote the principles of using only transparent, responsible, accountable systems.

OECD AI PRINCIPLES

2.60 In 2019, the Organisation for Economic Co-operation and Development (OECD) published its international principles on AI standards, which contain five 'value-based' principles and five recommendations.

2.61 The principles[72] are that:

1. AI should only be used for positive outcomes such as inclusivity and sustainability.
2. AI should be based on the rule of law and democracy. It should be human-centric by design and this should be protected with suitable safeguards and guardrails.
3. AI systems should be transparent; this is both in terms of their use and limitations.
4. AI systems should always be safe and secure. Systems should be put in place to safeguard this principle.
5. The creators of AI systems should have accountability.

2.62 The OECD[73] made five recommendations to policy makers, which included the need to invest in long-term AI research, the recognition that both work and society will change as a result of AI and the need for international co-operation.

HIROSHIMA AI PROCESS COMPREHENSIVE POLICY FRAMEWORK

2.63 The Hiroshima AI Process Comprehensive Policy Framework, which was agreed by the G7 leaders in 2023, comprises four different types of policies in respect of control of AI, including voluntary international principles for developers and those involved with AI systems.[74]

2.64 The 11 principles urge developers to develop AI systems in line with democratic principles and not to harm people. Any development should be in line with human rights law. The principles include taking steps to mitigate risks, continual monitoring of issues, public reporting of issues and limitations to try and form appropriate information sharing networks, creating appropriate governance,

72 https://www.oecd.org/en/topics/sub-issues/ai-principles.html.

73 Ibid.

74 https://digital-strategy.ec.europa.eu/en/library/hiroshima-process-international-guiding-principles-advanced-ai-system.

implementing proper cyber security systems and respect for intellectual property and data protection.

G7

2.65 In 2024, the G7 Technology Ministers met to consider the impact of AI on industry at which they made a declaration which included affirming

> 'our unwavering commitment to the principles of the rule of law, due process, democracy, and respect for human rights while harnessing the opportunities of innovation'[75]

A FOCUS ON LEGAL CONSIDERATIONS OF CYBER-PHYSICAL SYSTEMS AND ROBOTICS IN INDUSTRY 4.0

Legal considerations of cyber-physical systems and robotics

2.66 A cyber-physical system is a term used for systems which connect the real-world with the digital. It is a term used to describe smart robots, those typically integrated as part of Industry 4.0, which integrate a robotic system into sensors using internet of things or IT networks, or robots or AI, which then in turn interacts with the real-world. The EU provide a helpful definition of a cyber-physical system as an 'intelligent robotic systems, linked with the IoT, or technical systems of networked computers, robots and AI that interact with the physical world'.[76]

2.67 There is currently no one distinct law on either robots or cyber-physical systems in the UK or EU. Robots typically now incorporate some form of AI and therefore this aspect of the robot will be governed and considered in line with those relevant provisions discussed earlier in the chapter. The use of robots will fit within the existing regulatory system within the UK. Personal data will be dealt with under the UK GDPR, the Data Protection Act 2018 and those updates under the Data (Use and Access) Act 2025.

2.68 There are challenges with regulating robots because there will be unforeseen issues which a robot will face, and will not be able to properly respond to, as we still do not understand fully the evolution of robots, especially with

75 https://www.gov.uk/government/publications/g7-ministerial-declaration-deployment-of-ai-and-innovation/g7-ministerial-declaration.

76 https://www.europarl.europa.eu/RegData/etudes/STUD/2016/563501/EPRS_STU%282016%29563501_EN.pdf.

machine learning which is intensified by the 'black box'[77] effect.[78] The effective regulation of robots requires proper consideration of legal liability, ethics and technical engineering considerations concerning the capabilities and potential evolution of these system.[79] One of the main challenges is determining where the fault lies, especially where the system comprises mechanical elements as well as software. Where an incident happens does the fault lie with the software, the machinery or the user? Often this is not necessarily straightforward to determine given the complexities of the system. The Robotic Growth Partnership sums it up when it says:

> 'Our world is complex, non-linear, messy, turbulent and chaotic. Our nation is a complex system-of-systems … unravelling this complexity and engineering solutions to tackle challenges and realise opportunities requires systems thinking.'[80]

2.69 'Asimov's Law' is a fictional set of principles from his 1943 book *Runaround*, but these have now largely been adopted as being generally accepted fundamental principles for designers and operators of robots, not least through its reference within the European Parliament's resolution of 16 February 2017 with its recommendation to the Commission on Civil Law Rules on Robotics, and a broad reflection of the 'do no harm' principle within its Code of ethical conduct for robotic engineers.[81] 'Asimov's Law' directs that:

1. a robot must not injure or harm a human whether through its actions or inaction;
2. a robot must obey its orders from a human, save for where it conflicts with law 1; and
3. a robot must protect itself save for where it conflicts with law 1 or 2.

ETHICAL ASPECTS OF CYBER-PHYSICAL SYSTEMS

2.70 In a 2016 study,[82] prepared for the European Parliament on the ethical aspects of cyber-physical systems, experts considered that the key ethical issues in respect of cyber-physical systems expected between now and 2050 will be:

77 Which is where there is a lack of knowledge on the inner workings of these emerging technologies, which often result in a level of distrust but also means that it is difficult to regulate and to litigate without having a sophisticated understanding of the inner-workings of the technology.

78 Guerra, Parisi, and Pi (2022), 'Liability for robots I: legal challenge', Journal of Institutional Economics, 18: 331–343, https://www.cambridge.org/core/services/aop-cambridge-core/content/view/089EA1B996A5E8974643F8F1BDCD86BB/S1744137421000825a.pdf/liability_for_robots_i_legal_challenges.pdf.

79 Teresa Da Cunha Lopes, Main Issues Surrounding Robot Law (4 September 2023), available at SSRN: https://ssrn.com/abstract=4561516.

80 An independent expert group advising the UK Government.

81 (2015/2103) (INL) C252/239.

82 https://www.europarl.europa.eu/RegData/etudes/STUD/2016/563501/EPRS_STU%282016%29563501_EN.pdf.

1. the changes expected in employment and societal impact from this technology;
2. the safety concerns and how these can be mitigated. They considered ideas around liability for failed systems and cyber-security risks;
3. the concerns in respect of the right to privacy given the volume of data that will be generated with these systems; and
4. the ethical considerations around the impact of morals on cyborgs.

2.71 As part of this study, a legal expert for the European Parliamentary Research Centre concluded that due to these ethical concerns a legal framework is required for cyber-physical systems, which should include a code of conduct and ethics. They considered that the legal and regulatory issues which need to be addressed are:

1. data protection rights and privacy issues;
2. safety, including those in respect of the testing and operation of the systems;
3. liability issues, including considerations around strict liability and insurance;
4. cyber security issues;
5. issues with dual use of the system;
6. the risks of malicious use of the systems by criminals;
7. the public impact of the use of the systems;
8. certification and standardisation of the systems;
9. the need for risk assessments and safety standard;
10. intellectual property considerations;
11. regulatory standards; and
12. embedding law within the algorithms of the systems itself.

UK PERSPECTIVE

2.72 The Robotic Growth Partnership[83] released its report in 2022 on 'The Cyber-Physical Infrastructure – empowering innovation, people, robots and smart machines to enhance prosperity, resilience, sustainability and security'.[84] It advocates the need for developing agile cyber-physical systems, which are able to respond to opportunities that present themselves, and which need to be compatible with multiple different systems and fit within a wider infrastructure

83 An independent expert group advising the UK Government.

84 https://assets.publishing.service.gov.uk/media/6204e6ebe90e077f7392d446/cyber-physical-infrastructure-vision.pdf.

(be interoperable). The report highlights the need for policies, standards and regulations, which should all be baked into all systems by design.

2.73 The UK Government[85] shares the view that there is the need for a standards framework for cyber-physical systems, as well as the need for steps to be taken to develop a wider cyber-physical ecosystem. Its key concerns are around the importance of: (1) ensuring cyber-physical system security; (2) building resilient cyber-physical systems and data; (3) strengthening the resilience of the supply chain generally; and (4) properly dealing with the cyber-physical system and wider infrastructures where the cyber and real-life meet, which it considers is where it is likely to result in a higher degree of risk. It considers that the following principles should be deployed by developers and users of cyber-physical systems:

1. the use of effective security to boost the value of the system;
2. to implement security by design;
3. the need to mitigate the risks with effective security;
4. the importance of viewing the system as a whole; and
5. the use of best industry practices.

2.74 In 2024, the National Cyber-Physical Infrastructure held a series of round tables on issues relating to cyber-physical infrastructure, one of which was a Standards, Frameworks and Guidance workshop.[86] At this roundtable it was highlighted that having a framework is important as it promotes trust, but that such a framework should not stifle innovation nor be too prescriptive given the infancy of the technology. It also discussed the lack of clarity in the technology, and its relatively infancy, which both impacted on governance.

2.75 The March 2025 report prepared by the National Cyber-Physical Infrastructure Ecosystem – the 'National Cyber-Physical Infrastructure – Future Opportunities Plan 2025', again calls for a 'pro-innovation regulatory framework',[87] illustrating that there is the need for frameworks and standards, and the need for regulation, but again there is that call for a balancing act between sufficient clarity but not too onerous prescriptive requirements which may inhibit the ability of innovators to innovate. It therefore considers that any standards need to be able to adapt to the evolving technology, and must be relevant to real-life.

85 https://www.gov.uk/government/consultations/enabling-a-national-cyber-physical-infrastructure-to-catalyse-innovation/outcome/enabling-a-cyber-physical-infrastructure-to-catalyse-innovation-government-response-html.

86 https://digitaltwinhub.co.uk/download/ncpi-frameworks-guidance-and-standards/.

87 https://digitaltwinhub.co.uk/download/national-cyber-physical-infrastructure-future-opportunities-plan-2025/.

THE SMART MACHINE STRATEGY 2035

2.76 The Robotic Growth Partnership documented its 10-year plan in February 2025.[88] It considers that by 2035, the use of smart machines will be widespread across the UK and that by that date smart machines could in turn increase the UK gross asset value add by over £140 billion. The Robotic Growth Partnership calls for the establishment of an Office for Smart Machines and for kite mark systems to be brought in specifically for smart machines. It also felt that in order to generate support for smart machines, coordinated regulations needs to be addressed, as well as establishing industry standards.

2.77 Importantly, the Robotic Growth Partnership feels that there does become a point in time where humans in the loop are not appropriate for smart machines, nor necessarily even possible, as the systems start to evolve and eradicate the ability of humans to properly monitor. Therefore, it is vital that these machines are ethical, safe and have integrated governance by design.

THE EU PERSPECTIVE

2.78 The EU has been exploring some of the legal and ethical considerations around the development and use of robots for several years. There are calls in the EU for harmonised rules on cyber-physical systems, with the need for updated law and ethics to cover this space.[89] The JURI Committee[90] itself has rejected the idea that the challenge of trying to regulate a rapidly changing technology is a barrier to putting in place necessary safeguards now, and that steps should be taken to properly address the regulation of this technology.[91]

2.79 In 2017, the JURI Committee published its report on 'Civil law rules on robotics',[92] which recommended having specific EU legislation adopted on robots, and having a register for advanced robots which are monitored by an EU agency. It believes that it is now time to legislate robots, particularly where existing law will not be capable of being applied to the complexities caused by robots, such as questions around how to determine civil liability where there is autonomous decision-making in play. Whilst legislation may need to be redrafted again as the technology rapidly evolves, basic principles around civil liability needs proper consideration. Almost ten years has passed since this report, and we

88 https://www.gov.uk/government/publications/smart-machines-strategy-2035/smart-machines-strategy-2035.

89 (2018/C 252/25) Introduction (b) 'now that humankind stands on the threshold of an era when ever more sophisticated robots, bots, androids and other manifestations of artificial intelligence ("AI") seem to be poised to unleash a new industrial revolution, which is likely to leave no stratum of society untouched, it is vitally important for the legislature to consider its legal and ethical implications and effects, without stifling innovation'.

90 The Legal Affairs Committee.

91 https://www.europarl.europa.eu/RegData/etudes/ATAG/2017/599250/EPRS_ATA(2017)599250_EN.pdf.

92 Ibid.

still do not yet have a specific robot law in the EU or UK. This may be more to do with the focus of attention having been on AI for the last few years, but sight must not be lost that AI is only one form of technology integrated into robots and whilst this is certainly an important aspect driving the acceleration of this technology, it is not the only part of the technology.

2.80 The European Parliament resolution of 16 February 2017 with recommendations to the Commission on Civil Law Rules on Robotics (2015/2103 (INL)) (2018/C 252/25) highlighted many of the legal issues facing legislators with robots and the evolving technological developments in this space. These are that:

1. Laws on liability will need to evolve to adapt to the use of robots, especially as these become more and more autonomous;[93]
2. Contractual liability needs to evolve to fit advances in the innovation;[94]
3. Humans should retain oversight over these smart robots;[95]
4. There is the need for ethical principles to be set;[96]
5. Consideration is needed in respect of the intellectual property rights of robots but existing intellectual property laws could be applied;[97]
6. Existing data protection requirements will apply, such as the GDPR;[98]
7. Calls on considerations around autonomous vehicles,[99] drones,[100] care and medical robots are all needed;[101]
8. Legal consideration on liability is vital and there is an acute need for legal certainty;[102] and
9. There may be the need for compulsory insurance for robots such as with cars, to ensure that there is sufficient compensation available to recompense for harm.[103]

93 (2018/C 252/25) Introduction AB 'the more autonomous robots are, the less they can be considered to be simple tools in the hands of other actors … this, in turn, questions whether the ordinary rules on liability are sufficient or whether it calls for new principles and rules to provide clarity on the legal liability of various actors concerning responsibility for the acts and omissions of robots where the cause cannot be traced back to a specific human actor and whether the acts or omissions of robots which have caused harm could have been avoided'.
94 (2018/C 252/25) Introduction AG 'the shortcomings of the current legal framework are also apparent in the area of contractual liability insofar as machines designed to choose their counterparts, negotiate contractual terms, conclude contracts and decide whether and how to implement them, make the traditional rules inapplicable; … this highlights the need for new, efficient and up-to-date ones, which should comply with technological developments and innovations that have recently arisen and are used on the market'.
95 (2018/C 252/25) section 3.
96 (2018/C 252/25) section 11.
97 ((2018/C 252/25) section 18.
98 ((2018/C 252/25) section 19.
99 (2018/C 252/25) section 25.
100 (2018/C 252/25) section 30.
101 (2018/C 252/25) sections 31–35.
102 (2018/C 252/25) section 49.
103 (2018/C 252/25) section 57.

2.81 It is important to note that in many cases the EU AI Act[104] will apply in some respects and in some degree to robots, given these now typically do incorporate some form of AI. Further robots in the industrial space will have to interplay with staff, which is in part regulated under employment law.[105] Currently, we do not have such regulation across the board in Industry 4.0, however, as discussed in **Chapter 3**, many aspects are already regulated in one way or another.

TORTIOUS LIABILITY OF ROBOTS AND AUTOMATION

2.82 The idea of tort in the context of robots has been under-considered to date.[106] It is, however, an important area that needs to be properly addressed given the novel issues dealing with robots when considering tortious liability, largely come about because typically torts are designed for attributing blame where there are humans actively involved.[107] From a legal perspective, many of the concepts themselves in tortious liability rely on human concepts.[108] Therefore it is felt by some that there needs to be a new way of dealing with robots, which may be the combination of negligence and strict liability, as it is currently unclear whether under current legal theory the liability of robots should fall under product liability or negligence, and there may also be the need for what Guerra et al have called 'manufacturer residual liability' for robots.[109] The EU JURI Committee suggested in its 2017 report, for example, that in certain situations a strict liability approach in respect of robots should be taken, whilst in other circumstances liability should be put on the person tasked with managing the system.[110]

2.83 There is a distinction made between those robots which take on physical tasks and those which take on thinking tasks whereby the robot has some element of cognitive choice.[111] Robots are not simply just machines solely controlled by human actors. With the rise of AI, and its inclusion within cyber-physical systems, many of the Industry 4.0 robots can now be said to have taken

104 Regulation (EU) 2024/1689 of the European Parliament and of the Council of 13 June 2024 laying down harmonised rules on artificial intelligence and amending Regulations (EC) No 300/2008, (EU) No 167/2013, (EU) No 168/2013, (EU) 2018/858, (EU) 2018/1139 and (EU) 2019/2144 and Directives 2014/90/EU, (EU) 2016/797 and (EU) 2020/1828 (Artificial Intelligence Act).

105 Guerra, Parisi and Pi (n 78).

106 Ibid.

107 Ibid.

108 Ibid.

109 Ibid.

110 https://www.europarl.europa.eu/RegData/etudes/ATAG/2017/599250/EPRS_ATA(2017)599250_EN.pdf.

111 Guerra, Parisi and Pi (n 78).

on some level of cognitive tasks. This is because over time the involvement of humans decreases as the sophistication of the robots and automation increases. As a result, it becomes less and less easy to ascribe liability to a specific human individual.[112] As the machines become more and more sophisticated this balance will continue to shift, and consideration must be had where any 'tipping point' might lay.

2.84 Academics distinguish between those robots where there is an element of human control exerted over it, which should be subject to fault-based torts, and those where the robot is autonomous and develops through self-learning, where strict liability should be utilised; which is the same approach taken when dealing with liability caused by animals.[113] Using examples from autopilot technology, where in most cases manufacturers are not held liable given the extent of the regulation in the sector which firmly puts the responsibility on the pilots for the use of the autopilot, it may be that we see the emergence of regulation over the use of robotics rather than the strict regulation of the robots themselves, and importantly when it is important to shut-off the robot or not to use it.[114]

ELECTRONIC PERSONHOOD

2.85 As part of its 2020 Artificial Intelligence and Civil Liability study commissioned by the Juri committee,[115] the European Parliament considered the idea of electronic personhood. The report challenges the concept of 'electronic personhood', a term which currently has no accepted legal definition but is widely felt to be the creation of a new form of legal status for robots; although there are queries over whether this would go as far as distinct legal personality akin to limited liabilities of corporates or not.

2.86 The European Parliament recognised that there are many opponents of the idea of robots or AI attracting legal personality, and in most cases, there was no actual need to actually even have this because a real-life human can in many instances be identified as bearing responsibility for the system.[116]

112 Ibid.

113 https://ai-laws.org/2019/12/12/robotics-and-civil-liability-in-the-eu/.

114 Guerra, Parisi and Pi (n 78).

115 https://www.europarl.europa.eu/RegData/etudes/STUD/2020/621926/IPOL_STU(2020)621926_EN.pdf.

116 Ibid.

A FOCUS ON LEGAL CONSIDERATIONS OF EDGE COMPUTING IN INDUSTRY 4.0

2.87 Cloud computing is one of the most fundamental innovations which has enabled Industry 4.0 to take place and evolve. Within the EU, cloud services are considered as part of the core platform services under the Digital Markets Act 2022 and providers are afforded responsibility as gatekeepers. In the UK, the Cyber Security and Resilience (Network and Information Systems) Bill set to expand the Network and Information Systems Regulations 2018, will categorise certain data centres as essential services[117] and will see more clarity on the definition of cloud computing, as well as additional registration requirements introduced, stricter security requirements and enhanced reporting for cloud service providers.

2.88 Industry 4.0 and the industrial metaverse tend to utilise edge computing, as well as cloud computing, and even fog computing which is the middle-layer between the cloud and the edge,[118] often known as a cloud to edge continuum solution.[119]

2.89 Edge computing is an alternative to traditional forms of cloud computing. It means rather than data having to be transmitted to a centralised cloud data centre, it is effectively decentralised, utilising local devices, such as the IoT devices, and servers at the edge of the network typically in situ, or closer in proximity, for processing data rather than having to send all the data to one centralised cloud.[120] It is used within smart manufacturing to deal with, for example, monitoring any unusual actions of robots and making decisions based on the data it receives, and allowing devices such as those used for wind turbines to monitor and make decisions based on data it receives. Edge computing is utilised widely in smart agriculture, autonomous vehicles and healthcare to empower autonomy for devices to process specific data and then act upon it.[121]

2.90 The IEEE considers that edge computing can be utilised to mitigate some of the risks associated with cyber attacks.[122] It may also help address some of the risks experienced over the course of 2025 with cloud service outages such as the October 2025 AWS outage and November 2025 Cloudflare outage. Other experts caution, however, that it can instead just present different risks, effectively just

117 Clause 2(2)(a)-(d) of the proposed Cyber Security and Resilience (Network and Information Systems) Bill seeks to extend the Network and Information Systems Regulations 2018 to those persons providing data centres and that these be designated as critical suppliers.

118 https://azure.microsoft.com/en-us/resources/cloud-computing-dictionary/what-is-edge-computing.

119 https://www.berec.europa.eu/system/files/2024-03/BoR%20%2824%29%2052_Draft_Cloud_Report.pdf.

120 https://ieeexplore.ieee.org/document/10596039 and https://azure.microsoft.com/en-us/resources/cloud-computing-dictionary/what-is-edge-computing.

121 https://azure.microsoft.com/en-us/resources/cloud-computing-dictionary/what-is-edge-computing.

122 https://ieeexplore.ieee.org/document/10596039.

moving the risk away from the cloud providers and instead to software providers of IoT devices and sensors.[123]

2.91 Edge computing does have benefits in respect of data protection, given data does not then have to be transmitted to a centralised data centre. Concerns as set out above, however, concerning the vulnerability of the devices to cyber-attack, has an impact on the protection of data, especially where this is personal data.[124]

2.92 Under the new EU Data Act[125] protection is afforded to users of cloud and edge computing services, which includes interoperability rights and the ability to switch providers. A Cloud Rulebook has been created in the EU which is designed as a self-regulatory handbook of policies and standards for cloud providers in the EU.[126] This includes a certification scheme and a code of conduct. The EU has also developed standard contractual clauses for cloud and edge services which are contained in the Rulebook.[127]

A FOCUS ON LEGAL CONSIDERATIONS OF SEMICONDUCTORS IN INDUSTRY 4.0

2.93 Semiconductors underpin Industry 4.0. These are the computer chips which are powering the revolution, and commonly are made out of silicon. The EU Chips Act[128] came into force in September 2023. The EU Act seeks to establish a framework to deal with the supply of semiconductor chips across the EU, and was a response to the international three-year shortage of chips between 2020 to 2023. In 2025, the EU member states signed the Declaration of the Semicon Coalition where they committed to trying to progress towards a new Chips Act for the EU. The new Chips Act, known as the Chips Act 2.0, is a key priority for the EU and is expected to be adopted by mid-2027.[129]

2.94 The UK has also identified semiconductors as being part of its critical infrastructures[130] and certain companies carrying out activities within the semiconductor industry will fall under the National Security and Investment Act 2022.[131] The UK does not have widescale semiconductors manufacturing capabilities so instead imports these chips, typically from Taiwan which poses a risk in itself. In September 2025, it was announced that there would be £10

123 https://www.techuk.org/resource/opportunities-and-risks-of-edge-computing.html.
124 https://researchbriefings.files.parliament.uk/documents/POST-PN-0631/POST-PN-0631.pdf.
125 Regulation 2023/2854.
126 https://digital-strategy.ec.europa.eu/en/library/cloud-and-edge-computing-different-way-using-it-brochure.
127 Ibid.
128 Regulation 2023/1781.
129 https://www.europarl.europa.eu/RegData/etudes/BRIE/2026/785742/EPRS_BRI(2026)785742_EN.pdf.
130 https://researchbriefings.files.parliament.uk/documents/POST-PN-0721/POST-PN-0721.pdf.
131 Meaning certain sales and investment will require Government consent

million invested in semiconductor innovation in the UK and it is predicted that by 2030 in the UK this area will grow by 75%.[132] Similar to the EU, the UK has confirmed as part of its strategy on semiconductors that it will publish industry guidance for resilience in this market and establish a forum to identify issues early. In April 2024, the UK implemented export restrictions on the export of semiconductor materials out of the UK, which now require a specific licence to be exported.[133]

2.95 The Semiconductors Point of Contact (PoC) Group was set up by the G7 to enable collaboration and information sharing between members.[134] In December 2025, the G7 Industry, Digital and Technology Ministers highlighted the work being undertaken by the PoC Group and the need to protect the supply chain for semiconductor chips.

2.96 Semiconductors typically encompass multiple intellectual property rights including patent rights, design rights, copyright and trade secrets.

KEY TAKEAWAY POINTS

2.97 The key takeaway points in respect of the key legal considerations in Industry 4.0 and its technologies are:

- Legal considerations in Industry 4.0 primarily revolve around issues of liability, data security, privacy, and intellectual property rights. Legislators are keen not to stifle innovation by overly onerous legislation but novel issues will arise as the Industry 4.0 technologies continue to advance.
- Steps need to be taken to protect people in the industrial metaverse. Technology should be human-centric by design.
- Other key areas of concern include the digital divide and human rights, sustainability and environmental concerns, and competition law considerations.
- Steps can be taken to use contracts to try and mitigate some of the risks associated with a lack of governance and regulations on emerging technologies. There are concerns, however, where it may not be possible for there to be a contractual relationship between all the different parties making up the technology stack, as well as with the end-user, so sufficient care and attention is needed when preparing terms to carefully map out the different parties and relationships.

132 https://www.gov.uk/government/news/new-10-million-fund-to-support-uk-businesses-to-deliver-next-generation-of-semiconductors.
133 Under The Export Control (Amendment) Regulations 2024.
134 https://www.gov.uk/government/publications/g7-ministerial-declaration-deployment-of-ai-and-innovation/g7-ministerial-declaration.

- The Digital Regulation Cooperation Forum (DRCF) is a multi-regulator taskforce in the UK whose mission is to consider the specific impact of different emerging technologies on the different regulatory landscapes.

Chapter 3

Legal and regulatory frameworks for Industry 4.0

'Given the Fourth Industrial Revolution's extraordinarily fast technological and social change, relying only on government legislation and incentives to ensure the right outcomes is ill-advised. These are likely to be out-of-date or redundant by the time they are implemented.'

World Economic Forum White Paper on Values and the Fourth Industrial Revolution Connecting the Dots Between Value, Values, Profit and Purpose, Global Agenda Council on Values (2014–2016)[1]

3.1 It is vital that effective steps are taken now, as we embrace the digital revolution, to find an effective form of governance and regulation of emerging frontier technology so that we can protect people from harm but still enable digital progression. Whilst emerging technologies bring significant advantages, there are also considerable risks; trying to govern these technologies is extremely challenging given the pace of innovation.[2] This all presents unique challenges to regulators given the technologies continue to advance must faster than the regulators can react, the risks they bring may not be immediately obvious as they are themselves emerging risks, it typically all falls outside of the existing regulatory framework (or at least what it was designed to cover), and cuts across different sectors, fields and jurisdictions in new, and often unexpected ways.[3]

3.2 Industry 4.0 is not limited to one territory or one jurisdiction. This is a global phenomenon which has been met with different responses by lawmakers from different territories. Some jurisdictions, such as the EU have sought to adopt prescribed regulations for the different Industry 4.0 technologies, whilst the UK has adopted an 'innovation first' approach, preferring instead to try and utilise existing regulatory frameworks or alternative forms of control to avoid stifling innovation. Germany and the EU have gone down the path of strict regulations, whilst the USA and China have taken a more relaxed approach focused on commercial drivers.[4] This is even more of a challenge in practice where systems may integrate different components from different states, and its delivery or implementation may cross multiple different jurisdictions.

1 https://www3.weforum.org/docs/WEF_Values_and_the_Fourth_Industrial_Revolution_WHITEPAPER.pdf.
2 Gary E. Marchant (2020), 'Governance of Emerging Technology as a wicked problem', Vanderbilt Law Review, 73(6):1861–1877.
3 Ibid.
4 https://issues.org/wp-content/uploads/2019/04/Belton-et-al.-Smart-Factories-SP19-ISSUES-70-76.pdf.

3.3 *Legal and regulatory frameworks for Industry 4.0*

3.3 In the past, regulators have dealt with emerging technologies by either adapting existing regulations, or creating new regulations or trying to utilise industrial standards. Given the changes presented by Industry 4.0, however, and the pace of innovation as we progress through the digital revolution, it may be time for regulators to rethink how they can regulate this space, and instead focus on horizon scanning and working collaboratively with multiple different stakeholders nationally and transnationally, including industry bodies and other experts.[5] The Government of the United Arab Emirates[6] surmise that:

> 'The coming decade will test whether countries can align technological change and governance fast enough to stay competitive. Regulators that act early to design clear, adaptive rules, and companies that treat regulation as a strategic priority, will shape the standards, trust and markets of the future. Those who wait will compete on others' terms. The window for leadership in regulatory innovation is open now; those who act first will set the direction of global innovation and competitiveness.'[7]

3.4 The 2013 'Securing the future of German manufacturing industry – recommendations for implementing the strategic initiative Industrie 4.0' report considers that any regulation needs to balance innovation and compliance, the key being to consider the legal perspective of emerging technologies early to ensure that the issues are addressed swiftly at the outset.[8] What is of fundamental importance for industry, however, is to have some form of legal certainty, to enable innovators to innovate. How this is achieved in this landscape, however, does not have universal consensus. Whilst in theory this may sound promising, there still remains a distinct lack of effective governance or regulation covering Industry 4.0, and the changes being brought about by the digital revolution, despite good intentions.

3.5 There are challenges with regulating the technologies relating to Industry 4.0, because of the speed at which the technology is evolving, the complexity of the technology, the cross-border nature of Industry 4.0 and the need to balance the innovation against regulation.[9] Many consider that technology itself can also be utilised to help monitor and enforce compliance with regulations[10] and

5 https://reports.weforum.org/docs/WEF_The_Regulatory_Frontier_Designing_the_Rules_that_Shape_Innovation_2025.pdf.

6 In its World Economic Forum's 2026 White Paper prepared by the Government of the United Arab Emirates and the Boston Consulting Group –'The Regulatory Frontier: Designing the Rules that Shape Innovation' January 2026.

7 https://reports.weforum.org/docs/WEF_The_Regulatory_Frontier_Designing_the_Rules_that_Shape_Innovation_2025.pdf.

8 'Securing the future of German manufacturing industry – recommendations for implementing the strategic initiative Industrie 4.0' 2013, https://www.din.de/resource/blob/76902/e8cac883f42bf28536e7e8165993f1fd/recommendations-for-implementing-industry-4-0-data.pdf.

9 Da Cunha Lopes, Teresa, Main Issues Surrounding Robot Law (4 September 2023), available at SSRN: https://ssrn.com/abstract=4561516.

10 https://www3.weforum.org/docs/WEF_Technology_Policy_Responsible_Design_Flourishing_World_2024.pdf.

should be promoted as a tool for regulators to help ensure that regulations remain relevant and suitable.[11]

EMERGING TECHNOLOGY POLICY

3.6 It is importance that lawmakers implement suitable policies for the governance of emerging technologies[12] because effective technology policy should act as a 'guardrail' to protect society.[13]

3.7 The Global Future Council, part of the World Economic Forum, highlights the need to guide safe and responsible innovation through policy, which needs to balance the benefits of innovation, against its risks, which should be done through proactive governance reflecting the ethical underpinning principles and objectives of society.[14]

3.8 According to the Global Future Council, there are eight guiding principles for suitable technology policy:[15]

1. investment in early innovations to encourage responsible growth;
2. establishment of shared values and principles that need to be protected;
3. well balanced competition because restraints on competition are not beneficial to society;
4. an effective balance between innovation and national risks, such as risks around national security and safety;
5. the creation of policy which is borderless and interoperable. It considers that there should be a baseline of standards which does not conflict with other jurisdictions policies where possible;
6. adoption of a risk-based approach to regulation;
7. encouragement of a 'by design' approach for the development of technologies, so that the technology is designed with the specific principles baked into their design – such as privacy by design; and
8. ensuring that all policy is evidenced based.

11 https://www.oecd.org/content/dam/oecd/en/publications/reports/2025/04/oecd-regulatory-policy-outlook-2025_a754bf4c/56b60e39-en.pdf.

12 https://www.weforum.org/publications/technology-policy-responsible-design-for-a-flourishing-world/.

13 Ibid.

14 Ibid.

15 Ibid.

3.9 Policy should also be human centric so to empower citizens, protect their resilience, foster sustainability, reflect privacy principles and be developed with the support of multiple different interested stakeholders.[16]

EXISTING REGULATIONS

3.10 Any emerging technology, whether as Industry 4.0 or beyond, will typically first exist within the then current and established legal framework before new laws and regulations can be created.[17] This presents challenges in both enforcing the existing laws in respect of those emerging technologies, but also because there is then also a lack of legal certainty for those utilising the new technologies since any solution in trying to apply existing laws to new forms of technology will be an imperfect one.[18]

3.11 Whilst there may currently be little specific regulation concerning Industry 4.0 per se, many parts of industry, in which the technologies are being deployed, are already heavily regulated and many issues will also fall under more general regulation.

NEW REGULATION

3.12 The Institute of Electrical and Electronics Engineers (IEEE) calls for a focus on regulating the industrial metaverse, at both national and international levels.[19] Academics, however, caution that any regulation should facilitate innovation[20] and the OECD cautions regulators to include consideration of innovation-based risks into their regulatory impact assessments.[21]

3.13 One role of the World Economic Forum is to assist policy-makers with dealing with many of the issues around regulating emerging technologies, and it has created a number of initiatives which are focused on Industry 4.0 and emerging technologies, such as the AI Governance Alliance.[22] The World Economic Forum has established the Centre for Frontier Technologies and Innovation[23] which provides guidance and policies on emerging technologies and as part of the centre has established the Fourth Industrial Revolution Network.

16 Ibid.
17 'Securing the future of German manufacturing industry' (n 8).
18 Ibid.
19 https://ieeexplore.ieee.org/document/10596039.
20 E. A. Gromova, N. S. Koneva and E. V. Titova (2022), 'Legal barriers to the implementation of digital industry (Industry 4.0) components and the ways to overcome them', The Journal of World Intellectual Property, 25: 186–205, http://doi.org/10.1111/jwip.12215.
21 https://www.oecd.org/content/dam/oecd/en/publications/reports/2025/04/oecd-regulatory-policy-outlook-2025_a754bf4c/56b60e39-en.pdf.
22 https://www3.weforum.org/docs/WEF_Governance_in_the_Age_of_Generative_AI_2024.pdf.
23 https://centres.weforum.org/centre-for-frontier-technologies-and-innovation/home.

3.14 The World Economic Forum promotes the use of regulations for Industry 4.0, focusing on outcome-based regulation, or prescriptive regulations with enough flex to balance the existing regulatory system against the evolving emerging technology landscape, such as the 'right to innovate' in Italy.[24] In 2020, the World Economic Forum published a paper on the 'Agile Regulation for the Fourth Industrial Revolution: A Toolkit for Regulators'.[25] In the paper the World Economic Forum highlighted the need for regulators to move towards a more agile approach to regulation in the context of Industry 4.0 generally, so to ensure that regulations can be adapted swiftly to meet the rapidly changing needs borne out of the pace of innovation that will come about as a result of this mass industrial revolution. It identifies the following concerns:

1. 'the pacing problem …
2. The coordination problem … [and]
3. The responsibility problem'.[26]

3.15 The paper effectively provides a blueprint for regulators to follow to identify and manage the emerging risks in Industry 4.0. It is felt that there is the need for a new way of regulating these technologies not least because of the global regulatory failings which the Covid-19 pandemic highlighted.[27] The World Economic Forum highlights the importance of timing; if the regulation is too early then it may not be relevant, and if this is too late, the risks will be manifesting and multiplying and eventually will get out of control.[28] One practical suggestion for good governance is the use of what has been termed 'anticipatory regulation', being the consideration of the likely risks that will present themselves in respect of a particular technology and then using this to then guide regulation.[29] This does not necessarily mean that regulation has to immediately follow just because there may be some risk identified, and there should always be a period of observation and horizon mapping before there is a need to regulate.[30] There are risks with this approach if serious harm manifests itself during the observation period. Emerging technology, such as quantum computing, can produce serious risk of harm. The balance of knowing when to act, what to regulate, and when, is therefore extremely complex.

3.16 In its January 2026 white paper, the World Economic Forum together with the UAE Government considered the design of rules for encouraging innovation, and the opportunities in being able to use regulation to accelerate progress and

24 'Agile Regulation for the Fourth Industrial Revolution: A Toolkit for Regulators' (2020), https://www3.weforum.org/docs/WEF_Agile_Regulation_for_the_Fourth_Industrial_Revolution_2020.pdf.

25 Ibid.

26 https://www3.weforum.org/docs/WEF_Agile_Regulation_for_the_Fourth_Industrial_Revolution_2020.pdf.

27 Ibid.

28 Ibid.

29 Ibid.

30 Ibid.

innovation, by calling for suitable regulations to act as a catalyst for growth, provided these rules are unpinned with creating trust, are transparent and facilitate competition.[31] It suggests that regulators need to be able to combine foresight, collaboration and technical expertise, but also the need to act swiftly to establish themselves as leading jurisdictions for these pioneering emerging technologies.[32] The report highlights that there are varying degrees of risk, and with the changes brought about by the advances in emerging technology, regulators are no longer required to regulate specific organisations, but instead should focus on regulating activities regardless of who performs them.[33] Regulations need to adapt to the new emerging technologies, and the increased use of regulatory sandboxes and effective collaboration between regulators and innovators should be promoted as we move into Industry 4.0.[34] The World Economic Forum advocates for principle-based law which is agile and can adapt and evolve with the emerging technologies, together with the continual evolution and oversight of regulators and flexible laws.[35]

3.17 The World Economic Forum cautions

> 'Laws lose credibility when adaptation lags. When standards bodies take years to update their principles, they stop providing protection. When regulators interpret them differently across regions, companies face costly fragmentation. The worst outcome is a system that claims flexibility but creates uncertainty … Well-designed guardrails are not brakes – they are the runway for innovation and will define the competitive map of the future. Regulation has become a defining capability of competitiveness. Countries and companies that master it will determine how innovation scales and where economic power grows in the decade ahead.'[36]

THE ALAN TURING INSTITUTE FRAMEWORK AND SELF-ASSESSMENT TOOL

3.18 In January 2026, the Alan Turing Institute launched its framework for regulating AI in the UK. It is a voluntary regime, based on the UNESCO AI Readiness Assessment Methodology, aimed at providing regulators and policy-makers with an efficient way of assessing AI systems and being able to build out policies and regulatory frameworks.[37] The framework provides good practice for artificial intelligence (AI) systems, by again seeking to balance innovation against risk, and to assist regulators deal with AI where the responsibility for policymaking has been put on the existing regulators.

31 https://reports.weforum.org/docs/WEF_The_Regulatory_Frontier_Designing_the_Rules_that_Shape_Innovation_2025.pdf.
32 Ibid.
33 Ibid.
34 Ibid.
35 Ibid.
36 Ibid.
37 https://www.turing.ac.uk/news/new-guidance-will-help-uk-regulate-ai-effectively-and-responsibly.

3.19 The framework and self-assessment tool[38] are aimed at helping regulators understand and address the risk of AI in their sectors, and then use this tool to build out suitable regulations. The framework splits the issues into six distinct stages for regulators, as set out in Figure 3.1, from the initial objective, through formulation of the rules and then to devising the policies. Following on from this, there are 17 capabilities issues to be addressed relating to legal and administration, finances, technology, research, skills and then organisational concerns. The framework is then used within the tool, which the regulators can then use to score their readiness and capability in respect of the regulation of AI in their sector.

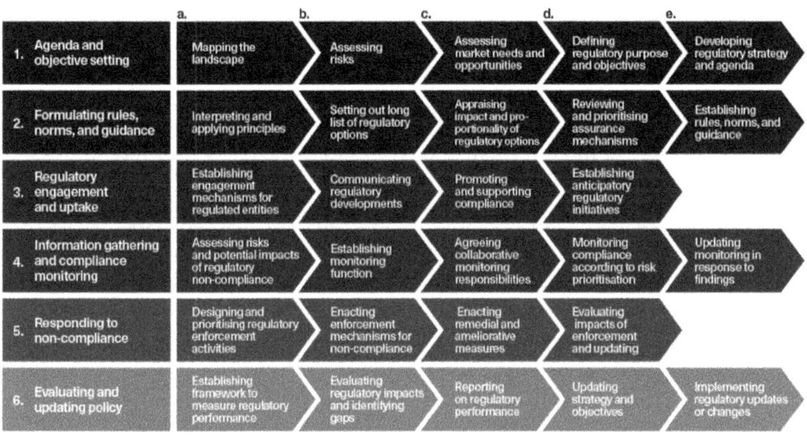

Source: C. D. Thomas and R. Beddard (2026), *The AI Regulatory Capability Framework and Self-Assessment Tool*, The Alan Turing Institute. © The Alan Turing Institute and reproduced with their kind permission. For more information, visit https://www.turing.ac.uk/.

Figure 3.1 The six regulatory stages under the AI Regulatory Capability Framework and Self-Assessment Tool

3.20 The framework and tool can be used by regulators to understand how to regulate AI in their sector, understand the gaps, help action to plug the gaps and then monitor their impact. The idea is to help regulators create suitable rules and polices based on key actions which should apply across all regulators.

THE GLOBAL REGULATORY INNOVATION PLATFORM

3.21 Despite the resistance of some countries to try and regulate emerging technologies and innovations, experts consider that rather than hinder innovation

38 https://storage.ghost.io/c/44/95/449506ca-034e-480f-9725-fcde08ef1cc1/content/files/2026/02/The-AI-Regulatory-Capability-Framework-and-Self--Assessment-Tool.pdf.

suitable regulations can actually encourage innovations to grow and prosper as it provides certainty and encourages responsible growth.[39] Any regulation should therefore be designed so that:[40]

1. the legal perimeters are clearly defined, typically taking a risk-based approach;
2. there are effective systems to identify learnings;
3. it facilitates the entry of new businesses into the sector;
4. there are suitable underpinning infrastructures created. This is going further than simply creating the rules but also creating distinct infrastructures such as creating open access API interfaces; and
5. there are systems in place which enable the regulations to adapt to advances in the innovations and technology. Any regulatory system should be agile.

3.22 Recognising the challenges of regulation of emerging technologies and innovations, given the speed of change, the World Economic Forum has also established the Global Regulatory Innovation Platform initiative to assist policy-makers in designing suitable regulations.

ORGANISATION FOR ECONOMIC CO-OPERATION AND DEVELOPMENT (OECD)

3.23 The OECD is mapping regulations in terms of AI and tracking common trends, such as where its focus is on the protection of fundamental rights and use of agile regulations balanced against voluntary codes and industry standards.[41]

3.24 The OECD Regulatory Policy Outlook 2025 considers the regulation of the future and believes that regulations need to be able to address emerging risks from new technologies, as well as still enable opportunities to be taken in respect of this new frontier.[42] It considers that regulation can actually help innovations and that a gap in regulation can actually prevent the growth of emerging technologies.[43] The main issue for regulators is the speed at which the technology is developing and the cross-border nature of the technology; in fact, regulators may not yet even know the extent of the risks presented by certain technologies, given the pace at which they are developing and the risks evolving.[44]

39 https://reports.weforum.org/docs/WEF_The_Regulatory_Frontier_Designing_the_Rules_that_Shape_Innovation_2025.pdf.

40 Ibid.

41 https://www.oecd.org/content/dam/oecd/en/publications/reports/2025/04/oecd-regulatory-policy-outlook-2025_a754bf4c/56b60e39-en.pdf.

42 Ibid.

43 Ibid.

44 https://www.oecd.org/content/dam/oecd/en/publications/reports/2025/04/oecd-regulatory-policy-outlook-2025_a754bf4c/56b60e39-en.pdf.

3.25 The OECD also promotes the use of risk-based regulation for emerging technologies but consider that governments should also appreciate the need for the continual assessment and approval of new regulations, as well as taking a proactive approach to regulation through effective horizon scanning and the use of anticipatory governance.[45] Importantly, the OECD stresses the need for an 'adapt-and-learn' approach to regulation and the need for collaboration between governments and regulators given the nature of the technology. What is clear is that it is not only the technology that is emerging and changing as part of the digital industrial revolution, but also the need for its regulation to also evolve to remain effective and relevant to emerging risks.

REGULATORY SANDBOXES

3.26 Regulatory sandboxes allow regulators to test out innovations in a virtual environment where there may be a lack of regulation or where it may be risky for the technology to be deployed in a live environment prior to regulatory sign-off. It enables the regulators to work with the innovators to build out the regulation around the innovations, and for pioneering innovators to build in a safe space with the knowledge and oversight of the regulators.

3.27 The World Economic Forum promotes the effective use of sandboxes, or what it terms as 'experimental regulation' in its white paper on 'Agile Regulation for the Fourth Industrial Revolution: A Toolkit for Regulators' because regulators need to be able to innovate and adapt alongside the innovation, which can be achieved through creative solutions such as testbeds, sandboxes and holding competitions to challenge the regulators perspective.[46]

3.28 Regulatory sandboxes have been successfully used in the UK, such as with the Financial Conduct Authorities 'Project Innovate',[47] the Solicitors Regulation Authority's 'LawTech' programme,[48] the ICO sandbox,[49] the MHRA AI Airlock[50] and the HSE industrial safetytech sandbox.[51] Sir Patrick Vallance, the former Minister of State for Science, Research and Innovation of the United

45 As some technologies, such as quantum computing, are too early to need comprehensive regulation but given the importance of the technology, it is important that this is in the minds of regulators.

46 https://www3.weforum.org/docs/WEF_Agile_Regulation_for_the_Fourth_Industrial_Revolution_2020.pdf.

47 https://www.fca.org.uk/news/press-releases/financial-conduct-authority-unveils-successful-sandbox-firms-second-anniversary.

48 https://www.sra.org.uk/solicitors/resources/innovate/common-queries-answered/.

49 https://ico.org.uk/for organisations/advice-and-services/regulatory-sandbox/our-key-areas-of-focus-for-the-regulatory-sandbox/.

50 https://www.gov.uk/government/collections/ai-airlock-the-regulatory-sandbox-for-aiamd.

51 https://solutions.hse.gov.uk/training/sandbox.

Kingdom also recommended the implementation of an AI sandbox in the 2023 UK Government policy on 'A pro-innovation approach to AI regulation'.[52]

3.29 Regulatory sandboxes are popular in the UAE.[53] The RegLab is a regulatory sandbox based in Dubai which was established in 2019 and allows emerging technology to be tested and 'incubated' in a safe environment and enables effective collaboration between the technology providers and regulators.[54]

VOLUNTARY CODES AND TECHNICAL STANDARDS

3.30 Within the technology sector there has always been a reliance on self-regulation through subscription to voluntary codes and standards. This continues within Industry 4.0 and the industrial metaverse.

3.31 Gromova et al[55] consider that there should be a drive towards self-regulation in Industry 4.0, and the World Economic Forum also highlight the benefit of using voluntary codes of conduct to assist regulation, and even the use of 'rules as code'.[56] The 2023 UK Government policy on 'A pro-innovation approach to AI regulation' itself also stresses the importance of technical standards on the control of emerging technologies, in particular in respect of AI.[57]

3.32 Often enterprise customers insist upon their contracting parties meeting specific standards or codes, therefore in many situations software providers and suppliers are being commercially required to meet specific codes or standards in order to fulfil contractual requirements, meaning that industry itself and economics are guiding controls over the technology and driving standards. Some of the key relevant existing standards include:

1. Standard ISO 42001 in respect of artificial intelligence management systems;
2. Standard ISO 23894 in respect of risk management of artificial intelligence;
3. IEEE 7001 standard for transparency of autonomous systems;
4. Standard ISO/IEC 22989:2022 on artificial intelligence;
5. Standard ISO/IEC 23053:2022 on framework for artificial intelligence systems using machine learning;

52 https://www.gov.uk/government/publications/ai-regulation-a-pro-innovation-approach/white-paper.
53 https://u.ae/fi/about-the-uae/digital-uae/regulatory-framework/regulatory-sandboxes-in-the-uae.
54 https://www.dubaifuture.ae/initiatives/future-design-and-acceleration/uae-regulations-lab.
55 Gromova, Koneva, and Titova (n 20).
56 https://www3.weforum.org/docs/WEF_Agile_Regulation_for_the_Fourth_Industrial_Revolution_2020.pdf.
57 https://www.gov.uk/government/publications/ai-regulation-a-pro-innovation-approach/white-paper.

6. Standard ISO/IEC 24029-2:2023 on the robustness of neural networks;
7. Standard ISO/IEC TS 6254:2025 on objectives and approaches on machine learning and artificial intelligence; and
8. Standard ISO/IEC TR 5469:2024 on AI system safety.

3.33 The International Electrotechnical Commission (IEC) considers that there are currently gaps in the technical standards for the industrial metaverse which need to be addressed since this causes issues with interoperability.[58] It recommends that there is the need to establish a dedicated working group to develop key standards on the industrial metaverse; this should also address key governance and regulatory standards which cover ethical considerations, standards on interoperability and for testing within the industrial metaverse.[59] Where voluntary industry codes are utilised to govern Industry 4.0, however, it is vital that there is full transparency and these codes are not utilised as a way to try and fetter competition or disproportionately hinder other businesses.[60]

ECONOMIC FREE ZONES AND PPPS

3.34 PPPs are public-private partnerships (PPPs). In PPPs, private sector businesses and the public sector collaborate together on specific innovations. Private investors are incentivised to invest in innovation, often with tax reliefs, and the PPPs in turn enable the injection of private capital funds through private companies into the innovation to be utilised in many cases in the public sector, or in a hybrid situation with a focus on public and private sector use. Many consider that PPPs can be utilised for sustainability purposes.[61] PPP are being used to fund the innovations of the future and are a popular mechanism to cross-pollinate the private and public sectors.

3.35 There has been a move towards virtual or digital-free zones in certain jurisdiction,[62] which enable testing in these areas and looser regulatory control. Economic free zones have been established, such as in the UAE and India.

THE 'WICKED PROBLEM FRAMEWORK'

3.36 Academics consider that there may in fact not be one ideal solution to regulate emerging technologies, instead there is what has been termed the 'wicked problem framework', a combination of substandard solutions which,

58 https://www.iec.ch/basecamp/industrial-metaverse.

59 Ibid.

60 https://www3.weforum.org/docs/WEF_Agile_Regulation_for_the_Fourth_Industrial_Revolution_2020.pdf.

61 https://unece.org/sites/default/files/2022-10/ECE_CECI_WP_PPP_2022_06-en.pdf.

62 https://www.wcoomd.org/-/media/wco/public/global/pdf/topics/facilitation/activities-and-programmes/free-zone/wco-fz-guidance_en.pdf?la=en.

when combined together, may provide a workable solution to the issues being faced given that traditional forms of regulation in isolation are just not suitable.[63] In doing this it is necessary to combine both the regulators and the private sector to be able to govern emerging technologies, and use some, if not all, of the four major forms of governance being soft law, precaution, resilience and liability.[64]

3.37 The 'Securing the future of German manufacturing industry – recommendations for implementing the strategic initiative Industrie 4.0' report, often considered the origins of Industry 4.0 theory, also believes that the best way to deal with Industry 4.0 is a combination of regulation, policies and technical standards, as well as producing model contracts and the harmonisation of international rules.[65] The World Economic Forum itself also considers that effective governance is a combination of regulation, codes, self-governance and standards to guide behaviour and address the risks in Industry 4.0.[66]

3.38 Gromova et al[67] also highlight the combined use of PPPs,[68] regulatory sandboxes and special economic zones to encourage the use of regulation to encourage the emergence and development of Industry 4.0.

INTERNATIONAL COOPERATION

3.39 Industry 4.0 technologies transcend traditional jurisdictional boundaries. Businesses strive for legal certainty to be able to operate, but this is extremely complex to achieve in Industry 4.0, especially in respect of cross-border interactions. Proper international cooperation on regulation is essential. In 2022, the OECD published its Recommendation of the Council on International Regulatory Cooperation to Tackle Global Challenges which builds on the Regulatory Policy Committee established in 2012.[69]

3.40 This difficulty has been recognised by Sir Geoffrey Vos MR, and in 2025 he announced the establishment of the International Jurisdiction Taskforce, for which he is the Chair.[70] The International Jurisdiction Taskforce was formed to consider the common international legal issues that emerging technologies present, predominantly blockchain and digital assets, across multiple jurisdictions and cross-border interactions.[71] When announcing the initiative Sir Geoffrey Vos

63 Marchant (n 2).
64 Ibid.
65 'Securing the future of German manufacturing industry' (n 8).
66 https://www3.weforum.org/docs/WEF_Agile_Regulation_for_the_Fourth_Industrial_Revolution_2020.pdf.
67 Gromova, Koneva, and Titova (n 20).
68 Examples they cite include robotics and supercomputers in the EU, as well as examples in Brazil and China.
69 https://legalinstruments.oecd.org/en/instruments/OECD-LEGAL-0475.
70 https://lawtechuk.io/ijt/launch-of-the-international-jurisdiction-taskforce-ijt/.
71 https://www.judiciary.uk/speech-by-the-master-of-the-rolls-the-international-jurisdiction-taskforce/.

MR said that the plan was to see whether it was possible to achieve private law alignment from key jurisdictions on emerging technology issues.[72] The Taskforce has representatives from private law jurisdictions, amongst others, of the UK, Australia, EU, and the USA.

COORDINATED REGULATION

3.41 Given the nature of Industry 4.0, and the cross-overs between different industries and existing regulatory issues, it is important to have cooperation between the different regulators.[73] In the UK the Digital Regulation Cooperation Forum (DRCF) embodies this principle. The DRCF is a multi-regulatory forum which come together to consider, and collaborate on, digital issues.[74] It comprises the financial regulator – the Financial Conduct Authority, the personal data regulator – the Information Commissioner's Office, Ofcom – the communications regulator, and the Competition and Markets Authority – the competition and anti-trust regulator. In addition, the DRCF has established the International Network for Digital Regulation Cooperation (INDRC) which sees further collaboration between Australia, Canada, Ireland, UK and Netherlands.[75]

3.42 The DRCF ran a pilot scheme in 2024 called the AI and Digital Hub, which was a multi-regulatory hub offering guidance to innovative businesses. In its October 2025 report on the findings from the pilot scheme, the DRCF considered that it helped to foster innovation and provided meaningful and flexible guidance to emerging technology businesses.[76]

THE UK INDUSTRY 4.0 REGULATORY LANDSCAPE

3.43 One of the reasons why innovative businesses historically have been attracted to the UK is because of its regulatory framework, but this needs to continually evolve to accommodate emerging technologies and encourage innovation.[77] In 2018, the Council for Science and Technology[78] wrote to the UK Prime Minister at that time about the need to reform regulation and the need for:

72 https://www.judiciary.uk/speech-by-the-master-of-the-rolls-to-the-lawtech-uk-conference-2025/.

73 https://www3.weforum.org/docs/WEF_Agile_Regulation_for_the_Fourth_Industrial_Revolution_2020.pdf.

74 https://www.drcf.org.uk/about-us.

75 https://www.drcf.org.uk/projects/projects/international-network-for-digital-regulation-cooperation-indrc.

76 https://www.drcf.org.uk/siteassets/drcf/pdf-files/insights-from-the-drcf-ai--digital-hub-pilot.pdf?v=406887.

77 https://assets.publishing.service.gov.uk/media/5bcf2d8940f0b604d1032880/cst-reforming-the-governance-of-technological-innovation.pdf.

78 Ibid.

1. effective horizon scanning;
2. dealing with the interplay between regulation, codes of practice and industry standards;
3. easy access to information about the regulations;
4. ongoing testing of regulations, for example, through sandboxing; and
5. international cooperation;

3.44 In response to the Council for Science and Technology's warning, the Secretary of State for Business, Energy & Industrial Strategy explained that:

> 'our regulators must … be open to experimentation … innovation does not fit around neat regulatory boundaries or processes. Our regulators must collaborate to provide joined-up, timely regulatory advice to innovators … [and] … must also be joined up with the broader landscape of industry codes, standards and guidance that shapes the development of innovation.'[79]

3.45 These words of caution must be heeded to ensure that UK remains an attractive environment for innovators. We find ourselves therefore in a somewhat uncertain regulatory landscape in so far as Industry 4.0 and emerging technologies are concerned. There is no one overarching Industry 4.0 regulator, and there is no suite of neatly packaged Industry 4.0 laws. Instead, much of the regulations remain somewhat siloed into traditional distinct areas, such as data protection, financial regulation and other professional regulations. Where this is not the case, however, is with the DRCF, which is discussed earlier in the chapter but which does start to see the coming together of key regulators to collaborate on distinct emerging technology issues. We must remember to keep in mind the question whether traditional regulatory sectors, which were important before the digital revolution, will still remain relevant in the emerging Industry 4.0 landscape and post-digital revolution. Given the seismic changes to society, it is anticipated that this will not be the case and regulators must keep abreast of the situation as the landscape changes.

THE REGULATORY ACTION PLAN

3.46 The UK Government published its policy paper in 2025 on a 'New Approach to ensure regulators and regulation support growth'.[80] The Government believes that regulation can inhibit innovation, and therefore its vision is to develop a system which balances safeguarding citizens, but still enables growth in emerging technologies. It considers that regulation should be proportionate

79 https://assets.publishing.service.gov.uk/media/5bcdda73ed915d431e833e41/beis-reforming-the-governance-of-technological-innovation.pdf.

80 https://www.gov.uk/government/publications/a-new-approach-to-ensure-regulators-and-regulation-support-growth/new-approach-to-ensure-regulators-and-regulation-support-growth-html.

and agile to be able to react to developments in technology and innovation. The plan is therefore to try and reduce the level and unnecessary complexity of regulations. This change has resulted in the abolition of the Payment Systems Regulator and the Office of the Regulator of Community Interest Companies, both of which have been consumed within other organisations. The plan also addresses reforms required to environmental regulation and health and safety regulation, both of which are key to Industry 4.0. The Government has stated that it wants to simplify the regulators' duties, make their roles more transparent and 'ensure … [the] … regulatory regime is fit for the age of AI'.[81]

REGULATION FOR THE FOURTH INDUSTRIAL REVOLUTION

3.47 In 2019, the Government published a white paper on 'Regulation for the Fourth Industrial Revolution'.[82] Whilst the make-up of the Government has changed multiple times since this date, not only with various different changes in the Conservative Government but also changes from Conservative to Labour in July 2024, and multiple changes in leadership, the paper reflects the same sentiment as the 2025 Government policy paper 'New Approach to ensure regulators and regulation support growth' as discussed above at para **3.46**. This is fundamentally that regulation needs to be balanced against innovation, and that it is not in the UK's favour to insist on overly prescriptive regulation in this area. The white paper highlights that the changes in technology bring new challenges for regulators and changes the technological landscape with new roles, new products and new risks. Traditional regulatory sectors may not be relevant to Industry 4.0 businesses and technologies, which may find themselves subject to multiple different regulatory systems if the status quo is maintained.

3.48 The strategy again highlights the international regard that is held of the UK regulatory system, and suggests that we are well-placed to adapt this for Industry 4.0, but that its important as this evolves that there is trust and confidence in the regulatory system that is deployed.[83] The paper acknowledges the need for an agile and flexible regulatory system, but cautions that it needs to ensure that it still protects citizens.[84] It considers that before regulating, it is important to first consider alternatives to regulations such as voluntary codes and standards.[85] Onerous regulations are not suitable for Industry 4.0 technologies, and where regulation is used it should be outcome-focused; however, in certain industries, which are synonymous with Industry 4.0, such as in automation and energy, regulation is still considered important.[86] What is important is that any

81 Ibid.

82 https://www.gov.uk/government/publications/regulation-for-the-fourth-industrial-revolution/regulation-for-the-fourth-industrial-revolution.

83 Ibid.

84 Ibid.

85 Ibid.

86 Ibid.

regulation, codes or standards keep pace with innovation to ensure that they remain relevant to businesses and society.[87]

THE REGULATORY INNOVATION OFFICE (RIO)

3.49 The RIO was established in October 2024, is part of the Department for Science, Innovation and Technology, and states that its mission is to 'transform the UK's approach to regulation so that it becomes the best place in the world to invest in and commercialise new technologies'.[88] Since 2024, the ROI has worked with over 150 businesses, worth over £100 billion, and has confirmed its key priorities are on defence and robotics.[89] The RIO encompasses the Regulatory Horizons Council, which is an expert committee tasked with advising the Government on regulatory reform,[90] and the Regulators' Pioneer Fund. Its aims include funding sandboxes, providing grants and advises on reform. The 2025 Regulators' Pioneer Fund projects included those with the Medicines and Healthcare Products Regulatory Agency (MHRA), Council for Licensed Conveyancers, Care Quality Commission, Environment Agency, Greater London Authority and the Information Commissioner's Office.[91]

AI

3.50 When discussing the regulation of AI and the use of AI, the Government promotes the need to balance protecting individuals from harm, as against encouraging innovation concluding that:

> 'The UK's current pro-innovation approach to regulation is a source of strength relative to other more regulated jurisdictions and we should be careful to preserve this. Well-designed and implemented regulation, alongside effective assurance tools, can fuel fast, wide and safe development and adoption of AI. Regulators themselves have an important role in supporting innovation … Government must protect UK citizens from the most significant risks … without blocking the path towards AI's transformative potential.'[92]

The AI Security Institute (previously called the AI Safety Institute) is considered to be the 'first state-backed organisation'[93] looking to advance 'safe, secure and beneficial' AI[94] through research and collaboration between industry and government.

87 Ibid.
88 https://www.gov.uk/government/organisations/regulatory-innovation-office/about.
89 https://www.gov.uk/government/news/red-tape-to-be-slashed-for-british-robotics-and-defence-innovators.
90 https://assets.publishing.service.gov.uk/media/6644c99cbd01f5ed32793c50/RHC_Charter__3_.pdf.
91 https://www.gov.uk/government/publications/projects-selected-for-the-regulators-pioneer-fund/projects-selected-for-the-regulators-pioneer-fund-2025.
92 https://www.gov.uk/government/publications/ai-opportunities-action-plan/ai-opportunities-action-plan.
93 https://www.aisi.gov.uk.
94 Ibid.

3.51 In January 2026, the Alan Turing Institute released its report 'AI Governance around the World' under which it maps out the governance responses in various countries including the UK, EU and Singapore.[95] In its UK report, the Alan Turing Institute considers that the UK is a proactive jurisdiction in terms of the governance of AI, through voluntary codes and standards from the National AI Strategy of 2021, through the pro-innovative framework in 2023 to the AI cybersecurity code of practice in 2025.[96]

3.52 The World Economic Forum calls on governments to ensure that they have established clear policies on AI and believes that the EU AI Act[97] will be the starting point for many other jurisdictions on how to regulate AI.[98] It urges policy makers to take a three-stage approach:[99]

1. Consider the current regulations and see where AI governance fits into these regulations and where there are still gaps. Priorities are data protection principles, intellectual property, consumer protection and competition law principles.
2. Create suitable AI governance, which should not be sector agnostic. There should be a collaborative approach between regulators.
3. Future-proof the regulation, to create agile regulations that will evolve with the technology. This should be done by way of effective horizon scanning.

3.53 There is no settled view on whether there is the actual need at this stage for a specific AI agency to deal with the regulation of AI, but what is important is the need for coordinated efforts, between agencies.[100] The World Economic Forum uses the UKs Digital Regulation Cooperation Forum (DRCF) as an example of such collaborative approach. It considers that it is a balancing act between over and under regulation in this space and that there are other ways of encouraging responsible AI use, including through financial incentives such as R&D relief.[101]

95 https://www.turing.ac.uk/research/research-projects/ai-governance-around-world.

96 A. Leone de Castris and C. Thomas (2025), 'AI governance around the world: United Kingdom', The Alan Turing Institute, http://doi.org/10.5281/zenodo.18172829.

97 Regulation (EU) 2024/1689 of the European Parliament and of the Council of 13 June 2024 laying down harmonised rules on artificial intelligence and amending Regulations (EC) No 300/2008, (EU) No 167/2013, (EU) No 168/2013, (EU) 2018/858, (EU) 2018/1139 and (EU) 2019/2144 and Directives 2014/90/EU, (EU) 2016/797 and (EU) 2020/1828 (Artificial Intelligence Act).

98 https://www3.weforum.org/docs/WEF_Governance_in_the_Age_of_Generative_AI_2024.pdf.

99 Ibid.

100 Ibid.

101 Ibid.

THE EU

3.54 The EU terms the key aspects of Industry 4.0 as 'web 4.0' and has undertaken a significant amount of work on web 4.0 and virtual worlds. It describes web 4.0 as 'an integration between digital and real objects and environments, and enhanced interactions between humans and machines'.[102] Web 4.0 sits within the 'Digital Decade' EU initiative which is focusing on ensuring that emerging technology innovations reflect fundamental European values.[103] The EU has confirmed that it is looking to create an EU ecosystem to build out the infrastructure for industrial use of Web 4.0 and are encouraging its member states to operate regulatory sandboxes to support Web 4.0.[104]

3.55 In its 2012 Industrial Policy communication, and its 2014 'For a European Industrial Renaissance' communication, the European Commission highlights that the use of Industry 4.0 technologies could be used to bring about renewed interest in manufacturing in Europe.[105] As part of these initiatives it established the following taskforces:

1. Advanced Manufacturing for Clean Production;
2. Strategic Policy Forum on Digital Entrepreneurship; and
3. Grand Coalition for Digital Jobs;

3.56 Furthermore, the EU launched the Virtual and Augmented Reality Industrial Coalition in 2022, a collaboration between industry and policy makers. It held a number of workshops between 2021 and 2023, and published the EU strategy on Web 4.0 and virtual worlds in July 2023.[106] The EU strategy[107] is entitled 'Communication from the Commission to the European Parliament, the Council, the European Economic and Social Committee and the Committee of the regions: An EU initiative on Web 4.0 and virtual worlds: a head start in the next technological Transition' and addresses the challenges identified in the Commission's March 2023 communication on the 'Long-term competitiveness of the EU: looking beyond 2030'.[108]

102 https://ec.europa.eu/commission/presscorner/detail/en/ip_23_3718.
103 https://digital-strategy.ec.europa.eu/en/policies/europes-digital-decade.
104 https://eur-lex.europa.eu/legal-content/EN/TXT/?uri=celex:52023DC0168.
105 https://www.europarl.europa.eu/RegData/etudes/BRIE/2015/568337/EPRS_BRI(2015)568337_EN.pdf.
106 https://digital-strategy.ec.europa.eu/en/policies/virtual-and-augmented-reality-coalition.
107 https://digital-strategy.ec.europa.eu/en/library/eu-initiative-virtual-worlds-head-start-next-technological-transition.
108 https://eur-lex.europa.eu/legal-content/EN/TXT/?uri=celex:52023DC0168.

EU AND DATA

3.57 The EU recognises the importance of data in driving the new industrial revolution[109] and has confirmed that the central part of its new Data Strategy is balancing the protection of citizens' rights against industrial innovations.[110] The EU has implemented the Data Governance Act[111] and the Data Act[112] which seek to go some way to address this balance, and released its Data Union strategy in the autumn of 2025 under which it addressed the need for a significant amount of data to be able to power AI and accordingly the need for reform to legislative frameworks to enable the same and address data scarcity.[113]

EU INDUSTRIAL POLICY ON AI AND ROBOTICS

3.58 The European Parliament resolution of 12 February 2019 on a comprehensive industrial policy on artificial intelligence and robotics[114] sets out suggestions and recommendations concerning robotics and digitalisation. The European Parliament acknowledges the benefits of the innovations that AI and robotics bring, especially in the areas of health, industry, transportation and construction, but highlights the need for proper policy provisions and regulation to mitigate against some of the risks. The policy cements the need for a proper legal framework and highlights the need for any such regulations to:

1. reflect the Charter of Fundamental Rights;
2. respect data protection and privacy;
3. be secure and incorporate suitable cybersecurity provisions;
4. safeguard the autonomy of humankind in the context of AI and be designed as human centric;
5. protect access to data;
6. ensure systems are ethical by design;
7. incorporate legal liability;
8. try and limit bias, but still recognising that there is always bias in data;
9. recognise the need for transparency in the systems; and
10. prioritise sustainability.

109 Recital (2) of the Data Governance Act 2022 states 'Over the last decade, digital technologies have transformed the economy and society, affecting all sectors of activity and daily life. Data is at the centre of that transformation'.

110 https://digital-strategy.ec.europa.eu/en/policies/strategy-data.

111 Regulation (EU) 2022/868 of the European Parliament and of the Council of 30 May 2022 on European data governance and amending Regulation (EU) 2018/1724 (Data Governance Act).

112 Regulation (EU) 2023/2854 of the European Parliament and of the Council of 13 December 2023 on harmonised rules on fair access to and use of data and amending Regulation (EU) 2017/2394 and Directive (EU) 2020/1828 (Data Act).

113 https://eur-lex.europa.eu/legal-content/EN/TXT/PDF/?uri=CELEX:52025DC0835.

114 (2018/2088 (INI)).

3.59 The policy further promotes the need for regulatory sandboxes, with regulators working with innovators to work out some of the key issues in these fields as they evolve. This means that the technologists can then help to identify concerns and the regulators can react to these issues with the technologists, both working in a collaborative approach.

EUROPEAN HIGH PERFORMANCE COMPUTING JOINT UNDERTAKING

3.60 In a similar example of this collaborative approach to monitoring and regulating frontier technology, the European High Performance Computing Joint Undertaking (EuroHPC JU) was established in 2018 and is focused on fuelling the EUs supercomputing network.[115] It focuses on quantum computing efforts as well as AI factories, which are important applications in industry and sees the coming together of multiple countries, the EU and private stakeholders.[116] It is regulated under Regulation 2026/150.[117]

THE DIGITAL OMNIBUS

3.61 The EU recognises that many of its laws and regulations may be out of date due to the digital revolution being experienced with Industry 4.0 and beyond. Accordingly, the EU's Digital Omnibus[118] is a proposal to amend and update a number of EU laws through a digital rulebook. The proposal calls for 'innovation-friendly'[119] updates to unlock opportunities, including those relating to data, AI, and cybersecurity.

3.62 The EU has also introduced the voluntary AI Pact through the EU AI Office, which requires its signatories to agree their commitment to three core principles prior to the full implementation of the AI Act:

1. to have an AI governance strategy in place;
2. map out the high-risk areas of the business under the EU AI Act; and
3. upskill staff on AI.

115 https://www.eurohpc-ju.europa.eu/about/discover-eurohpc-ju_en.

116 Ibid.

117 Regulation (EU) 2026/150 of 16 January 2026 amending Regulation (EU) 2021/1173 on establishing the European High Performance Computing Joint Undertaking.

118 Proposal for a Regulation of the European Parliament and of the Council amending Regulations (EU) 2016/679, (EU) 2018/1724, (EU) 2018/1725, (EU) 2023/2854 and Directives 2002/58/EC, (EU) 2022/2555 and (EU) 2022/2557 as regards the simplification of the digital legislative framework, and repealing Regulations (EU) 2018/1807, (EU) 2019/1150, (EU) 2022/868, and Directive (EU) 2019/1024 (Digital Omnibus).

119 https://eur-lex.europa.eu/legal-content/EN/TXT/?uri=CELEX:52025PC0837.

3.63 Those that have signed up to the Pact include Google, IBM, Nokia, OpenAI, Microsoft and Samsung.[120]

KEY TAKEAWAY POINTS

3.64 The key takeaway points in respect of the legal and regulatory frameworks for Industry 4.0 are:

- The changes being brough about by Industry 4.0 demand a rethink of existing regulatory frameworks and governance.
- The pace of change and cross-border nature of the technologies presents challenges for policy makers and regulators.
- The UK has adopted an 'innovation first' approach in terms of the regulation of emerging technologies.
- There should be effective governance of emerging technologies to protect society from the harms and risk of harm presented by these technologies.
- There are multiple ways in which regulators are dealing with Industry 4.0, including trying to use existing regulations, bringing in new regulations, using alternative forms of managing innovations such as regulatory sandboxes, voluntary codes and standards.
- The Regulatory Innovation Office (RIO) is tasked with transforming the regulation of innovation in the UK.
- Industry 4.0 and pioneering frontier technology present significant challenges to regulators and lawmakers. There may not be a perfect solution, and it may be that there must be a rethink over traditional methods of governance and regulation to be fit for the future.

120 https://digital-strategy.ec.europa.eu/en/policies/ai-pact.

Chapter 4

Digital twins

'The digital twin is the foundation upon which all the potential of Industry 4.0 and IIoT technologies is built. Simply put, the digital twin is the future.' [1]

Dr Andreas Kaufmann, R. Stahl

4.1 Digital twins are the (current) backbone of the industrial metaverse, and are synonymous with Industry 4.0, having already been utilised in many different industries, from a railway network in Egypt[2] to exploring space.[3] Whilst it is fair to say that over the last 10 years the sophistication of digital twins has skyrocketed, brought about by the advancement in emerging technologies such as edge computing and artificial intelligence (AI). The idea of the 'digital twin' can be traced back to the 1970s and the NASA simulation of Apollo 13.[4]

4.2 Digital twins offer invaluable knowledge and learning about the real-life objects. They can do this safely and efficiently through creating a virtual replica of the object or series of objects.[5] Digital twins are being used for a variety of different use cases including smart cities, manufacturing, aviation and medicine.[6] There are, however, a myriad of legal issues and considerations which effect digital twins, many of which have not been fully explored nor addressed, in part due to the evolving nature of the technology and its adoption.

4.3 The long-term vision of the industrial metaverse is a network of digital twins, which connects various different object together within a wider network and digital twin ecosystem. This has been termed the 'internet of twins' by Capgemini[7] or a composite twin.[8] The Alan Turing Institute considers that it is the linking of digital twins into these 'ecosystems of digital twins (EDT)'[9] which

1 https://r-stahl.com/en/us/industries/innovations/digital-nameplate-industry-40/.
2 https://assets.new.siemens.com/siemens/assets/api/uuid:e36f2de7-f3c4-481f-bb20-9791dc12bbec/the-emergent-industrial-metaverse-update-2024.pdf.
3 NASA's digital twin of the Mars Rover, https://assets.new.siemens.com/siemens/assets/api/uuid:e36f2de7-f3c4-481f-bb20-9791dc12bbec/the-emergent-industrial-metaverse-update-2024.pdf.
4 https://www.turing.ac.uk/research/harnessing-power-digital-twins.
5 https://www.turing.ac.uk/blog/what-are-digital-twins-and-why-do-we-need-them.
6 Barricelli, Casiraghi, and Fogli (2019), 'A Survey on Digital Twin: Definitions, characteristics, applications and design implications', IEEE Access, https://ieeexplore.ieee.org/stamp/stamp.jsp?arnumber=8901113.
7 https://assets.new.siemens.com/siemens/assets/api/uuid:e36f2de7-f3c4-481f-bb20-9791dc12bbec/the-emergent-industrial-metaverse-update-2024.pdf.
8 https://www.amrc.co.uk/files/document/406/1605271035_1604658922_AMRC_Digital_Twin_AW.pdf.
9 https://www.turing.ac.uk/research/research-projects/ecosystems-digital-twins.

is technologically extremely challenging and they recommend a 'system of systems engineering' approach.[10] This is also extremely challenging from a legal perspective, as we effectively bring in a new layer of capabilities which transcend the real-life and the digital.

4.4 Given their considerable importance to Industry 4.0, many consider that digital twins should be part of the critical national infrastructure of the UK.[11] Yet, however, despite their fundamental importance there still remains a distinct lack of laws or regulations specifically concerning digital twins, their adoption, use or control. Significant attention is needed to protect national sovereignty over both the technological infrastructure and the data.

4.5 At this time, there are still technological challenges with the digital twin technology which is thought to be limiting their adoption, as well as other limitations such as cyber-security concerns, ethical issues, human rights concerns, collaboration issues, and their significant development costs.[12] It is vital that where digital twin technology is being developed that effective licensing and contractual provisions are implemented to ensure that clear responsibilities and divisions are agreed. As the use of digital twins increases, we can expect that direction will come initially from insurers over the division and allocation of risk and responsibilities, and then from regulators and lawmakers given the critical nature of the systems.

WHAT IS A DIGITAL TWIN?

4.6 At a rudimentary level digital twins are generally considered to be a sophisticated virtual digital replication of a physical thing using real-time data to gain insights.[13] The data is collected from the real-life object, typically via the Internet of Things (IoT) sensors and this is fed into the digital twin. The data from the digital twin is then fed back into the real-life object. A digital twin can be utilised to model and test various different scenarios in a virtual environment. It typically utilises AI and seeks to establish a continuous loop of data flowing between the real-life object and the digital twin. Digital twin technology is intrinsically linked with the idea of Big Data and IoT sensors, since for the technology to work coherently it relies on a significant amount of data, which is obtained and transmitted through the IoT device.

4.7 There is not yet, however, a globally recognised definition of a 'digital twin' and warnings have been made that the term should not just become a buzz

10 Ibid.
11 TechUK, June 2025 Green Paper on 'Digital Twinning of Everything and Everyone', https://www.techuk.org/resource/reimagining-infrastructure-with-digital-twins.html.
12 https://post.parliament.uk/digital-twins-dynamic-models-that-respond-to-real-time-data/.
13 Ibid.

word.[14] As discussed further below at para **4.14**, there are practical challenges and risks with the lack of a unified definition of a digital twin, especially where these are designed to sit within a wider network of digital twins.[15]

4.8 There have been multiple different attempts to try and define a digital twin. The definition of a digital twin published by the Defence Science and Technology Laboratory, a branch of the Ministry of Defence, focuses on the need for a digital twin to be independent from, but linked to 'a real-world process, environment or object', which is being accurately mimicked in real-time and in turn it can be used to predict the impact and effect in real-time on the object.[16]

4.9 TechUK, on the other-hand, defines a digital twin as 'a relevant, virtual representation of the state and behaviour of something physical or non-physical with a functional output in the real-world'.[17]

4.10 Academics have sought to distinguish the idea of a digital twin from other types of technologies, like CAD software, and that they believe that digital twins must have a continuous connection between the real-life object and the digital twin, and the capacity to store and process this continuous data.[18]

4.11 Thales, who is one of the industrial partners of the UK Digital Twin Centre, consider that:

> 'A digital twin is much more than just a virtual model – it's a dynamic, digital replica of a physical system or process, linked through a two-way data exchange. This means the model doesn't just mirror the physical asset – it evolves with it … [the]… extreme level of accuracy and feedback loop is what sets digital twins apart from traditional models or simulators.'[19]

4.12 The National Digital Twin Programme considers that, whilst there are similarities, there should be clear distinctions between digital twins, 'digital models', 'digital shadows', 'simulations' and 'control systems'.[20] They believe that a digital twin should never include features in the virtual space which are not replicable in the real-world, as fundamentally a digital twin should be fully synchronised with the real-world object.[21] In addition, they believe that a digital

14 https://www.amrc.co.uk/files/document/406/1605271035_1604658922_AMRC_Digital_Twin_AW.pdf.

15 https://www.ndtp.co.uk/resources/digital-twin-definition/.

16 https://www.gov.uk/government/publications/digital-twin-definition/digital-twin-official.

17 TechUK Green Paper (n 11).

18 Barricelli, Casiraghi, and Fogli (n 6).

19 https://www.thalesgroup.com/en/countries-europe/united-kingdom/news/thales-and-uk-digital-twin-centre-shaping-future-beyond.

20 Digital models are typically not linked to the real-world object; digital shadows, is the term used for a model that does not influence the real-world object, so the data flows only from the real-world object to the virtual model but not back again; simulations, are not connected to the real-world object; and control systems are used to describe devices that do not allow for predictions. See https://www.ndtp.co.uk/resources/digital-twin-definition/.

21 https://www.ndtp.co.uk/resources/digital-twin-definition/.

twin should set clear parameters over what features it reflects of the real-world object (and what features it does not reflect if this is the case), and therefore they can either operate in a fully connected state[22] or a 'semi-conducted' state, which is effectively a part digital twin, part simulation.[23, 24] On this basis the NDTP consider that the features of a digital twin are that it:[25]

1. must represent a real-world object; the real-world object must be the exact counter-part to the digital twin;
2. the data needs to flow both ways, from the real-world object to the digital twin and from the digital twin into the real-world object;
3. must mirror the real-world object – meaning that it must perform in the same way as the real-world object, without bias; and
4. is an accurate predicator, including once it integrated into a network of digital twins.

4.13 Finally, whilst it is not vital that a digital twin incorporates AI capabilities, the idea of digital twins have now become synonymous with AI given the considerable benefits this technology adds to digital twins. This is not, however, to say that a digital twin must be wholly autonomous and academics do stress that human involvement is still very much required within the process, not least to utilise the digital twin as a tool and to interpret and utilise its data and learnings.[26]

WHY IT MATTERS

4.14 The precise definition and scope of a digital twin is important, especially where it needs to fit into a wider network of digital twins. This is because in most cases the real-world objects themselves do not sit in isolation; they sit within a wider infrastructure and within a sophisticated real-world network with multiple different parts of a wider system. For digital twins to become successful, and to see widespread adoption, there must be a level of interoperability, to allow digital twins to work within a wider infrastructure. Having a clear scope and definition therefore as to what is meant by a digital twin, with clear defining features and requirements enable this technology to be properly built, used and maintained.

22 A fully connected system is where the digital twin has a two-way data loop, with the all-necessary relevant data from the real-world object being processed and used by the digital twin, and then all the relevant data from the data twin feeding into the real-world object.
23 A 'semi-conducted' system is where the digital twin is effectively just processing one part of a process, and not all parts of the process.
24 https://www.ndtp.co.uk/resources/digital-twin-definition/.
25 Ibid.
26 Barricelli, Casiraghi, and Fogli (n 6).

THE REGULATION OF DIGITAL TWINS

4.15 There is a lack of policy globally on digital twins[27] and currently no single regulation in the UK that specifically covers digital twins. They will, however, for now fall under numerous existing regulations, covering the different technologies and industries. For example, medical digital twins, are likely to be considered as medical devices and fall under the Medicines and Healthcare products Regulatory Agency (MHRA) regulations in the UK and the European Medicines Association (EMA) in the EU.[28] Further, whilst many digital twins are currently in their formative stages, many will have future uses which involve some consumer use, at some stage of the process; however, this will not necessarily be all digital twins where it does apply the digital twin will be subject to consumer protection regulations.

4.16 Given the importance of digital twins being able to meet specific security and technological criteria so that they can be trusted within an ecosystem, we should start to see a shift in focus in the future towards the specific regulation of a digital twin especially as further use of this technology is adopted in the mainstream. Standardisation is important for digital twins. This is to enable the *federation* of the different systems, which can then fit together to create a wider digital twin or system of digital twins. The focus over the last few years has been mainly developing technical specifications rather than addressing concerns over the underpinning regulation and legal accountability. These concerns, however, must be properly considered and addressed before we can hope for widespread implementation of this technology into wider infrastructure. The idea of trust is fundamental when dealing with federated digital twins fitting into a wider network of digital twins,[29] which would benefit from specific regulations with technological stipulations.

4.17 It is unlikely that there will be a dedicated digital twin regulator in the near term. Instead, as seems to be the trend of regulators dealing with digitalisation generally, it is more likely that we will see the different existing regulators look to bring digital twins expressly into their scope as their use increases across multiple different sectors. Regulators will need to assess whether a digital twin is appropriate to meet the threshold of its regulations, and some regulators are already starting to work with different technical catapults to understand the inner workings of digital twins.[30]

4.18 At this stage, given many of the digital twin projects sit within already largely regulated sectors such as energy and medicine, the technology is extremely sophisticated, and there are significant costs associated with

27 https://www.techuk.org/resource/reimagining-infrastructure-with-digital-twins.html.

28 L. Asciak, J. Kyeremeh, and X. Luo, et al (2025), 'Digital twin assisted surgery, concept, opportunities, and challenges', npj Digit Med, 8(32), https://doi.org/10.1038/s41746-024-01413-0.

29 TechUK Green Paper (n 11).

30 Ibid.

their development, the majority of large digital twin projects operate through catapults and programmes such as the National Digital Twin Programme. These programmes tend to include some degree of collaborative involvement of existing regulators within the projects. For example, the National Digital Twin Programme includes partnerships with the Department for Transport, Met Office, Ofgem, NHS England, the Royal Airforce, and the Department for Science, Innovation and Technology.[31] Given the relatively small scale of digital twin adoption at this time significant oversight can still be exerted by regulators. This may change as the technology itself becomes more accessible and its costs decrease.

4.19 For now, whilst there is a gap in specific regulation concerning digital twins it is imperative that those dealing with them ensure that there are effective contracts in place stipulating key areas of liability as well as expected specifications and technical requirements to ensure that the wider network is not detrimentally impacted by one digital twin.

4.20 Digital twins themselves present considerable opportunities for regulators. They can act as an environment to test and simulate real-life issues and obstacles[32]. Technologists have confirmed that digital twins can enable regulators to stress test their own rules within a simulated environment, so they can analyse the suitability and impact of these rules.[33]

4.21 Finally, TechUK interestingly considers that once the digital twin systems mature, we may even start to see self-regulating digital twins.[34] Some thought is therefore required over embedded rules, governance and ethical decision making within the technology itself. Sight should not be lost over the importance of protecting critical national infrastructure, and preserving human relationships and community.

'DIGITAL TWINNING OF EVERYTHING AND EVERYONE'[35]

4.22 TechUK is the trade association for technology in the UK and helps to guide Government policy and laws.[36]

4.23 In June 2025, it published its Green Paper on 'Digital Twinning of Everything and Everyone', which highlights that the UK needs to be at the cutting edge of developing the underlying infrastructure for the implementation of digital twinning if it wants to try and establish itself as a global leader in this

31 https://www.ndtp.co.uk/collaborations/.
32 https://www.techuk.org/resource/digital-twins-and-public-policy.html.
33 https://www.techuk.org/resource/guest-blog-digital-twins-and-virtual-testing-of-regulatory-remedies.html.
34 https://www.techuk.org/resource/reimagining-infrastructure-with-digital-twins.html.
35 Ibid.
36 https://www.techuk.org.

area. The Green Paper proposes an ambitious roadmap for the UK Government to 2050 and makes the following Government recommendations:[37]

1. make digital twins a priority;
2. produce clear guidance;
3. focus on UK hardware and infrastructure. As we move through 2026 and beyond, the debate concerning data sovereignty has only intensified as a critical national priority;
4. create a national digital twinning network (NDTN) utilising public-private partnerships;
5. establish a government body to oversee digital twin strategy and funding;
6. set guidelines on data collection, storage and usage, which should seek to facilitate responsible data sharing;
7. create a framework which enables digital twins to fit together with other emerging technologies;
8. have a clear position to achieve 'national-scale federated digital twins by 2050';
9. encourage the creation of open-source data with federated digital twins, rather than closed systems;
10. set the standards for digital twins;
11. create a 'One Project One District One City One Nation approach';
12. encourage the development of digital twins and provide guidance to these organisations;
13. ensure there is a fully ready work-force competent to utilise the digital twins. As discussed in **Chapter 16**, investment in education in this area is paramount to ensure there is a suitably trained work-force; and
14. create a government department to deal with digital twins and metaverse technologies.

4.24 The Green Paper further acknowledges that more is needed to be done in respect of establishing infrastructure for the adoption of digital twins in the UK, including the need to establish a suitable framework, establish standards and suitable governance, which is agile and suitable for interoperability.[38]

37 TechUK Green Paper (n 11).
38 Ibid.

INTERNATIONAL REGULATION OF DIGITAL TWINS

4.25 Internationally, Asia is leading the way in terms of the adoption of digital twin technology.[39] In 2023, China launched its 'three-year action plan for the Industrial innovation and development of the metaverse',[40] and is focused on the rapid adoption of digital twin technology, which fits squarely within the 'Digital China' strategy of the Chinese Communist Party.[41] Considerable support is being provided by the Government in China for the development of AI, heavy investment is being made by industry, and in 2024 it published comprehensive guidelines entitled 'Guidelines for the Construction of a Comprehensive Standardisation System for National Artificial Intelligence Industry.[42] Lessons should be taken from the focus on digital twin infrastructure by China.

4.26 Japan has initiated its plan for 'Society 5.0',[43] which via its Ministry of Land, Infrastructure, Transport and Tourism, is where the entire real-life ecosystem will be recreated as a digital twin 'through a highly integrated system of cyberspace and physical space'.[44]

DIGITAL TWIN CATAPULTS

4.27 At this stage digital twin technology is still being developed and refined. Much of the framework and guidelines are therefore being created at this stage through the various different technological catapults, rather than through direct regulation. The focus is very much still on developing the technologies, their capability and the way in which the planned innovation can come to fruition to revolutionise different sectors. Sight should not, however, be lost as to the importance of embedding effective governance within the technology, as well as considering the importance of future regulation as the systems themselves are built out. Much in the same way as the concept of 'privacy by design' has revolutionised data protection principles, the systems must be designed with foresight to protect future users and future society from its outset.

4.28 There have been numerous different digital twin initiatives over the last ten years. In 2018, the National Digital Twin Programme (NDTP) was created, and in 2020 the Digital Twin Hub (DT Hub), which is as part of the University of Cambridge, was formed.[45] The DT Hub devised the 'Gemini Principles', which,

39 https://futureiot.tech/ai-driven-digital-twins-to-unlock-asias-operational-excellence/.

40 https://www.china-briefing.com/news/china-releases-three-year-action-plan-for-metaverse-industry-development/.

41 Joshua Baughman (2023), 'Enhancing the Battleverse: The People's Liberation Army's Digital Twin Strategy', Military Cyber Affairs, 6(1), Article 1, http://doi.org/10.5038/2378-0789.6.1.1091.

42 https://reports.weforum.org/docs/WEF_Blueprint_to_Action_Chinas_Path_to_AI-Powered_Industry_Transformation_2025.pdf.

43 https://info.tokyo-digitaltwin.metro.tokyo.lg.jp/docs/roadmap/roadmap_docs_en.pdf.

44 https://www8.cao.go.jp/cstp/english/society5_0/index.html.

45 https://digitaltwinhub.co.uk.

as discussed below at para **4.59**, set a benchmark for the ethical standards for digital twins and an important early steps towards the regulation of digital twins.

4.29 The UK Digital Twin Centre, based in Belfast, opened in May 2025 to promote the strategic partnerships between research and industry within a standard digital twin framework.[46] The Alan Turing Institute, has been exploring digital twins since 2015,[47] and established the Turing Research and Innovation Cluster in Digital Twins (TRIC-DT) in 2023[48] with the mission to 'democratise' access to an open, reproducible and trustworthy ecosystems of digital twins'[49] and is tasked with trying to establish best practices in digital twins.[50]

4.30 Finally, the Twinning Capability for the Natural Environment (TWINE) project is an initiative led by the Met Office and Natural Environment Research Council and includes supporting various projects looking at marine ecosystems and water hazards.[51]

THE NATIONAL DIGITAL TWINS PROGRAMME (NDTP)

4.31 The NDTP is a long-term government initiative on digital twins, which started in 2018. It is seeking to establish the rules and underpinning infrastructure to be able to create an interconnected and interoperable network of digital twins, called the 'National Digital Twin' (NDT).[52]

4.32 The NDTP is looking to create a blueprint for digital twins in the UK, to try and create a safe, trusted and secure network of digital twins, that is ethical, sustainable and long-lasting.[53] The idea is to create an 'ecosystem of multi-domain, multi-sector digital models including digital twins, connected via securely shared, interoperable data and information of a known quality'.[54] The idea is not to create just one isolated digital twin, but to create the framework, standards and rules for the UK, to enable users to create digital twins that are able to fit into the wider digital twin infrastructure, and which will eventually become the NDT.

4.33 Based on feedback from 40 different stakeholders, the NDTP identified the following seven key features which they felt were important practical requirements and expectations when building a digital twin: (1) safety; (2)

46 https://www.digicatapult.org.uk/programmes/programme/uk-digital-twin-centre/.
47 https://www.turing.ac.uk/research/harnessing-power-digital-twins.
48 https://www.turing.ac.uk/research/research-projects/tric-dt.
49 Ibid.
50 https://www.turing.ac.uk/research/research-projects/trustworthy-and-ethical-assurance-digital-twins-tea-dt.
51 https://www.ukri.org/news/digital-twin-projects-to-transform-environmental-science/.
52 https://www.gov.uk/government/collections/the-national-digital-twin-programme-ndtp.
53 Ibid.
54 https://www.ndtp.co.uk/about-ntdp/.

security; (3) trustworthiness; (4) ethics; (5) sustainability; (6) adaptability; and (7) interoperability:[55]

THE NDT FRAMEWORK

4.34 The NDTP has established a set of guiding principles for the NDT[56] which are:

1. that every project must have a measurable benefit in line with the NDTs strategic priorities;
2. to create open-source solutions, which can be utilised;
3. to act honestly and transparently;
4. to create digital twins which are accessible and inclusive;
5. to bridge the skill and culture gap;
6. to develop rules and frameworks for the digital twins; and
7. to create governance for the digital twins

THE INFORMATION MANAGEMENT FRAMEWORK

4.35 The Information Management Framework (IMF), developed by the Centre for Digital Built Britain as part of the NDTP, forms the technical specifications for the NDTP to meet the requisite technological standards, but also incorporates some ethical and legal standards.[57] This framework comprises the foundational data model, the reference data library and integration architecture. Taking account of some of the early legal considerations relating to digital twins is important for the NDTP, and in 2021 a series of roundtables were held to consider the main legal considerations for digital twins and their early adoption, focusing on the governance of digital twin, data protection and intellectual property rights.[58]

THE NDT

4.36 The creation of a National Digital Twin (NDT), as set out above at para **4.31**, is the goal of the NDTP. The NDT is designed to be made up of lots of smaller digital twins, known as federated digital twins. The aim is to set the foundations, rules, expectations of the technology, ethics and governance via the NDTP, so to enable industry, academic and government organisations to build

55 https://www.ndtp.co.uk/resources/digital-twin-development-attributes/.
56 https://www.ndtp.co.uk/about-ntdp/.
57 https://digitaltwinhub.co.uk/information-management-framework-imf/.
58 https://digitaltwinhub.co.uk/forums/discussion/the-national-digital-twin-legal-implications/.

digital twins which are technologically, ethically and legally compatible. This will in turn enable these different networks of digital twins, or federated digital twin, to fit into the wider NDT. To achieve all this, the infrastructure is being built and developed as open-source[59] on a distributed ledger.[60] The code is currently available under an open-source licence.[61]

4.37 The NDT is designed to facilitate trusted data-sharing. This means that the digital twins have to firstly be capable of data-sharing, and secondly this data must also be trustable. The system is being designed to operate so that each individual digital twin is managed by its own organisation, which can use the data for its own needs,[62] as well as data being exchanged with other digital twins[63] via a managed infrastructure which is being built as part of the NDTP.[64]

4.38 In short, what is being created is an interconnected web of linked digital twins, all capable of sharing their data with each other, which in turn enable the extrapolation and use of that data to be able to learn about the different digital twins. Therefore, whilst the digital twin will mirror the real-life object, the NDT will itself mirror the real-life interconnectivity of the different real-life objects.

4.39 It is envisaged that there will be multiple federations of different digital twins, which are then linked to other federated digital twins to create a wider underpinning digital twin infrastructure. Just like the interwoven realities of real-life objects and systems, which do not sit in insolation themselves but within a wider system.

THE INTEGRATION ARCHITECTURE (IA) NODE

4.40 The Integration Architecture (IA) nodes, which are the foundations for the individual digital twins, has been developed and tested as part of the NDTP.[65] It is currently being rolled out for implementation and use by different organisations.[66] The focus is now on developing the integration and interoperability between the different IA nodes[67] beyond 'an experimental framework'.[68]

4.41 In terms of initial registration and control over the wider NDT, the individual AI nodes, which effectively are the parts of each digital twin that are controlled by individual organisations, will have to be registered and there will

59 The open-source infrastructure is termed the Integration Architecture (IA).
60 https://www.gov.uk/government/publications/what-a-digital-twin-is-and-how-you-can-contribute/what-a-digital-twin-is-and-how-you-can-contribute.
61 https://www.ndtp.co.uk/for-developers/.
62 Known as the IA Node https://www.ndtp.co.uk/integration-architecture/.
63 To their IA Nodes https://www.ndtp.co.uk/integration-architecture/.
64 Which is known as the IA Management Node https://www.ndtp.co.uk/integration-architecture/.
65 https://www.ndtp.co.uk/integration-architecture/.
66 Ibid.
67 The development of the IA management nodes.
68 https://www.ndtp.co.uk/integration-architecture/.

be a monitoring requirement.[69] This is effectively a form of licensing programme to register the distinct digital twins forming part of the overall NDT. This is important preparatory foundational work that is being undertaken and considered as part of the wider NDT, and an example of how pragmatic measures are being implemented to control who is able to access and link into the wider NDT. We should expect that as the technology itself, and its regulation, are further developed that we will see strict criteria over auditable requirements for an individual node or digital twin to be able to join the wider NDT that goes further than mere technical capability and has some focus on the entity controlling the digital twin, its governance and safeguards.

DIGITAL TWIN DEMONSTRATOR PROGRAMMES

4.42 In 2022, the Government established a series of demonstrator programmes to test various digital twins in the real-world and how they will work in real-life.[70] The case studies include:

1. **Retrofitting in housing** – the IRIS project.[71] IRIS was successfully completed and is ready for wider adoption. This project was designed to identify homes which required energy efficiency improvements, pulling data from EPC data and Ordnance Survey data. This digital twin can demonstrate the effect of the different improvements on the different houses, so that these can be trialled virtually and modelled out in the digital twin, before improvements are made in real-life. It has created relevant API interfaces, as well as the relevant IA. IES:Building is an Information Exchange Standard (IES) that has been created as part of the project. It is expected that in the future the digital twin will be able to also incorporate other data such as Met Office data. With changes being brought about as a result of climate change, and weather changes, this is an important project for the future in and of itself,
2. **Energy systems** – the NOVA project.[72] The NOVA project is a digital shadow focused on the expansion of renewable energy, and is the early stages of a 'Virtual Energy System' (VES) (as discussed below at para **4.45**). The project has seen the engagement of regulators and other important key stakeholders, such as Scottish & Southern Electricity Networks (SSEN) and Ofgem. The aim of the project is to explore the ability to generate, use and store energy such as solar, tidal and wind. The hope is to try and use this project to understand how energy digital twins generally can deal with the high volume of data produced from a wide variety of different sources. It also highlights the importance that digital twins can play in the UK's 'Net Zero' commitments.

69 Ibid.
70 https://www.ndtp.co.uk/demonstrators/.
71 https://www.ndtp.co.uk/demonstrators/iris-domestic-retrofitting/.
72 https://www.ndtp.co.uk/demonstrators/nova-energy-system/.

3. **Emergency planning** – the L!SA,[73] VISTA[74] and SALUS projects. The Local Incident Services Application (L!SA)[75] has been tested and is ready for scale. It is designed to log emergencies, and to provide for real-time monitoring. It was tested in 2024 on a simulated outbreak of avian influenza and in 2025 at the Isle of Wight Festival. The VISTA[76] project is focused on the monitoring of assets during national emergencies. The focus is on infrastructure like the road networks and energy supplies. It uses sensors to obtain real-time data for disaster planning and mitigation purposes, and feeds into wider standards.[77] SALUS[78] is in the early development stages and is aimed at dealing with emergency planning for vulnerable people. It centralises and shares real-time data from multiple agencies.

4.43 The Isle of Wight, dubbed the 'digital island',[79] has been used to trial part of the NDTP demonstrator programme.[80] The NDTP has been divided into tranches, the second tranche ran until March 2025, and during which time the project sought to establish the initial architecture and test real-world use cases.[81]

4.44 The third stage of the programme, which will last until around 2030, is focused on building out the programme at scale and finalising the different underpinning frameworks.[82] After this, the project will reach the final stages and should cumulate in a clear framework and widescale adoption of digital twins.

VIRTUAL ENERGY SYSTEM (VES OR VIRTUALES)

4.45 Real-life energy systems do not sit in isolation; they have to interact with other parts of a wider infrastructure and within existing systems. This presents significant opportunity and challenge for digital twins. The VES is the UKs connected energy digital twin infrastructure which is being developed and run by the National Energy Supply Operator (NESO).[83]

4.46 It is being designed to enable different federated energy digital twins to connect together to replicate the wider infrastructure, just as it would in real-life.

73 https://www.ndtp.co.uk/demonstrators/lsa-incident-management-response/.
74 https://www.ndtp.co.uk/demonstrators/vista-asset-resilience-emergency-planning-and-response/.
75 https://www.ndtp.co.uk/demonstrators/lsa-incident-management-response/.
76 https://www.ndtp.co.uk/demonstrators/vista-asset-resilience-emergency-planning-and-response/.
77 The Information Exchange Standard (IES).
78 https://www.ndtp.co.uk/demonstrators/salus-vulnerable-people/.
79 Isle of Wight Council Digital Strategy 2022 to 2027, Believe in digital, to believe in great, https://www.iow.gov.uk/documentlibrary/download/digital-strategy-2022-2027.
80 https://www.iow.gov.uk/news/The-Isle-of-Wights-Digital-Twin.
81 https://www.ndtp.co.uk/about-ntdp/.
82 Which are identified as being 'legal, security, safety, ethics, sustainability and commercial' frameworks, https://www.ndtp.co.uk/about-ntdp/.
83 https://www.neso.energy/about/our-projects/virtual-energy-system.

4.47 *Digital twins*

The infrastructure is being built as open-source, subject to centralised governance, and with an interoperable set of systems.[84] Part of the drive behind the establishment of the VES is the push towards net zero. Figure 4.1 shows the VES model, with the connections between the power supply, operating system and use.

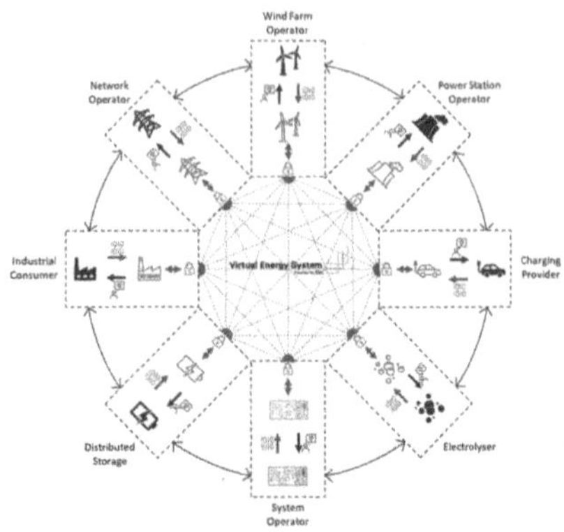

Source: NESO, Virtual Energy System - Creating a governance framework (August 2023), https://www.neso.energy/document/285406/download. Reproduced with the kind permission of NESO (https://www.neso.energy/). © NESO

Figure 4.1 VES interconnected model

4.47 The VES needs an overarching governance framework. NESO considers that a collaborative approach should be taken to develop this governance; however, there also still needs to be effective regulation and oversight.[85]

4.48 NESO considers that using a co-led model is the most appropriate way to govern the VES.[86] This model requires a new type of governance model, with a new independent regulator tasked with specifically monitoring the digitalisation of the energy sector, which it terms the 'Orchestrator' with a novel industry-led 'Expert Advisors'.[87]The governance framework is being built on the following guiding principles:[88]

1. accountability and responsibility;
2. collaboration and engagement with stakeholders;
3. agility and responsiveness;
4. being inclusive;
5. being innovative and empowering; and
6. being transparent and legitimate;

84 Ibid.
85 https://www.neso.energy/document/285406/download.
86 Ibid.
87 Ibid.
88 Ibid.

4.49 The VES itself is, however, another example of where traditionally highly regulated sectors are utilising digital twin technology and therefore the importance and need for effective governance and regulation are already accepted principles and commonplace. Whilst issues around the governance and regulation of digital twins in the energy sector are important, they are not unexpected or novel. Those operating in these sectors expect regulation, strict policies, procedures and governance. More focus is needed on those sectors which traditionally have not been as heavily regulated. This is where investment is needed to ensure that there is a cultural change in those sectors to abide by regulation, governance, licensing requirements and to take heed of regulatory oversight.

OTHER TYPES OF DIGITAL TWINS

Destination Earth (DestinE)

4.50 DestinE is a European Commission initiative to create a digital twin of the Earth and is designed to study the correlation between natural phenomena and human behaviour.[89] This project incorporates the EU data strategy, which aims to create a 'single market for data'[90] across the EU as part of the Common European Data Spaces initiative.

Odyssey Programme

4.51 The Odyssey Programme was carried out by the Alan Turing Institute in 2020 in response to the covid-19 pandemic. The project utilised air quality data collection techniques and devised algorithms and models to look at the busyness of London during lockdown.[91] This project showed the ability to be able to innovate and utilise sensors and data collections in multiple ways, rather than for their original purpose. This is because the sensors were adapted from being used to collect air pollution levels to monitor the level of people at those specific points. The results were used to implement specific responses and measures in areas where it was identified that social distancing was either not working or not being properly carried out so that interventions could be quickly deployed.

Medical digital twins

4.52 Digital twin technology is being frequently utilised in medicine. It has been termed 'digital twin assisted surgery' and the IoT sensors as 'Internet of

89 https://digital-strategy.ec.europa.eu/en/policies/destination-earth.
90 https://digital-strategy.ec.europa.eu/en/policies/strategy-data.
91 https://www.turing.ac.uk/about-us/impact/helping-london-navigate-lockdown-safely.

Medical Things' (IoMT).[92] Digital twin technology is being used to recreate organs, cells and even the entire body. Digital twins can be used to assist with surgery[93] and with drug trials.[94] It is also being used for medical education and training purposes.

Energy

4.53 The energy sector is an important area for digital twin technology. TechUK released a White Paper on Digital Twins in Energy in 2021 which highlights the significant opportunities in this sector given the need to transition to net zero and the numerous issues experienced in this area as a result of covid-19.[95]

4.54 Unasys Navitas is a digital twin of energy infrastructure of the Teesside industrial area, combining solar farms, green hydrogen plant and power stations. It is known as a 'system of systems' which means that it models the entire system, including the different energy and road infrastructures.[96]

Defence

4.55 Digital twins are a useful new addition to the UK's defence arsenal.[97] They form part of the evolving DefTech or Defence Tech sector[98] and have helped to accelerate the trial and testing of new weapons, as well as reduce the costs associated with the research and development stage. They are also helpful to identify and strategise simulated attacks, and plan logistics and war tactics.[99] With a renewed focus on defence, as a result of recent global conflicts, we have seen a focus on investing in the digitalisation of defence including the Commercial X project,[100] and the Future Capabilities Innovation (FCI).[101]

92 Asciak, Kyeremeh, and Luo et al (n 28).
93 Ibid.
94 https://www.bbc.co.uk/news/articles/cq8v73dkne3o#:~:text="With%20a%2090%25%20failure%20rate,Sanofi's%20global%20head%20of%20research.
95 https://www.techuk.org/resource/new-techuk-whitepaper-highlights-the-power-of-digital-twins-in-the-energy-sector.html
96 https://www.unasys.com/blog/unasys-navitas-a-game-changer.
97 https://www.techuk.org/resource/future-defence-success-in-the-uk-will-depend-on-digital-twins.html.
98 DefTech: Technology transforming Defence, November 2024, https://www.techuk.org/asset/00E4D031%2D7B4E%2D4875%2D8D3C9D92DF2C084B/.
99 https://www.techuk.org/resource/future-defence-success-in-the-uk-will-depend-on-digital-twins.html.
100 https://www.gov.uk/guidance/ministry-of-defence-commercial-commercial-x.
101 https://des.mod.uk/what-we-do/army-procurement-support/future-capability-group/.

Challenges with digital twins

4.56 Despite the many positives of digital twins, there are also negatives. These include issues around ethics, cyber-security, data protection, the significant costs associated with their design and implementation, the digital divide, a lack of regulation (and by virtue of this, mistrust in the systems), the fact that they are typically not readily easy to use (they are nowhere close to being a 'plug and play' technology, instead require an extensive amount of underpinning infrastructure) and the technology is still developmental.[102]

4.57 These concerns are well-known by policy makers. The UK Government recognises that the lack of a unified frameworks is a challenge of digital twins,[103] as well as the challenges around the reliability of the technology, legal issues around privacy, intellectual property rights, integrity and accountability, and the difficulties to access and then form collaborations.[104] The US Government Accountability Office has also flagged issues with digital twins as being (a) the issues with the use and reliance on cloud computing; (b) issues around ownership of data and privacy; (c) technical issues which could in turn end up resulting in a digital twin which is discriminatory or incorrectly functioning; (d) cybersecurity concerns and their vulnerability to attack; (e) the high costs needed to update infrastructure; and (f) the lack of developed laws and regulations.[105] Recently, there has been a significant focus on sovereign systems which can be shielded from foreign state interference or subject to third party state restrictions.

Ethics and digital twins

4.58 Ethics is very important in respect of digital twins, not least because of the areas in which they tend to operate.[106] There are a number of different projects which are looking at trying to understand the ethical challenges of digital twins. The National Digital Twin Project considers that it is vital for the National Digital Twin to sit within a 'robust ethical framework'[107] given the need to safeguard human rights, be a force for good and to ensure that they create an inclusive society. The NDTP strategy adopts the ethical principles that have been more widely considered around AI and data. Its strategy highlights the need for digital twins to be human-centrically designed, with a focus on inclusivity and

102 Barricelli, Casiraghi, and Fogli (n 6).

103 https://www.gov.uk/government/publications/rapid-technology-assessment-digital-twins/rta-digital-twins.

104 https://post.parliament.uk/digital-twins-dynamic-models-that-respond-to-real-time-data/#heading-6.

105 https://www.gao.gov/products/gao-23-106453?utm_campaign=usgao_email&utm_content=daybook&utm_medium=email&utm_source=govdelivery.

106 C. Burr, J. Anderson, S. Arana, D. Block, J. Byrne, R. Goodman, C. Gavidia-Calderon, I. Habli, N. Moreira, S. Niederer, N. Polo, and D. Wagg (2024), 'Trustworthy and Ethical Assurance of Digital Twins: Putting the Gemini Principles into Practice', Alan Turing Institute, https://doi.org/10.5281/zenodo.14216050.

107 https://www.ndtp.co.uk/wp-content/uploads/2025/07/NDTP-Ethics-Strategy.pdf.

sustainability. They should be designed to be transparent, robust, secure, safe and accountable. Digital twins must be built with human rights in mind.[108]

4.59 The Centre for Digital Built Britain established the Gemini Principles in 2018 as a guiding mandate for ethical digital twins.[109] These principles have now been adopted as the safe and ethical design principles for digital twins, and are frequently referred to whenever the adoption of digital twin technology is discussed. The three key ethical principles being: (1) the focus must be on the public benefit; (2) they must be trustworthy; and (3) it must function effectively.

The Gemini Principles consider that digital twins should have a clear purpose, be trustworthy and function effectively. To be able to achieve this the purpose of the digital twin should always be for the public benefit, create value and provide insight. To be trustworthy, the digital twin must be secure, open and built on quality data. To function effectively, the digital twin must be federated and capable of connecting to standard connected systems, have transparency in terms of ownership governance and regulation; and be able to evolve.[110]

4.60 The Digital Twin Hub[111] has established the 'Gemini Firebox', as a practical playbook for digital twins to be able to be built in real-life with industrial stakeholders and in line with the Gemini Principles.[112]

Trustworthy and ethical assurance of digital twins

4.61 The Alan Turing Institute considers that, whilst the Gemini Principles have helped to guide the discussions around the need for ethical digital twins, there is, however, the need to go further and now create an 'assurance ecosystem'.[113] It is leading a project called the Trustworthy and Ethical Assurance of Digital Twins (TEA-DT) which is part of its open-source Trustworthy and Ethical Assurance (TEA) Platform, and through which it intends to use its research to further develop ethical guidance and standards for those building digital twins.[114] Through holding key stakeholder roundtables, it has concluded that building ethical digital twins goes further than simply producing a set of principles, it

108 Ibid.

109 https://www.cdbb.cam.ac.uk/system/files/documents/TheGeminiPrinciples.pdf.

110 Ibid.

111 A digital twin catapult now part of the Connected Places Catapult but previously part of the University of Cambridge, https://digitaltwinhub.co.uk/the-digital-twin-hub/.

112 Burr et al (n 106).

113 Ibid.

114 https://www.turing.ac.uk/research/research-projects/trustworthy-and-ethical-assurance-digital-twins-tea-dt.

needs more than this; digital twins should all deploy the principle of being ethical by design.

4.62 The Alan Turing Institute further believes that all stakeholders should be participating in the process of designing the ethical underpinnings of the systems. These values need to reflect shared and representative values across the society in which the digital twin will sit.

4.63 The main issue, however, is that there is no one universal ethical standard. The lines of ethics and morality are interwoven into the fabric of society. It is often intangible, and difficult to define. Yet these boundaries must be drawn if we want to be able to guide the development of ethical digital twins. If, however, we only rely on those stakeholders with vested interest in the outcomes then how much should we expect commercial objectives to influence these ethical principles?

Contracting and digital twins

4.64 Most digital twin projects are collaborative, with multiple stakeholders involved in the process of design, implementation and operation. Traditional specialisms tend to still be siloed, for example, when considering energy digital twins, we see a range of experts come together such as engineering and energy specialists and software development and data experts. This is likely to change as the jobs of the future change, as discussed further in **Chapter 12**; however, this will take some time to achieve as we progress through the digital industrial revolution. It is imperative therefore that each party involved in a digital twin is contractually linked, to ensure that there is parity of contract for all parties, and that risk and liability between the different components are clearly and expressly set out. Collateral contracts are useful to ensure that owners and operators of facilities can enforce against all parties involved in the development and operation of the digital twin infrastructure.

4.65 Furthermore, any contract should also deal expressly with the ownership of any background intellectual property, as well as any intellectual property created through the project and data use and ownership. Further challenges are presented due to the cross-border and international nature of these collaborations.

Data and privacy

4.66 Data is an integral part of digital twins. The issue of personal data is therefore key in respect of digital twins, and is addressed further in **Chapter 7**. The design and operation of digital twins must be premised on the fundamental underpinnings of data protection regulations. This can become complex when considering some of the different use cases of digital twins especially within the healthcare sector. Privacy by design is essential, whereby a privacy impact assessment at each stage of the design and implementation is imperative, clearly establishing the lawful basis for the collection and processing of any personal data, as well as effective, proportionate and suitable safeguards for their safekeeping.

4.67 In the EU the Data Governance Act[115] establishes the Common European Data Spaces, which is designed to help with the sharing of data. This covers both personal data and non-personal data. In addition the EU's Data Act[116] deals with the harmonisation of access and use of data across the EU and is relevant to digital twins noting in recital 4 that the purpose of the Act is:

> 'to respond to the needs of the digital economy and to remove barriers to a well-functioning internal market for data, it is necessary to lay down a harmonised framework specifying who is entitled to use product data or related service data, under which conditions and on what basis'.

Cybersecurity

4.68 The security of a digital twin is of paramount national importance and should be built with data security in mind.[117] They are extremely vulnerable to cyber-attacks, especially those digital twins which are embedded into key infrastructure like the energy systems and defence systems.[118] The industrial metaverse and digital twin technology is vulnerable to criminal groups, including to terrorist organisations, given the vast access that hold to incredibly sensitive and important infrastructure data.[119]

4.69 The National Cyber Security Centre considers that some of the main vulnerabilities of digital twins are the sensors, the use of AI and the significant amount of data that are being collected.[120]

4.70 It is therefore important for the UK to create its own network, hardware and infrastructure to reduce the risk of concerns around foreign state interference, similar to the concerns raised in respect of Huawei in 2023 concerning 5G networks.[121] In a radically changing world, with innovation outpacing regulation, significant global unrest, changing national priorities, a shift in critical raw resources and growing imbalances, data sovereignty and sovereignty over underlying infrastructure are now fundamental considerations for all governments.

115 Regulation (EU) 2022/868 of the European Parliament and of the Council of 30 May 2022 on European data governance and amending Regulation (EU) 2018/1724 (Data Governance Act).
116 Regulation (EU) 2023/2854 of the European Parliament and of the Council of 13 December 2023 on harmonised rules on fair access to and use of data and amending Regulation (EU) 2017/2394 and Directive (EU) 2020/1828 (Data Act).
117 TechUK Green Paper (n 11).
118 https://www.ncsc.gov.uk/blog-post/digital-twins-secure-design-development.
119 https://www3.weforum.org/docs/WEF_Metaverse_Cybersecurity_2024.pdf.
120 https://www.ncsc.gov.uk/blog-post/digital-twins-secure-design-development.
121 TechUK Green Paper (n 11).

Technological challenges, safety risks and liability

4.71 One of the central legal considerations in respect of digital twins is their impact, and wider potential impact as their use continues to grow, on product liability and safety laws, and therefore it is imperative that there is clear accountability and transparency, and all operational data is fully traceable and properly recorded.[122] There are still technological challenges with digital twins, and their sensors, especially in certain sectors such as medicine.[123] Current iterations of digital twins still fail to offer proper interoperability and do not seamlessly integrate with other forms of technology.[124]

4.72 For safety reasons, the real-life object should not be wholly reliant on the digital twin to function and should be able to continue to operate independently of the digital twin in emergency scenarios.[125]It is also vital with any such system that there remains a 'human-in-the-loop' accountable for oversight of the technology and its operation.

4.73 The division of legal liability is a serious consideration in respect of digital twins. As discussed in **Chapter 2**, the Law Commission is currently reviewing the laws around product liability in the UK in the wake of emerging technologies. Any reform, if needed, however, will not necessarily be quick and therefore as discussed above it is vital to consider these issues and reflect the same within the contracts. EU legislation, however, does already now recognise the impact of Industry 4.0 technologies on product liability. The new EU Product Liability Directive[126] categorises software as a product for the purpose of this EU legislation, and the software developers as manufacturers, bringing them directly within the scope of the regulations and strict liability regime, avoiding any ambiguity about software falling under product liability laws as there had been in the past.

Insurance

4.74 It is vital for all components of the digital twin to be fully insured, and that this is coordinated in a similar vein to construction projects generally with consideration over subrogation risks between the multiple parties. The insurance sector does, however, identify that digital twins can help to mitigate and minimise

122 Clementson, Teng, Wood, and Windmall (2021), 'Legal Considerations for Using Digital Twins in Additive Manufacture – A Review of the Literature', Advances in Manufacturing Technology, XXXIV: 91–96.

123 https://www.nature.com/articles/s41746-024-01413-0.

124 TechUK Green Paper (n 11).

125 https://www.gov.uk/government/publications/what-a-digital-twin-is-and-how-you-can contribute/what-a-digital-twin-is-and-how-you-can-contribute.

126 Directive (EU) 2024/2853 of the European Parliament and of the Council of 23 October 2024 on liability for defective products and repealing Council Directive 85/374/EEC.

risks by enabling modelling out real-life issues in the virtual landscape.[127] Insurers are using digital twins themselves to determine the underwriting of claims and to predict risks,[128] as well as assess and process claims.

Litigation

4.75 The *Topalsson* cases are the first swathe of cases concerning digital twins in the UK.

4.76 The case of *Topalsson GmbH v Rolls-Royce Motor Cars Ltd*[129] was heard in the first instance in the UK in the High Court in 2023 and concerned a contractual dispute between car manufacturer Rolls-Royce and Topalsson, a German company specialising in digital twin engines. Rolls-Royce contracted with Topalsson to create a digital twin for the new Rolls-Royce Ghost. The decision principally deals with the interpretation of the contract and whether Rolls-Royce was entitled to terminate the contract due to delays to the project and the reported failure of Topalsson to achieve agreed milestones.

4.77 Topalsson appealed the decision of O'Farrell J, the first instance judge who was sitting in the Technology and Construction Court, resulting in the Court of Appeal case of *Topalsson GmbH v Rolls-Royce Motor Cars Ltd* [2024] EWCA Civ 1330. The appeal related to the interpretation of the contractual cap for liability. The Appeal Court found that the €5,000,000 cap applied to both parties based on the contractual interpretation of the contract.

4.78 *Topalsson GmbH v Rolls-Royce Motor Cars Ltd and Matthew Scott*[130] deals with an application made by Rolls-Royce to set aside an order made in December 2024 concerning US copyright proceedings initiated by Topalsson and an order made concerning disclosure of Rolls-Royce material. The case identifies that litigation has ensued in the UK, US and German courts arising out of the relationship between Topalsson and Rolls-Royce. The cases in Germany relate to a criminal complaint made by Topalsson for copyright infringement and proceedings between Topalsson and its insurers, Hiscox.

4.79 In the US, Topalsson issued proceedings against Rolls-Royce Motorcars Limited, Rolls-Royce North America LLC, BMW and five dealerships in the US. The proceedings were discontinued against Rolls-Royce Motorcars Limited and struck out against Rolls-Royce North America LLC and BMW. The US case concerns allegations made by Topalsson that their software was being infringed. The software in question enables the real-time configuration of vehicles so that customers can see different customisations of the vehicles. After the contract

127 https://axaxl.com/fast-fast-forward/articles/digital-twins-how-a-double-life-can-help-prevent-losses.

128 https://www.theactuary.com/2024/04/04/power-two-digital-twins-insurance.

129 [2023] EWHC 1765 (TCC).

130 [2025] EWHC 1584 (KB).

with Topalsson was terminated, it was alleged by Topalsson that Rolls-Royce contracted with their competitor, called Mackevision. Topalsson considered that the configurator that was being used was actually an infringement of their copyright. Topalsson was successful in some parts of its application that Rolls-Royce be subjected to part of a letter of request for disclosure relating to the US proceedings. .

4.80 Whilst the focus of the UK cases appears in the main to be on contractual interpretation, what the *Topalsson* case highlights most interestingly is some of the niche commercial issues being faced in this sector, which would not normally be public knowledge. It demonstrates the considerable sums being spent on innovation in respect of private digital twin technology, as well as the significant consequential losses which are likely to arise should something go amiss during the course of the delivery of a contract. Therefore, illuminating the need for careful drafting of any contract covering digital twins. It is important that the contract:

1. includes a clear and properly enforceable cap on liability;
2. includes where there is a cap on liability, what is not limited (eg, under the Topalsson contract the liability cap did not cover a breach of the intellectual property clause);
3. distinguishes clearly where each party assumes liability and where they do not;
4. clearly sets out when the different sections of the project are considered to be delivered/completed and the terms of the acceptance criteria;
5. properly deals with intellectual property rights and any period of exclusivity to prevent; and
6. makes clear what it means for a section or project to be considered completed in the context of, say, the asset digital twin, federated digital twin and then the wider system; which may not be immediately obvious at the start.

4.81 The case itself also shows the international nature of Industry 4.0, and the likelihood that any litigation in this space will play out across multiple jurisdictions and courts, with different procedural rules and varying types of liability. Further, the case highlights that the technical ability required to create enterprise level digital twins is significant, as demonstrated by the fact that Rolls-Royce used three different suppliers to try and create the solution it wanted.

4.82 Finally, the 2025 case[131] brought by Topalsson against its original UK litigation lawyers, highlights the considerable sums that are involved in emergent

131 *Topalsson Gmbh v CMS Cameron Mckenna Nabarro Olswang LLP* [2025] EWHC 118 (SCCO).

digital twin technology litigation.[132] Interestingly, this case also disclosed that the original litigation was being funded in part by its insurers and in part by the German Government – again, highlighting the critical importance being placed on digital twin technology, and infrastructure by different governments and states.

KEY TAKEAWAY POINTS

4.83 The key takeaway points in respect of digital twins are:

- They are one of the key technologies in Industry 4.0, typically combining IoT devices and AI. They can also include other types of technology such as augmented reality, and they may gather data from other systems such as wearable devices.
- Data is the driving force behind digital twins. This brings with it concerns around data protection, privacy, risk of cyber-attacks, risks to trade secrets, data sovereignty and confidential information.
- In addition to the above, other key legal challenges facing digital twins include a lack of regulation, human rights concerns, intellectual property concerns, liability concerns and product liability considerations.
- Focus has been on the technological blueprints for digital twin infrastructure, but sight must not be lost on the need to also build regulatory governance in line with this. Much has already been done on developing ethical principles, such as the Gemini Principles; however, more is still needed.
- Effective contracts are vital for digital twins. These should clearly establish expectations around the divisions of liability. Contracts should be developed in line with insurers to ensure that insured risks and levels of liability are properly reflected within the contracts. Careful consideration must be had around the privity of contract, and third-party rights when contracting in this space.
- Key UK digital twin projects are:
  - the National Digital Twin Programme (NDTP): concerned with developing rules around the National Digital Twin;
  - the National Digital Twin (NDT): the goal to create a network of federated (individual) digital twins;
  - Virtual Energy Systems: the National Energy Supply Operator (NESO) project to create a connected energy digital twin infrastructure; and
  - demonstrator programmes: tested on the Isle of Wight, the real-life digital twin tests including the IRIS project, the NOVA project, L!SA, VISTA and SALUS.

132 Which in this case between 2019 and 2022 was £2,151,614.41 with estimated fees trial fees of £3.7 million.

Chapter 5

Smart factories and manufacturing

> *'We will revolutionize how products and experiences are designed, manufactured and serviced. On the path to the industrial metaverse, this next generation of industrial software enables customers to experience products as they would in the real world: in context, in stunning realism and – in the future – interact with them through natural language input.'*[1]
>
> Roland Busch, President and CEO of Siemens

5.1 Smart factories are revolutionising the manufacturing sectors; connected systems which allow for the exchange of data between the real-life and the virtual in real-time. The value of Industry 4.0 and the industrial metaverse across the maintenance, design, monitoring, logistics, quality control and manufacturing process is significant. Siemens has created a factory in China which is increasing productivity by 20% and space efficiency by 40%,[2] and BMW's 31 factories in the industrial metaverse have resulted in 30% more efficiency.[3] Future manufacturing facilities must be able to respond to future crisis' and pandemics, which can be effectively achieved through digitalisation and technological solutions showcasing examples of the deployment of smart manufacturing techniques, such as Foxconn in China which reduced costs by 30% and was able to increase the creation of new products by 29%.[4]

5.2 The Industry 4.0 technologies of the Internet of Things (IoTs), artificial intelligence (AI), additive manufacturing (such as 3D printing), robotics and wearable devices are transforming the manufacturing sector.[5] XR is now being used within factories to enable industrialists to develop, test and iterate ideas in a virtual space, free from health and safety hazards and costly errors, especially when trialling new ideas have historically caused numerous challenges, whether this is the cost of using precision machinery, or working on expensive or scarce raw materials, or the numerous health and safety concerns posed by these trials in a live industrial setting.[6]

1 https://www.siemens.com/global/en/company/insights/siemens-and-nvidia-bringing-the-real-and-digital-worlds-together.html.
2 https://assets.new.siemens.com/siemens/assets/api/uuid:e36f2de7-f3c4-481f-bb20-9791dc12bbec/the-emergent-industrial-metaverse-update-2024.pdf.
3 https://www.weforum.org/publications/navigating-the-industrial-metaverse-a-blueprint-for-future-innovations/.
4 https://centres.weforum.org/centre-for-advanced-manufacturing-and-supply-chains/home.
5 https://www3.weforum.org/docs/WEF_Impact_of_the_Fourth_Industrial_Revolution_on_Supply_Chains_.pdf.
6 https://ieeexplore.ieee.org/document/10596039?denied=.

5.3 Different countries treat the idea of smart manufacturing differently, which may itself be borne out of the fact that different nations treat manufacturing itself differently. This presents its own challenges for interoperability, and reinforces why international standards are important to be able to benchmark expectations. The key legal considerations in respect of cybersecurity, data protection, intellectual property and trade secrets in respect of smart factories are, however, largely universal. Using Audi's smart manufacturing plant in San José Chiapa, Mexico as an example, the existence of innovative technology and a suitably certain regulatory framework now very much influence the location of new manufacturing plants.[7] In 2024, 72% of advanced manufacturing companies were based in China, USA or the EU, with the world leaders being China.[8]

5.4 As discussed further in this chapter, it is the automotive industry which is leading the way in the adoption of this technology, with 85% of all electric vehicle production in 2024 using digital twin technology.[9]

WHAT IS A SMART FACTORY?

5.5 A smart factory is a term coined to describe the use of smart technology, synonymous with Industry 4.0, within the manufacturing process. Smart factories are designed to offer personalised manufacturing, enabling manufacturers to be able respond to demands at an individualised level.

5.6 We are now at the stage where the costs of these types of technology systems are no longer prohibitive, resulting in a digital revolution across the entire manufacturing process and the commercial adoption of these technologies.[10] China has strongly embraced the idea of smart factories and smart manufacturing believing that 'AI is not seen as a standalone technology, but as infrastructure. It is the invisible layer that will underpin the next phase of industrial transformation'[11] referred to as 'AI+' and the idea that AI will become an underpinning fundamental of all manufacturing, and through the entire process.

5.7 In its September 2025 report on 'Physical AI: Powering the New Age of Industrial Operations', the World Economic Forum envisages the future of manufacturing with real-time AI robots assembling and packaging products,

7 World Economic Forum, 'Beyond Cost: Country Readiness for the Future of Manufacturing and Supply Chains', December 2024 https://reports.weforum.org/docs/WEF_Beyond_Cost_2024.pdf.

8 https://joint-research-centre.ec.europa.eu/jrc-news-and-updates/advanced-manufacturing-industry-growing-significantly-eu-2024-07-02_en.

9 https://www.weforum.org/publications/navigating-the-industrial-metaverse-a-blueprint-for-future-innovations/.

10 https://hub.unido.org/sites/default/files/publications/UNIDO%20-%20Guidelines%20for%20the%20establishment%20of%20a%20Smart%20Factory%20Lab_Automotive%20Sector_Final.pdf.

11 https://www.weforum.org/stories/2025/06/how-china-is-reinventing-the-future-of-global-manufacturing/.

factories planned and controlled by robotics, raw materials and parts being moved around the facility and monitored via AI, quality control being carried out by the robotic systems and the systems themselves monitoring and then carrying out any repairs or maintenance, using robotics and drones.[12]

5.8 Manufacturing is already evolving. Manufacturers are no longer reliant only on visual inspections and instead use AI for quality assurance and to identify defects. We are already seeing the use of IoT sensors, automatic warehouse management, eLabels, smart quality, automated planning, AGVs (automated guided vehicles), MES (manufacturing execution systems), RFID (radio-frequency identification),ERP (enterprise resource planning), simulations, virtual commissioning, digital twins, paperless productions, and real-time monitoring and dashboards as part of the smart supply chain.[13] At smart facilities we are seeing the use of cloud computing, high performance networks, AI/ machine learning, and the vertical and horizontal integration of emerging technologies.[14] The various different technologies being deployed include automation, robotics, predictive maintenance, AGV, self-describing machine, additive manufacturing and agile equipment, and staff are now using mobile devices, smart glasses, wearable technology, digital assistants, digital workplace and virtual reality.[15]

5.9 The industrial metaverse is already being used throughout various manufacturing processes and through different platforms. It is being used for tracking objects through the manufacturing process, for quality control, for maintenance, to interact with IoT sensors and devices, to provide remote interactions and assistance, to be able to see within a structure, such as look at the underlying infrastructure, and for training.[16] Augmented reality and virtual reality is also being used to troubleshoot issues at smart factories and for training, as well as for carrying out remote maintenance.[17]

5.10 We are also seeing a mix of different robotic systems within the manufacturing process, and the emergence of robots-as-a-service (or RaaS), which have been made possible by the significant recent advancements in robotics, including on how they are trained, their ability to be able to grip materials, their ability to be autonomous and their virtual deployment.[18] Technology such as physical AI, are now enabling highly perceptive, dexterous, intelligent robotics with in-built real-time automation powered by AI.[19] It is expected that robotic

12 https://reports.weforum.org/docs/WEF_Physical_AI_Powering_the_New_Age_of_Industrial_Operations_2025.pdf.

13 https://hub.unido.org/sites/default/files/publications/UNIDO%20-%20Guidelines%20for%20the%20establishment%20of%20a%20Smart%20Factory%20Lab_Automotive%20Sector_Final.pdf.

14 Ibid.

15 Ibid.

16 https://ieeexplore.ieee.org/document/10596039.

17 https://www.iiot-world.com/augmented-reality/augmented-reality-remote-maintenance/.

18 https://reports.weforum.org/docs/WEF_Physical_AI_Powering_the_New_Age_of_Industrial_Operations_2025.pdf.

19 Ibid.

systems will take on more and more tasks which are hazardous for humans[20] as well as those which are costly or where there is a deficit of suitable staff.

A SMART FACTORY LAB

5.11 The United Nations Industrial Development Organisation (UNIDO) prepared guidelines for the establishment of a smart factory lab, which was largely built out of learnings from the automotive sector.[21] The guidelines are designed to help establish new smart factory labs, which are effectively a sandbox to facilitate innovation in this space and to act as a testbed for new smart factories and its technology. The UNIDO considers that the use of smart factory labs helps to develop regulations and industrial standards, as well as provide suitable workforce training and testing of the technology. The idea is to develop a collaborative framework for different size of industries.

5.12 It is estimated that the cost of setting up a smart factory lab is between €1.5 million to €3 million.[22]

5.13 Legal and regulatory issues must be considered when setting up a smart factory lab, these are principally intellectual property rights, data protection rights, cyber security, health and safety, quality standards, supply chain regulations, environmental law and licensing.

FACTORY OF THE FUTURE

5.14 The transition to Industry 4.0 and automation is expected to increase efficiency by around 30% through the use of innovative technologies such as 3D printing, AI and XR.[23] The World Economic Forum describes a factory of the future, as having processes which are automated and connected, likely via IoT but they may also utilise other technologies such as digital twins and the deployment of 3D printing; there will be a change in the roles of the human operators and the machinery. This will see a move away from humans having to carry out the dirty, difficulty tasks that will instead be replaced by the machines and technology; and there will be a move to a more efficient and sustainable operation, which should, it is hoped, result in a more pleasant and eco-friendly environment.[24]

20 Ibid.
21 https://hub.unido.org/sites/default/files/publications/UNIDO%20-%20Guidelines%20for%20the%20establishment%20of%20a%20Smart%20Factory%20Lab_Automotive%20Sector_Final.pdf.
22 Ibid.
23 https://www.weforum.org/stories/2017/01/factory-of-the-future-clean-high-tech/.
24 Ibid.

5.15 We already have smart factories in the UK. As part of The Global Combat Air Programme, BAE Systems has created its 'Factory of the Future' in Lancashire.[25] The factory relies heavily on IoT devices and uses a range of technologies including 3D printing and robotics.[26] Atlas Copco also opened its Smart Factory Innovation Centre in Wolverhampton in 2024.[27] The Centre demonstrates the assembly line as well as a full smart factory, highlighting the need for a flexible and agile manufacturing processes.[28]

5.16 Significant investment has been made into smart factories in the USA. Deloitte, together with SAP and Witchita State University, has created a smart factory in Witchita which is 'an experimental space and innovation playground'.[29] The space, which opened in 2022, uses AI, XR, 3D printing, Iot and robotics, and sees a collaboration within the ecosystem between, amongst others Deloitte, AWS and Siemens. Deloitte has built a network of smart factories, with sites in the USA, Canada, Japan and Germany.[30]

5.17 There are also important international innovations in smart factories. The Smart Manufacturing Innovation Centre[31] is an initiative between the University of Novi Sad, Serbia and the UNIDO, which is a research centre established in 2024 to iterate for Industry 4.0. It offers a range of services to enable research and development in smart manufacturing aimed at industry, academics and government bodies.[32] It provides a testbed to test, train and study innovations in smart manufacturing in a research environment.[33]

THE 'META-FACTORY'

5.18 A meta-factory is a virtual factory, which exists in the metaverse. The term was first-coined by Hyundai and Unity who collaborated in 2022 to create the first meta-factory.[34] A meta-factory will typically utilise Industrial Internet of Things (IIoT) devices and autonomous vehicles, as well as edge computing, 6G, and be co-ordinated by workers known as 'meta operators'.[35]

5.19 One of the key use cases for the industrial metaverse is in manufacturing.[36] Processes typically combine XR technologies with digital twins. Virtual prototyping is being used by Kia Motors and General Motors to design and then

25 https://www.baesystems.com/en-uk/uk-businesses/air/factory-of-the-future.
26 Ibid.
27 https://www.atlascopco.com/en-uk/itba/expert-hub/innovate/smart-factory-innovation-centre.
28 Ibid.
29 https://www.deloitte.com/an/en/alliances/sap/about/smart-factory.html.
30 https://www.thesmartfactory.io.
31 https://www.unido.org/smart-manufacturing-innovation-center-smic.
32 https://smic-rs.com/about-us/.
33 Ibid.
34 https://www.hyundaimotorgroup.com/en/tag/2161.
35 https://ieeexplore.ieee.org/document/10596039.
36 https://www.iec.ch/basecamp/industrial-metaverse.

iterate their new products, and pharmaceutical business Syntegon Technology GmbH combines XR with cyber-physical systems and digital twins to virtually craft products, inspect them and then adapt them as needed with input from multiple parties.[37]

5.20 The industrial metaverse is already being used to: (a) remotely maintain manufacturing plant systems, including operators using smart glasses; (b) for immersive training on how to use different machinery, but also training for emergency situations; (c) predictive maintenance, meaning that by using digital twin technology and AI, the system can monitor the equipment in real-time and then determine when maintenance should be scheduled and carried out; and (d) for various collaborations in real-time in a shared space between different people and organisations.[38]

STANDARDS AND INDUSTRIAL FRAMEWORKS

5.21 Industry level technical standards are essential for smart factories, which should cover issues such as dealing with the different types of products, procedures, processes and services, especially if interoperability is to be achieved as they will set out the minimum expectations and technical requirements.[39] It is typical for enterprise level businesses to stipulate that certain standards must be met, meaning that there are typical commercial considerations driving compliance with industry standards.

5.22 The Reference Architectural Model Industrie 4.0 (RAMI 4.0) was prepared by the German Electrical and Electronic Manufacturers' Association as a framework for the transition to Industry 4.0 for manufacturers.[40] It highlights that whilst Industry 3.0 is based on hardware and a hierarchy of different isolated sections, Industry 4.0 sees the move towards a more flexible system, with more equality between different levels, and where each aspect has an 'administrative shell' that enables it to be independently controlled.[41] German Electrical and Electronic Manufacturers' Association promotes the need for each aspect of the system to be built with 'security by design' and highlights that Industry 4.0 in manufacturing is a multidisciplinary field, bringing together mechanical engineering, electronics and IT.[42] The RAMI 4.0 is a technical guide for standardised key common shared guidelines regarding underpinning technological infrastructures and communication structures, cyber security, data

37 Ibid.
38 Ibid.
39 https://issues.org/wp-content/uploads/2019/04/Belton-et-al.-Smart-Factories-SP19-ISSUES-70-76.pdf.
40 https://ec.europa.eu/futurium/en/system/files/ged/a2-schweichhart-reference_architectural_model_industrie_4.0_rami_4.0.pdf.
41 Ibid.
42 Ibid.

protection, and the software languages being used in smart manufacturing.[43] There are also other standards which have been created, either to supplement RAMI 4.0[44] or for different parts of the systems such as the IIoT aspects.[45] Critics of the RAMI 4.0 model however, consider that it fails to take into consideration the human elements within the smart factory.[46]

5.23 There are benefits in creating open standards to try and facilitate an interoperable system, which would drive down costs, promote competition, and drive-up usage, to integrate multiple systems, especially cross-border and to rapidly progress the transition towards Industry 4.0; there is unlikely, however, to be one universal set of agreed standards.[47]

UK PERSPECTIVE ON SMART MANUFACTURING

5.24 In April 2025, the UK Government published its research and analysis titled 'The wider economic impact of emerging technologies in the UK'. The report was the result of the Sunak Government commissioning PwC to report on behalf of the Government Office for Science on the impact of emerging technologies on the UK.[48] The report itself considers the adoption of many of the Industry 4.0 technologies, including AI, digital twins, robotics and virtual reality, and concluded that conservative estimates put the likely potential investment into the UK that these Industry 4.0 technologies will generate at £60 billion.[49] Some of the challenges it identified however, with the adoption of Industry 4.0 technologies are the gaps in skilled workers that have the necessary knowledge to operate these systems, and the significant costs of adopting the technology.[50]

5.25 In June 2025, the UK Government released its Modern Industrial Strategy which includes a £4.3 billion investment into innovation in manufacturing.[51] The Strategy again emphasises the Government's focus on industrial metaverse technologies such as AI, XR and automation, and highlights that in order to facilitate this innovation, regulations will be simplified. Advanced manufacturing

43 https://www.plattform-i40.de/IP/Redaktion/EN/Downloads/Publikation/rami40-an-introduction.pdf?__blob=publicationFile&v=7.
44 Such as the Fraunhofer Layer model.
45 Such as the Industrial Internet Consortium IIRA reference architecture.
46 Yong et al, 'Industry 4.0 Reference Architectural models: critical review and opportunities', International Journal of Advanced Research in Engineering Innovation, vol, no 4, 40 – 49, – http://myjms.mohe.gov.my/index.php/ijarei.
47 Yong et al (2021), 'Industry 4.0 Reference Architectural models: critical review and opportunities', International Journal of Advanced Research in Engineering Innovation, 4: 40–49, http://myjms.mohe.gov.my/index.php/ijarei.
48 https://www.gov.uk/government/publications/the-wider-economic-impacts-of-emerging-technologies-in-the-uk/the-wider-economic-impacts-of-emerging-technologies-in-the-uk-html#introduction.
49 Ibid.
50 Ibid.
51 https://assets.publishing.service.gov.uk/media/68595e56db8e139f95652dc6/industrial_strategy_policy_paper.pdf.

areas such as the automotive industry, agri-tech and advanced materials are all a focus of modernising manufacturing, and the Government considers that business investment in this space by 2035 may reach £39 billion.[52] Investment is being promoted in areas such as robotics, AI, digital twins and IoTs.

5.26 Finally, the UK Government has committed a £40 million investment into Robotic Adoption Hubs as part of the Made Smarter Adoption programme.[53] This all clearly demonstrates the significant value and importance of smart manufacturing on UK public policy and agenda as we move through the digital revolution.

EU PERSPECTIVE ON SMART MANUFACTURING

5.27 From as far back as 2015, the EU was predicting that smart manufacturing would speed up manufacturing processes by 120% and may increase production levels by as much as 20%.[54]

5.28 The European Commission believes that it is important to set rules and expectation around smart factories and smart manufacturing at a supra-national level like the EU, as well as developing strategic partnerships with other nations and that all stakeholders need to build a connected infrastructure.[55] Given the collaborative nature of smart factories' ecosystems, any relationships should be properly documented in clear contracts to reflect the different relationships and assumptions being made by each of the parties.[56]

5.29 There is no one comprehensive smart factory regulation; however, many of the different technologies are regulated by the EU, for example, the use of AI will fall under the EU AI Act,[57] and the health and safety requirements of smart machinery fall under Regulation 2023/1230.[58]

52 Ibid.

53 Ibid.

54 https://www.europarl.europa.eu/RegData/etudes/BRIE/2015/568337/EPRS_BRI(2015)568337_EN.pdf.

55 European Commission report (2015), 'Platform for Connected Factories of the Future', https://ec.europa.eu/information_society/newsroom/image/document/2015-48/workshop_report_platforms_oct15_finaldocx_12361.pdf.

56 Ibid.

57 Regulation (EU) 2024/1689 of the European Parliament and of the Council of 13 June 2024 laying down harmonised rules on artificial intelligence and amending Regulations (EC) No 300/2008, (EU) No 167/2013, (EU) No 168/2013, (EU) 2018/858, (EU) 2018/1139 and (EU) 2019/2144 and Directives 2014/90/EU, (EU) 2016/797 and (EU) 2020/1828 (Artificial Intelligence Act).

58 Regulation (EU) 2023/1230 of the European Parliament and of the Council of 14 June 2023 on machinery and repealing Directive 2006/42/EC of the European Parliament and of the Council and Council Directive 73/361/EEC.

'MADE IN CHINA 2025' – CHINA'S PERSPECTIVE ON SMART MANUFACTURING

5.30 It is important to consider China's perspective and position in respect of the Industry 4.0 movement given the industrial might of China. The 'Made in China 2025', a 2015 Chinese initiative, combined China's prowess in industry and manufacturing, with the smart revolution of Industry 4.0.[59] The plan put innovation at the heart of manufacturing. Whilst the label 'Made in China 2025' is no longer promoted due to an international backlash, it is clear that the underlying policy has been successful. It is felt that as we look forward to Made in China 2035:

> 'the divide between "tech" and "industry" dissolves entirely. AI doesn't just assist manufacturing: it becomes part of its DNA. Robotics not only automates tasks but shapes how products are conceived, iterated, and delivered. Materials science converges with biotechnology and environmental engineering to create self-healing composites, energy-generating fabrics, or waste-neutral production loops.'[60]

WORLD ECONOMIC FORUM'S PERSPECTIVE ON SMART MANUFACTURING

5.31 The World Economic Forum has established the Centre for Advanced Manufacturing and Supply Chains given the fundamental global importance of these industries.[61] It considers that the changes to the manufacturing industry is being driven by numerous factors including international tensions, the environment and technology, and calls for advanced manufacturing techniques and solutions to be made readily available across all businesses, including SMEs (small to medium-sized enterprises).[62]

THE GLOBAL LIGHTHOUSE NETWORK

5.32 The World Economic Forum created a peer-to-peer scheme for pioneering manufacturing businesses in 2018, which it has then studied since that time, with the support of McKinsey & Company, to try and understand what these 'best in show' organisations have been doing as a 'playbook' for digital adoption and transformation in manufacturing, so that other factories and manufacturing organisations can learn from them and adopt their processes as we move into the

59 https://www.csis.org/analysis/made-china-2025.

60 https://www.weforum.org/stories/2025/06/how-china-is-reinventing-the-future-of-global-manufacturing/.

61 https://centres.weforum.org/centre-for-advanced-manufacturing-and-supply-chains/home.

62 World Economic Forum briefing paper (2023), 'Advanced Manufacturing: A New Narrative', https://www3.weforum.org/docs/WEF_Advanced_Manufacturing_A_New_Narrative_2023.pdf.

fourth industrial revolution.[63] The scheme grew from 16 sites in 2018 to 189 by 2025.[64]

5.33 What is considered to set many of the 'Lighthouses' apart from other manufacturing businesses has been their mindset in terms of the use and adoption of cutting-edge emerging technologies, such as AI.[65] Factories who now collaborate with the Lighthouse scheme are able to scale up their digital transformation at pace, within around six months, but most of them agree it is fundamentally the people within the business who are key to its successful adoption of emerging technologies.[66] Further, it was identified that businesses within the Lighthouse scheme tended to strategically and meticulously breakdown each separate part of their operations, consider each aspect in turn, and then decide how improvements could be made. They also prioritised promoting the adoption of these technologies to their staff and invested significantly in encouraging the use of new and novel systems by their staff.[67] Communication is key, and Coca-Cola in Singapore is one such example of this, with its focus on consistent corporate messaging for all staff to encourage them to adopt the new technologies, which included communicating the messaging around the adoption of emerging technology using VR experiences as well as traditional engagement via newsletters. Further Schneider Electric in China has used smart glasses in order to gather staff feedback on the structural changes within the organisation, seamlessly and effectively using appropriate technology solutions to even address some of the challenges.[68]

QUANTUM

5.34 The World Economic Forum is tracking the advent of quantum computing on manufacturing and details three use cases – the Ford Otosan plant which is using quantum annealers for scheduling the production of custom vehicles, the use of quantum diamond microscopes within the creation of microchips in Munich, and the use of quantum secured fibre optic networking technology at the Port of Rotterdam.[69]

5.35 It is imperative for those in manufacturing, especially smart manufacturing, to be considering quantum now, given both its benefits for their business via quantum computing and quantum sensing, but also given the

63 https://www.weforum.org/stories/2024/07/technology-and-talent-in-manufacturing-global-lighthouse-network/.

64 https://reports.weforum.org/docs/WEF_Global_Lighthouse_Network_2025.pdf.

65 Ibid.

66 Ibid.

67 Ibid.

68 Ibid.

69 https://www.weforum.org/stories/2025/10/what-every-manufacturing-leader-know-about-quantum-technologies/.

considerable security risks it presents to them. [70] There is an urgent need to now invest in quantum security measures considering that smart factories have a vast amount of data on offer, and there are serious safety and security risks if this is attacked[71].

COLLABORATIONS

5.36 Collaborations are key for the seismic changes to manufacturing as a result of Industry 4.0.[72] Effective collaboration is demonstrated in practice by the Deloitte Smart Factory, which has created an ecosystem of different partners who bring different expertise to the operations.

5.37 A smart factory sees the convergence of traditional manufacturing and computing, and accordingly there is the need for a range of different specialists within smart manufacturing, that traditionally would not work together (although it is expected that job roles in manufacturing will change as a result of the innovations).[73] There is also commercial pragmatism in why we see collaborations between technology and industry in this sector given the costs of smart factories.[74]

5.38 It is imperative therefore that there are effective contractual relationships between the different parties within the smart manufacturing facility, from its installation, through its operation and ongoing maintenance. Effective KPIs (key performance indicators) will ensure that sufficient uptime is maintained, and a suitable disaster plan must be in place. Given the considerable sums involved, much of this conversation will be led by insurers; however, this does all need to be carefully coordinated to ensure that all risk is properly covered, and liability is not inadvertently limited. Software providers traditionally seek to license their software with specific requirements and restrictions. It is a different form of relationship traditionally than other types of contracts, where there is more contractual bargaining powers built in. When collaborating in respect of smart factories, it should be seen more as a joint venture style relationship, utilising collaboration agreements setting out the role and responsibilities of each party, though noting the risk of joint liability under English partnership law[75] that is typically expressly avoided when contracted in this territory.

70 https://reports.weforum.org/docs/WEF_Quantum_Technologies_Key_Opportunities_for_Advanced_Manufacturing_and_Supply_Chains_2025.pdf.

71 Ibid.

72 https://www3.weforum.org/docs/WEF_Impact_of_the_Fourth_Industrial_Revolution_on_Supply_Chains_.pdf.

73 https://reports.weforum.org/docs/WEF_Physical_AI_Powering_the_New_Age_of_Industrial_Operations_2025.pdf.

74 https://www.techuk.org/resource/smart-manufacturing-the-solution-to-the-uk-s-productivity-puzzle.html.

75 Partnership Act 1890.

TECHNOLOGICAL RISKS OF SMART FACTORIES

5.39 Where manufacturing plants do implement Industry 4.0 technologies, some of the technological risks include: issues with interoperability and a lack of standardisation between the different technologies and providers; cybersecurity concerns, since systems need to be secure for the human actors, but also must embed information security; the fact that there is not always ready availability of underlying IT infrastructure nor sufficiently fast internet; the systems are complex; and there are normally also some form of organisational issues caused by the reluctant adoption by the workforce, especially where there are concerns that they are being replaced.[76]

INDUSTRIAL SAFETY

5.40 It is estimated that 3 million people per year die as a result of accidents or illness in the manufacturing industry; the use of AI and frontier technology has revolutionised safety in this sector through real-time monitoring, hazard detection devices and predictive technology.[77] For example, the use of AI proximity sensors and vision safety systems on forklifts in smart factories, which, when adopted by a Malaysian automotive manufacturer resulted in a decrease in near misses of 43% in six months. In addition, there were no collisions at all reported in a Singaporean factory that was using this technology.[78] Further, the use of computer vision, a form of AI, for industrial safety with monitoring in real-time of compliance via CCTV or other forms of monitoring technology resulted in a 50% drop of near-misses in a Hong Kong factory.[79]

5.41 Industry is now even able to connect AI detection technology via IoT sensors, which alert a worker via a wearable device, like a smart watch, and deploy technology to shut down systems automatically when needed.[80]

5.42 It is important that health and safety rules and regulations keep pace with these technological advancements. Whilst there are many examples of emerging technologies being deployed to help with safety within manufacturing, there are also new risks being introduced as a result of the change in the way safety is being managed. EU Regulation 2023/1230, for example, updates safety regulations to cover new forms of machines in the digital age with less human involvements and covers 'safety risks stemming from new digital technologies',[81] including

76 Frank Herrmann (2018), 'The Smart Factory and its risks', System, 6(4): 38, https://doi.org/10.3390/systems6040038.

77 https://industrytoday.com/how-ai-is-rewiring-workplace-safety-in-manufacturing/.

78 Ibid.

79 Ibid.

80 https://www.viact.ai/post/ai-in-manufacturing-safety?utm_source=Post&utm_medium=SocialMedia&utm_campaign=AIinManufacturingSafety.

81 Regulation (EU) 2023/1230, Recital 12.

having to take 'proportionate measures' to protect products from malicious third parties.[82]

5.43 The Health and Safety Executive has confirmed that its remit, and accordingly in its view, the Health and Safety at Work etc Act 1974 already covers any risks presented by new technologies in the workplace, regardless of whether these risks were known to exist when the legislation came into effect or not.[83] Whilst their guidance relates specifically to AI,[84] its application will be much wider across all the emerging Industry 4.0 technologies. It considers that its regulations are sufficiently flexible to cover these innovations. It is important, however, that risk assessments are properly updated to accurately reflect the risks which arise through the incorporation of emerging technologies within the traditional manufacturing setting. Risk as well as benefits must be properly evaluated.

CYBERSECURITY

5.44 Traditionally the manufacturing industry is a cybersecurity target, and it will be yet more so with the introduction of Industry 4.0 technologies such as IoT and AI within this sector. With the digitalisation of manufacturing there is a significant amount of interconnectivity between systems, both on-site and off-site, with a vast amount of data now being exchanged at multiple touchpoints, including between relatively small enterprises and large enterprises within the industrial metaverse space and Industry 4.0.[85] There are multiple cybersecurity risks to smart factories, at different levels and across all aspects of business, including: the use of ransomware being deployed; social engineering attacks; supply chain attacks; insider threat attack and denial of service attacks.[86] This is not to say that the cybersecurity risks are risks only to smart factories; old manufacturing systems are also vulnerable to attack but manufacturers are often reluctant to replace these since they still may operate and function well.[87] This in itself presents a challenge since we will see a variety of different states of digitalisation, some that will adopt the changes early, and those that will be more delayed. Where these have to interact the cybersecurity risk will be elevated.

5.45 The manufacturing sector is under prepared for cyber security breaches, and this is a key area that needs to be addressed as we move into Industry 4.0. It

82 Ibid, Recital 25.
83 https://www.hse.gov.uk/news/hse-ai.htm.
84 https://www.hse.gov.uk/news/assets/docs/understand-how-ai-is-used-in-hse-regulated-sectors.pdf.
85 See World Economic Forum (2024), 'Building a Culture of Cyber Resilience in Manufacturing', https://www3.weforum.org/docs/WEF_Building_a_Culture_of_Cyber_Resilience_in_Manufacturing_2024.pdf. The report confirms that the manufacturing sector was actually the most targeted sector by cyber attacks for the three years up to its report in 2024.
86 Ibid.
87 Ibid.

is estimated that the cost per industrial cyberattack is $4.73 million, with wider ramifications permeating more than just the organisation that has been attacked given the interrelated nature of manufacturing in Industry 4.0 and its global impact.[88] Vulnerabilities include the low level of downtime in manufacturing, the rapid speed at which manufacturers are moving over to Industry 4.0 technologies and because there is no one set of principles or universal standards for cyber security in manufacturing.[89]

5.46 The World Economic Forum calls for 'cybersecurity by design'[90] in smart manufacturing which requires: prioritising cyber resilience in all aspects of the business; ensuring that cyber resilience is reflected across the staff, training, culture, the processes and assets; and the system is being effectively managed.[91] As part of this approach it is imperative to have suitable governance in place, with clear policies, allocations of roles and commitment to cybersecurity across the organisations at all levels.[92] There should also be proper resources allocated to the cybersecurity aspect of the business, with continual monitoring of systems and risks.[93] Siemens uses what it calls a 'zero-trust' method, which is effectively limiting those who have access to its data.[94] This is often overlooked by organisations, who fail to consider who actually needs, and should, have access to what data, and is a more effective way of dealing with risks than trying to deal with enforcing breaches after the fact.

5.47 All smart factory organisations need to have suitable incident management plans and have suitable policies and checklists in place which are relevant and adapted to the specific requirements of the business.[95] All relevant stakeholders in the business must be identified, and then consideration had over what minimum cybersecurity requirements should be in place across the entire process,[96] which should be properly documented and contained within contracts with each stakeholder. In addition, there should be regular compliance audits undertaken throughout the process and any procedure should be agile, and continually reviewed to ensure that it is suitable for the business and the current threats.

5.48 The World Economic Forum does call out a number of positive examples of good cyber security measures being implemented within the smart manufacturing space, for example, Unilever's role of 'Global Factory

88 Ibid.
89 Ibid.
90 https://initiatives.weforum.org/cyberresilienceindustries/manufacturing.
91 World Economic Forum (n 83).
92 Ibid.
93 Ibid.
94 https://www.weforum.org/stories/2024/01/advanced-manufacturing-improve-supply-chain-resilience-cybersecurity/.
95 World Economic Forum (n 83).
96 World Economic Forum (n 83).

Cyber Security Leader',[97] as well as having 'Regional Security Champions';[98] the effective use of internal regulation that has been implemented across Volkswagen Group; the use of cyber-attack exercises carried out by Henkel; the use of employee targets at Schneider Electric which incorporates cyber security achievements and principles; and the security by design principles deployed by Siemens as part of its Siemens Product PKI.[99]

SUSTAINABILITY

5.49 Environmental considerations are a driving force in smart manufacturing. One reason for this is because manufacturing is currently responsible for around one-fifth of global carbon emissions.[100] There are numerous projects being explored to try and combat this issue. One such initiative is being carried out by the World Economic Forum through its Centre for Advanced Manufacturing and Supply Chains, who are exploring how the carbon footprint for the manufacturing industry could be reduced by data sharing, and together with industry leaders such as Siemens, have created a digital tool which shows CO_2 emissions for each stage of the supply chain, relying on a multi-collaboration across the supply chain to share this data.[101] It is initiatives like these which further drive the digital revolution. It is through the use of Industry 4.0 technologies that innovators, regulators and policy-makers have this data, which can then be analysed and suitable targets and measures implemented.

5.50 Sustainability in manufacturing is important for both small to medium-sized enterprises (SMEs) and enterprise businesses alike[102]. In fact, embedding environmental sustainability into SME manufacturing businesses can help to reduce costs and monitor key data indices around sustainability and the environmental impact of the business can be an additional source of revenue and drive effective public private partnerships.[103]

5.51 Given the collaborative aspect of smart manufacturing, seeing a range of sizes in stakeholder businesses within the supply chain, sustainable manufacturing should be promoted to all size businesses. There is the need, however, for greater support for SMEs in sustainable manufacturing, which includes better access to resources and policies which are relevant and suitable for the size of their business; in many cases environmental and sustainability policies are aimed at larger businesses and difficult to utilise for SMEs without significant adaptation.[104]

97 World Economic Forum (n 83).
98 World Economic Forum (n 83).
99 World Economic Forum (n 83).
100 https://www.weforum.org/impact/carbon-footprint-manufacturing-industry/.
101 Ibid.
102 https://reports.weforum.org/docs/WEF_Sustainability_Meets_Growth_2025.pdf.
103 Ibid.
104 Ibid.

5.52 Environmental policy in manufacturing should reward sustainable choices, rather than be punitive.[105]

KEY TAKEAWAY POINTS

5.53 The key takeaway points in respect of smart factories and manufacturing are:

- Manufacturing is already being revolutionised by Industry 4.0 technologies. There is already a digital revolution happening. Manufacturing is a core objective of most current governments, so there is a focus to improve efficiencies, reduce costs and increase national manufacturing capabilities; all of which are achieved through digital transformation. In the UK, pioneering frontier technology is a key part of the Modern Industrial Strategy and considerable sums have been committed to its implementation.
- One of the key adopters of Industry 4.0 technologies within manufacturing, and effectively throughout the supply chain, has been the car industry. Many examples can be taken from the automotive industry by other now embracing this revolution.
- Rules and regulations need to keep pace with the changes to manufacturing brought about by these emerging technologies. This requires the collaboration of both technologists, industry and regulators.
- Standards and international frameworks are vital in smart manufacturing, to ensure interoperability between different technologies and to maintain the same consistent level of standards across industry. This is important where we see products passing through multiple different manufacturing processes, and vital that there is consistency across the board, as well as embedding high levels of safety and security.
- Given the emergent nature of the technology, and lack of regulation and case law, examples of good practice are drawn from recognition in industry and the World Economic Forum's Global Lighthouse Network, which act as 'best in show' examples of different organisations who have incorporated Industry 4.0 technologies within smart factories and across manufacturing.
- The collaborative nature of smart factories means that effective contracting is important within this sector. Key issues such as intellectual property ownership, data use and ownership, risk, liability and insurances all need to be properly reflected.
- Emerging technologies can have a positive impact on industrial safety within manufacturing; however, risk assessments need to be updated to ensure that new technologies and their risks are properly reflected. The

105 Ibid.

existing regulations and rules in place by the Health and Safety Executive still remain in force and have the capability to adapt to this new horizon.

- Cyber security is a fundamental risk in smart factories. Effective measures need to be embedded into the design and operation from the outset. Technological safeguards, as well as effective policies and procedures are essential.

Chapter 6

The digital supply chain

'We're unlocking a future where autonomous trucks make supply chains more efficient and reliable. That's the kind of value shippers across the industry are looking for—and why we're committed to building a more intelligent and resilient freight network.'[1]

Lior Ron, Founder and CEO of Uber Freight

6.1 It is not only the manufacturing industry which has been given an overhaul in the industrial metaverse. The supply chain has also followed suit. Eighty-six per cent of businesses when questioned have said that they are looking at digitally transforming their supply chain.[2] Whether this is the deployment of electronic trade documents, which has for centuries very deliberately relied on paper-form documents, the use of sophisticated end-to-end tracking of goods, the use of drones and robotics within warehouses to deliver goods, digital twins that are being used to revolutionise the supply chain[3] or last-mile delivery solutions – fundamental changes continue to be made to the supply chain as a result of the digital revolution.

6.2 The changes brought about by the advancements in the different technologies have forced legal changes in an industry which, at its heart are the legal rights concerning possession, bailment and liens; effectively protections brought about (and only capable of being in place) by holding the physical goods and which have come about to protect those within logistics who are unpaid for their services or end up left with storing someone else's heavy bulky goods.

6.3 Cyber-physical systems is a term used for systems which connect the real-world and digital world. It includes digital twins, robots and autonomous vehicles. It is effectively the blending of the real-life and digital. This is the coming together of multiple different technologies as part of a system. The use of digital twins has brought great efficiencies within the supply chain, including reducing transport and labour cost by 10%.[4]

1 https://www.uberfreight.com/blog/driverless-freight/.
2 https://www.mckinsey.com/featured-insights/mckinsey-explainers/what-is-digital-twin-technology.
3 https://www.mckinsey.com/capabilities/quantumblack/our-insights/digital-twins-the-key-to-unlocking-end-to-end-supply-chain-growth.
4 https://www.mckinsey.com/featured-insights/mckinsey-explainers/what-is-digital-twin-technology.

6.4 The Made Smarter Digital Supply Chain Innovation Hub run by Digital Catapult is looking specifically at digitalising the supply chain.[5] The Alan Turing Institute is also developing the system of systems digital twin for large fleets as part of the UK Research and Innovation Strategic Priorities Fund.[6] It identifies that fleets of delivery vehicles using digital twin technology enable the sharing of data from individual vehicles so that decisions can be taken in respect of the collective set of vehicles, such as in respect of maintenance scheduling.[7]

6.5 Digital twin technology is also being deployed in retail, at the other end of the supply chain. This includes installing Internet of Things (IoT) sensors in bricks and mortar stores, which collects data, which is then analysed by the stores and utilised for planning within the stores, as well as replacing human cashiers.[8] Digital twins are also being deployed to assist with 'shop-floor management and control (SMC)'.[9]

6.6 The Robotic Growth Partnership uses Ocardo as an example of end-to-end digitalisation of the supply chain, blending robots within its warehouses, digital twins running simulations of the warehouse and the use of artificial intelligence (AI) to identify issues such as demand, as well as reduce fraud.[10] There is not only one solution, but the blending of multiple different technologies to revolutionise the supply chain for the next industrial revolution.

6.7 In the EU, the Digital Product Passport (DPP) was implemented under the Ecodesign for Sustainable Products Regulation 2024.[11] Under the regulations, over time, a digital passport will become mandatory for different products, starting with some batteries from 2027.[12] The passport will digitally register and then share life-cycle product information, which will be available throughout the supply-chain and by the customers. The rules are yet to be drawn up for these but the passport is being designed for transparency and to promote sustainability.[13] The DPP is one of the first steps in recognising the importance of integrating digital information within the supply-chain and the resulting product.

5 https://www.digicatapult.org.uk/programmes/programme/made-smarter-innovation-digital-supply-chain-hub/.
6 https://www.turing.ac.uk/research/research-projects/ecosystems-digital-twins.
7 https://www.turing.ac.uk/sites/default/files/2023-05/turing_asg_whitepaper_digitaltwins.pdf.
8 https://www.bcs.org/articles-opinion-and-research/making-retail-smarter-with-digital-twins/.
9 C. Zhuang et al (2025), 'Digital twin-based smart shop-floor management and control: A review', Advanced Engineering Informatics, 65 (Part A), 103102.
10 An independent expert group advising the UK Government.
11 Regulation (EU) 2024/1781 of the European Parliament and of the Council of 13 June 2024 establishing a framework for the setting of ecodesign requirements for sustainable products, amending Directive (EU) 2020/1828 and Regulation (EU) 2023/1542 and repealing Directive 2009/125/EC.
12 Under the new EU Battery Regulation 2023/1542 of the European Parliament and of the Council of 12 July 2023 concerning batteries and waste batteries, amending Directive 2008/98/EC and Regulation (EU) 2019/1020 and repealing Directive 2006/66/EC.
13 https://www.deloitte.com/uk/en/services/consulting-risk/perspectives/digital-product-passports-are-just-around-the-corner.html.

6.8 This chapter explores the digitalisation of the supply chain from the legal intricacies of international trade document, through the revolutionary work being done by the Digital Container Shipping Association (DCSA) and whose General Counsel has contributed towards this chapter, to the use of AI and automation for deliveries and logistics.

CYBERSECURITY IN THE SUPPLY CHAIN

6.9 The current Network and Information Systems (NIS) Regulations 2018 do not currently apply specifically to the supply chain. The UK is, however, in the process of updating its cyber security regulation, and in April 2025 released its policy paper on 'Cyber security and resilience policy statement'.[14] The Secretary of State for Department for Science, Innovation and Technology has announced the need for a Cyber Security and Resilience Bill to address some of the threats and concerns which have been identified to the UK infrastructure from cybercriminals. Currently cybersecurity requirements fall under the NIS Regulations 2018, which are limited in their scope and application. The new legislation will bring more entities into the scope of the regulation, which will include the supply chain, as it was specifically referenced in the Kings Speech in 2024.[15] The supply chain is vulnerable and remains a target for cybercriminals looking to disrupt the supply of goods and food in the UK.

INTERNATIONAL TRADE DOCUMENTS

6.10 International trade still relies heavily on what are termed 'documentary intangibles',[16] this is where rights and obligations pass via the transfer of the possession of a document. This means that the person with possession of the document is able to demand the deliverance of the obligations owed by the other party. These are unique types of documents in which title is actually transferred by virtue of the transfer of the paper itself, given the paper itself embodies the rights. The law concerning these rights date back to medieval law.[17] It means that the holder of the document can rely on the rights in the document without having to carry out any further investigations. The document itself can be used as security,[18] the documents are afforded protection in respect of torts in the same vein as other types of property,[19] and you are able to recover damages in respect of the rights in the documents themselves.[20] This is an area which is rich for innovation as part of the digital revolution.

14 https://www.gov.uk/government/publications/cyber-security-and-resilience-bill-policy-statement/cyber-security-and-resilience-bill-policy-statement.

15 Ibid.

16 Sometimes referred to as 'documents of title'.

17 *Goodwin v Robarts* (1875) LR 10 Exch 337.

18 Given the rights of bailment apply: *Carter v Wake* (1877) 4 Ch D 605.

19 Such as negligence: *Smith v Lloyds TSB Group Plc* [2001] QB 541.

20 *OBG Ltd v Allan* [2007] UKHL 21, [2008] 1 AC 1.

6.11 In international trade there are often in excess of 100 pages of paper documents for each consignment, dealing with the goods passing between multiple different parties, from logistic companies, to insurance companies. It is estimated that four billion paper documents are created a year in international trade.[21]

DOCUMENTS OF TITLE

6.12 Documents of title were considered by the Law Commission in its 2021 consultation on electronic trade documents.[22] There are various different documents of title, used for different purposes throughout the supply chain.

6.13 A bill of exchange is title to money.[23] In international trade, a bill of exchange is typically used as payment, for finance and as evidence of the sums due.[24] Bills of exchange are governed by the Bills of Exchange Act 1882 and the Law Commission has highlighted concerns around this legislation.[25]

6.14 A bill of lading deals with issues concerning the shipping of goods by sea. It documents that the person transporting the goods (carrier) has actually received the goods, gives certain rights against the carrier, gives possession of the goods whilst at sea[26] and allows the person with possession of the bill of lading the right to take receipt of the goods from the carrier. It is governed under the common law, the Carriage of Goods by Sea Act 1971, the Sale of Goods Act 1979, and the Carriage of Goods by Sea Act 1992.[27] It was considered that section 1(5) of the Carriage of Goods by Sea Act 1992 required that a bill of lading must be in paper form unless it was decreed otherwise by the Secretary of State.[28] Typically, a bill of lading is in three counterparts, frequently done using carbon paper,[29] although this practice had been criticised for a very long time.[30]

6.15 A warehouse receipt, used to reclaim goods stored at a warehouse is not considered as a document of title[31] but is 'effectively … [a] … document

21 Law Commission (2021), Consultation Paper no. 254: Digital Assets: electronic trade documents: a consultation paper, https://webarchive.nationalarchives.gov.uk/ukgwa/20250109104304mp_/https://cloud-platform-e218f50a4812967ba1215eaecede923f.s3.amazonaws.com/uploads/sites/30/2021/04/Electronic-trade-documents-CP.pdf.

22 Ibid.

23 A cheque is a bill of exchange but is not the only form of a bill of exchange. There are statutory requirements which have to be met to qualify as a bill of exchange.

24 Law Commission, Consultation Paper no. 254 (n 21).

25 Ibid.

26 *Lickbarrow v Mason* (1787) 2 TR 63.

27 Law Commission, Consultation Paper no. 254 (n 21).

28 Ibid.

29 Or more accurately, NCR paper.

30 *Glyn Mills Currie & Co v The East and West India Dock Company* (1882) 7 App Cas 591.

31 Law Commission, Consultation Paper no. 254 (n 21).

of title'.[32] The exception being warehouse warrants issued by the London Metal Exchange which are considered as a proper document of title as a result of London Metal Exchange regulations. Whilst not technically a document of title, the Law Commission included warehouse receipts within the scope of their review. The Law Commission also covered marine insurance policies which fall under the Marine Insurance Act 1906[33] and cargo insurance certificates which are dealt with under the common law, and in principle are transferable to the person holding the paper certificate.[34]

ELECTRONIC TRADE DOCUMENTS

6.16 From 2021 onwards, the Law Commission started to explore the idea as to whether international trade documents, like the bill of lading and bill of exchange,[35] could be digitalised.[36] The reason why this warranted the involvement of the Law Commission was because many of these documents[37] required the act of being 'possessed'[38] and at that time electronic documents were incapable of being 'possessed' since they are considered as being intangible property.[39] As a result, electronic documents could not be considered delivered, held, be documents of title nor negotiable instruments, be bailed, nor be capable of possessory security and therefore were not protected against certain torts such as trespass and conversion.[40] The Law Commission distinguished between those documents which transferred title, and those which were just evidence of the transfer.[41]

6.17 The Law Commission was concerned that unless changes were made to accommodate electronic documents then English law would lose its high status

32 *Niru Battery Manufacturing Co v Milestone Trading Ltd* [2003] EWCA Civ 1446.
33 Although acknowledging that it had already considered that there was probably scope for such documents being in electronic form in its 2010 report.
34 *Koskas v Standard Marine Insurance Co* (1927) 27 Ll L Rep 59, 60.
35 The Law Commission considered the following documents: bill of exchange; promissory notes; bill of lading; ship delivery orders; warehouse receipts; marine insurance policies; cargo insurance certificates (Law Commission, Consultation Paper no. 254 (n 21)), and in its report expanded these specific lists further to include mate's receipts (Law Commission (2022), Electronic Trade Documents: Report and Bill HC 1188 Law Com No. 405. https://webarchive.nationalarchives.gov.uk/ukgwa/20250109113011mp_/https://cloud-platform-e218f50a4812967ba1215eaecede923f.s3.amazonaws.com/uploads/sites/30/2022/03/Electronic-Trade-Documents-final-report-ACCESSIBLE-1.pdf.
36 Although the Law Commission prefer the term 'electronic documents'.
37 Being 'documentary intangibles'.
38 The concept of possession was considered in *The Manchester Ship Canal Co Ltd v Vauxhall Motors Ltd* [2018] EWCA Civ 1100 and required 'factual possession' and 'intention to possess'.
39 *OBG Ltd v Allan* [(n 20); *Your Response Ltd v Datateam Business Media Ltd* [2014] EWCA Civ 281, [2015] QB 41.
40 Law Commission, Electronic Trade Documents: Report and Bill HC 1188 (n 35).
41 Certain documents like air waybills and sea waybills are not documents of title and were already largely done electronically.

in international trade, since in most international shipping transactions English law is used.[42] Electronic trade documents were already recognised in France, the USA, Germany, South Korea, Australia, Singapore, Abu Dhabi and Bahrain. The Law Commission highlighted that at this time parties were deploying complex, multilayer contractual provisions to try and workaround the legal issue with electronic documents under English law, meaning the law at this time simply did not reflect the real-life position, and was making it unnecessarily complex, inefficient and costly.

6.18 In its 2022 report, the Law Commission recommended that electronic trade documents be legally recognised as being the same as paper trade documents provided specific criteria was met and all rights flowing from the act of being possessed should apply to electronic documents.[43] In 2023, the Government passed the Electronic Trade Documents Act 2023.

6.19 The Law Commission in its report considered the idea of designating some documents as 'trade documents' capable of being possessed in an electronic form as a matter of law[44]. This was intended to cover all of the documents of title except bearer bonds and uncertified securities. Further, it highlighted that the intention to possess was an important part of possession.[45] The Law Commission and the courts each considered that there was the need for statutory reform to permit electronic trade documents, rather than just try and deal with it through the common law[46], nor was it felt suitable to make these changes via subordinate legislation. Given the significant legal changes, only statutory law reform was felt necessary.

6.20 This is a pivotal point for Industry 4.0. It brings international trade documents into the modern times and was estimated that it would create £224 billion in savings and £25 billion in economic growth by 2024.[47] It is important to note, however, that the updated statutory position does not prevent international trade documents remaining in paper form and there is no requirement which compels electronic trade documents.[48] Meaning, in practice there is now a choice between electronic documents or paper form.

42 The Law Commission concludes that between 50–80% of shipping documents were subject to English law, Law Commission, Electronic Trade Documents: Report and Bill HC 1188 Law Com No. 405 (n 35).

43 Ibid.

44 Ibid.

45 Ibid.

46 *Your Response v Datateam Business Media Ltd* [2014] EWCA Civ 281 and OBG Ltd v Allan (n 20).

47 https://lawcom.gov.uk/project/electronic-trade-documents/#1-Problem.

48 Law Commission, Electronic Trade Documents: Report and Bill HC 1188 Law Com No. 405 (n 35).

THE ELECTRONIC TRADE DOCUMENTS ACT 2023

6.21 The Electronic Trade Documents Act 2023 was passed on 20 September 2023.

6.22 Section 3 of the Act confirms that:

1. electronic trade documents can be possessed, indorsed and possession can be parted;[49]
2. electronic trade documents have the 'same effect as an equivalent paper trade document';[50] and
3. 'Anything done in relation to an electronic trade document has the same effect (if any) in relation to the document as it would have in relation to an equivalent paper trade document'.[51]

6.23 The exceptions to those provisions under section 3 are contained at section 5, which include where the document, or the terms, itself show an intention that section 3 should not apply[52] – therefore bringing the concept of the intention to possess back into the spotlight.

INTERPRETING QUALIFYING ELECTRONIC DOCUMENTS AND POSSESSION

6.24 The Law Commission's report can assist in the interpretation of Acts of Parliament originating from the Law Commission. This is useful for expanding the key concepts set out under the new statute, especially with regards to qualifying electronic documents and the idea of possession.

6.25 In considering what should be considered as a qualifying electronic document, the Law Commission[53] felt that there were seven 'gateway' criteria, which are that:

1. the electronic documents must contain all information that is required of the original underlying paper versions;
2. the electronic trade document should be contained on a reliable system. That system should have operational rules and security measures, be independently audited, and have regulatory oversight and industry standards;
3. the documents must have integrity so that they cannot be interfered with and must be trusted as being authentic;

49 Section 3(1) of the Electronic Trade Documents Act 2023.
50 Section 3(2) of the Electronic Trade Documents Act 2023.
51 Section 3(3) of the Electronic Trade Documents Act 2023.
52 Section 5(1) of the Electronic Trade Documents Act 2023.
53 Law Commission, Electronic Trade Documents: Report and Bill HC 1188 Law Com No. 405 (n 35).

4. the document must be capable of being controlled and that control should be exclusively controlled by one person (or persons jointly) controlling the document at any one time;
5. the document must be divestible. This means that once the document is transferred that control also transfers and the original person who was holding the document can no longer control it;
6. the document must be capable of being identifiable as the document itself and distinguishable from copies; and
7. the document must be able to be uniquely associable with the person controlling it.

6.26 For trade documents to be capable of being possessed electronically, the Law Commission felt that this required the documents to have only one person able to control the document at any one time; and upon them being transferred the person who originally had control of the document then loses this control.[54] This is not simply an email and email attachment.[55] What was envisaged by the Law Commission was a sophisticated technology system since the law already permitted electronic signatures unless specifically excluded under the specific legislation concerning the relevant requirements of the document.[56]

6.27 It is for this reason, as discussed further below at para **6.28**, digital ledger technology, such as blockchain lends itself perfectly to the role. The gateway criteria set out above at para **6.25**, and view as to possession, are very similar in nature to the original concerns that belied the idea of decentralised cryptocurrency before the invention of BitCoin and were expressed in the White Paper of Satoshi Nakamoto.[57]

BLOCKCHAIN FOR ELECTRONIC TRADE DOCUMENTS

6.28 Being technologically neutral means that the Electronic Trade Documents Act 2023 is not limited by future technological innovations. The Law Commission does, however, consider that smart contracts on the blockchain could meet the necessary criteria for an electronic trade document provided it was able to be read by someone, even if this was in code.[58]

54 Ibid.

55 Ibid.

56 They considered that electronic signatures would be permitted for both marine insurance policies and bills of exchange, both of which were highlighted as potentially complex by the Law Commission.

57 https://bitcoin.org/bitcoin.pdf.

58 Law Commission, Electronic Trade Documents: Report and Bill HC 1188 Law Com No. 405 (n 35).

6.29 Some of the main issue stems from the previous legal position that property could only be a thing in action or thing in possession.[59] This position was causing numerous difficulties to the Law Commission when considering several updates needed for the digital revolution. This has now, however, been remedied through the Property (Digital Assets etc) Act 2025 which now absolutely confirms on a statutory footing that digital assets, such as cryptoassets can be property. The common law has already accepted this position as well.[60] This means that trade documents can effectively be tokenised using the blockchain.

THE ELECTRONIC BILL OF LADING: AN INTERNATIONAL CROSS BORDER PERSPECTIVE

6.30 Few instruments in the history of commerce have demonstrated the same durability, legal sophistication, and global reach as the bill of lading. Emerging from 14th-century mercantile practice, it remains the cornerstone of carriage of goods. At its core, as discussed briefly above at para **6.14**, the bill of lading performs three interrelated legal functions, each essential to international trade and transport law.

6.31 Firstly, the bill of lading serves as evidence of receipt. When a carrier issues a bill of lading, it acknowledges having received the goods being transported in apparent good order and condition. This receipt function is vital for both the shipper (typically an exporter/seller) and consignee (typically an importer/buyer), providing *prima facie* proof of what was shipped and the state of the cargo at loading. Courts across jurisdictions have confirmed that statements on the bill serve as binding evidence.

6.32 Second, the bill of lading serves as evidence of an underlying contract of carriage between the shipper and carrier, particularly once the goods are loaded and the document is issued. While an underlying charterparty or preliminary booking agreements may govern initial arrangements, the bill serves as the operative contract for third parties who later acquire it and might become party to that contract. Its terms and conditions of carriage, incorporated in the bill itself, define rights and obligations concerning *inter alia* carriage, delivery, and liability.

6.33 Finally, and significantly, as discussed above at para **6.14**, the bill of lading operates as a document of title. Possession of the bill equates to constructive possession of the goods represented by that bill. By endorsement and delivery, the bill enables transfer of ownership or security interest in the goods while it remains in transit. This negotiability underpins trade finance, allowing letters of credit, pledges, and sale of goods afloat.

59 *Colonial Bank v Whinney* (1885) 30 Ch D 261, 285.
60 *D'Aloia v Persons Unknown* [2024] EWHC 2342 (Ch).

6.34 In effect, the bill of lading bridges the physical and the commercial. It links tangible cargo moving across oceans with intangible legal rights and financial flows across borders.

THE CHALLENGE OF DIGITALISATION

6.35 Digitising such a venerable instrument is not merely a technical upgrade, it is a profound legal transformation. The shift from paper to electronic bills of lading (eBLs) raises a set of interlocking challenges.

THE POSSESSION PROBLEM

6.36 At the heart of the issue lies the concept of possession. Under common law, possession implies physical control of a tangible object coupled with intent to possess. Electronic records such as electronic bills of lading, being intangible, cannot be 'possessed' in the traditional sense. Without statutory intervention, electronic documents risk falling outside the legal definitions that underpin their negotiability.

6.37 Several jurisdictions have addressed this. The UK's Electronic Trade Documents Act 2023, following the United Nations Commission on International Trade Law (UNCITRAL) Model Law on Electronic Transferable Records (2017) (MLETR), creates a legal fiction: an electronic trade document can be 'possessed' if a reliable system is used to ensure core principles such as singularity, integrity, and control. Adoption of equivalent legislation has been moderate, with only 12 jurisdictions enacting MLETR-inspired laws as of November 2025, yet momentum is large and several additional jurisdictions are in the process of legislation.

EQUIVALENCE AND EVIDENTIARY INTEGRITY

6.38 A second challenge concerns functional equivalence. That is, ensuring that electronic documents perform the same evidentiary and legal functions as paper ones. This requires robust systems to prevent duplication, alteration, or unauthorised access. Without universal recognition of such systems, carriers and banks may hesitate to accept electronic bills of lading, fearing legal uncertainty or non-recognition in foreign courts.

LEGAL FRAGMENTATION

6.39 The maritime industry is inherently international. Each voyage crosses multiple jurisdictions, each with its own contract law, carriage conventions, and rules of evidence. Without harmonised recognition of electronic bills of lading, the same shipment may be electronically valid in one jurisdiction but legally void in another. This jurisdictional variance has been a major impediment to widespread adoption.

LEARNINGS AND PRECEDENTS

6.40 The (traditional, paper) bills of lading has been around for centuries, and therefore the subject of countless use-cases and disputes in every corner of the world. This has caused well-established learnings and practices, as well as an abundance of legal cases which have in turn created a solid basis for relative legal certainty and acceptance from all stakeholders participating in international trade.

6.41 By contrast, the electronic bills of lading is quite a new concept. As of November 2025, there has not been a single court case around the world which has dealt with the electronic bills of lading and how it has treated the challenges described above at para **6.35**.

6.42 In the absence of judicial precedents, the responsibility for establishing commercial certainty has fallen to industry bodies. The Digital Container Shipping Association (DCSA) has taken a leading role in creating this certainty through the standardisation of digital trade documentation.

DCSA AND THE STANDARDISATION OF ELECTRONIC BILLS OF LADING

6.43 The DCSA was founded in 2019 by several leading ocean container carriers, representing together about 75% of all containerised trade, to accelerate digital transformation through common, open standards. Its mission is to enable interoperability and data exchange across the container shipping ecosystem, a prerequisite for the industrial metaverse of global logistics.

THE DCSA ELECTRONIC BILLS OF LADING STANDARD

6.44 In 2024, DCSA released its Bill of Lading Standard 3.0, defining the structure, semantics, and data exchange protocols for digital bills. Built on The United Nations Centre for Trade Facilitation and Electronic Business (UN/CEFACT) multimodal reference data models, the standard provides a common digital language for electronic bills of lading issuance, transfer and surrender. It ensures that data elements such as consignee details, shipment identifiers and contractual clauses are machine-readable, secure and aligned with international trade norms.

6.45 Crucially, the DCSA standard is technology-agnostic. It does not prescribe a specific blockchain or platform architecture. Rather, it sets out business and data interoperability requirements. This allows carriers, banks, and technology providers to develop or adopt compliant solutions without being locked into proprietary systems.

ALIGNMENT WITH LEGAL FRAMEWORKS

6.46 DCSA's work explicitly aligns with MLETR principles and national implementations like the UK Electronic Trade Documents Act 2023. The standard supports the core legal requirements of *singularity*, *integrity*, and *control*, ensuring that an electronic record can serve as a unique, transferable title document. By providing a technical layer that satisfies these legal tests, DCSA enables carriers and customers to operate within compliant frameworks, regardless of which jurisdiction their trade touches.

INDUSTRY ADOPTION

6.47 DCSA's member carriers have committed to issuing 100% of their bills of lading electronically by 2030. The DCSA eBL standard is now integrated into the operational systems of carriers, freight forwarders, and electronic bills of lading platform providers, accelerating a shift that promises substantial gains in efficiency, fraud reduction, and sustainability.

6.48 As of November 2025, DCSA's member carriers issue more than 12% of their bills of lading in electronic format, with exponential growth on the horizon.

INTEROPERABILITY: THE NEXT FRONTIER

6.49 If standardisation was the first milestone, interoperability is the true enabler of the digital trade ecosystem. The legal value of a bill of lading, be it paper or electronic, depends on its ability to circulate freely. In the paper world, transfer is made by endorsement and handing over of the document. In the digital world, transfer requires inter-platform trust and legal recognition.

THE LANDSCAPE OF EBL PLATFORMS

6.50 Over the past decade, several technology providers have emerged, each offering digital title registries based on distinct architectures. Some use distributed ledger technology (DLT), others rely on secure centralised databases.

6.51 Each platform creates a closed ecosystem where electronic bills of lading can circulate, but transfers between systems is not natively supported, neither technically nor legally. As a result, the digital document risks losing its legal continuity when crossing platform boundaries.

THE LEGAL CHALLENGE OF TRANSFER BETWEEN SYSTEMS

6.52 When an electronic bill of lading is moved between platforms, several legal risks arise:

- Continuity of title: The transferee must obtain exactly the same legal rights as if the bill had been endorsed and delivered in paper form. Any break in control could invalidate the transfer.
- Singularity: There must never exist two versions of the same bill on different systems. Establishing and maintaining a single authoritative version is technically complex.
- Recognition of control: Each platform may define 'control' differently, and legal systems may not recognise cross-platform control transfers as satisfying possession requirements under MLETR or national laws.
- Evidence and auditability: Courts or banks must be able to verify control across systems, even if they operate under different governance models or jurisdictions.

TECHNICAL CHALLENGES

6.53 Technically, interoperability requires common data models, secure application programming interfaces (APIs), and trusted identity frameworks. The DCSA eBL standard provides the data model, but additional layers, covering authentication, transfer protocols and audit logs, are necessary for seamless exchange.

6.54 A key technical challenge is the creation of a 'handover protocol' that allows one system to relinquish exclusive control while another system assumes it, with cryptographic assurance that no duplicates exist. This process must be verifiable, tamper-evident, and compliant with legal definitions of 'possession'.

DCSA'S WORK ON INTEROPERABILITY

6.55 Recognising that the absence of interoperability risked fragmenting the digital trade landscape, DCSA, in collaboration with industry stakeholders and specifically the electronic bills of lading platform providers, has developed a standard (technical and legal) for interoperability.

THE INTEROPERABILITY FRAMEWORK

6.56 The DCSA Interoperability Framework defines how electronic bills of lading platforms can exchange control of a document in a legally valid and technically secure manner. It consists of:

- common API specifications for handover and verification;
- digital identity and authentication standards;
- audit trail requirements to demonstrate the continuous chain of control;
- common user terms for ensuring a proper and valid transfer of rights and obligations between users of different platforms; and
- governance rules for liability, dispute resolution, and compliance.

6.57 The framework does not centralise control. Rather, it provides a federated trust model. Each platform retains autonomy but adheres to common rules for interoperation, akin to how email systems interconnect through shared protocols (SMTP, IMAP) while operating independently.

LEGAL VALIDATION AND THE ROLE OF DCSA

6.58 From a legal perspective, DCSA's interoperability model was designed to ensure compliance with MLETR Article 11, which allows for the transfer of control through 'reliable methods'. Legal validation required demonstrating that a cross-platform handover preserves:

1. singularity – only one authoritative version exists;
2. integrity – the content of the document remains unaltered; and
3. control – the transferee gains exclusive control while the transferor loses it.

6.59 To that end, DCSA engaged with leading maritime law firms and regulators to ensure the framework could withstand judicial scrutiny. The association also collaborates closely with BIMCO (the Baltic and International Maritime Council), ICC (the International Chamber of Commerce), Swift (the Society for Worldwide Interbank Financial Telecommunication), and FIATA (the International Federation of Freight Forwarders Associations), through the establishment of the Future of International Trade (FIT) Alliance, to harmonise contractual and documentary references to electronic bills of ladings across the supply chain.

LEGAL IMPLICATIONS FOR THE INDUSTRIAL METAVERSE

6.60 The broader context of this development lies in the industrial metaverse – the convergence of digital twins, smart contracts, and virtual trade ecosystems.

Within this landscape, electronic bills of lading represent more than digitisation of a paper form. It becomes a tokenised legal object, a verifiable digital twin of property rights in goods.

AUTOMATED TRADE

6.61 With interoperability, electronic bills of lading can interact seamlessly with other digital trade instruments, such as electronic certificates of origin, warehouse receipts, or insurance policies, within decentralised networks. Smart contracts can automate release of goods, payment under letters of credit, or enforcement of sanctions, provided the underlying digital assets are legally recognised.

6.62 The DCSA eBL framework therefore serves as a foundational layer for the automation of trade law performance, where legal events (such as endorsement or surrender) can trigger real-time digital actions.

6.63 The more interconnected these systems become, however, the greater the complexity of jurisdictional and private international law questions. Which court has competence over a dispute arising from a cross-platform transfer? Which law governs control of a digital title document residing on a distributed ledger?

6.64 DCSA advocates for contractual harmonisation, at least in the immediate term, ensuring that platform terms incorporate clear governing law and dispute resolution clauses consistent with international conventions. In parallel, engagement with the United Nations, other inter-governmental organisations (such as the World Trade Organisation and the World Customs Organisation), governments and other non-governmental organisations, ensures that industry experience informs future legislation and iterations of legal instruments and related guidance.

THE PATH AHEAD

6.65 The transition from paper to electronic bills of lading mirrors the evolution of maritime law itself; from tangible parchment to distributed ledgers. Yet, while technology may transform the medium, the underlying legal principles endure: certainty, negotiability, and trust.

6.66 Widespread adoption of MLETR-based legislation remains the single most important enabler. As of 2025, about 12 jurisdictions, including the UK, Singapore, and France, have enacted enabling laws. DCSA continues to engage with governments, shippers, electronic bills of lading platform providers, banks, and industry bodies to advocate for global legal recognition of electronic bills of lading.

6.67 The container shipping industry's commitment to full electronic bills of lading adoption by 2030 will unlock estimated savings of $6.5 billion in direct costs annually[61] while reducing 28,000 tonnes of CO_2 emissions from paper and courier logistics. More importantly, it will embed digital trust and transparency in global supply chains, which are core attributes of the industrial metaverse.

6.68 The electronic bill of lading epitomises the journey from document to data, from possession to control, and from fragmentation to interoperability. Through the coordinated efforts of DCSA and its partners, what was once a theoretical construct is now a functioning component of the industrial metaverse – a digital ecosystem where trade, law, and technology converge.

6.69 The enduring lesson of the electronic bill of lading is that law does not stand apart from innovation. It evolves with it, translating ancient principles into new digital realities. As maritime commerce sails further into the metaverse, the bill of lading in electronic, interoperable, and legally secure form remains its most trusted compass.

AUTONOMOUS LOGISTICS

6.70 It is estimated that by 2032 there will be 4.7 million delivery robots in operation.[62] These range from autonomous vans, and 'last mile' robots, to warehouse autonomous vehicles and drones, all of which are used to prepare, move and deliver consignments and are often referred to as 'autonomous logistics'.[63] We already live in a society, at least for now, where not only our workplace is being shared with these autonomous systems, but also our streets. In order to safeguard the public, and encourage safe innovation, there needs to be effective regulation and licensing for these technologies, especially when these delivery robots need to use the pavements, roads or skies.[64]

6.71 The use of autonomous vehicles in the freight and logistic industries could bring considerable benefits in a sector where there are low margins, yet there is still a distinct lack of practical underpinning infrastructure for these types of system to gather widespread adoption, for example, there is still a distinct failing in being able to easily charge delivery robots, which is having an impact on their adoption.[65]

61 https://dcsa.org/newsroom/dcsas-member-carriers-commit-to-a-fully-standardised-electronic-bill-of-lading-by-2030.
62 https://vivatechnology.com/news/autonomous-delivery-robots-delivering-the-future-of-logistics.
63 Ibid.
64 https://hansard.parliament.uk/commons/2023-05-23/debates/4B1A37B1-E54E-40C4-A7BE-EED56A1DC1BF/AutonomousLast-MileDelivery.
65 https://committees.parliament.uk/publications/41454/documents/203901/default/.

6.72 The following sets out some examples of autonomous logistics which are being deployed across the supply chain.

AMAZON

6.73 Amazon is deploying a range of smart warehouse technology. It is using around 750,000 mobile robots in its US fulfilment centres, which are controlled centrally by its digital warehouse management system.[66] Amazon currently uses nine different types of robots throughout their logistic supply chain including a range of technology such as AI, robotics and computer vision.[67]

6.74 Proteus[68] is 'Amazon's first autonomous robot'[69] which is used to move packages around within its fulfilment centres. The tech giant boasts that the robot moves about freely within the fulfilment centre and has integrated sensor technology enabling it to avoid objects and can undertake two 10-hour shifts a day with 15-minute battery charges every two hours. It uses bespoke Amazon developed technology called simultaneous localisation and mapping (SLAM).

6.75 Sequoia is a robotic system which helps with storing stock, retrieving this stock from the stored location within the fulfilment centre and making this accessible to its real-life staff to pack.[70]

6.76 Hercules is used to move pods of products around the fulfilment centre to the specific employees picking the products for packing.[71] Hercules uses a 3D camera to make decisions about its route within the fulfilment centre to avoid staff and other items in the centre.[72] Unlike Proteus, Hercules relies on markers on the floor of the site, which also act as a safety perimeter for human staff.[73]

6.77 Titan is similar to Hercules but can lift heavier items.[74]

6.78 Vulcan picks stock from the top and bottom shelves in the fulfilment centres and can also move objects around on the shelves to make space.[75] Amazon claims that this is the first of its robots with the sense of touch, using the combined technology of robotics and physical AI. It can also identify where it is not able to move something and alerts a human member of staff to assist.

66 https://www.aboutamazon.com/news/operations/amazon-robotics-robots-fulfillment-center.
67 Ibid.
68 https://www.aboutamazon.com/stories/amazon-robotics-autonomous-robot-proteus-warehouse-packages.
69 Ibid.
70 https://www.aboutamazon.com/news/operations/amazon-robotics-robots-fulfillment-center.
71 Ibid.
72 Ibid.
73 Ibid.
74 Ibid.
75 Ibid.

6.79 Sparrow selects specific individual items and sends these to staff to be packaged.[76] This technology deploys a lot more specificity than the other robots as it selects individual products, from effectively a pick-face type of setup. Sparrow uses computer vision and AI.

6.80 Robin[77] sorts the packages once they are packaged and before they are put onto the dock and loaded into the lorries. Both Robin and Cardinal[78] use AI and computer vision. Cardinal selects the packages and gets it ready for loading based on reading its label.

6.81 Amazon also uses packaging automation to package items, and to create made-to-measure paper bags to fit the products using sensors.

6.82 Finally, DeepFleet is used to coordinate the robots within the fulfilment centres.[79] This uses AI to optimise the use of the robots within the fulfilment centres. The technology is designed to learn from the data it produces to continue to improve operations within the fulfilment centres.

6.83 Amazon's 'smart' fulfilment centres show clearly the combined resources of real-life staff and robots, which work together to make tasks swifter, and easier for the human staff. As discussed further in **Chapter 12,** there are many employment challenges and opportunities presented by Industry 4.0, which is demonstrated here.

6.84 As discussed in **Chapter 5**, it is important that health and safety rules and regulations keep pace with technological advancements. In the UK, the health and safety of a smart warehouse facility will fall under the Health and Safety Executive and the Health and Safety at Work etc. Act 1974 will apply. It is vital that the risks presented by these robots and smart systems in the warehouse are properly reflected in risk assessments. Further, cyber-security concerns, as they are in smart manufacturing facilities, continue to apply within the smart logistic space.

SMART DELIVERY

6.85 A number of delivery companies are expanding their smart delivery offerings. For example, DHL is utilising 3,000 robots within its supply chain across the UK and Europe,[80] and the Roboat Project in the Netherlands used

76 Ibid.
77 Ibid.
78 Ibid.
79 https://www.aboutamazon.com/news/operations/amazon-million-robots-ai-foundation-model.
80 https://www.iotworldtoday.com/robotics/dhl-adding-1-000-more-robots-in-uk-748m-expansion?utm_source=superhuman&utm_medium=newsletter&utm_campaign=robotics-special-robots-ride-the-subway&_bhlid=0d369d7e921f29aa0f03ee0db19d749bfd38ee59.

autonomous canal boats for logistics operations.[81] DPD has created an 'end-to-end robotic warehouse automation solution'[82] and is using autonomous vehicles called an Ottobot to deliver parcels.[83] Whilst the vehicles currently only deliver within a mile of the depots, known as the 'last-mile delivery'[84], to try and combat security concerns, the robots hold the parcels inside a special compartment which are accessed with a code.[85]

6.86 Freight has not escaped the digital revolution. Uber has partnered with multiple different businesses to offer smart logistic services[86] and one such innovation is a collaboration with Aurora to offer autonomous lorries, which are currently used to haul loads between Dallas and Houston in the USA with 'Uber Freight'.[87] Uber has created an entire logistic system within which its autonomous freight vehicles sit and which has integrated software which enables users to book, track and make changes to a delivery. Further, in 2024 the Chinese delivery company ZTO purchased 400 autonomous trucks to use in its express delivery services.[88] The trucks are 'equipped with an autonomous driving system, multiple laser radars, and 11 cameras … are agile in movement, automatically stopping at red lights and for pedestrians, and can navigate around obstacles … [they are] … controlled by a mobile app … [and are] … capable of carrying 600 to 800 parcels at a time'.[89] The trucks have their speed restricted to 40kph and the doors for the parcels are opened using QR codes.[90]

6.87 Finally, Amazon is also utilising drone technology to deliver goods, known as Prime Air,[91] which uses software which enables the drones to determine and verify that the location is correct, monitors the location to ensure that the area is free of people and animals, and then uses perception software to navigate the delivery of the parcel.[92]

6.88 One benefit of autonomous logistic vehicles is combating the restraints on driving hours that apply to human drivers, as well as accommodation costs,[93]

81 https://reports.weforum.org/docs/WEF_Combatting_Congestion_2025.pdf.
82 https://www.geopost.com/en/news/dpd-uk-partners-with-deus-robotics/.
83 https://scw-mag.com/news/revolutionizing-deliveries-dpd-introduces-locker-robots-in-the-uk/.
84 https://logistics.org.uk/logistics-magazine-portal/logistics-magazine-features-listing/auto-restrict-folder/21-09-23/are-ai-robots-the-future-solution-for-last-mile-de.
85 https://sustainability.dpd.co.uk/our-innovation/autonomous-deliveries.
86 https://www.uberfreight.com/?uclick_id=336bba77-0312-4835-8d5d-d1bc702e4410.
87 https://www.uberfreight.com/blog/driverless-freight./
88 https://www.iotworldtoday.com/transportation-logistics/self-driving-tech-company-completes-delivery-of-400-autonomous-trucks#close-modal.
89 https://www.shqp.gov.cn/english/news2023/20240906/1208985.html.
90 https://english.taizhou.gov.cn/NewsCenter/art/2024/art_344952651643499b8ade26a652a318b4.html.
91 https://www.aboutamazon.com/news/transportation/amazon-drone-deliver-package.
92 Ibid.
93 S. Sindi and R. Woodman (2021), 'Implementing commercial autonomous road haulage in freight operations: an industry perspective', Transportation Research Part A: Policy and Practice, 152: 235–253.

In addition, suggestions have been made that autonomous freight vehicles may move to overnight deliveries to ease congestion; however, in doing so it may result in increased noise during these times.[94]

6.89 In order to promote the extended use of autonomous deliveries globally, there needs to be a suitable regulation in place to deal with the management and safety of innovations in this space.[95] Estonia, as far back as 2017, already changed its laws to deal with robots and humans sharing the same routes.[96]

AUTONOMOUS VEHICLES IN PUBLIC AREAS

6.90 The Law Commission commenced its autonomous vehicle project in 2018, which resulted in the Automated Vehicles Act 2024.[97] The Law Commission report on autonomous vehicles, which was published in 2022, acknowledges that it is pre-dating the technology itself being in a final settled form given the nature of the emerging technology; however, considerations around the legal position were requested by the autonomous vehicle industry itself to try and provide some certainty.[98] It is therefore acknowledged that the safety of autonomous vehicles in public spaces will be an ongoing and continuous process given the agile nature of the technologies and the manner in which the industry is evolving.[99]

6.91 The Law Commission was focused on the road use of the autonomous vehicles, which within Industry 4.0, includes last-mile delivery and driverless freight vehicles. It did not, however, consider non-public areas such as the use of autonomous vehicles in warehouses and acknowledged that further consideration was still required around the use of autonomous vehicles in freight.[100]

6.92 The central consideration for all autonomous vehicles is their safe deployment and use.[101] There must be sufficiently clear information provided to any user of an autonomous vehicle, and whilst the UN Regulation 155 on Cyber Security and Cyber Security Management System may be sufficient to

94 https://researchbriefings.files.parliament.uk/documents/POST-PB-0062/POST-PB-0062.pdf.

95 World Economic Forum (2025), 'Combatting Congestion: How Cities and Companies are Innovating First-and Last-Mile Transport', https://reports.weforum.org/docs/WEF_Combatting_Congestion_2025.pdf.

96 T. Hoffmann and G. Prause (2018), 'On the regulatory framework for last-mile delivery robots', Smart Manufacturing, Digital Supply Chains and Industry 4.0, https://www.mdpi.com/2075-1702/6/3/33.

97 Law Commission (2022), Law Com No. 404 HC1068, Automated Vehicle: joint report, https://webarchive.nationalarchives.gov.uk/ukgwa/20250109114535mp_/https://cloud-platform-e218f50a4812967ba1215eaecede923f.s3.amazonaws.com/uploads/sites/30/2022/01/Automated-vehicles-joint-report-cvr-03-02-22.pdf.

98 Ibid.

99 Ibid.

100 Ibid.

101 It is estimated that autonomous vehicles will prevent 60,000 accidents and save almost 4,000 lives between 2024 and 2040, see https://post.parliament.uk/autonomous-transport/.

deal with the threat of cybersecurity on autonomous vehicles, regulators should still specifically address cybersecurity concerns relating to autonomous vehicles.

6.93 The Law Commission considered issues around liability, safety and road traffic.[102] It distinguished between those vehicles that required a driver at some point in the journey and those which had no requirement for a driver at all. The focus was on regulation as opposed to imposition of unnecessary criminal liability akin to human road traffic offences.[103] The Law Commission recommended the introduction of an 'in-use' regulator. The Centre for Connected and Autonomous Vehicles (CCAV), part of the Department for Transport and Department for Business and Trade, oversees the legal frameworks for autonomous vehicles in the UK, and implements the Automated Vehicles Act 2024.[104]

AUTOMATED VEHICLES ACT 2024

6.94 The Automated Vehicles Act 2024 sets the framework for autonomous vehicle use in the UK. It is, however, designed to be just a framework, which the Law Commission felt should where possible be flexible and agile.[105] Secondary legislation to build upon the Act is necessary, especially around the safety principles that need to be implemented.[106]

6.95 The legislation brings about three new entities:

1. Authorised self-driving entity, which is the vehicle manufacturer or software developer who develops the vehicle and makes it available for authorisation to use on the roads. This entity is responsible for the self-driving vehicles and ensuring that it meets the necessary criteria and responsibilities.[107]
2. User-in-charge which, where relevant, is the person in the vehicle. Some of the vehicles used within the industrial metaverse will not have a user-in-charge. Under the legislation, there are rules around the transition period between the user-in-charge being engaged and the autonomous aspect of the vehicle.[108]
3. The no user-in-charge operator, which is a licenced entity who is responsible for overseeing a vehicle where there is no user-in-charge.[109]

6.96 Under section 2(1) of the Automated Vehicles Act 2024, the Secretary of State is required to prepare a statement of principles ensuring:

102 Law Commission, Law Com No. 404 HC1068 (n 97).
103 Ibid.
104 https://www.gov.uk/government/organisations/centre-for-connected-and-autonomous-vehicles/about.
105 Law Commission, Law Com No. 404 HC1068 (n 97).
106 https://researchbriefings.files.parliament.uk/documents/POST-PB-0062/POST-PB-0062.pdf.
107 Section 6 of the Automated Vehicles Act 2024.
108 Section 7 of the Automated Vehicles Act 2024.
109 Section 12 of the Automated Vehicles Act 2024.

1. that autonomous vehicles are at least as safe as 'that of careful and competent human drivers';[110] and
2. the safety of road in Great Britain must 'be better as a result of the use of authorised automated vehicles on roads than it would otherwise be'.[111]

6.97 Under the Automated Vehicles Act 2024, most of the liability has been placed on the licensed operators, especially where there is no-user-in-charge,[112] but there are issues concerning liability with autonomous freight vehicles due to the numerous different entities around and involved.[113]

6.98 The Law Commission called on the Secretary of State for Transport to set out a safety standard for autonomous vehicles and update the Highway Code to reflect the use of autonomous vehicles.[114] In 2022, the Highway Code was updated to reflect the concept of a self-driving vehicle. The CCAV has published a Code of Practice for trialling automated vehicles,[115] which we expect to be updated once the trial phase is completed.

6.99 The vehicles itself should be capable of collecting and storing certain data which would be beneficial in the event of a collision, being time and location data. This data should be stored safely and in a form which can be utilised by insurers and in respect of civil claims.

AUTHORISATION, REGULATION AND LICENSING OF AUTONOMOUS VEHICLES

6.100 The authorisation of vehicles generally is dealt with under various trade laws and international agreements. The Law Commission, however, called for additional authorisation for autonomous vehicles under UK law.[116] It would then be at this stage that decisions would be taken over whether the vehicle was self-driving or not. This is relevant to autonomous vehicles used within the supply chain, including last-mile delivery and automated logistic vehicles utilised within warehouse facilities.

6.101 The Law Commission recommended the use of a regulator to deal with monitoring the use of autonomous vehicles[117] and that a safety scheme should

110 Section 2(2)(a) of the Automated Vehicles Act 2024.
111 Section 2(2)(b) of the Automated Vehicles Act 2024.
112 Section 12 of the Automated Vehicles Act 2024.
113 https://researchbriefings.files.parliament.uk/documents/POST-PB-0062/POST-PB-0062.pdf.
114 Law Commission, Law Com No. 404 HC1068 (n 97).
115 https://www.gov.uk/government/publications/trialling-automated-vehicle-technologies-in-public/code-of-practice-automated-vehicle-trialling.
116 Law Commission, Law Com No. 404 HC1068 (n 97).
117 Section 3 of the Automated Vehicles Act 2024 provides for the eventual collection and sharing of information and data with the regulator once it is in force and there are offences under section 20 for non-compliance.

be established.[118] It acknowledges that this is likely, however, to be an evolving framework, responding to real-life issues which will inevitably arise.[119]

6.102 When there is no user in charge then there also should be a licensed operator.[120] These operators would supervise the vehicles and, amongst other responsibilities, would be responsible for insuring the autonomous vehicles and for demonstrating the safety of the vehicle.[121] To be able to apply for a licence there should be reputational and financial requirements.[122] This is likely to be more relevant for those autonomous vehicles used within the supply chain.

STRICT LIABILITY

6.103 Some academics consider that that last-mile robots, should be subject to strict liability road traffic liability if they want to be able to share the roads or pavements with other users.[123]

UN'S WORKING PARTY ON ROAD TRAFFIC SAFETY

6.104 The United Nations Economic Commission for Europe has established a Working Party on autonomous and connected vehicles that has produced a framework document on automated/autonomous vehicles. The framework document is technological-neutral,[124] and is trying 'to deliver safe and secure road vehicles in a consistent manner, and to promote collaboration and communication amongst those involved in their development and oversight'.[125]

6.105 The overarching principle is that '"an automated/autonomous vehicle shall not cause any non-tolerable risk", meaning that … [it] …shall not cause any traffic accidents resulting in injury or death that are reasonably foreseeable and preventable'.[126]

118 Law Commission, Law Com No. 404 HC1068 (n 97).
119 Ibid.
120 Ibid.
121 Ibid.
122 Ibid.
123 Hoffmann and Prause (n 96).
124 Framework 2.4, Economic Commission for Europe Inland Transport Committee, 180th Session, Revised Framework document on automated/autonomous Vehicles ECE/TRANS/WP.29/2019/34/Rev.2, https://docs.un.org/en/ECE/TRANS/WP.29/2019/34/REV.2.
125 Framework 3.6, Economic Commission for Europe Inland Transport Committee, 180th Session, Revised Framework document on automated/autonomous Vehicles ECE/TRANS/WP.29/2019/34/Rev.2, https://docs.un.org/en/ECE/TRANS/WP.29/2019/34/REV.2.
126 Framework 3.7, Economic Commission for Europe Inland Transport Committee, 180th Session, Revised Framework document on automated/autonomous Vehicles ECE/TRANS/WP.29/2019/34/Rev.2, https://docs.un.org/en/ECE/TRANS/WP.29/2019/34/REV.2.

AUTONOMOUS VEHICLES IN NON-PUBLIC AREAS

6.106 The description of the Automated Vehicles Act is 'An Act to regulate the use of automated vehicles on roads and in other public places; and to make other provision in relation to vehicle automation'.[127] The Law Commission did not consider it necessary to consider the use of autonomous vehicles within non-public areas such as warehouses and ports, both important in Industry 4.0, since existing health and safety legislation such as the Health and Safety at Work etc Act 1974 and laws on occupational liability already provided sufficient cover to deal with autonomous vehicles in these areas.[128] It is, however, important that the legislation evolves to cover emerging risks.

6.107 Autonomous vehicles, robots and drones used in the workplace will all fall under section 6 of the Health and Safety at Work etc. Act 1974. This provision puts a duty on manufacturers and suppliers who provide any equipment for use at work to ensure:

1. 'It will be safe and without risks to health at all times when it is being set, used, cleaned or maintained by a person at work';[129]
2. necessary testing and examination have been carried out on the equipment; and[130]
3. suitable information is provided about the designed use of the product, its testing and any conditions or requirements to ensure it is safe and without risk.[131]

6.108 The Lifting and Operations and Lifting Equipment Regulations 1998 (LOLER) concerns the regulation of safe lifting equipment. LOLER will apply to robots used in lifting, but where these are not likely to be used in dangerous situations then the extensive examination required under regulation 9(3) may not apply.[132] This is likely to be the case where the lifting robot is not operated near staff and is fully fenced off.[133] The British Safety Council considered the use of robots within industry, and felt that it does bring challenges especially with 'cobots' which operate in conjunction with human workers and wearable technology such as exoskeletons integrating human and robot power and risks around human error, speed, force and power limits, system failures and ergonomic issues.[134] It remains important that as we proceed through the digital revolution, where existing regulation concerning health and safety are utilised,

127 In addition, section 39(2) defines 'relevant incidents' as something occurring on a road or other public place.
128 Law Commission, Law Com No. 404 HC1068 (n 97).
129 Section 6(1)(a) of the Health and Safety at Work etc. Act 1974.
130 Section 6(1)(b) of the Health and Safety at Work etc. Act 1974.
131 Section 6(1)(c) of the Health and Safety at Work etc. Act 1974.
132 https://www.hse.gov.uk/work-equipment-machinery/faqs.htm.
133 Ibid.
134 https://www.britsafe.org/safety-management/2023/are-you-ready-for-the-next-industrial-revolution.

that these remain relevant and that effective safeguards are in place to monitor the changes and effective responses. Regulators should keep in mind the option of using technology itself to monitor and address such risks.

6.109 What is important is ensuring that sufficient insurance coverage is in place to cover the use of autonomous vehicles and robots in these areas, and any harm or liability which arise as a result are suitably covered.

DATA

6.110 A significant volume of data is collected from autonomous vehicles, estimated to be around 4,000 GB a day.[135] This will include personal data, which is subject to the Data Protection Act 2018. One of the key data protection considerations relating to delivery robots is the significant amount of personal data that will be collected on its journeys. This will include not only the delivery information but also all information obtained on the route. Given the significant volume of images and sounds, typically gathered by the robot on route and for the purpose of evidencing delivery and any issues, experts call into question whether delivery robots can be properly be said to have been built with privacy by design.[136]

EQUALITY

6.111 All decisions concerning autonomous vehicles need to comply with the Equality Act 2010, and should not detrimentally impact those with protected characteristics; Equality should be embedded within autonomous vehicles.[137] This is a vital consideration as we progress through the digital revolution.

LEGAL CONSIDERATIONS WITH DRONE DELIVERIES

6.112 The use of drones in the UK is regulated by the Civil Aviation Authority. In May 2025, the Civil Aviation Authority concluded its consultation around drone regulation in the UK. It considered that rules and regulation should be relaxed to encourage greater adoption of drones in the UK[138] as currently to be able to fly a drone beyond the visual line of slight (BVLOS) you need authorisation from the Civil Aviation Authority.

135 https://researchbriefings.files.parliament.uk/documents/POST-PB-0062/POST-PB-0062.pdf.
136 Hoffmann and Prause (n 96).
137 Law Commission, Law Com No. 404 HC1068 (n 97).
138 https://www.caa.co.uk/newsroom/news/updated-rules-confirmed-to-support-safe-growth-of-drone-sector/#.

6.113 As part of its BVLOS sandbox, the Civil Aviation Authority included projects with Amazon Prime Air on drone deliveries.[139]

FUTURE OF FREIGHT

6.114 In 2022, the Department for Transport commenced its Future of Freight Plan[140] as a response to Covid-19 and the Ukrainian war, both of which heavily disrupted the freight and logistic sectors.[141] Under the plan a £7 million fund was created and an innovation group as part of the Freight Council. The plan identified a lack of awareness of the need for innovation in the industry and for the potential pace of change. It predicted a rise in the use of AI and blockchain technologies, confirming that private investments were already being made by those in industry into distribution centres and ports. The plan considers that the UK should be leading the way in this space, and requires a flexible form of regulation to be able to achieve this.

KEY TAKEAWAY POINTS

6.115 The key takeaway points in respect of the digital supply chain are:

- There are many examples of innovation within the supply chain, from automation within the warehouse facilities to autonomous deliveries and freight being deployed.
- Historically, most international trade documents required paper documents given the unique rights and obligations these documents of title acquired. Following the Law Commissions report, the UK implemented the Electronic Trade Documents Act 2023 which gives electronic trade documents the same equivalence as paper trade documents provided certain criteria are met. Much is needed internationally to address these challenges.
- A lot of work has been done on the idea of the electronic bill of lading. The Digital Container Shipping Association (DCSA) has taken a prominent role in setting international standards for digital trade documentation, and promoting the widespread adoption of electronic bills of lading to its members.

139 https://www.caa.co.uk/newsroom/news/new-trials-set-to-help-unlock-drone-deliveries-and-inspections-in-the-uk/.

140 https://researchbriefings.files.parliament.uk/documents/POST-PN-0692/POST-PN-0692.pdf.

141 https://assets.publishing.service.gov.uk/media/62b9a2ec8fa8f53572e3db68/future-of-freight-plan.pdf.

- The Automated Vehicles Act 2024, which was passed following the Law Commission report into autonomous vehicles, will cover the use of autonomous vehicles used for deliveries as part of the supply chain. In the workplace, the use of autonomous vehicles will still fall under the Health and Safety at Work etc. Act 1974, and where lifting is being done by a robot, it will fall under the Lifting and Operations and Lifting Equipment Regulations 1998 (LOLER).

Chapter 7

Cybersecurity, data protection and privacy in Industry 4.0

'You cannot wait until a house burns down to buy fire insurance on it. We cannot wait until there are massive dislocations in our society to prepare for the Fourth Industrial Revolution.'[1]

Professor Robert J. Shiller, Professor of Economics, Yale University

7.1 Cybersecurity is fundamental to the safe and resilient adoption of Industry 4.0 and the emerging industrial metaverse. These paradigms rely on highly interconnected systems that integrate Industrial Internet of Things (IIoT) devices, cloud platforms, digital twins, and immersive environments, creating unprecedented opportunities for efficiency and innovation. This interconnectivity, however, also expands the cyber 'attack surface', exposing critical industrial processes and valuable intellectual property to exploitation. Compromise of such systems has already, and will continue to, disrupt operations, degrade safety, and facilitate large-scale theft of proprietary knowledge.

7.2 Industry 4.0 and the industrial metaverse present significant cybersecurity risks, in particular in respect of privacy, virtual assets, safety and in respect of political systems.[2]

7.3 Robust cybersecurity is therefore essential not only to safeguard industrial assets but also to preserve trust, competitiveness, and national resilience in the digital economy. A challenge for governments and industry around the globe is to keep track of the current threat landscape surrounding our critical infrastructure, as well as predicting future threats and delivering timely guidance and effective regulation to industry to mitigate those threats.

7.4 The following sections outline some of the key cybersecurity threats associated with Industry 4.0 and its emerging technologies.

ATTACK SURFACE EXPANSION

7.5 When an adversary is conducting reconnaissance of a target organisation, they will likely seek to identify multiple, if not all, potential entry points to

1 https://be.stantonchase.com/wp-content/uploads/2016/09/Leadership-in-Fourth-Industrial-Revolution.pdf.

2 https://www3.weforum.org/docs/WEF_Metaverse_Cybersecurity_2024.pdf.

obtain initial access. In cybersecurity, the sum of these entry points is known as the organisation's 'attack surface'. It encompasses all potential vulnerabilities, entry points, and pathways that a threat actor could exploit to compromise that organisation.

7.6 As Industry 4.0 has evolved from the increasing connectivity of industrial systems to IIoT devices, the attack surface is no longer confined to traditional IT systems but has now expanded to include internet-enabled smart devices responsible for controlling and monitoring operational technology (OT).

7.7 IIoT devices are now being embedded within supervisory control and data acquisition (SCADA) systems, distributed control systems (DCS), programmable logic controllers (PLCs), and safety instrumented systems (SIS). These devices collect critical telemetry from, and in some cases transmit control signals to, their host systems. While this integration has unlocked efficiencies far beyond what was possible when many industrial control system (ICS) environments were first deployed, it has also expanded the attack surface, creating new pathways for adversaries to exploit and disrupt.

7.8 This shift is underpinned by a broader industry trend; the past five years have seen rapid growth in the adoption of IIoT devices, particularly in the manufacturing sector,[3] as organisations seek to capture the efficiency gains promised by Industry 4.0. This trajectory is expected to continue, fuelled by the exponential growth of industrial data. As that data is systematically analysed and fused with technologies such as artificial intelligence (AI), it will deliver increasingly advanced insights, but also create further dependencies and potential vulnerabilities.

7.9 The risks associated with this convergence are not theoretical. In late 2023, an internet-exposed Unitronics PLC operated by the Municipal Water Authority of Aliquippa, in the United States, was compromised by a threat actor linked to an adversary nation-state.[4] The PLC, responsible for regulating water pressure, served as the initial access point. From here the attackers were able to pivot across the network, eventually gaining control over additional assets, including those managing CCTV systems. This incident demonstrated how a single exposed IIoT-connected control point can jeopardise both operational continuity and broader organisational security.

7.10 These developments underline why attack surface management (ASM) is becoming a critical discipline for organisations operating digitally transformed ICS environments. Each additional sensor, actuator, or controller connected via IIoT expands the attack surface, demanding continuous visibility, mapping, and monitoring across IT and OT domains. Effective ASM involves not only

3 https://www.grandviewresearch.com/industry-analysis/industrial-internet-of-things-iiot-market.
4 https://cyberlaw.ccdcoe.org/wiki/Cyber_incident_against_a_water_authority_in_Pennsylvania_(2023).

identifying exposed devices and prioritising vulnerabilities but also enforcing segmentation and access controls; ensuring that IoT-driven efficiencies are not gained at the expense of systemic cyber risk.

FINANCIALLY MOTIVATED ATTACKS

7.11 Financial gain remains the dominant motivation behind most modern cyberattacks, with ransomware being the most prevalent method. Ransomware is a form of malicious software that, once executed on a computer or network, encrypts specified file types and renders them inaccessible. Attackers then demand a ransom, often in cryptocurrency transferred via dark web channels, in exchange for decryption keys. Increasingly, adversaries also exfiltrate sensitive data before encryption and threaten to release it publicly if payment is withheld, a tactic commonly referred to as a double-extortion attack.

7.12 Although ransomware campaigns are not exclusive to Industry 4.0 environments, they are widely regarded as one of the most significant existential threats facing modern enterprises, particularly in the manufacturing sector.[5] The increasing digitisation and automation of production facilities have created a strong dependency on interconnected IT and OT assets to maintain business continuity. Consequently, adversaries do not necessarily need to compromise industrial control systems directly to cause disruption. By targeting conventional IT infrastructure that underpins automation and process management, attackers can halt production lines, disrupt supply chains, and inflict substantial financial and reputational damage. This cyber-physical dependency amplifies the potential impact of ransomware in Industry 4.0, transforming what was once a predominantly data-centric threat into one capable of directly undermining industrial resilience and operational safety.

7.13 As an example, Jaguar Land Rover, a global luxury car maker has been a pioneer of smart factories, using Industry 4.0 technology such as IIoT devices to collect data from car manufacturing equipment and analysing that data using AI to cut waste and predict future issues.[6] These Jaguar Land Rover smart factories are a demonstrable example of the efficiencies and insight that Industry 4.0 technology delivers to businesses. A recent cyber-attack against Jaguar Land Rover has, however, demonstrated the inherent vulnerability of internet-enabled industrial processes being affected following the compromise of conventional IT environments.[7]

7.14 In late August 2025, Jaguar Land Rover was hit by a ransomware attack. The impact of the attack was significant enough for Jaguar Land Rover to close

5 https://www.dragos.com/blog/dragos-industrial-ransomware-analysis-q2-2025/.

6 https://www.tcs.com/what-we-do/industries/manufacturing/video/tcs-jlr-fireside-chat-future-manufacturing-mobility.

7 https://www.bbc.co.uk/news/articles/c0q75q4l87no.

its car production factories in several countries around the world, completely shutting down manufacturing operations and severely impacting supply chain partners. In the UK alone, these factories were producing approximately 1,000 vehicles per day, resulting in an estimated loss to Jaguar Land Rover of £50 million per week.[8] The cost to the wider UK economy, however, was even greater; in late October 2025, the UK's Cyber Monitoring Centre (CMC), reported that the attack had cost the UK economy £1.9 billion due to the overall impact on both Jaguar Land Rover and its substantial supply chains. In its report, the CMC stated the Jaguar Land Rover attack was likely 'the most economically damaging cyber event' seen in the country.[9]

7.15 Due to the scale and sophistication of the attack, the UK National Cyber Security Centre (NCSC) and National Crime Agency (NCA) are reported to be leading an investigation into possible links to an adversarial nation-state.[10] Although those responsible have not yet been identified, this attack demonstrated how adversaries can use malicious software, ostensibly used to hold victims to ransom payments, to cause catastrophic impact to industrial processes.

7.16 The unfortunate byproduct of Industry 4.0, is the ever-increasing attack surface, presenting a variety of new entry points for attackers to exploit. The effectiveness of ransomware to cripple an organisation, and in many cases cause physical consequences in the real-world, means that those responsible for industrial operations need to be prepared for these incidents, and it would be wise to consider these types of incidents as inevitable. Risk management, backup strategies, simulation exercises and attack surface management (to name a few) should all form part of a business's incident response preparation activities.[11]

INDUSTRIAL ESPIONAGE

7.17 Building on the foundations of Industry 4.0, the concept of the industrial metaverse has emerged, denoting the use of immersive virtual environments to enhance design processes, operational efficiency, and strategic decision-making across industrial domains. Central to this paradigm is the digital twin: a virtual representation of a physical system that continuously mirrors real-world conditions through real-time data integration. Such models often contain detailed technical blueprints, proprietary process data, and performance metrics, all intellectual assets typically derived from extensive research, years of development, and substantial financial investment. These characteristics render digital twin environments not only critical enablers of industrial innovation but

8 https://www.reuters.com/sustainability/boards-policy-regulation/jaguar-land-rover-hack-cost-uk-economy-25-billion-report-says-2025-10-22/.

9 https://www.ft.com/content/6f2923b3-2a4b-4c9b-9cde-eb5f0d5b9ce3.

10 https://www.telegraph.co.uk/politics/2025/10/11/russia-suspected-jaguar-land-rover-cyber-attack/.

11 https://www.hunt-ir.com/huntirs-blog/preparation-essentials.

also highly attractive targets for malicious actors, potentially including state-sponsored groups engaged in industrial espionage.

7.18 Industrial espionage is a prevalent risk within today's cyberthreat landscape.[12] In 2025, multiple state-sponsored threat groups conducted a coordinated campaign targeting Taiwan's semiconductor ecosystem.[13] The primary objective is alleged to have been the acquisition of proprietary design data, processing knowledge, and supply-chain intelligence. Adversaries employed spear phishing[14] lures themed around academia and investment, which led to the deployment command and control[15] (C2) implants and backdoor malware[16] for persistent access. This campaign is one of countless examples of sophisticated state-sponsored efforts to exfiltrate intellectual property from high-value industrial targets.

7.19 Adversarial nation-states pursue corporate espionage as a means of securing economic and geopolitical advantage. In contrast to traditional intelligence operations that prioritise political or military secrets, corporate espionage is directed at commercially valuable knowledge and data. The underlying motivation is multifaceted; the illicit acquisition of intellectual property can accelerate domestic innovation, reduce dependency on foreign technologies, and strengthen the competitiveness of strategically significant industries. Digital sovereignty is an emergent theme.

INDUSTRIAL SABOTAGE

7.20 Several nation-states have developed advanced offensive cyber capabilities in recent years.[17] The emergence of Industry 4.0, with its heavy reliance on interconnected digital technologies, has expanded the potential for software to be weaponised.

7.21 Since 2010, several cyber weapons targeting industrial control systems (ICS) have been discovered and publicly documented. The most prominent early example is Stuxnet,[18] uncovered in 2010 and widely regarded as the first cyber weapon designed to cause physical damage. It targeted Iran's Natanz nuclear facility by exploiting multiple zero-day vulnerabilities in Microsoft Windows and spreading through removable media. Once deployed, Stuxnet reprogrammed Siemens PLCs controlling uranium enrichment centrifuges, causing destructive speed fluctuations while feeding false telemetry to operators.

12 https://reports.weforum.org/docs/WEF_Global_Cybersecurity_Outlook_2025.pdf.
13 https://www.proofpoint.com/us/blog/threat-insight/phish-china-aligned-espionage-actors-ramp-up-taiwan-semiconductor-targeting.
14 https://attack.mitre.org/techniques/T0865/.
15 https://attack.mitre.org/tactics/TA0101/.
16 https://attack.mitre.org/techniques/T1505/003/.
17 https://www.ncsc.gov.uk/collection/ncsc-annual-review-2024/chapter-01.
18 https://www.cisa.gov/news-events/ics-advisories/icsa-10-272-01.

7.22 Since Stuxnet, several highly sophisticated cyber weapons have been discovered, designed to target operational technology (OT).[19] In 2016, a type of malware known as CrashOverride[20] (aka Industroyer), specifically designed to target OT by leveraging industrial communication protocols, was used to attack the Ukrainian electrical transmission network, causing wide-spread blackouts in Kyiv.[21] Other notable ICS-targeting malware families include TRITON,[22] which attempted to disable safety instrumented system (SIS), and PIPEDREAM,[23] a modular toolkit capable of compromising multiple industrial environments.

7.23 The examples above show how state-sponsored threat actors can now employ offensive cyber operations to disrupt the critical national infrastructure of their adversaries, achieving effects comparable to conventional military action without the physical destruction of infrastructure.

7.24 As nations become increasingly reliant on digital technologies to provide efficiencies and automation within industry, the development of cyber weapons by adversarial nation-states, designed to target those technologies, will almost certainly continue and become a more prevalent threat.

REGULATION, FRAMEWORKS AND STANDARDS

7.25 In 2024, the CEO of the NCSC, Dr Richard Horne, highlighted a widening gap between the cyber threats facing the UK and the nation's ability to defend against them in critical sectors.[24] The recent investment in infrastructure and data centres to support the growth of AI further illustrates the trajectory of Industry 4.0.[25] As such, it is critical that appropriate and proportionate cybersecurity controls evolve alongside the development of our critical infrastructure, with their effectiveness governed by intelligent regulation and overseen by UK regulators.

7.26 The UK's regulatory baseline in this area is the Network and Information Systems (NIS) Regulations 2018,[26] which aligns with the EU's, now repealed, Directive 2016/1148 (the original NIS Directive). These regulations are designed

19 https://www.ncsc.gov.uk/blog-post/what-is-ot-malware.

20 https://www.cisa.gov/news-events/ics-alerts/ics-alert-17-206-01.

21 https://www.welivesecurity.com/2022/06/13/industroyer-cyber-weapon-brought-down-power-grid/.

22 TRITON (aka TRISIS) is ICS-targeting malware discovered in 2017 that aimed at Safety Instrumented Systems (SIS) in a Saudi petrochemical plant. Designed to disable safety controllers, it risked causing catastrophic physical damage and loss of life.

23 PIPEDREAM (aka INCONTROLLER) is an advanced ICS malware toolkit discovered in 2022, attributed to Russia-linked actors. Modular and multifaceted, it targets multiple PLC vendors and OT protocols, enabling reconnaissance, manipulation, and disruptive control of industrial devices. Analysts warn it represents a highly capable, ready-to-deploy cyber weapon against critical infrastructure assets.

24 https://www.ncsc.gov.uk/speech/ncsc-annual-review-launch-2024-ceo-dr-richard-horne.

25 https://blogs.microsoft.com/on-the-issues/2025/09/16/microsoft-30-billion-uk-ai-future/.

26 https://www.legislation.gov.uk/uksi/2018/506.

to strengthen the operational resilience of critical industrial sectors, referred to as 'operators of essential services', which include infrastructure providers across transport, energy, drinking water, health, and digital services.

7.27 In July 2024, the UK Government announced the Cyber Security and Resilience Bill, intended to propose amendments to the UK NIS Regulations 2018 following the EU's updated Directive 2022/2555 (NIS2).[27] This was followed in April 2025 by the publication of the Cyber Security and Resilience Policy Statement, setting out the Government's legislative proposals to tackle the evolving cyber threat landscape surround the UK.[28] Among its proposals are plans to broaden the scope of regulation to include managed service providers and supply chain partners, ensuring that proportionate measures, such as contractual obligations, security assessments, and continuity planning, are in place to prevent vulnerabilities in the supply chain from undermining essential or digital services.

7.28 To help essential services meet these obligations, the NCSC developed the Cyber Assessment Framework (CAF),[29] which provides a structured approach to strengthening cybersecurity across four key areas: risk management, protection against cyberattacks, detecting cybersecurity events, and minimising the impact of cybersecurity incidents. The CAF has also been adopted by many regulators, (aka 'competent authorities'), as the framework for assessing compliance with the NIS Regulations. In August 2025, the NCSC published version 4.0 of the CAF,[30] which introduced updated guidance across several key areas. These include understanding attacker motivations and behaviours, embedding secure software development practices throughout the lifecycle, enhancing security monitoring and threat hunting to reduce attacker dwell time, and addressing AI-related risks, both the malicious use of AI by attackers and the possibility of AI systems themselves becoming targets.

7.29 It is not just governments who publish support frameworks for industry. The International Society of Automation (ISA) and the International Electrotechnical Commission (IEC) maintain a series of standards known as the ISA/IEC 62443 series.[31] These standards offer guidelines specifically designed to secure industrial networks from cyberattacks. A key principle of these standards is a 'shared responsibility' model, identifying the need to align people, processes, and technology to ensure the safe, secure and reliable operation of ICS.

7.30 Cybersecurity threats evolve rapidly, often outpacing regulatory frameworks and standards. A key challenge for both government and industry is that guidance and regulation tend to lag the threat landscape; by the time new

27 https://eur-lex.europa.eu/legal-content/EN/TXT/?uri=CELEX:32022L2555.

28 https://www.gov.uk/government/publications/cyber-security-and-resilience-bill-policy-statement/cyber-security-and-resilience-bill-policy-statement.

29 https://www.ncsc.gov.uk/collection/cyber-assessment-framework#whatcaf.

30 https://www.ncsc.gov.uk/files/NCSC-Cyber-Assessment-Framework-4.0.pdf.

31 https://www.isa.org/standards-and-publications/isa-standards/isa-iec-62443-series-of-standards.

policies are introduced, adversaries have already advanced their tactics. This is why businesses cannot rely solely on compliance with regulation as proof of security. They must continually adapt their own defences to keep pace with the evolving threat environment, recognising that regulatory compliance does not necessarily equate to effective protection.

THE UK CYBER-SECURITY GOVERNANCE LANDSCAPE

7.31 The current UK framework for dealing with cyber threats is a mix of regulation, policy and legislation, including: the Computer Misuse Act 1990; the 2014 Cyber Essentials Scheme; the NIS Regulations 2018; the Cyber Assessment Framework 2018, updated August 2025; the FCA Principles for Business 2018; the Telecommunications (Security) Act 2021; the UK Cyber Security Council 2021; the Product Security and Telecommunications Infrastructure Act 2022; and the UK Telecoms Lab 2023.

7.32 In addition, some regulators, such as the Financial Conduct Authority (FCA) also have their own expectations and standards on cybersecurity.

7.33 Criticisms which have been levied against the existing framework include the fact that it does not apply to all aspects of the supply chain, has resulted in patchy reporting, exposes human vulnerabilities, lacks accountability on software providers, lacks accountability on boards, and regulators lack actual power.[32] In addition there is a distinct lack of uptake in cyber insurance policies meaning commercially businesses are not incentivised to prioritise cyber security protection.[33]

THE NATIONAL CYBER SECURITY CENTRE

7.34 The National Cyber Security Centre (NCSC) is part of GCHQ and is tasked with trying to deal with cybersecurity risks for the UK.[34] Its guidance on AI and machine learning highlights the need for developers to build systems with security in mind.[35]

CYBER SECURITY AND RESILIENCE BILL

7.35 The Cyber Security and Resilience Bill is currently making its way through Parliament, and has been introduced by the UK Government because:

32 https://researchbriefings.files.parliament.uk/documents/POST-PN-0753/POST-PN-0753.pdf.
33 Ibid.
34 https://www.ncsc.gov.uk/section/about-ncsc/what-we-do.
35 https://www.ncsc.gov.uk/collection/machine-learning-principles.

> 'The digital revolution is transforming our Critical National Infrastructure and our essential public services. It offers an extraordinary opportunity – to make our people and our country better off. However, it may also bring new and dangerous vulnerabilities.'[36]

7.36 Given the changes caused by Industry 4.0, the existing regulations are not fit for purpose, and accordingly the new updated Cyber Security and Resilience Bill is intended to try and address the gaps by bringing more organisations within the scope of the regulations and then strengthening the process.[37]

THE EU

7.37 The EU has established the ENISA, which is the EU agency tasked with dealing with cybersecurity frameworks across the EU.

7.38 The Cyber Solidarity Act 2025[38] came into force in February 2025. The Regulation seeks to align cybersecurity regulation against changes in technology and industry, including cyberespionage. The Regulation calls on investment in strengthening cybersecurity infrastructure and responses to threats.

7.39 In April 2025 the EU launched a consultation on revising the Cybersecurity Act 2019. One key area for change is in respect of the supply chain. The EU Cybersecurity Act 2019 established an EU Cyber Certification which is a unified framework for certification of cybersecurity. Under the framework, the EU adopted the EU Cybersecurity Certification Scheme on Common Criteria, which is a voluntary scheme for certain products such as firewalls, operating systems and routers.[39] In January 2026 the EU Commission published its updated proposals to revise the Cybersecurity Act,[40] known as The Cybersecurity Act 2. The updates are felt necessary to deal with the threats from emerging technology and Industry 4.0, both of which present vulnerabilities to systems, but also present opportunities for other actors misusing these emerging technologies such as AI, to penetrate systems.

7.40 The Cyber Resilience Act came into force on 10 December 2024, and deals with cybersecurity standards for digital products in the EU. The main obligations will start to take effect from December 2027.

36 https://www.gov.uk/government/publications/cyber-security-and-resilience-bill-policy-statement/cyber-security-and-resilience-bill-policy-statement.

37 Ibid.

38 Regulation (EU) 2025/38 of the European Parliament and of the Council of 19 December 2024 laying down measures to strengthen solidarity and capacities in the Union to detect, prepare for and respond to cyber threats and incidents and amending Regulation (EU) 2021/694 (Cyber Solidarity Act).

39 https://digital-strategy.ec.europa.eu/en/policies/cybersecurity-certification-framework.

40 https://digital-strategy.ec.europa.eu/en/library/proposal-regulation-eu-cybersecurity-act.

DATA PROTECTION AND PRIVACY

7.41 The risk to privacy and to data in the industrial metaverse are both key areas of risk, and governance should be modernised to address these new technologies.[41] In particular, there is the need to update the way in which users understand how data is collected in this new landscape, developing updated security features which are relevant to these new technologies and focusing on creating cross-border ethical frameworks to set expectations in this field.[42]

7.42 The 2021 UNESCO AI ethical standards highlight the need to protect privacy and data protection doctrines in Industry 4.0 and to properly assess the impact of privacy concerns when using these technologies.[43]

7.43 UN Regulation 77/211, which was adopted on 15 December 2022 by the General Assembly, affirms article 12 of Universal Declaration of Human Rights. It recognises that there is the need to address the issues caused by emerging technologies on the right to privacy, which is caused by issues such as monitoring, surveillance and hacking. The Resolution further recognises that there is the need to properly explore the impact of these new technologies on the right to privacy and what safeguards are required to protect citizens from a degradation of their rights, and from discrimination and misuse of their data. Suitable safeguards should be implemented by those designing, implementing and using these technologies.

7.44 The Resolution further reminds us that emerging technology should take into consideration human rights, and their impact on individuals and that:

> 'in the digital age, technical solutions to secure and to protect the confidentiality of digital communications and transactions, including measures for strong encryption, pseudonymization and anonymity, are important to ensure the enjoyment of human rights, in particular the rights to privacy'.[44]

7.45 The Resolution also suggests that states should adopt suitable safeguards for emerging technologies,[45] prevent violations of privacy,[46] provide suitable guidance to businesses on the need to respect the human right to privacy,[47] and that businesses should adopt the Guiding Principles on Business and Human Rights: Implementing the United Nations 'Protect, Respect and Remedy' Framework,[48]

41 https://www3.weforum.org/docs/WEF_Metaverse_Cybersecurity_2024.pdf.
42 Ibid.
43 https://www.unesco.org/en/artificial-intelligence/recommendation-ethics.
44 General Assembly UN Resolution 77/211 adopted 15 December 2022.
45 Ibid, 7(b).
46 Ibid, 7(c).
47 Ibid, 7(l).
48 Ibid, 8(a).

to ensure that there are suitable safeguards in place to protect privacy,[49] and that systems implement privacy-by-design principles.[50]

KEY TAKEAWAY POINTS

7.46 The key takeaway points in respect of Cybersecurity, Data Protection and Privacy in Industry 4.0 are:

- One of the main threats to Industry 4.0 is cybersecurity. The nature of the technology makes it an expansive target for attack.
- Cybersecurity breaches, such as the 2025 attack on Jaguar Land Rover, have significant financial impacts not only on the company targeted, but also have wider ramifications.
- The current regulations of cybersecurity in the UK is the Network and Information Systems (NIS) Regulations 2018, however, these are out of date and proposals have been made to update these through the Cyber Security and Resilience Bill.
- Given the abundance of data in the industrial metaverse, privacy and protection of personal data is a paramount consideration, and a challenge that has to be continually monitored and properly addressed.

49 Ibid, 8(c).
50 Ibid, 8(d).

Chapter 8

Intellectual property in Industry 4.0

> *'The last two decades have seen an explosion of technologies that are transforming how we work and live in an increasingly interconnected digital world. The emergence and merging of frontier technologies is at the heart of what is sometimes termed the Fourth Industrial Revolution or Industry 4.0. Frontier technologies are changing how we do business, how we innovate and create and the rate of change is increasing exponentially.'*[1]
>
> World Intellectual Property Office

8.1 Intellectual property (IP) rights are a crucial strategic tool for companies. The commercial importance of securing and exploiting such rights continues to increase as the value of companies in the digital economy increasingly resides in intangible, rather than tangible, assets. A recent World Intellectual Property Office (WIPO) study found that 84% of the value of the top firms in the UK comes from intangible assets.[2] This rises to 90% in the US. Capturing that value is therefore key, and IP rights provide one mechanism for achieving this.

8.2 Nonetheless, there are questions around the relevance and suitability of various existing IP rights in the context of commercial operations in a virtual reality (VR) or augmented reality (AR) environment. For instance, issues arise relating to the territorial nature of IP rights, the difficulty of obtaining IP protection for software-based innovation, challenges around defining a suitable scope of protection afforded by a given IP right, the detectability of third-party infringement, ownership, freedom to operate, and the fast pace of development in this sector.

8.3 This chapter seeks to provide an overview of different IP rights, and what they may be used to protect in a VR/AR context, particularly in the context of so-called 'Fourth Industrial Revolution' or 'industrial metaverse' technologies such as the Internet of Things (IoT), cloud computing, artificial intelligence (AI) and blockchain. The chapter also considers the various perceived issues with existing IP rights as to whether they are well-founded and, if so, what solutions may be desirable. Case studies are presented to highlight how different IP rights may be utilised in different scenarios.

1 https://www.wipo.int/en/web/frontier-technologies.

2 https://www.wipo.int/en/web/global-innovation-index/w/blogs/2025/the-value-of-intangible-assets-of-corporations.

OVERVIEW OF IP RIGHTS

8.4 Different types of IP right exist to offer protection for different types of intellectual assets within companies. IP rights may be split into two broad categories: those that require an applicant to go through a registration process to obtain the right; and those that do not (ie, the right subsists automatically). In the first category are IP rights such as patents, trademarks, registered designs and domain names. In the other category are IP rights such as copyright, unregistered design rights, common law trademarks, confidential information and database rights.

8.5 Patents are for protecting technical inventions or solutions to technical problems. The patent system aims to encourage and accelerate innovation by giving a patent owner the right to prevent a third party from making use of the patented invention for a defined period of time, typically up to 20 years. In return, the patent owner is required to publish technical details of how to implement the invention. To obtain granted patent protection, the claimed invention in a patent application needs to be novel and inventive over the state of the art (ie, everything in the public domain prior to the patent application being filed).

8.6 Trade marks relate to branding, such as a company name or a branded product or service. Trade marks are signs, like words and logos, that distinguish the goods and services of one company from another company in the marketplace. To obtain trade mark protection, the sign must not be identical or confusingly similar to a previously registered mark. The sign also must not be wholly descriptive of the goods and services to which the sign relates, must not wholly contain common usage words (eg, 'the', 'a', etc), must not deceive the public, and must have distinctiveness.

8.7 Registered designs are for protecting the shape or visual appearance of a product. Design protection can be used to protect features of a product such as its shape, configuration, colours, lines, contours, etc. For a registered design to be valid, its features must be novel and have individual character, although this is not examined as part of the application process in the UK and EU. The owner of a registered design can prevent third parties from making, selling or using products incorporating the design. In a virtual world context, registered design protection can be obtained for features of graphical user interfaces, icons, animations and elements of augmented reality environments.

8.8 Copyright is for protecting original creative works. Specifically, copyright is for protecting the expression of an idea, rather than the idea itself. It can be used to protect literary, artistic, musical and dramatic works. Copyright can be a powerful tool in a virtual world environment. For instance, copyright subsists in source and object code for software applications, as well as design materials such as flowcharts and specifications, provided they reflect creativity on the part of the author.

8.9 Confidentiality can be used as a strategy where maximum commercial benefit comes from not disclosing generated IP to third parties or where protection via other IP rights is not available. Confidential information can be regarded as a broad concept that covers any information having a quality of confidence and which is disclosed in circumstances importing an obligation of confidence.

8.10 Trade secrets are becoming ever more important as a strategic tool for protecting a company's IP. Trade secrets may be regarded as a subset of confidential information and are protected under specific statute. In particular, in order for information to qualify as a trade secret, it must: be secret; have commercial value because it is secret; and be the case that reasonable steps have been taken to keep the information secret. Given the higher standard to qualify as a trade secret, while a company may keep a wide range of proprietary information confidential, trade secret status may be reserved for the company's most valuable and tightly controlled information.

PATENTS IN THE INDUSTRIAL METAVERSE

8.11 Patent protection is available for inventions that are new, inventive and are capable of industrial application. In the UK and Europe, however, there are categories of invention that are not eligible for patent protection. These are:[3]

1. a discovery, scientific theory or mathematical method;
2. a literary, dramatic, musical or artistic work or any other aesthetic creation whatsoever;
3. a scheme, rule or method for performing a mental act, playing a game or doing business, or a program for a computer; and
4. the presentation of information.

8.12 This list of categories is exhaustive. Furthermore, inventions are only excluded from patentability to the extent that the subject matter claimed in a patent application relates to one or more of these categories 'as such'.

8.13 Some of these categories are excluded from patentability because of their overlap with other forms of IP right. For instance, the appropriate form of IP protection for literary, dramatic, musical or artistic works is copyright. Other aesthetic creations may be eligible for registered design protection, as may presentations of information.

8.14 Challenges arise when seeking patent protection for software-related innovation, not least as a result of the 'program for a computer' exclusion. It may be argued that the original intention of this excluded category was to prevent any crossover with copyright protection, which is available for source code of

3 UK Patents Act 1977 (as amended), section 1(2).

a computer program. However, in practice this exclusion is applied much more broadly than merely to the expression of an idea in this context (eg, source code), and in fact captures many computer-implemented inventions. This can lead to issues where there may not necessarily be an appropriate IP right available for certain types of software innovation.

8.15 The EPO's approach to assessing whether a claimed invention relates to excluded subject matter as such involves a consideration of the technical contribution provided by a claimed invention. In particular, the EPO applies the so-called 'two-hurdle approach'. The first hurdle involves assessing whether the claimed subject matter as a whole falls into one or more of the categories of invention not eligible for patentability. In practice, this hurdle is typically relatively simple to overcome. For instance, provided that a claimed invention is directed to or uses technical means, such as a computer processor, then it does not fall into the 'program for a computer' excluded category 'as such'. In a notable recent decision from the UK Supreme Court,[4] the approach to be taken by the UKIPO in this regard is to be brought in line with the EPO.

8.16 The second hurdle involves asking whether the claimed invention is inventive. The EPO uses their so-called 'problem-solution approach' to assess inventive step. This involves three main stages:

1. determining the 'closest prior art',
2. establishing the 'objective technical problem' to be solved, and
3. considering whether or not the claimed invention, starting from the closest prior art and the objective technical problem, would have been obvious to the skilled person.

8.17 Step 2 above involves identifying the distinguishing features of the claimed subject matter relative to the closest prior art document, identifying the technical effect resulting from the distinguishing features, and formulating the technical problem based on the identified technical effect.

8.18 Only distinguishing features of claimed subject matter that contribute to the technical character of an invention can be taken into account for the assessment of inventive step. Patent claims can legitimately include 'non-technical' features as well as 'technical' features, where non-technical features may be regarded as features that would, in isolation, relate to one or more of the excluded subject matter categories as such.

8.19 For claimed inventions that include a mix of technical and non-technical features, such as many computer-implemented inventions, a further step needs to be performed prior to assessing inventive step according to the second hurdle. In particular, it first needs to be identified which of the claim features contribute

4 *Emotional Perception AI Limited (Appellant) v Comptroller General of Patents, Designs and Trade Marks (Respondent)* [2026] UKSC 3.

to the technical character of the claimed invention, referred to as the COMVIK approach.[5] It is noted that features that are non-technical in and of themselves, and so do not make a technical contribution in isolation, may still make a technical contribution when considered in combination with other claim features. As such, any novel technical features, and novel non-technical features that contribute to the technical character of the invention, are taken into account for the inventive step assessment in the second hurdle of the two-hurdle approach.

8.20 The EPO has deliberately left the term 'technical' undefined as it deems it necessary to leave the term open to further development as technology evolves. The EPO has, however, adopted a relatively consistent approach to assessment of inventive step using the COMVIK approach for a couple of decades now, meaning that the case law built up over that period paints a relatively clear picture of what may and may not be deemed technical by the EPO.

8.21 Referring to the 'computer program' exclusion, it has been argued that a computer program running on a computer is inherently technical. It has however been made clear by the EPO that a computer program must produce a 'further technical effect' when run on a computer, that goes beyond normal physical interactions between computer software and hardware. For instance, computer-implemented methods for controlling an anti-lock braking system in a car, determining emissions by an X-ray device, compressing video, restoring a distorted digital image, or encrypting electronic communications produce further technical effects in this regard. Also, if a computer program is designed and adapted based on the specific architecture of the computer on which it is to be executed, rather than being designed irrespective of the hardware on which it is to be run, then this may be indicative of a further technical effect.

8.22 As well as the 'program for a computer' exclusion, another one of the excluded categories that is often relevant to AR/VR technology is the 'mathematical method' exclusion. This has become particularly pertinent in recent years with the rise of AI-based innovation. This is because the EPO considers AI and machine learning to be based on computational models and algorithms that are per se of an abstract mathematical nature, and so the approach the EPO takes to assessing AI-based innovation in this regard is the same as the one it takes for mathematical methods.

8.23 Similarly to above, it is typically relatively trivial to draft a patent claim involving mathematical methods that as a whole is not directed to excluded subject matter (eg, by claiming a technical means, such as a computer processor), for implementing the mathematical method.

8.24 For the steps of a mathematical method to be taken into account for the assessment of inventive step, they must contribute to the technical character of the claimed invention. There are two ways in which this may be achieved: by

5 EPO Board of Appeal decision T0641/00.

application of the mathematical method to a specific technical application; and by adaptation of the mathematical method to a specific technical implementation.[6]

8.25 Specific technical applications of mathematical methods may typically involve contact with the real world at the input and/or output of the computational device implementing the mathematical method. For instance, at the output side, specific technical applications may include control of a specific technical system based on the determination performed by the mathematical method (eg, automatic control of a car braking system). On the other hand, at the input side, specifical technical applications may include the use of real-world sensor measurements to perform analysis (eg, use of physiological sensor data to determine energy expenditure of a subject). Specific applications of mathematical methods in technical fields, such as cryptography, image processing, video/image/noise compression, are allowable. The claimed application or use of the mathematical method, however, must be specific: claims using the output of a mathematical method to control a generic technical system, for instance, will not be allowed.

8.26 Specific technical implementations of mathematical methods may typically mean that the mathematical method is specifically adapted based on the internal functioning of the computer hardware on which it is to be executed. If the mathematical method can be executed on any generic hardware then it is not being implemented in a specific technical manner. On the other hand, if the mathematical method is designed to exploit particular technical properties of the hardware on which it is to be executed, then this may be regarded as being implemented in a specific technical manner. The technical properties could be memory storage capacity, network bandwidth, available computational processing power/efficiency, etc. Claimed subject matter that merely provides a more efficient algorithm for performing a mathematical method on a generic computer processor will not be regarded as providing a technical contribution.

CASE STUDY 1

8.27 A company uses computer numerical control (CNC) machines to operate industrial machinery, such as lasers, routers and grinders, in order to fabricate parts with high precision. A collection of sensors are used to monitor various aspects of the operation of the CNC machines. The collected sensor data is processed to determine or predict the occurrence of faults in the operation of the CNC machines. A proprietary algorithm is used to determine whether a fault has occurred.

8.28 The company provides its employees with remote training on how to operate the CNC machines and how to deal with identified faults. The provision of remote training is convenient when employees are located a significant

6 EPO Guidelines for Examination G-II 3.3, https://www.epo.org/en/legal/guidelines-epc/2024/g_ii_3_3.html.

geographical distance from the CNC machines. The company uses VR technology to provide the remote training, which allows for a more immersive and interactive experience when training is being delivered remotely. In particular, three-dimensional virtual models, or digital twins, of the CNC machines are constructed, which trainees and instructors can view and explore using individual VR headsets. When faults with the CNC machines are identified, sensor data relating to the fault is captured and stored. Then, when training is being delivered using the VR equipment in relation to fault detection and correction, a distinctive visual layout is provided on the VR headsets that show the digital twin of the relevant part of the CNC machines adjacent to real sensor data (eg, video footage, obtained during occurrence of the fault under consideration).

8.29 The company may be able to seek patent protection for one or more aspects of its operations. It is unlikely that patent protection is available in the UK or Europe for the 'proprietary algorithm' (used for fault detection) in and of itself. This is because it is likely to fall under one or both of the 'mathematical method' and 'computer program' exclusions from patentability. However, patent protection may be available to a method of fault identification that combines the real-world sensor data with the algorithm for performing the determination. Furthermore, if the output of the algorithm included controlling the CNC machines in some way (eg, automatic shutdown of the equipment when a fault is detected, or controlling a robotic arm to operate the machinery), then combining the algorithmic determination with this real-world automatic control may also be patentable. In each case, the beneficial effects of more accurate fault detection are achieved by virtue of the details of the proprietary algorithm. As such, sufficient detail of the algorithm would need to be included in a patent application, and this would eventually be made available to the public. This would be a relevant consideration for the company when deciding whether to file for patent protection for aspects including the proprietary algorithm.

8.30 Assuming that the VR equipment itself is standard, then patent protection may not be available for any of the hardware aspects of the arrangement. Also, the mere concept of using VR equipment for training users to use industrial equipment would be likely to lack novelty. Furthermore, the way in which a digital twin of the CNC machine is displayed next to actual sensor data/video footage of a fault occurrence may not be eligible for patent protection as it may be deemed to be excluded as a 'presentation of information' as such. Patent protection may, however, be available for a method or system where capture of sensor data/video footage of (a relevant part of) the industrial equipment is triggered upon automatic detection of a fault with the equipment, where the captured sensor data/video footage is stored and is subsequently retrievable by a trainer using a VR headset while training users also wearing VR headsets to display alongside a digital twin of the equipment on a VR display during a training session. In this way, users can be trained in an interactive environment on how to deal with such fault scenarios should they arise during future operation, while being presented with actual video footage of such a fault occurring previously at the industrial equipment, as well as other relevant sensor data associated with the fault as captured during the previous fault.

8.31 As a general point, if an innovative aspect of a system or method is excluded from patentability in and of itself (eg, a proprietary algorithm or a novel way to display information to a user on a VR headset), then it is useful to consider how the innovative aspect fits into an overall system or method being performed. If the invention is framed with such additional context, specifically, if the additional context brings out the technical contribution provided by the innovative aspect, then this may be enough to transform the innovative aspect into one in which patent protection may be obtained.

ADDITIONAL CONSIDERATIONS FOR PATENTING AI IN THE INDUSTRIAL METAVERSE

8.32 The increase in the development and use of AI-based technology is being witnessed across almost every sector of the economy, and the industrial metaverse is no exception. For instance, AI methods are being used for predictive maintenance of industrial machinery, for training of robotic machinery, for the design of equipment parts and components, for supply chain optimisation, etc. Innovation around AI-based technology in this context can be found in both development of the underlying AI models and in adaptation of known AI models to new use cases.

8.33 When considering whether to seek patent protection for AI-related innovation, all of the above-outlined considerations relating to novelty, inventive step and excluded subject matter apply. Indeed, the EPO considers AI models to be based on abstract mathematical methods and so assesses the technical contribution of AI models using the same approach as for mathematical methods described above.[7]

8.34 Nonetheless, there may be additional considerations for AI-related subject matter. One such consideration may relate to sufficiency of disclosure in a patent application. The 'sufficiency' requirement arises from the 'patent bargain' underlying the patent system: in return for a patent applicant benefiting from a defined period of exclusivity for an invention, they must disclose in the patent application at least one way of carrying out the invention. The idea here is that inventors are encouraged to publish details of their inventions, thus advancing human knowledge, while being rewarded with a period of exclusivity.

8.35 In Europe, a patent application must disclose an invention in a manner that is sufficiently clear and complete for it to be carried out by a person skilled in the art.[8] The 'person skilled in the art' or, simply, the 'skilled person', is a

7 Ibid.

8 European Patent Convention, Article 83, https://www.epo.org/en/legal/epc/2020/a83.html.

legal construct of a hypothetical individual, or team of individuals, used as a benchmark to assess various aspects of patentability of an invention. They are regarded as being a skilled practitioner in the technical field of the invention, have common general knowledge in the technical field, have access to all information in the state of the art, and be capable of routine experimentation. They are not, however, imaginative or capable of inventive activity.

8.36 The EPO's Guidelines for Examination provide more detail on what is needed to meet the sufficiency requirement:

> 'A detailed description of at least one way of carrying out the invention must be given. Since the application is addressed to the person skilled in the art, it is neither necessary nor desirable that details of well-known ancillary features are given, but the description must disclose any feature essential for carrying out the invention in sufficient detail to render it apparent to the skilled person how to put the invention into practice.'[9]

8.37 The EPO's Guidelines for Examination further indicate what would be regarded as insufficient disclosure in this regard: 'Sufficiency of disclosure cannot be acknowledged if the skilled person has to carry out a research programme based on trial and error to reproduce the results of the invention, with limited chances of success.'[10]

8.38 For more traditional 'deterministic' or 'predictable' computational and mathematical method inventions, a functional description of each step or feature of the method would typically be considered to satisfy the sufficiency requirement, without needing to describe how the steps are to be programmed in the computer.

8.39 This may not, however, be 'sufficient' for AI-related inventions, which may be more 'probabilistic' or less predictable in nature. In particular, the described functionality of an AI system may be achieved only for certain trained parameters of the AI system (eg, weighting values at nodes, or when certain training data is used to obtain the system parameters).

8.40 As such, for AI inventions it is important to consider: has the skilled person really been provided with enough information in the patent specification to be able to implement the invention to achieve the desired functionality without undue burden? Whereas a relatively high-level, functional description of an algorithm may be sufficient for mathematical or computational methods of a more predictable or deterministic nature, for AI inventions training data or model parameters may need to be disclosed in more detail for the skilled person to be able to reproduce the invention and achieve the described functionality in order

9 EPO Guidelines for Examination F-III 1, https://www.epo.org/en/legal/guidelines-epc/2025/f_iii_1.html.

10 EPO Guidelines for Examination F-III 3: https://www.epo.org/en/legal/guidelines-epc/2025/f_iii_3.html

for the sufficiency of disclosure requirement to be met. For instance, one or more examples of specific sets of training data or model parameters may be provided.

8.41 An important point here is that a purported technical effect associated with a claimed invention, which can be indicative of inventive step, in a patent application must be achieved across the entire scope of the claimed invention. This may be problematic for AI-based inventions where small changes to model weights or hyperparameters may significantly impact the result obtained. The EPO Guidelines clarify that insufficient disclosure:

> 'can be found in the field of artificial intelligence if the mathematical methods and the training datasets are disclosed in insufficient detail to reproduce the technical effect over the whole range claimed. Such a lack of detail may result in a disclosure that is more like an invitation to a research programme.'[11]

8.42 This may place an additional, and perhaps burdensome, requirement on patent applicants. For more deterministic, predictable computer-implemented inventions, it has typically been sufficient to merely allege a technical effect achieved by a claimed invention, as this is perhaps more apparent to the skilled person by mere inspection. For more probabilistic, unpredictable computer-implemented inventions, such as AI-based innovation, however, such an assertion may not be sufficient. Instead, evidence in the form of experimental results may be needed to support an assertion of technical effect across the entire breadth of a patent claim. While the inclusion of such evidence is commonplace for chemical- and pharmaceutical-based patent applications, it has thus far been less common in engineering- and software-based patent applications.

8.43 If there is a slightly elevated requirement for AI inventions in terms of how much detail needs to be disclosed in a patent application, then this raises additional considerations for patent applicants. For instance, if more detail that will eventually be made public needs to be disclosed, then it may be that a company decides that the 'patent bargain' is not worth it in this instance. Instead, they may decide to keep the inventive concept confidential and not seek patent protection.

8.44 Also, if defining a scope of protection to be sought via a patent application that is broad enough to be commercially useful is not possible because it cannot be shown without undue burden that a purported technical effect is achieved across the entire scope, companies may decide that filing a patent application is not worthwhile. In general, patent protection is most useful when protection is obtained at a functional, rather than implementational, level, as this tends to make easy workarounds less likely or possible, resulting in stronger patent protection.

8.45 A final point on AI-related innovation specifically is in relation to inventorship. The rights to obtaining patent protection lie in the first instance with the inventor(s), and these rights typically flow automatically by law to the

11 Ibid.

employer of the inventor(s). In the UK, an inventor is an 'actual deviser' of the invention (i.e. someone who contributed substantially to the inventive concept, and did not merely provide a support role, eg, carry out routine experimentation, during conception).

8.46 It has been speculated that some AI systems are now, or soon will be, capable of inventive creation without human input. Leaving aside whether this is, or will be, the case, the UK Supreme Court has confirmed that an inventor named on a patent application must be a human.[12] This has been confirmed in almost every other jurisdiction in which this question has been tested. A question therefore arises as to whether patent protection should be available to AI-generated inventions and, if so, how. Indeed, it is at least the case that, at present, patent applicants are incentivised to downplay the part any AI system plays in the inventive process.

CASE STUDY 2

8.47 A company operates in the field of drug discovery. Drug discovery is the process of identifying candidate compounds for progression to the next stage of drug development (eg, pre-clinical trials). Such candidate compounds are required to satisfy certain criteria for further development. Modern drug discovery involves the identification and optimisation of initial screening 'hit' compounds. In particular, such compounds need to be optimised relative to required criteria, which can include the optimisation of a number of different properties. The properties to be optimised can include, for instance: efficacy/potency against a desired target; selectivity against non-desired targets; low probability of toxicity; and, good drug metabolism and pharmacokinetic properties (ADME). Only compounds satisfying the specified requirements become candidate compounds that can continue to the drug development process.

8.48 The drug discovery process can involve making/synthesising a significant number of compounds during the optimisation from initial screening hits to candidate compounds. In particular, those compounds which are synthesised are measured to determine their properties, such as biological activity. The number of compounds, however, that could be made as part of a particular drug discovery project will far outnumber, likely by orders of magnitude, the number of compounds that can be synthesised and tested. The results of the measurements of synthesised compounds are therefore analysed and used to inform a decision on which compounds to synthesise next to maximise the likelihood of obtaining compounds with further improved properties relative to the various criteria required by a candidate compound.

8.49 The synthesis and subsequent measurement of biological activity of one or more compounds at a particular stage is referred to as a design cycle of the

12 *Thaler v Comptroller-General of Patents* [2023] UKSC 49.

drug discovery process. Typically, a set of compounds is synthesised and tested at each design cycle of the process as this is more efficient than synthesising and testing a single compound at a time. However, a level of available resources usually means that there is an upper limit on the number of compounds in a set that can be synthesised at any given design cycle.

8.50 During a drug discovery project, many hundreds or even thousands of compounds typically are synthesised across several design cycles before a candidate compound is found. This is a lengthy, expensive, and inefficient process: synthesis of a single compound can cost thousands of pounds, and it can take three to five years on average to obtain a single candidate compound.

8.51 The use of computational methods greatly increases the level of analysis that may be performed on already-synthesised compounds relative to that which could be performed by a medicinal chemist alone. In particular, AI methods can be used to evaluate numerous design parameters in parallel, at a level that is beyond the capabilities of a human, to identify relationships between parameters and desired properties, such as biological activity levels. The AI methods can then use these identified relationships to make a better prediction as to which compounds are more likely to exhibit a greater number/level of desired properties relative to required criteria of a candidate compound. Once a compound has been synthesised, its now-known properties can be used to update/retrain the AI model, such that its prediction accuracy continues to increase. Such AI methods can be used to reduce the number of design cycles, and so reduce the number of compounds that need to be synthesised, to obtain a compound that achieves a desired combination of properties, as required of a candidate compound, thereby achieving an associated reduction in cost and time of a drug discovery project.

8.52 The company has developed a new AI model that provides more accurate predictions of the properties that are exhibited by a compound, once synthesised, based on structural features of the compound. This means that fewer design cycles need to be performed to identify candidate compounds, thereby saving significant time and cost. The AI model is general in the sense that it is not limited to predicting certain types of property (eg, biological activity), and is not limited to identifying candidate compounds for drugs for certain types of disease.

8.53 The company wishes to seek patent protection for its AI model. The model in and of itself will not be eligible for patent protection in the UK or Europe as it will be deemed to be a mathematical method as such. It may be possible to obtain patent protection for an overall drug design method that makes use of the AI model to select the next compounds to be synthesised. Note, however, that the purported technical effect of identifying candidate compounds (ie, compounds with desired properties) in fewer design cycles is only achieved when one or more design cycles are actually performed. As such, a patent claim may need to recite not only computational steps of using the AI model, but also real-world steps of making/synthesising compounds that have been selected based on the predictions. This may be important from an infringement point of view. A competitor company who also develops AI models for drug discovery may not perform in-lab synthesis themselves, but instead partner with a further company to do this. It may be more difficult to show and assert infringement when the activities of two different companies need to be taken into account for infringement of a patent claim.

8.54 As the novel part of the invention lies in the AI model, then sufficient detail of how the AI model works needs to be included in the patent application in order to meet the sufficiency of disclosure requirement. Indeed, if the effect of more accurate prediction of compound properties relies on using specific combinations of input data, specific model architectures, or specific model weights and parameters, then this must be detailed in the patent application so that the skilled person would be able, without undue burden, to replicate the invention and achieve the beneficial effect.

8.55 Furthermore, the purported technical effect of improved accuracy prediction needs to hold across the entire scope of the patent claim. Given the probabilistic nature of AI methods, relatively small changes in model parameters, for instance, may impact the prediction accuracy of the AI model but such changes/modifications may nonetheless be covered by relatively broad, functional language typically used in patent claims.

8.56 The company may need to include testing or experimental data across a range of different embodiments covered by the patent claim to evidence the presence of the purported technical effect across the full scope of the claimed subject matter. These different embodiments may include the use of different model parameter values, different combinations of input parameters, and use of the model to predict different types of properties. Of course, in some cases this may be relatively burdensome for the company should the data not necessarily be available at the time of filing the patent application. In Europe, in some cases it is possible to file experimental data after a patent application has been filed. Such post-filed data can, however, only be used to evidence the presence of a technical effect already described in the patent application as filed.[13] The company must therefore ensure that such details are included in the patent application as filed.

CHALLENGES WITH PATENT PROTECTION IN THE INDUSTRIAL METAVERSE

8.57 Obtaining commercially useful patent protection for innovation in a virtual world context, such as in the industrial metaverse, can be difficult because some of the categories of subject matter that is excluded from patentability are often relevant and invoked in this context.

13 Enlarged Board of Appeal Decision, *Sumitomo Chemical Company Limited v Syngenta Limited*, G2/21: G0002/21 23 March 2023.

8.58 Additional challenges may arise in this context. IoT technologies have brought together different industries that would previously have not been operating in the same business context and would not have been in competition. One example of this is in the field of connected vehicles, in which wireless communications technology developed by telecommunications companies is incorporated into, and/or otherwise used by, vehicle manufacturers in their vehicles. Connected vehicles are vehicles equipped with communication technologies that allow them to exchange data with other vehicles (V2V), infrastructure (V2I) and networks (V2X). This connectivity can be used for information sharing (eg, to provide real-time traffic updates, hazard warnings and remote diagnostics). Indeed, many autonomous vehicles are connected and, while autonomous vehicles may primarily use vehicle sensor data and satellite navigation data to make driving decisions, connectivity can complement autonomy by improving situational awareness and traffic coordination.

8.59 Traditional vehicle manufacturers are heavy users of the patent system, with all of the main players having large patent portfolios in various territories. These patent portfolios have in the past, however, been used mostly for defensive purposes. That is, each manufacturer has a strong negotiating position should contentious proceedings arise, but active enforcement of patent rights has been relatively rare.

8.60 Traditional telecommunications companies are also heavy users of the patent system and have built large portfolios. Much of their technological development revolves around standardised technology such as wireless communication (4G, 5G, etc) and video codecs. Patents declared as SEPs (standards essential patents) are critical for interoperability, and licensing under FRAND (fair, reasonable, and non-discriminatory) terms often leads to disputes when parties disagree on royalty rates or licensing conditions. Telecoms companies actively defend their portfolios, with litigation often being used as leverage in licensing negotiations.

8.61 With connected vehicles, these two industries, and their differing approach to using the patent system, have been brought together. Vehicle manufacturers want their vehicles to use the relevant wireless communication technology, and telecoms companies want to receive licensing royalties for such use.

8.62 One approach that has evolved in recent years is the creation of new patent pools that include relevant patented technology from telecoms companies that can be accessed by vehicle manufacturers. This one-stop shop ensures that vehicle manufacturers and telecoms companies do not need to enter into separate licensing negotiations for the use of different required patented technology, which also reduces the potential for litigation.

8.63 Avanci is the most prominent example of an entity that operates global licensing platforms for SEPs covering cellular technologies used in connected cars. Avanci aggregates SEPs from major telecom companies (eg, Qualcomm, Ericsson, Nokia, Huawei) and offers vehicle manufacturers a single licence for technologies essential to 2G, 3G, 4G, and 5G connectivity. This includes cellular vehicle-to-everything (C-V2X) standards, which enable vehicles to communicate with infrastructure, other vehicles, and devices.

8.64 The dispersed nature of the industrial metaverse also makes questions around freedom-to-operate (FTO) relative to existing patent rights more complex. To assess FTO, it is important for companies to understand which territories they operate in, which may be non-trivial in a virtual world and/or cloud computing context, to ensure that a proper FTO assessment in each relevant territory can be performed. Even when territorial scope is clear, the increasing interconnectedness and collaboration between different industries that would traditionally have been separate (eg, wireless technology and automotive, pharmaceuticals and software developers) means that defining a suitable scope for FTO analysis becomes more difficult and, indeed, can mean more extensive and far-reaching analysis is needed.

TRADE SECRETS IN THE INDUSTRIAL METAVERSE

8.65 Trade secrets are a particular type of confidential information protected under specific statute (eg, the Trade Secrets (Enforcement, etc.) Regulations 2018 in the UK, and Directive 2016/943[14] in the EU). There is no formal registration requirement to obtain trade secret protection. For information to be considered a trade secret under these statutes, however, it must: be secret; have commercial value because it is secret; and be the case that reasonable steps have been taken to keep the information secret. Information may be protected as a trade secret indefinitely provided that these conditions continue to be met.

8.66 In an industrial metaverse context, various types of information and innovation may be generated that are suitable for trade secret protection. For instance, this could include digital twin models, simulation algorithms, process automation logic, arrangement of IoT hardware, etc.

8.67 In one sense, trade secrets can be regarded as a relatively risky form of IP protection in that if the relevant information enters the public domain, whether accidentally, maliciously, or in any other manner, there is no option to row back time and make the information secret again.

8.68 Although there is no formal registration requirement, companies who wish to protect certain innovation as a trade secret must take certain steps internally to ensure that it can be shown, if needed, that the information in

14 Directive (EU) 2016/943 of the European Parliament and of the Council of 8 June 2016 on the protection of undisclosed know-how and business information (trade secrets) against their unlawful acquisition, use and disclosure.

question satisfies the above requirements. This may typically take the form of a trade secrets register that documents all of the information/secrets within a company that are regarded as being trade secrets. Some practical points for generating and maintaining a trade secret register may include the following:

1. The register needs to be a live document that is kept up-to-date.
2. Perform regular audits of what is in the register to determine whether items should be kept or removed. Why is a specific item valuable?
3. Take reasonable steps to ensure the register is not leaked. This will typically at least include limiting access within a company and building in password protection.
4. Assign responsibility to keep the register up-to-date (eg, member of IP team or other employee if there is no such team in the company).
5. Keep the process of maintaining the register simple and clear. This makes it more likely that people responsible for maintaining the register do actually engage with the process.
6. Train those people who need to maintain a trade secret register about what to include, what to remove, how often to audit, etc.
7. For a given item include enough detail in the register to identify what is protected and who has access. Include a pointer as to where to go to find full details. For instance, include the title of a secret in the register but not full details. If full details are included in the register then it becomes more likely that it is not kept up-to-date over time.

8.69 Other points to consider for companies in relation to trade secret protection include the following:

1. Not everything in a company that is not in the public domain should be labelled as a trade secret. If everything is labelled a secret then perhaps nothing is really regarded as being a trade secret.
2. Have a policy for what is labelled confidential and what is not. Similarly to above, if every document or communication within a company is labelled as confidential then this may reduce the weight of a confidential label on a genuinely confidential document.
3. Do not use non-disclosure agreements (NDAs) to share trade secrets with potential collaborators. An NDA may be thought of as a preparatory document for companies to determine whether they want to work together. Sharing of trade secrets likely needs a different type of agreement, which typically comes further down the line than an NDA.
4. It is possible to protect negative results (eg, experiments with undesired results) as a trade secret when there is value in knowing these results.
5. It is generally a good idea to require employees to read and sign a company trade secret policy that outlines what their responsibilities are to keep trade

secrets confidential, etc. It can also be a good idea to require employees leaving the company to sign the same.

6. For employee exits, ensure that Human Resources know what trade secrets the exiting employee knows so that it can be communicated to them what their responsibilities/obligations are. It helps to be able to identify what information the exiting employee can take with them and what information they cannot.
7. When onboarding, ask a new employee for details of any patents or patent applications on which they are named as an inventor. It is likely that there is trade secret information belonging to the previous employer alongside the information disclosed in the patent application. As such, this should be kept separate from similar projects to avoid potential trade secret infringement.
8. It can be a good idea to set up alarms/alerts in your document management system when unusually large amounts of information is being accessed or downloaded.

8.70 Although it may be more typical to license patent rights compared to trade secrets, it is nonetheless possible for a company to generate a revenue stream by licensing its trade secrets. When considering whether to license a trade secret it is crucial, however, to bear in mind: how easy it will be to keep an idea secret; how commercially valuable the idea is to the business; and the likely evolution of that value over time.

8.71 These considerations help divide trade secrets into two groups: those which concern features of a product or process which may best generate revenue by providing a competitive edge in the market and those which may provide more financial benefit through licensing. The first group includes trade secrets which can reliably be kept secret, are financially valuable, and are likely to maintain their value over time. The second includes those trade secrets which are commercially valuable but may not hold their value over time, such that the available window for generating profit therefrom is limited, or may be difficult keep secret. Members of the second group are likely to provide greater benefit as licensed trade secrets given their reduced longevity. In one case, the information protected by the trade secret may be at risk of leaking into the public domain, such that its secrecy is time-limited. In the other case, advancements from competitors may surpass that which is protected by the trade secret, such that the opportunity for generating increased profits through a market-leading product or service is time-limited.

8.72 For instance, in the context of the industrial metaverse, an AI model may slowly leak specific underlying features, or elements of training data, when responding to user queries. Therefore, these features of the AI model may only present limited windows for generating profit. If trade secrets regarding these features were, however, licensed to third parties, more profit may be generated in this window. Moreover, the licensing payments may even extend beyond a time at which the licensor predicts the profitability window closing.

8.73 When licensing a trade secret, the licensing agreement must clarify a number of key elements to maximise the value of the license to the licensor. The licensee must be made aware of their obligations regarding confidentiality and any measures they are expected to put in place to maintain secrecy. Failure to do so may lead to the secret being leaked into the public domain unwittingly by the licensee.

8.74 Moreover, a licensing agreement must clearly define precisely what information is to be held in confidence. If this is unclear, then the licensee may openly discuss information which they are unaware is intended to be kept secret. The licensing agreement should also include a description of the licensor's right to audit the requirements placed on the licensee. This ensures that both the licensor and licensee are in agreement regarding checking the maintenance of the information as a secret and having appropriate measures in place to do so.

8.75 Crucially, when negotiating the license, the payment structure should be clearly laid out and designed to mirror the evolution of value of the trade secret to the licensee. For instance, it is often the case that the majority of the value of obtaining a licence for a trade secret is realised upon the initial transfer of the secret. In such cases, payments should generally be front-loaded.

PATENTS V TRADE SECRETS (AND CONFIDENTIAL INFORMATION)

8.76 For innovation in fields such as AI, IoT, blockchain and cloud computing, a decision typically needs to be made as to whether patents or trade secrets (or other confidentiality) are the most appropriate form of IP protection for the innovation. Indeed, it is often the case that a combination of the two is appropriate (eg, patent protection to protect inventions at the functional level), while keeping specific implementation details confidential. Copyright protection may be relevant in this context too, given that it subsists in source code.

8.77 Patents are a relatively strong and safe form of IP protection. When drafted properly, patents offer broad protection of an invention, and no public disclosures of the invention after filing a patent application can impact the validity of the eventually granted patent. Also, it may be easier to enforce patents than trade secrets given that for trade secret enforcement it will in the first instance need to be shown that a trade secret actually exists. Furthermore, patents may be used more readily to add value to a company given that it is easier to license, sell and market patents relative to trade secrets.

8.78 Nonetheless, these advantages of patents need to be balanced against some potential drawbacks. These include the costs involved with drafting a patent application and prosecuting it through to grant, which can be substantial. Also, there is always a risk that a patent application is not granted, or is granted in a form offering a narrower or different scope of protection from what would be desired from a commercial point of view. In the context of software innovation in a virtual world context, the patentability of an invention from an excluded subject matter viewpoint needs to be assessed carefully before deciding whether to file a patent application. Furthermore, the level of disclosure of an invention in order to meet the sufficiency requirements, particularly in the context of AI inventions, may be deemed to be not worth the payoff of a possible granted patent.

8.79 Given the advantages of patent protection, a general strategy may be to seek patent protection for inventions where it is possible to do so, and then fill in the gaps where patent protection is not viable by using trade secret protection, or even mere confidentiality.

8.80 One approach for determining whether to file a patent application for an invention or whether to keep a secret may be to involve considering the following:

1. whether the invention is new;

2. whether the invention is commercially valuable;

3. whether the invention would be detectable when implemented.

8.81 For an invention in which each of points 1–3 above hold, then filing a patent application would generally be advisable. If only points 1 and 2 hold, then keeping the invention as a trade secret may be the preferred course of action. If only points 1 and 3 hold, then making the invention available to the public by way of defensive disclosure may be the preferred route, to ensure that no third parties can subsequently obtain patent protection for the same invention. If only point 1 holds, then keeping the invention confidential, but not necessarily as a trade secret, may be the appropriate action.

8.82 Returning for a moment to a situation in which only points 1 and 2 hold (ie, where an invention may be difficult to detect when implemented, which may be particularly relevant to industrial metaverse technology), it may still be a strategically prudent decision to file a patent application. Although it may be difficult to enforce any eventually granted patent rights in such a case because of the difficulty of detecting infringement, there are other reasons that companies obtain patent protection. Patents, and even patent applications, can be used as marketing tools and be used to increase the value of a company, which can be particularly useful during investment rounds or as part of a merger or acquisition.

8.83 A concrete example of another example for which patent protection may be sought in the UK is that it can be used to reduce a company's corporation tax liability from the headline rate to a lower rate under the so-called 'Patent Box' regime. The UK Patent Box is a tax relief on profits made from the exploitation of products or processes that incorporate patented technology. In particular, the Patent Box reduces the UK corporation tax payable on qualifying profits from the headline rate (of currently 25%) to as low as 10% (but typically somewhere in between).

8.84 To be eligible to make a Patent Box claim, a company must: be liable to UK corporation tax; make a profit from exploiting inventions covered by granted patents; own, or have an exclusive licence for, the relevant patents; and, have undertaken qualifying development on the relevant patents. In practice, such qualifying development means that the company has made a significant contribution to either: the creation or development of the patented invention; or, a product or process incorporating the patented invention.

8.85 The patents in question must be granted by the UKIPO, the EPO or by one from a particular list of European Economic Area countries. In order for a profit to be taken into account in the reduced corporation tax calculation, it must come from activities such as selling products or providing services that are covered by a patent or which incorporate a patented invention, and licensing out or selling the relevant patent rights.

8.86 Obtaining patent protection can be a relatively lengthy process, typically, three to five years, and involves some financial outlay. The Patent Box savings that could be available should, however, in most cases more than cover the cost to obtain a patent. Also, while Patent Box relief cannot be claimed until granted patent protection is obtained, the tax reduction calculation can include the period that a patent application was pending prior to grant, making the Patent Box and patents eligible for Patent Box relief valuable indeed.

CASE STUDY 3

8.87 A start-up software company has developed a predictive maintenance system for predicting faults with an industrial machine. A proprietary AI model is used to predict faults based on sensor data. The system provides for real-time predictive maintenance of industrial machines but with low data transmission rates. The system makes use of one or more edge/local processing devices, equipped with dedicated trained AI models, to make inferences about an operational state of an industrial machine based on sensor data indicative of machine operation received by the edge device. The system beneficially provides for identifying locally when the inference/prediction about the operational state of a machine changes, and only initiates communication across a (wireless) network when such a change is identified.

8.88 Indeed, the system further benefits from communicating only information related to the inference change/event, rather than the raw sensor data or other parameters associated with the change/event. The system can furthermore identify when the inferred change results in abnormal or anomalous machine operation. The system is advantageous not only in that sensor data processing is performed locally/at the edge, but also in that only a relatively small selection of processed information is transmitted across a network (eg, to the Cloud) and the processed information that is transmitted is in a low data size format/representation. Data transmission across a network can thereby be significantly reduced (eg, to the order of kilobytes of data, rather than terabytes), while still performing effective, real-time monitoring and maintenance of the industrial machine.

8.89 The start-up company wishes to test and further develop the system in collaboration with an OEM (original equipment manufacturer) that manufactures edge devices in which the proprietary AI model can be incorporated.

8.90 The start-up company should file for patent protection covering the overall functionality of the system (ie, predicting faults locally and communicating event data across a network only when needed). This has clear technical benefits of reduced data transmission when performing predictive maintenance.

8.91 The start-up company should keep details of the proprietary AI model confidential. It seems that the AI model is of significant commercial value as it provides for improved fault predictions and there is third-party interest in testing and developing the AI model. As such, the start-up may wish for the AI model to be regarded as a trade secret. The start-up should take all of the necessary steps to ensure that details of the AI model would be recognised as a trade secret, and that steps are taken to ensure these details remain secret.

8.92 Ownership questions also arise. At the start of the collaboration, all of the background IP should be clearly identified, and it should be agreed where ownership and entitlement to file for patent protection, for instance, lies for any innovation that comes out of the collaboration.

8.93 In order to facilitate the collaboration, the start-up may consider offering a temporary licence for the patent rights to the OEM for the duration of the collaboration, so that the OEM can use the overall functionality of the system during testing and development. If the collaboration is to continue into production, with the OEM manufacturing a product incorporating aspects of the overall functionality covered in the patent, then the start-up may consider offering a more long-term licence, which may be exclusive, to the OEM, or may even considering selling the patent rights to the OEM if the start-up is moving towards a different area of development.

8.94 Also, in order to further develop the system as part of the collaboration, the OEM may need access to details of the AI model. In this case, the start-up may consider offering the OEM a temporary licence to the trade secret covering the AI model. Care must be taken to ensure that the scope of the licence is well defined and that the OEM understands its responsibilities when using the trade secret. In the future, the start-up may consider licensing or selling a piece of software incorporating the AI model.

TRADE MARKS IN THE INDUSTRIAL METAVERSE

8.95 The rise of virtual marketplaces such as Roblox and blockchain-based assets like NFTs (non-fungible tokens) has introduced new challenges and opportunities for trade mark protection. In the UK and EU, trade marks for virtual goods and services can be registered under existing frameworks, but applicants should carefully select the correct classes and terminology to reflect the digital nature of these offerings.

8.96 Virtual goods, such as digital clothing, accessories or art, are generally classified under Class 9, which covers downloadable digital files and software. For instance, 'downloadable virtual clothing for use in online environments' would fall under Class 9 rather than Class 25 (which is reserved for physical clothing). Similarly, NFTs themselves are typically considered digital tokens and also fall under Class 9, often described as 'downloadable digital files authenticated by non-fungible tokens'.

8.97 For services provided within virtual environments, such as operating a virtual retail store or hosting virtual events, the relevant classes mirror those for physical services but should specify their virtual nature. This may include Class 35 for retail services, described as 'retail services featuring virtual goods', or Class 41 for entertainment or educational services in virtual worlds.

8.98 The distinction between trade mark protection for virtual and physical goods/services lies in the description. While the Nice Classification system remains the same, applicants should clearly indicate that the goods or services are virtual or digital. Failure to do so may result in objections or limited protection. For instance, registering 'clothing' without specifying 'virtual' may not cover avatars' outfits in Roblox.

8.99 Both the UKIPO and EUIPO accept applications for virtual goods and services, and recent guidance confirms that existing classes can accommodate these new realities. Companies should, however, anticipate evolving practice and ensure their specifications are precise to avoid ambiguity in what a trade mark application is intended to cover.

8.100 Enforcing trade mark rights in a virtual world context presents additional hurdles compared with a physical world context. Infringement may occur across decentralised platforms, often operated by entities across the world, complicating questions of jurisdiction and enforcement. Identifying infringers can be difficult when pseudonymous accounts and/or blockchain anonymity are used. Moreover, platforms may lack robust IP enforcement mechanisms, requiring rights holders to rely on contractual terms or platform-specific takedown procedures. These factors make proactive monitoring and clear contractual protections essential for brand owners.

CASE STUDY 4

8.101 A UK-based clothing company with a long-standing reputation and registered trade marks in the UK and EU for physical clothing launches a metaverse platform. The platform allows users to purchase virtual versions of its garments for avatars. The company uses its established trade mark for the virtual offering, assuming its existing registrations provide adequate protection. Shortly after launch, an EU start-up introduces a similar virtual clothing platform under a confusingly similar name. While the marks are not identical, the similarity causes consumer confusion, with users frequently misdirected when searching for virtual clothing. The UK company fears brand dilution and reputational harm in this emerging digital space.

8.102 If the existing registrations cover physical clothing (Class 25), then they may not extend to virtual goods (Class 9) or related services (Classes 35 and 41). Also, cross-border enforcement may be complicated by the start-up's EU base and the decentralised nature of Metaverse platforms.

8.103 There are several steps that the UK-based company may consider to improve its position:

1. Review current trade mark registrations to confirm scope. If virtual goods and services are not included, then file new applications in the UK and EU (eg, in Class 9, 35, 41, as appropriate).
2. Document instances of confusion, misdirected traffic, and any reputational harm. Screenshots, user complaints, and analytics showing diversion strengthen enforcement claims.
3. Send a cease-and-desist letter asserting rights and requesting rebranding. Highlight the likelihood of confusion and potential infringement under UK and EU law.
4. Use takedown mechanisms offered by the platform. Many platforms have IP enforcement policies similar to those for physical goods.
5. Implement a proactive IP strategy for emerging technologies, including monitoring NFT marketplaces and virtual platforms for misuse.

COPYRIGHT IN THE INDUSTRIAL METAVERSE

8.104 In the UK and EU, copyright protects original works of authorship, including literary, artistic, musical and visual creations. Within the metaverse, this extends to 3D models, virtual environments, avatars, textures, digital artwork and code underpinning interactive experiences. Copyright subsists automatically upon creation – meaning in the UK and EU, registration is not required.

8.105 The author of a work enjoys exclusive rights to reproduce, distribute, communicate to the public and adapt the work. For metaverse content, this means copying or modifying virtual assets without permission may constitute infringement. Works generated by AI may raise questions of authorship, but current UK and EU law generally attributes authorship to the human who made the arrangements for creation.

8.106 Enforcement in virtual spaces can be challenging due to decentralisation and anonymity. Rights holders can rely on traditional remedies such as injunctions and damages through UK or EU courts. Additionally, platform-level enforcement is critical: most metaverse platforms provide takedown procedures similar to those under the EU's Digital Services Act[15] and UK online safety frameworks. Proactive monitoring, contractual terms with platform operators, and technological measures (eg, watermarking) are essential to deter infringement.

8.107 One area in which copyright has become an issue in this context is in the use of copyrighted material to train LLMs (large language models) that are used as chatbots (eg, ChatGPT, Gemini, etc). In particular, the tech companies developing these LLM tools have used web scrapers to scrape material from web pages that is then used to train the LLM models.

8.108 There is a question as to whether this indeed constitutes copyright infringement, which needs the existence of a copy of the work. While it may be possible to get a trained LLM to reproduce individual items of training data as an output, this is an edge case. Nonetheless, these acts by tech companies have initiated a movement by the creative industries to push back against what they deem to be a threat to their entire industries.

8.109 The recent EU AI Act[16] imposes mandatory copyright compliance for providers of general-purpose AI models such as LLM chatbots. It explicitly states that any use of copyright-protected content for training requires authorisation from the rightsholder unless an exception applies. In particular, AI model providers must use lawfully accessible data only, must respect opt-out mechanisms where rights holders reserve their rights in a machine-readable form (eg, robots.txt or similar standards), and must publish a summary of training data sources and maintain internal copyright policies. The level of detail required to meet the summary of training sources requirement remains to be seen.

15 Regulation (EU) 2022/2065 of the European Parliament and of the Council of 19 October 2022 on a Single Market For Digital Services and amending Directive 2000/31/EC (Digital Services Act).

16 Regulation (EU) 2024/1689 of the European Parliament and of the Council of 13 June 2024 laying down harmonised rules on artificial intelligence and amending Regulations (EC) No 300/2008, (EU) No 167/2013, (EU) No 168/2013, (EU) 2018/858, (EU) 2018/1139 and (EU) 2019/2144 and Directives 2014/90/EU, (EU) 2016/797 and (EU) 2020/1828 (Artificial Intelligence Act).

IP IN THE INDUSTRIAL METAVERSE

8.110 The industrial metaverse presents new challenges around protecting and enforcing IP rights. Existing IP frameworks are still the best mechanism that we have to encourage innovation and protect innovators. Indeed, when used properly IP rights perhaps offer an even bigger opportunity in terms of monetisation and commercial advantage in the context of metaverse technologies compared to some more traditional technologies. Nonetheless, IP rights need to be able to adapt to these new technologies. For instance, it is important that IP protection is available for new technologies such as AI, and these technologies do not slip between the realm of different current IP rights (eg, copyright and patents). In some cases, changes in law may be needed, and at the time of writing, the Patent Eligibility Restoration Act of 2025 continues to progress through Congress in the US, with this Act aiming to reduce the scope of subject matter that is considered ineligible for patent protection. Elsewhere, developments in case law in Europe and the UK can ensure that innovation in new technologies is deemed technical and therefore patentable.

KEY TAKEAWAY POINTS

8.111 The key takeaway points in respect of IP in Industry 4.0 are:

- Currently traditional IP rights will apply to Industry 4.0, which include patents, design rights, copyright, trade secrets, confidential information and trade marks. There are, however, limitations with these as the law needs to keep pace with these emerging technologies and inventions.
- There are legal and practical challenges with patenting some of the Industry 4.0 technologies, not least the amount of disclosure required, and the 'patent bargain' which requires publishing details of the inventions for the benefit of the public.
- Suitable steps are needed to protect IP when there are collaborations between multiple parties.
- Trade secrets are an effective tool in the industrial metaverse. There are strict requirements for these to be classified as trade secrets; however, these can be licensed for use, or retained for use only for the business. When these are licensed, it is vital that the licence is effectively prepared.
- In real-life, companies in the industrial metaverse are likely to use multiple different IP rights in conjunction with each other to cover different aspect of risk and protection.
- When used in the industrial metaverse, it is vital that trade marks cover the virtual aspects of the goods and services to afford the appropriate protection.
- Copyright challenges exist in the training of AI LLM, and we are still waiting on judicial determination or legislative reform to address the position finally on this.

Chapter 9

Smart contracts and contracting in the industrial metaverse

> *'Automation is not a threat to the UK economy; it is one of the greatest untapped opportunities that we have. From boosting productivity to creating high-quality and high-skilled jobs, automation can power our growth, competitiveness and resilience.'*[1]
>
> John Slinger MP

9.1 At a time where much legal uncertainty remains on the subject of Industry 4.0, and globally there is a lack of regulations and determined case law, then the most effective way to try and mitigate against some of these risks is through effective contracts which commercially establish those tricky areas in terms of liability and the parties' different expectations. In fact, basic contractual principles which are often overlooked by seasoned contract lawyers as being trite start to regain importance where we are literally rewriting the way in which businesses can interact. Whilst in principle the use of contracts and reliance on private contract law in the industrial metaverse may give some degree of certainty to stakeholders, and opens the door to effective communications with insurers to underwrite the exposure to risk that will always be present in these evolving markets, what is of fundamental importance is remembering the underpinning contractual principles that remain the benchmark for contracting whether in real-life, through code, or autonomously.

9.2 In the digital space of the industrial metaverse we start to see new forms of contracts, concepts and legal considerations. From the idea of autonomous artificial intelligence (AI) agents being able to enter into contracts without human oversight, to the use of smart contracts concluding chains of contracts as part of the technology itself and contract management records being retained within the blockchain or on a distributed ledger.

9.3 What is of great importance is that lawyers, and the judiciary, keep firmly abreast of the new ways and forms of contracting, and the legal issues that these present.

1 https://hansard.parliament.uk/commons/2025-04-22/debates/3BA9B457-33DC-4EE1-B3A8-510ED3315E9D/AutomationEconomicBenefits.

CONTRACTS AND THE DIGITAL REVOLUTION

9.4 The EU has acknowledged that there are various issues and considerations in respect of contracts as we embark on the digital revolution, especially in respect of emerging technologies and autonomous contracting.[2] The EU Commission notes in particular the emerging use of AI within the contractual process, from pre-contractual discussions through to its autonomous use to conclude contracts.[3]

9.5 The European Parliament's project 'Novel forms of contracting in the digital economy' is important horizon scanning for the key contractual issues that the EU considers of greatest importance as we embark on Industry 4.0.[4]

9.6 Academics consider that the fact that contracts are transacted by emerging technology itself should not be a barrier to them having contractual force, provided they meet the same requirements of a contract under contract law, nor do they believe you need to open discussions around the need for the technology itself to be treated as having had autonomy, nor the need for legal personality.[5]

9.7 Mik considers that the fact that emerging technologies can conclude contracts is not in and of itself a concern in respect of contract formation, and that confusion should not be had between technological narrative and names and their actual legal status. For example, an AI agent may not be an agent in the true legal sense, just as autonomous piece of software does not necessarily mean that there is actual autonomy.[6] She rejects the idea that contracts concluded autonomously should view the software as a separate legal entity, not least because the rendering of liability in this vein would be commercially worthless since the algorithm itself would not have assets to pay over as damages should they be in breach. Even in technological advanced situations humans will have had some input, even if this was to programme a rule for a future time, and that the software is always merely an existential tool of the human, and should be regarded as such when considering contracts concluded autonomously or through emerging technologies.[7]

9.8 The Law Commission, however, in its introduction paper to the idea of AI and the law, confirmed that it would be considering the impact of AI across most areas of law, the novelty of which is principally caused by the lack of

2 https://commission.europa.eu/topics/business-and-industry/doing-business-eu/contract-rules/digital-contracts/innovative-technologies-and-data-contracts_en.

3 https://commission.europa.eu/document/download/a88859a5-2d87-49f7-a3bd-ab2d041b61b1_en?filename=JUST_template_comingsoon_standard_12.pdf.

4 https://www.europarl.europa.eu/doceo/document/BUDG-DT-729851_EN.pdf.

5 Eliza Mik (2020), 'From Automation to Autonomy: Some Non-existent Problems in Contract Law' Journal of Contract Law, 36: 205–226, available at SSRN: https://ssrn.com/abstract=3635346.

6 Ibid.

7 Ibid.

legal personality of AI, and it will also be considering whether that needs to be reformed or not.[8]

AUTONOMOUS CONTRACTING

9.9 Autonomous contracting, with varying degrees of human involvement, is a key concern in the industrial metaverse, and has been seen as an important topic for consideration by both the EU and UN.

THE EU

9.10 As part of its 2025 report commissioned to explore the novelty of autonomous contracting, the EU Commission has made it clear that it needs to review whether there is the need to update national laws and EU harmonised regulations to deal with the intricateness of autonomous contracting.[9] As the technology further evolves, we are likely to see automation with less and less human oversight, and not just pre-programmed automations. The EU Commission considers that this may present even more challenges under the current laws and regulations than the early stages of autonomous contracting does today, especially as we do not necessarily know what changes we can expect from the technology as it continues to evolve and becomes more and more autonomous[10]. The EU Commission strongly considers that there should always be human oversight of all AI contracting systems for them to be trustworthy, notwithstanding the legal obligation under the EU AI Act[11] which requires human oversight under article 14(3) for high-risk systems.[12]

9.11 The EU Commission raises concern (1) that there may become a disparity in respect of autonomous contracting when dealing with different size organisations, (2) around hallucinations when contracting and the incorporation of sensitive data, (3) where the AI technology being utilised means that the output is effectively just a prediction, as represented in Figure 9.1. The risk of contractual mistakes in autonomous contracting is also a serious concern, and the risk that such mistakes may become a perpetuating issue and become part of the training data, often referred to a 'black box effect', where the complexities of the

8 Law Commission (2025), 'AI and the Law: A Discussion Paper', https://cdn.websitebuilder.service.justice.gov.uk/uploads/sites/54/2025/07/AI-paper-PDF.pdf.

9 https://commission.europa.eu/document/download/a88859a5-2d87-49f7-a3bd-ab2d041b61b1_en?filename=JUST_template_comingsoon_standard_12.pdf.

10 Ibid.

11 Regulation (EU) 2024/1689 of the European Parliament and of the Council of 13 June 2024 laying down harmonised rules on artificial intelligence and amending Regulations (EC) No 300/2008, (EU) No 167/2013, (EU) No 168/2013, (EU) 2018/858, (EU) 2018/1139 and (EU) 2019/2144 and Directives 2014/90/EU, (EU) 2016/797 and (EU) 2020/1828 (Artificial Intelligence Act).

12 https://commission.europa.eu/document/download/a88859a5-2d87-49f7-a3bd-ab2d041b61b1_en?filename=JUST_template_comingsoon_standard_12.pdf.

system make it exceptionally difficult to understand how the system is learning leading to concerns around bias.[13]

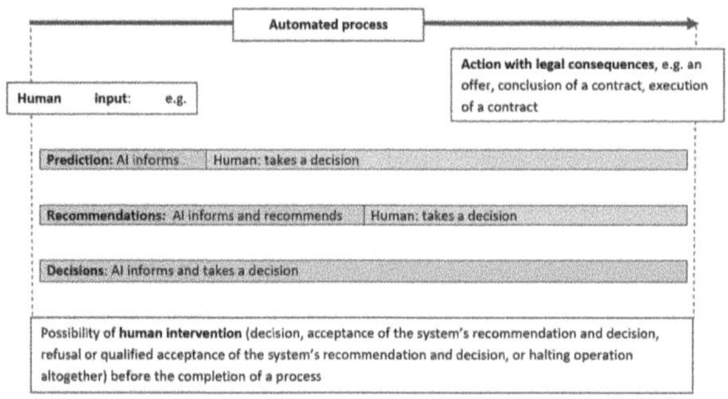

Source: S. Amaral-Garcia, N. Duch Brown, E. Navajas Cawood, and K. Pogorzelska (2025), 'Novel forms of contracting in the Digital Economy (CoDE) AI-enabled autonomous contracting', European Commission, Bruxelles, JRC145138. © European Union, 2025.[14]

Figure 9.1 Visualisation of automated contracting

9.12 As part of its 2025 report into autonomous contracting, the EU Commission specifically considered the use of autonomous AI contracting along the supply chain. This is where it believes that AI automation has significant benefits, such as its use by Amazon fulfilment centres and the future potential of machine to machine contracting within the supply chain.[15]

9.13 The EU has established a forum specifically in respect of AI contracting given the 'questions around potential needs for adaptations of private law, notably contract law to the needs of the digital economy'.[16]

ENGLISH LAW

9.14 Under English Law, we expect that the same position will be applied to autonomous contracting as the Law Commission applied to smart contracts, that is that the common law should be suitable to adapt to the new challenges presented by autonomous contracting; the underlying principles concerning contract law are well settled and technology agnostic. What still will be important, however, will be identifying clearly the different stages of the contracting process, and if (or where) the principles of offer and acceptance can be said to take place, and how this is evidenced. Interesting debate is to be had on the principle concerning

13 Ibid.

14 https://commission.europa.eu/document/download/a88859a5-2d87-49f7-a3bd-ab2d041b61b1_en?filename=JUST_template_comingsoon_standard_12.pdf.

15 Ibid.

16 https://commission.europa.eu/topics/business-and-industry/doing-business-eu/contract-rules/digital-contracts/innovative-technologies-and-data-contracts_en.

the intention to create legal relationships where this is carried out via autonomous agents.

9.15 The issue of AI on the law was considered by the Law Commission in 2025.[17] Given the significant impact of AI in all aspects of law, the paper was purposively a top-level approach to the topic, with acknowledgment that further consideration would become necessary in the future in many different areas impacted by AI. We should expect the issue of autonomous contracting to be considered by the Law Commission in due course, especially with the rise of agentic AI and the risks associated with the same. This may, however, fall more onto a broad consideration of the issue of legal personality of AI and its ability to enter into contracts on its own behalf. More immediate consideration is needed over how the courts should interpret contracts prepared by AI where the parties later contend that it does not accurately reflect the intention of the parties.

THE UNCITRAL MODEL LAW ON AUTOMATED CONTRACTING

9.16 In 2024 the UN published its Model Law on Automated Contracting which was adopted by the General Assembly under resolution 79/119, and under which it acknowledged that the uncertainty concerning the legal effect of autonomous contracts is detrimental to international trade.[18] The UN further released its guide to enacting the Model Law to assist with the implementation of the Model Law. The UN considers that the Model Law should supplement existing state laws on contracting, to make it abundantly clear that existing laws and rules should still apply to automated systems in the same way as they do to non-automated systems, and maintain the freedom of contract principles as in traditional contracts.[19]

9.17 Under the Model Law an "automated system" is defined as 'a computer system that is capable of carrying out actions without the necessary review or intervention of a natural person'.[20] AI agents would fall under this definition, as would other systems used within Industry 4.0, in particular those concerning smart supply chain management.

9.18 The Model Law has been designed as a technological neutral[21] attempt to try and create a uniform approach to dealing with contracts being formed or modified or terminated under an automated system.[22] It critically acknowledges that contracts should not be invalid purely on the basis that they are created using an automated system[23] nor where it does not have a person involved in the

17 Law Commission (n 9).
18 https://www.un-ilibrary.org/content/books/9789211542646/read.
19 Ibid.
20 Article 1(a) General Assembly resolution 79/119.
21 Article 4 General Assembly resolution 79/119.
22 Articles 2 and 3 General Assembly resolution 79/119.
23 Article 5(1) General Assembly resolution 79/119.

process.[24] Further autonomous contracts can be valid even if they consist purely as software code,[25] and the rule of law cannot be avoided on the basis that an automated system was used.[26]

9.19 It goes further to confirm that actions can still be attributed under a contract carried out by an automated system in accordance with the process that is agreed between the parties under the contract,[27] or, where it is not detailed, then it should be attributed to the person who is using the system to carry out that action,[28] regardless of whether the outcome that resulted was unexpected or not.[29] The Model Law provides optional wording to deal with unexpected actions and a blanket position that the parties cannot rely on an unexpected action unless they have agreed otherwise.[30]

SMART CONTRACTS

9.20 A smart contract, despite its name, is not automatically a contract. It is effectively just a piece of software code which brings about an effect automatically. Take the early form of a smart contract, the vending machine, the user makes its selection, pays the price and the machine automatically concludes the transaction and provides the chosen goods. This works in exactly the same way, albeit at a more rudimental level, as a smart contract; the code is programmed to bring about an effect when that pre-programmed trigger is activated. The definition of a smart contract is not settled in law, with the Law Commission even changing its idea on the defining features of a smart contract given the acknowledgment that it should not be incumbent solely on existing technology and instead be wide enough to cover the idea of smart legal contracts which do not necessarily rely on distributed ledger technology and have varying degrees of automation and human involvement.[31]

9.21 It is important to note that a smart contract will only become an actual contract where it meets the legal requirements of a contract, being the need for offer, acceptance, consideration, intention to create legal relations, capacity and sufficient certainty. Without meeting these legal requirements, a smart contract is simply just code.

9.22 Smart contracts bring considerable opportunities in Industry 4.0, and are part of a complex puzzle, especially where there is the practical need for

24 Article 5(2) General Assembly resolution 79/119.
25 Article 6(1) General Assembly resolution 79/119.
26 Article 10 General Assembly resolution 79/119.
27 Article 7(1) General Assembly resolution 79/119.
28 Article 7(2) General Assembly resolution 79/119.
29 Article 7(3) General Assembly resolution 79/119.
30 Article 8 General Assembly resolution 79/119.
31 https://webarchive.nationalarchives.gov.uk/ukgwa/20241223105348/https://lawcom.gov.uk/project/smart-contracts/.

efficiency and transparency. As we progress further into the industrial metaverse and the digital revolution, we can expect to see an increase in the use of smart contracts. Smart contracts and the blockchain are already being utilised for supply chain financing.[32]

9.23 The Law Commission advised the Government in 2021 on the issue of smart legal contracts, concluding that the current UK contract law remain broadly suitable to deal with smart legal contracts and supported the position of Sir Geoffrey Vos and the UKJT Legal Statement that (1) the common law was well equipped to deal with smart legal contracts, (2) there was no need for extensive legal reforms to deal with these types of contracts, and (3) there was no need to introduce novel rules of contract interpretation.[33] That said, lawyers still need to be aware that where smart legal contracts or other forms of autonomous contracts are utilised, there is likely to be the inclusion of software coding and other technological data such as meta data that may not be in natural language. From an evidential perspective, therefore, it is likely that in such circumstances there will be the need to include technological experts to explain this code to a court, especially where it forms the terms of the contract itself.[34]

9.24 There are also significant considerations that must be had when dealing with a dispute around the proper meaning and interpretation of code utilised within a smart contract, with the Law Commission expressing the view that the appropriate test would be to determine what the 'term would mean to a reasonable person with knowledge and understanding of code – that is, a "reasonable coder"... by reference to what the code, in that person's reasoned opinion, appeared to instruct the computer to do'.[35]

9.25 The legal remedy of rectification is likely to be of significant relevance in the context of smart legal contracts, especially where there is an error within the code resulting in an unexpected result. This is, however, a discretionary remedy, and as such will ultimately turn on its facts. Further, you may also see injunctive relief and that of specific performance turning on the issues contained in a smart contract and compelling some forms of automated performance itself.[36]

9.26 The EU Commission has also studied the civil law rules which apply to smart contracts and the lack of national laws of member states in place governing these.[37] It noted that some states had specific prescribed forms for specific

32 https://swoopfunding.com/uk/blog/blockchain-technology-in-supply-chain-finance/.

33 https://webarchive.nationalarchives.gov.uk/ukgwa/20241223105348/https://lawcom.gov.uk/project/smart-contracts/.

34 Ibid.

35 Ibid.

36 https://webarchive.nationalarchives.gov.uk/ukgwa/20241223105348/https://lawcom.gov.uk/project/smart-contracts/.

37 https://commission.europa.eu/document/download/16774905-32c7-49cd-a632-fe4fefdfa4c4_en?filename=JUST_template_comingsoon_standard_10.pdf.

contracts, which could be covered off using a smart contract provided these are carefully considered.

CONCERNS WITH SMART CONTRACTS

9.27 Smart contracts are revolutionary, but there are significant issues associated with these, and 'overcoming these challenges requires not just innovative technology but a comprehensive strategy that includes robust security measures, clear legal standards and adaptive economic policies'.[38]

9.28 Code needs to be properly checked before it is used, with proper measures and audits properly embedded into the process when smart contracts are being adopted since one of the main vulnerabilities of smart contracts is the risks of perverse outcomes where there are coding errors, which presents significant risk of dispute.[39]

9.29 There are also concerns about risks associated with 'oracles'[40] which are used within smart contracts, especially where this information is flawed or defective and results in a skewed resulting smart contract.[41] Therefore, express terms should be included within the agreement that makes it clear where liability should sit in such circumstances. This is important within the industrial metaverse, where smart contracts are deployed and are activated upon certain triggers, typically from external data from an Internet of Things (IoT) or an external source. Where those triggers are wrong or contain faulty information where should the fault lie? Considerations around this will depend to some extent on whether the provider and maintainer of the 'oracle' is complicit in its use for this purpose and party to the contract, and whether there are any express provisions dealing with its use.

DIGITAL ECONOMY AGREEMENTS

9.30 Digital economy agreements are agreements between states, similar to trade agreements, but deal with trying to harmonise digital trade between states. For example, the UK-Singapore Digital economy agreement (DEA) and the Chile, New Zealand and Singapore Digital Economy Partnership Agreement.[42] These are relatively new types of trade arrangements, and are considered a good

38 The World Economic Forum (2024), 'The Rise of Smart Contracts and Strategies for Mitigating Cyber and Legal Risks', https://www.weforum.org/stories/2024/07/smart-contracts-technology-cybersecurity-legal-risks/.

39 Ibid.

40 Which are the data sources which trigger the outcome on the smart contract, such as weather forecasting data from the met office.

41 https://webarchive.nationalarchives.gov.uk/ukgwa/20241223105348/https://lawcom.gov.uk/project/smart-contracts/.

42 https://www.weforum.org/stories/2022/08/digital-economy-agreements-trade/.

approach for the demands of Industry 4.0 and the agile way in which these technologies are evolving.[43]

9.31 The UK-Singapore DEA specifically recognises the need to establish a framework given the pace at which the digital economy moves, and the need for strategic cooperation in respect of this between nations.[44] One significant benefit of trade agreements is the ability to deal with uniformity in dealing with cross-border contracts concluded and/or signed electronically,[45] as discussed below at para **9.33**. It is envisaged that the scope of a DEA can be expanded to cover emerging technologies such as contracts concluded within a virtual industrial metaverse, supply chain contracts concluded autonomously and electronic trade documents being concluded on the blockchain.

CONTRACT ISSUES IN INDUSTRY 4.0

9.32 Despite the technological advances, there are still various contractual restraints that need to be resolved as we progress further into Industry 4.0. The fundamental concerns being the ability of contract law to deal with real-time cross-border transactions which can now be negotiated, executed and completed in an exceptionally short time-frame, digitally, using multiple forms of technology and with a lack of human involvement.

9.33 Not all jurisdictions are equipped at this stage with dealing with electronic contracts, let alone those completed autonomously or with minimal human involvement, for example, some international contracts still require notarisation or have specific formalities or 'wet ink' signing requirements, all of which typically present logistical barriers for emerging technology. There is still no universal approach to electronic contracts, despite a lot of work having been done by the World Economic Forum and the UN on digital trade, and it is expected that these divergences will only seek to deepen as we move more and more into Industry 4.0 and the way in which contracts technologically can be concluded continue to evolve.[46] In addition, there are still interoperability concerns in respect of digital signing tools, and a range of different regulatory approaches between jurisdictions, again which all present challenges in Industry 4.0.[47]

43 Ibid.

44 https://assets.publishing.service.gov.uk/media/6229f350e90e0747aa8eb6ad/CS_Singapore_1.2002_UK_Singapore_Digital_Economy_Agreement.pdf.

45 The World Economic Forum (2017), White Paper 'Making Deals in Cyberspace: What's the Problem?', https://www3.weforum.org/docs/WEF_White_Paper_Making_Deals_in_Cyberspace.pdf.

46 Ibid.

47 Ibid.

UNCITRAL MODEL LAW ON ELECTRONIC COMMERCE

9.34 Although advances in e-commerce technologies do present some challenges, the UNCITRAL Model Law on Electronic Commerce framework published by UNCITRAL does still remain relevant as we progress through Industry 4.0, especially its main principles that electronic contracts, and electronic communications, should be considered valid, and treated in the same way as paper transactions.

9.35 The Model Law on Electronic Commerce was enacted in December 1996 under General Assembly resolution 51/162 and deals with electronic commerce through data exchanges and maintains that data messages should have the same legal effect as other forms of communications,[48] and that this extends to where information is referred to within the data message as opposed to being contained in full.[49] Data messages should be considered as fulfilling requirements as being in writing where it is accessible in the future,[50] and electronic signatures should be valid provided they meet the key criteria that the individual can be identified and it is reliable.[51] The framework further confirms that contractual offer and acceptance can be concluded electronically[52]

COLLABORATION

9.36 The industrial metaverse is built on collaborations. The biggest being the collaboration between Siemens and Nvidia, which continues to grow.[53] As discussed further in **Chapter 8**, there are fundamental contractual intellectual property consideration that need to be addressed within any collaboration agreement, not only who will own the background IP and foreground IP in respect of the project, but limitations around exploitation of the data and restrictions on what each party can and cannot do. Effective contractual provisions are essential in any collaboration.

9.37 It is not only commercial ventures that collaborate in the industrial metaverse. We frequently see collaborations involving universities, as well as a mix of businesses. The Lambert Toolkit acts as a set of model framework agreements for collaborative research projects in the UK, and was initially aimed at providing a framework agreement for collaborations between business and universities. The agreements provide a starting point for dealing with IP ownership. Caution should, however, be had to the model agreements when being used for emerging technologies given these have not been specifically

48 Article 5 General Assembly resolution 51/162.
49 Article 5 bis General Assembly resolution 51/162.
50 Article 6 General Assembly resolution 51/162.
51 Article 7 General Assembly resolution 51/162.
52 Article 11 General Assembly resolution 51/162.
53 https://www.nvidia.com/en-gb/industries/industrial-sector/siemens/.

updated since 2017,[54] and were originally published in 2005.[55] The framework agreements are a helpful starting point for considering the contribution of the different parties to a collaboration. Regard is however needed especially where AI is being utilised within the project, and the contract needs to be able to consider and address some of the specific issues around these, such as ownership rights and right to use training data, and where liability should reside for issues caused by the underlying large language models.

NEGOTIATING CONTRACTS

9.38 Emerging technologies are now also being deployed to negotiate contracts. Walmart trialled the use of chatbots to negotiate certain supplier contractual terms in 2021 and reported positive feedback from over 80% of its suppliers that took part.[56] As part of the three-month trial Walmart was able to reach an agreement with 64% of those participating and reported savings of 1.5% of costs.[57] In 2023, Luminance negotiated an NDA (non-disclosure agreement), demonstrating the benefits of AI negotiations for straight-forward contracts at this stage.[58]

9.39 Disparity is, however, likely to occur in negotiations concluded autonomously between smaller organisations and Big Tech, who will receive the benefit of the learnings and a vast degree of information from the algorithms being utilised to negotiate the deals.[59] Further, it is expected that there will be a greater impact on smaller organisations in dealing with the fundamental shift in negotiations when humans are less involved, or not involved at all and the nuances found in human-to-human negotiations.[60]

KEY TAKEAWAY POINTS

9.40 The key takeaway points in respect of contracting in the industrial metaverse are:

54 https://www.gov.uk/guidance/model-agreements-for-collaborative-research.

55 Intellectual Property Office (2013), 'Collaborative Research between Business and Universities: the Lambert Toolkit 8 years on', https://assets.publishing.service.gov.uk/media/5a74d87540f0b65f61322b32/ipresearch-lambert.pdf.

56 https://commission.europa.eu/document/download/a88859a5-2d87-49f7-a3bd-ab2d041b61b1_en?filename=JUST_template_comingsoon_standard_12.pdf.

57 https://procureconsupplychain.wbresearch.com/blog/walmart-ai-chatbot-automate-supplier-negotiations.

58 Horst Eidenmüller (2025), 'The Advent of the AI Negotiator: Negotiation Dynamics in the Age of Smart Algorithms' Journal of Business & Technology Law, 20(1): 1, available at https://digitalcommons.llaw.umarlyland.edu/jbtl/vol20/iss1/1.

59 Ibid.

60 Ibid.

- The private law, and contracts, are one area where there is still some level of certainty that can be maintained for businesses as we move into the Industry 4.0. That said, there are still likely to be obstacles that have to be overcome as a result of the emerging technology, not least the debate over whether some form of legal personality should be afforded to autonomous systems and whether issues of capacity are relevant in the digital revolution.
- International digital economy agreements can be deployed to agree some of the cross-border limitations, as well as provide a framework for dealing with specific technology.
- Principles have been set at EU and UN level to call on the recognition of autonomously concluded contracts, subject to safeguards.
- Smart contracts are not in and of themselves contracts. They can become contracts provided that they fulfil the legal requirements of a contract. Caution must be had to issues presented by smart contracts in contracting, including determining where liability should sit if something goes wrong, especially where this is data either extracted from an 'oracle' or an IoT device.
- Success has been seen in contracts negotiated autonomously via AI. Safeguards will be required to ensure that they are proper programmes to set clear limits and protocols.

Chapter 10

Environmental law and Industry 4.0

> *'The industrial metaverse has the potential to revolutionize the real world in ways that few technologies can. In this digital world, machines, factories, buildings, cities, vehicles, and entire traffic systems can be mirrored and simulated, enabling virtual testing that conserves resources. The industrial metaverse will help develop sustainable products, as well as more efficient and sustainable factories, buildings, and cities. It will enable the democratization of engineering, allowing everyone to innovate without fearing risks or high additional costs.'*[1]
>
> Peter Körte, Chief Technology & Strategy Officer, Siemens

10.1 There are many environmental benefits of emerging technologies and Industry 4.0. That is not, however, to say that there are not also negatives. The average semiconductor manufacturing facility uses up to 38,000 cubic metres of water a month, which is equivalent to 16 Olympic swimming pools, and over 1 trillion litres of water a year, and data centres use the equivalent energy needed to power California.[2] In manufacturing 3D printing reduces the amount of raw materials used in the manufacturing process, which results in less waste, but it uses more energy than traditional manufacturing.[3] Some dispute that there is conclusive evidence that Industry 4.0 detrimentally impacts sustainability in the long-term,[4] yet it is probably too early to know, what is clear is that the emerging technologies of Industry 4.0 do expend a significant amount of energy and other critical resources.[5]

10.2 Regardless, technology businesses do now have the opportunity to make a positive impact on nature and the environment, and this should be taken up by them not least since, in turn, this will also have a positive knock-on financial impact.[6] Sustainability and environmental consideration are vital considerations for all businesses, not least as the 'younger generations care deeply about

1 MIT Technology Review Insights, 'The emergent industrial metaverse' (2024) https://assets.new.siemens.com/siemens/assets/api/uuid:e36f2de7-f3c4-481f-bb20-9791dc12bbec/the-emergent-industrial-metaverse-update-2024.pdf.
2 World Economic Forum, Nature Positive: Role of the Technology Sector Insight Report 2025 https://reports.weforum.org/docs/WEF_Nature_Positive_Role_of_the_Technology_Sector_2025.pdf.
3 World Economic Forum, Impact of the Fourth Industrial Revolution on Supply Chains (2017) https://www3.weforum.org/docs/WEF_Impact_of_the_Fourth_Industrial_Revolution_on_Supply_Chains_.pdf.
4 Oláh et al, 'Impact of Industry 4.0 on Environmental Sustainability' (2020) Sustainability 12(11).
5 World Economic Forum (n 3).
6 World Economic Forum (n 2).

sustainability'.[7] Many large technology businesses consider it their responsibility to protect the environment and nature through technological advances.[8]

10.3 Policy-makers, do also still need to adopt suitable specific regulation and frameworks to try and mitigate the risks of Industry 4.0 and emerging technologies on the environment given the significant and lasting impact these technologies cause.[9] The adoption of green technologies is now an expectation in many industries rather than just an ideal.[10] Most states are alive to environmental issues facing the world, and have been for some time, with many now having made climate change commitments.[11] This does now, however, still have to be balanced by them with economic considerations and international security concerns given geopolitical changes.[12] Many of the barriers experienced by those seeking to implement green technologies on a large scale, and secure investment and adoption, can be addressed with suitable regulation, the promotion and deployment of 'green finance', and the implementing of global frameworks to set expectations and offer some level of certainty to businesses and innovators.[13]

10.4 Industry 4.0 technology businesses appreciate that they fit within a wider supply chain and business infrastructure, often climate sensitive and sustainability issues are driven by economic drivers from enterprise clients. Sustainability and environmental considerations should be embedded within all businesses, and not simply used as a 'green-washing' marketing opportunity.[14]

10.5 A move to industry 5.0 is often considered to be more focused on sustainability; however, for the purpose of this book, sustainability and environmental matters are considered in the context of the digital industrial revolution as a broader concept than trying to pinpoint those distinct benefits of Industry 4.0 compared to Industry 5.0 and beyond.

7 https://reports.weforum.org/docs/WEF_Green_Procurement_Playbook_2025.pdf.

8 Such as initiatives by Microsoft to utilise novel cooling systems which recycle over 90% of the water in their system and some of the largest data centres have committed to use 100% renewable power https://reports.weforum.org/docs/WEF_Nature_Positive_Role_of_the_Technology_Sector_2025.pdf and Siemens have committed to reaching net zero greenhouse gas emissions by 2050 and is pioneering global initiatives such as its 2021 Zero-Carbon Pioneer Initiative in China https://reports.weforum.org/docs/WEF_Accelerating_Value_Chain_Decarbonization_for_Corporate_Growth_Perspectives_from_Asia_2025.pdf.

9 World Economic Forum (n 2).

10 https://reports.weforum.org/docs/WEF_Scaling_the_Industrial_Transition_2025.pdf.

11 Such as the net zero declaration made by the UK that it aims to achieve net zero by 2050 https://commonslibrary.parliament.uk/research-briefings/cbp-9888/ and China's commitment to reduce emissions by 7-10% by 2035 https://www.weforum.org/videos/china_climate_goal/.

12 https://reports.weforum.org/docs/WEF_Making_the_Green_Transition_Work_for_People_and_the_Economy_2025.pdf.

13 https://reports.weforum.org/docs/WEF_Green_Logistics_Innovation_for_Emerging_Markets_Driving_Competitiveness_and_Shared_Value_2025.pdf.

14 https://www.weforum.org/stories/2025/11/10-years-on-why-some-companies-deliver-on-climate-and-others-don-t/.

ENVIRONMENT ACT 2021

10.6 The Environment Act 2021 sets the framework for environmental law in the UK. It provides for the Secretary of State to set numerous targets,[15] as well as environmental monitoring requirements.[16] The Environment Act 2021 establishes the Office for Environmental Protection,[17] which monitors the implementation of environmental law[18] and advise on changes to environmental law.[19]

10.7 The Environment Act itself requires continuous monitoring in certain areas, such as for storm overflows and sewage disposal works[20] and recycling rates,[21] all of which see a move towards the incorporation of emerging technologies and Industry 4.0 technologies. Many of the national digital twin projects, as discussed in **Chapter 4**, are seeking to address the impact of disasters caused by climate change, such as floods and adverse weather systems. In addition, the Environment Agency is itself also looking to try and utilise emerging technology to try and deal with droughts, and are working with the Alan Turing Institute to create models and incorporate AI as a potential solution.[22]

INNOVATION IN ENVIRONMENTAL PROTECTION

10.8 We are now starting to see environmental bodies themselves also embrace the digital revolution. The Office for Environmental Protection 2024/2025 progress report, which was presented to Parliament in January 2026, calls on the Government to set clear regulations to show the importance of environmental protection, to stimulate growth and innovation and improve practices,[23] recognising the importance of innovations and emerging technology in trying to deal with environmental responses.

10.9 The Government's revised Environmental Improvement Plan was published in December 2025[24], and introduces the use of innovative technology both for regulators, such as the Environment Agency, to monitor those it

15 Sections 1–15.
16 Section 16 Environment Act 2021.
17 Section 22 Environment Act 2021.
18 Section 29 Environment Act 2021.
19 Section 30 Environment Act 2021.
20 Section 82 Environment Act 2021.
21 Section 58 Environment Act 2021.
22 https://www.gov.uk/government/news/latest-science-used-to-tackle-drought-as-rainfall-drives-recovery.
23 Office for Environmental Protection, 'Progress in improving the natural environment in England 2024/2025 January 2026' www.gov.uk/official-documents.
24 https://www.gov.uk/government/publications/environmental-improvement-plan-2025/environmental-improvement-plan-eip-2025.

regulates,[25] and for industry to improve outcomes, especially in areas such as farming pollution and water efficiencies.[26]

10.10 The Digital Waste Tracking initiative, which was introduced under the Environment Act 2021, sees the waste industry in the UK start to transition to digitalisation as part of the digital revolution. The scheme requires the move to digital record-keeping between 2026 and 2027.[27] Innovative Industry 4.0 technologies, such as blockchain and distributed ledger technology (DLT) lend themselves perfectly to the preservation of such data and the need for its integrity in an untampered format.

THE EU

10.11 Article 37 of the Charter of Fundamental Rights of the European Union requires that environmental protection be enshrined within EU policies.[28] The bedrock of the EU's current environmental regulation is the Green Deal which was initiated in 2019. The aim is to halve emissions by 2030 and be carbon neutral by 2050. The policy introduces the Climate Law,[29] and focuses on commitments for the EU on green energy, global competitiveness and trying to reduce carbon emissions.

10.12 The European Climate Law[30] came into force on 29 July 2021 and complements the European Green Deal set out above at para **10.11**, and seeks to achieve the commitments made by the EU as part of the Paris Agreement.[31]

10.13 Interestingly, the Climate Law itself considers that one of the benefits of the regulation is its promotion of the EU's leadership in innovation to combat climate change[32] and considers that there is a currently 'a clean-tech race' between key global powerhouses including the USA, China and India.[33]

25 Such as remote monitoring of farms for regulatory breaches.
26 https://www.gov.uk/government/publications/environmental-improvement-plan-2025/environmental-improvement-plan-eip-2025.
27 https://www.gov.uk/government/publications/digital-waste-tracking-service/digital-waste-tracking-service.
28 Charter of Fundamental Rights of the European Union 2000/C 364/01.
29 https://commission.europa.eu/strategy-and-policy/priorities-2019-2024/european-green-deal_en.
30 Regulation (EU) 2021/1119 of the European Parliament and of the Council of 30 June 2021 establishing the framework for achieving climate neutrality and amending Regulations (EC) No 401/2009 and (EU) 2018/1999 (European Climate Law).
31 Adopted under the United Nations Framework Convention on Climate Change.
32 Recital 7.
33 https://commission.europa.eu/topics/competitiveness/green-deal-industrial-plan_en.

GREEN DEAL INDUSTRIAL PLAN

10.14 As part of the Green Deal, the EU introduced the Green Deal Industrial Plan in 2023. There are four pillars to the Green Deal Industrial Plan, which was described by President von der Leyen as:

> 'first of all, a conducive regulatory environment for the net-zero industries; second, national and EU funding; third, ensuring proper skills for the green transition; and fourth, an ambitious trade agenda'[34]

10.15 The Green Deal Industrial Plan is designed to support EU industries achieve net-zero, and introduces a more streamlined regulatory framework, such as the Net-Zero Industry Act and the Critical Raw Materials Act, as well as providing for greater funding opportunities for green technology businesses.[35]

10.16 The Green Deal Industrial Plan aims to foster innovation in green technologies and to upskill staff on net-zero technology.[36]

NET-ZERO INDUSTRY ACT

10.17 The Regulation of the European Parliament and of the Council on establishing a framework of measures for strengthening Europe's net-zero technology products manufacturing ecosystem and amending Regulation 2018/1724 was adopted in June 2024.[37]

10.18 One of the fundamental objectives of the Net Zero Industry Act is to accelerate the compliance process to reduce administration and speed up the regulatory processes for technology businesses.[38] The focus is on clean-tech and the manufacture of clean-tech, all of which are in some part utilised within Industry 4.0. Key aspects of the regulation is the drive towards greater digitalisation and the industrial metaverse within the EU, in particular, a deep focus on the technologies around batteries.[39]

10.19 The Net Zero Industry Act establishes the Net-Zero Europe Platform to monitor the implementation and enforcement of the Act.[40]

34 https://ec.europa.eu/commission/presscorner/detail/en/statement_23_521.

35 https://commission.europa.eu/topics/competitiveness/green-deal-industrial-plan_en.

36 https://ec.europa.eu/commission/presscorner/detail/en/qanda_23_511.

37 Regulation (EU) 2024/1735 of the European Parliament and of the Council of 13 June 2024 on establishing a framework of measures for strengthening Europe's net-zero technology manufacturing ecosystem and amending Regulation (EU) 2018/1724.

38 https://ec.europa.eu/commission/presscorner/detail/en/statement_23_521.

39 https://commission.europa.eu/topics/competitiveness/green-deal-industrial-plan/net-zero-industry-act_en.

40 Ibid.

NET-ZERO INDUSTRY ACADEMIES

10.20 Net-Zero Industry Academies are established under the Green Deal Industrial Plan as a way of upskilling staff on green technologies.[41] The EU is hoping that the academies will train 100,000 within its first three years, one of which is the InnoEnergy Skills Institute.[42] As discussed further in **Chapter 12**, one of the greatest challenges of Industry 4.0 is the upskilling of staff for the digital revolution, to ensure that the technology is properly adopted in a streamlined manner.

GLOBAL

10.21 Given issues caused by climate change, and nature generally, we have seen a range of different international policies adopted. These policies, reflect the fact that we are going through a digital revolution. For example, UN Resolution 70/125 states that the UN 'recognize that increasing use of information and communications technologies both generates certain environmental benefits and imposes certain environmental costs, which we aim to reduce'.[43]

10.22 The United Nations Sustainable Development Goals (SDG), adopted in 2015 by the UN, includes the use of innovation to overcome environmental and economic issues[44] and for industry to take climate action.[45] Specifically, Goal 9 promotes the building of a resilient, inclusive, sustainable industrial infrastructure and use innovation.[46] Resolution 77/320[47] highlights that emerging technology can help to achieve the SDG. Furthermore, the UN General Assembly resolution 'Seizing the Opportunities of Safe, Secure, and Trustworthy Artificial Intelligence Systems for Sustainable Development'[48] considers that the non-military use of artificial intelligence (AI) can accelerate the SDG and sustainable development.

10.23 The United Nations Conference on Trade and Development considered Industry 4.0 against the SDG in 2022.[49] Its report focuses not only on environmental considerations caused by emerging technologies, but also sustainability and poverty generally in line with the SDG. The report finds that developing countries in particular need to take advantage of Industry 4.0 and develop suitable policies as soon as possible to maximise opportunities and minimise the potential harms, and further that the use of industry 4.0 by

41 https://ec.europa.eu/newsroom/growth/items/823315/en.
42 Ibid.
43 Resolution 70/125, 1 February 2016, item 20.
44 Goal 9.
45 Goal 13.
46 https://sdgs.un.org/goals/goal9.
47 Adopted on 25 July 2023.
48 UN RES/78/265.
49 As was requested by it at the November 2021 meeting of the Science and Technology for Development Commission.

developing countries can help to minimise the impact of industrialisation on the environment.[50] The use of Industry 4.0 to be able to reduce waste, and promote energy efficiencies, should all be embedded into national policies.[51]

10.24 There are many other benefits of the industrial metaverse that can be used to help achieve the SDGs, including using the industrial metaverse to address:

1. poverty through low-cost education;
2. hunger through its use in agriculture, to help with the supply chain and improve farming;
3. health through medical education and its use within healthcare;
4. education through providing cost-effective virtual education;
5. equality through education such as on women's health;
6. clean water by use of education and digital twins;
7. clean energy through digital twins;
8. economic growth through creating virtual workplaces and marketplaces;
9. innovation through testing and trialling products virtually; and
10. facilitate sustainable living through smart cities and digital twins in city and town designs.[52]

10.25 The 2021 UNESCO AI ethical standards emphasise the need for AI systems to protect the environment and state at standard 18:

> 'All actors involved in the life cycle of AI systems must comply with applicable international law and domestic legislation, standards and practices, such as precaution, designed for environmental and ecosystem protection and restoration, and sustainable development. They should reduce the environmental impact of AI systems, including but not limited to its carbon footprint, to ensure the minimization of climate change and environmental risk factors, and prevent the unsustainable exploitation, use and transformation of natural resources contributing to the deterioration of the environment and the degradation of ecosystems'. [53]

10.26 The UNESCO AI ethical standards go even further at standards 84–93 concerning the environment and ecosystems. Under these provisions the standards expect an impact assessment be carried out to consider the impact of the AI system on the environment, both directly and indirectly. The standards specifically highlight the importance of considering the carbon footprints of any AI system, and its impact on raw materials and energy use. The standards highlight the need for the Member States to ensure that AI systems comply with

50 https://unctad.org/system/files/official-document/dtlstict2022d4_en.pdf.
51 Ibid.
52 https://www.iec.ch/basecamp/industrial-metaverse.
53 https://unesdoc.unesco.org/ark:/48223/pf0000381137.locale=en.

environmental law and adopting a precautionary principle, promote the desire to try and use energy saving options.

TECHNOLOGY FOR GOOD

10.27 Use of the different Industry 4.0 technologies, and the integration of technological systems, is beneficial for companies striving to achieve sustainable goals, especially in reducing inefficiencies (which impact negatively on the environment) and to achieve greater monitoring and transparency for record-keeping and analysis.[54] Emerging Industry 4.0 technologies are being utilised to try and address climate change, such as projects building forecasting weather systems with AI,[55] and using sensors to monitor melting icecaps.[56] Industry 4.0 technologies are also seeking to address natural destruction and biodiversity, such as the REEFStoration project, at the Fullerton Ocean Park Hotel, which utilised 3D printed tiles embedded with fragments of coral.[57]

10.28 The OECD updated its recommendations on digital technologies and the environment in 2025.[58] Under these recommendations, the OECD considered:

> 'that digital technologies and their underlying infrastructure can help advance environmental sustainability and combat climate change across sectors, including by increasing energy efficiency, managing scarce resources, monitoring environmental standards and fostering systemic behavioural change …'[59]

10.29 Under the recommendations, the OECD[60] suggests that policies should be created to enhance tech for good and reduce the detrimental environmental impact of emerging technologies. In addition, environmental impact assessments should be carried out, technology utilised for monitoring and modelling of the environment and the technologies environmental impact; and technology should be built as environmentally sustainability by design.[61] Finally, it recommends focusing on the education and upskilling people on green tech and the use of technology for the environment,[62] again reiterating the position that Industry 4.0, as a distinct industrial revolution, requires a change in people, their way of working and education.

54 https://reports.weforum.org/docs/WEF_Green_Procurement_Playbook_2025.pdf.
55 https://www.turing.ac.uk/science-innovation/environment-and-sustainability.
56 https://www.turing.ac.uk/blog/democratising-environmental-forecasting-age-ai.
57 https://reports.weforum.org/docs/WEF_Reimagining_Real_Estate_2024.pdf.
58 https://legalinstruments.oecd.org/en/instruments/OECD-LEGAL-0380.
59 Recitals to OECD's Recommendation of the Council on Digital Technologies and the Environment https://legalinstruments.oecd.org/en/instruments/OECD-LEGAL-0380.
60 https://legalinstruments.oecd.org/en/instruments/OECD-LEGAL-0380.
61 Ibid.
62 Ibid.

GREEN LOGISTICS

10.30 Environmental innovation in the logistic sector, termed 'green logistic' is trying to combat greenhouse gas emissions which, for traditional logistics are responsible for 11% of all global emissions.[63] The global logistic market is anticipated to be worth $8 trillion by 2028 and therefore is a powerful driver of global economic policies.[64] Industry 4.0 sits squarely within the drive for green logistics, and those innovations discussed in **Chapter 6** are some of those seeking to effect change, including automations and 'last mile delivery', which both seek to reduce carbon emissions as a result of their increased efficiencies.[65]

10.31 As an example of 'green logistics' in action, Tianjin Port Second Container Terminal is an automated container shipping port which not only utilises green energy from its wind and solar energy systems, to achieve 100% self-sufficiency and 100% carbon emissions, but also uses specialist robots and autonomous cranes, which are all managed via a centralised system.[66]

MARITIME

10.32 A significant amount of work is already being done to transition to a greener maritime sector, utilising green tech innovations of Industry 4.0. The Maritime Decarbonisation Strategy emphasises the Government's plan to promote the use of technology to cut emissions in the maritime sector and as part of this it has established the UK Maritime Innovation Hub which launched in April 2026.[67] The UK Maritime Innovation Hub, effectively a regulatory sandbox for the marine industry, lists one of its aims is to 'bridge innovation and regulation'.[68] The Maritime and Coastguard Agency (MCA) is also exploring what improvements are required to their regulations to address digital innovation;[69] however, in line with the general attitude of regulating digital innovation, its strategy highlights the reluctance to impede innovation through its policy and regulation, but instead that the Innovation Hub will be used to monitor and enforce compliance.[70]

10.33 The UK SHORE is a UK Government initiative that was established in 2022 to try and reduce greenhouse gas emissions in the maritime sector to

63 https://reports.weforum.org/docs/WEF_Green_Logistics_Innovation_for_Emerging_Markets_Driving_Competitiveness_and_Shared_Value_2025.pdf.
64 Ibid.
65 Ibid.
66 Ibid.
67 https://assets.publishing.service.gov.uk/media/67f4dcb3c2fea2548f4eff64/dft-maritime-decarb-strategy-25.pdf.
68 https://ukshipregister.co.uk/uk-maritime-innovation-hub.
69 https://www.gov.uk/government/publications/mca-areas-of-research-interest/areas-of-research-interest-2025.
70 https://assets.publishing.service.gov.uk/media/67f4dcb3c2fea2548f4eff64/dft-maritime-decarb-strategy-25.pdf.

zero by 2050.[71] The initiative looks to support and invest in innovative emerging technologies to try and drive clean tech in the industry, given the impact of shipping globally on greenhouse gas emissions is higher than that of the UK.[72] The UK National Clean Marine Research Hub, which is a collaboration between 14 UK universities, is designed to try and help decarbonise the shipping sector, with one of its aims being to utilised digitalisation to reduce emissions.[73]

10.34 The UK has also committed to the Clydebank Declaration which is the creation of 'green corridors', which are zero-emission routes between two ports, and in doing so innovative technologies are also being deployed, demonstrating the transition to Industry 4.0 in all maritime sectors, and their use for positive environmental changes as well as innovation and sector disruption.[74]

DIGITAL TWINS

10.35 Digital twins are already being used for environmental initiatives,[75] such as Akila, which is a digital twin aimed at monitoring carbon neutrality targets for the estate management market.[76] The platform is focused on collecting data that relates to carbon emission targets so that changes can be made and then monitored efficiently.[77]

10.36 Digital twins are also being used to look at a wide array of different types of environmental and climate related challenges, such as the SyncED-Ocen project, which is a digital twin using AI to look at harmful alga along the UK coastlines, and FLOODTWIN which assists with the prediction and management of flooding,[78] initially of the Humber Estuary.[79]

GREEN ENERGY AND INDUSTRY 4.0

10.37 Industry 4.0 has the potential to effect environmental change in line with the UN SDG, the move towards green energy and the use of renewable energy in industrial processes.[80] The United Nations Industrial Development Organization

71 https://www.gov.uk/government/speeches/the-future-of-uk-shipping-office-for-reducing-emissions-uk-shorec.
72 https://iuk-business-connect.org.uk/programme/uk-shipping-office-for-reducing-emissions/.
73 https://www.clean-maritime-research-hub.org/about/#our-vision.
74 https://assets.publishing.service.gov.uk/media/67f4dcb3c2fea2548f4eff64/dft-maritime-decarb-strategy-25.pdf.
75 https://www.ukri.org/news/digital-twin-projects-to-transform-environmental-science/.
76 https://reports.weforum.org/docs/WEF_Shaping_Tomorrow_Responsible_Innovation_for_a_Brighter_Future_2025.pdf.
77 https://www.akila3d.com.
78 https://www.ukri.org/news/digital-twin-projects-to-transform-environmental-science/.
79 https://www.hull.ac.uk/research/projects/floodtwin.
80 https://www.unido.org/sites/default/files/2017-08/REPORT_Accelerating_clean_energy_through_Industry_4.0.Final_0.pdf.

calls for a 'joined-up' approach in using the digital revolution of Industry 4.0 to drive changes to the energy system towards sustainability.[81] There is, however, the need for effective regulations and infrastructure, to cover both Industry 4.0 and a move to clean-tech energy.[82]

NATURE

10.38 Many large technology businesses are promoting a 'nature-positive' approach. The idea of a 'nature-positive' approach is to increase nature by 2030 and beyond.[83] This is using a sustainability by design attitude to address the impact of their technology on nature, as well as the use of technology to try and protect the natural world, given the reliance of all businesses on nature.[84]

10.39 The Kunming-Montreal Global Biodiversity Framework was adopted on 19 December 2022 at COP15 in Montreal, Canada, and promotes the use of innovation to try and address biodiversity concerns.[85]

10.40 The World Economic Forum has created a Nature Positive Transitions initiative which promotes a nature-positive approach for businesses to use to try and preserve the Earth's natural resources. Over $44 trillion of GDP is dependent on nature[86] and therefore it is no longer an altruistic pursuit to try and preserve the Earth's resources, but fundamentally rooted in economic considerations. This is especially so with emerging technologies, which, as discussed later in the chapter are heavily reliant on key natural resources and critical raw material such as silicon and water.

10.41 The World Economic Forum makes seven recommendations for preserving nature in Industry 4.0. Whilst focusing specifically on the semiconductor manufacturing industry, data centres and hardware, the recommendations are, however, applicable to all emerging technologies as we transition through the digital revolution. They are:

1. To be mindful of water use, undertake a proper review of the water available at the site and use systems to minimise water waste;
2. Focus on using circular systems to minimise depletion of natural resources and avoid pollution;
3. Reduce emissions and waste through leaks;

81 Ibid.
82 https://www.unido.org/sites/default/files/2017-08/REPORT_Accelerating_clean_energy_through_Industry_4.0.Final_0.pdf.
83 Ibid.
84 https://reports.weforum.org/docs/WEF_Nature_Positive_Role_of_the_Technology_Sector_2025.pdf
85 Target 20.
86 https://initiatives.weforum.org/nature-positive-transitions/home.

4. Promote restoration as a principle, whether this is to the land or the habitat or ecosystem;
5. Use sustainable energy;
6. Have a sustainable supply chain;
7. Secure stakeholder engagement on promoting sustainability and a nature first approach.[87]

10.42 It is important that technology processes and policies encourage sustainability and take into consideration environmental and sustainability issues, remembering at all times that some processes are irreversible and some resources are finite and therefore once depleted are gone forever.[88] Policy for Industry 4.0 should therefore be based on what is termed 'equitable sustainability', a system which understands and appreciates the constraints imposed by the use of natural resources such as energy use and considers the carbon footprint of the technology being deployed in the manner proposed.[89]

NEGATIVE IMPACTS

10.43 Whilst many technologies are seeking to try and improve nature or mitigate climate change, there are also many negative impacts of the digital revolution and adoption of Industry 4.0 technologies on the environment. For example, within the semiconductor industry over a trillion litres of water is used globally, the manufacture of these chips creates a significant amount of waste and greenhouse gas emissions, and the process uses many critical raw materials, such as rare metals and minerals.[90]

DATA CENTRES

10.44 There are serious environmental concerns around data centres, as they use a significant amount of energy and water.[91] Most data centres use on average over 7 million litres of water a day and 1 GW of power; and the uptake in data

87 https://reports.weforum.org/docs/WEF_Nature_Positive_Role_of_the_Technology_Sector_2025.pdf.

88 World Economic Forum, 'The Global Future Council (2024) White Paper on Technology Policy: Responsible Design for a Flourishing World' https://www3.weforum.org/docs/WEF_Technology_Policy_Responsible_Design_Flourishing_World_2024.pdf.

89 Ibid.

90 https://reports.weforum.org/docs/WEF_Nature_Positive_Role_of_the_Technology_Sector_2025.pdf.

91 https://www.berec.europa.eu/system/files/2024-03/BoR%20%2824%29%2052_Draft_Cloud_Report.pdf.

centres are expected to grow 20% year on year until 2030.[92] One reason for the vast use of water is the need to cool the data centres given the high temperatures being produced by the cables, and to preserve the infrastructure. In many locations in the USA, new data centres have been opposed due to environmental concerns.[93]

10.45 In 2018, data centres used over 2% of the energy in the whole of the EU, and it is therefore vital to have suitable commitments to promote sustainable centres from the data centre community itself.[94] The Energy Efficiency Directive 2023,[95] which is part of the EU Green Deal policy, puts an obligation on data centres above a certain threshold to publish their energy footprint,[96] the aim of which is to raise awareness within the industry, to stakeholders and the public.[97] Under the Directive, a common framework is to be created to rate sustainability of data centres.[98] On 14 March 2024, the EU Commission approved Delegated Regulation C(2024)1639 on the first phase of the establishment of a common Union rating system for data centres,[99] which provides for annual reporting requirements on energy consumption, power use, temperatures, waste heat use, water use and renewable energy use.[100]

WATER

10.46 Experts predict that by 2030 there will be a freshwater deficit of 56%, which in turn impacts Industry 4.0, as, amongst other things, 'ultra-pure water' is required for the production of semi-conductor chips.[101] The World Economic Forum has established the Water Futures Community Platform which is designed to address global water challenges[102] given the need to include multiple stakeholders and international partners in any solution, including in collaboration between technologists and law-makers.[103] Digital twin technology, and nanotechnology, are being utilised to innovate water systems and to improve these.[104]

92 https://reports.weforum.org/docs/WEF_Nature_Positive_Role_of_the_Technology_Sector_2025.pdf.
93 Ibid.
94 Recital (13) EU/2023/1791.
95 EU/2023/1791.
96 Recital (85) EU/2023/1791.
97 Recital (87) EU/2023/1791.
98 Recital (153) EU/2023/1791.
99 https://data.consilium.europa.eu/doc/document/ST-7842-2024-INIT/en/pdf.
100 Recital (9) EU/2023/1791.
101 https://www.weforum.org/stories/2025/12/water-growth-era-of-ai/.
102 https://initiatives.weforum.org/water-futures/home.
103 https://reports.weforum.org/docs/WEF_Water_Futures_Mobilizing_Multi_Stakeholder_Action_for_Resilience_2025.pdf.
104 Ibid.

10.47 The EU Water Framework Directive[105] currently deals with the regulation of water within the Union identifying:

> '(1) Water is not a commercial product like any other but, rather, a heritage which must be protected, defended and treated as such …
>
> (4) Waters in the Community are under increasing pressure from the continuous growth in demand for sufficient quantities of good quality water for all purposes.'

10.48 It is likely, however, that this framework will be updated in line with the RESource EU Action Plan, which is the EU's plan to address critical raw materials depletion within the EU.[106]

WASTE

10.49 It is estimated that e-waste will reach 82 billion kg a year by 2030.[107] It is therefore not only the use of natural resources that needs to be considered when responding to the challenges of Industry 4.0, but also how waste is produced by these emerging technologies, the need for effective regulation to deal with this waste and to encourage the creation of truly sustainable technology.[108]

10.50 In 2022, India adopted E-Waste Management Rules which impose regulatory controls on the disposal of waste in the technology sector. In the UK electrical waste is dealt with under the Waste Electrical and Electronic Equipment Regulations 2013 (as amended by the Waste Electrical and Electronic Equipment (Amendment, etc.) Regulations 2025) which puts obligations on distributors in terms of dealing with waste electrical and electronic equipment, and which is overseen by the Office for Product Safety and Standards.

CRITICAL RAW MATERIALS

10.51 Industry 4.0 relies on a significant amount of precious and rare metals and minerals. It is estimated, for example, that data centres will have used up 6% of all global gallium and 2.4% of all germanium by 2035.[109] Semi-conductors, which are the high performing computer chips used within Industry 4.0, contain silicon, gold, silver, gallium, iron, tin and germanium; data centres use aluminium, steel and copper within their systems, and battery systems, used within robotics,

105 Directive 2000/60/EC.

106 https://single-market-economy.ec.europa.eu/document/download/01c448d6-dc93-40d7-9afe-4c2af448d00c_en.

107 https://reports.weforum.org/docs/WEF_Nature_Positive_Role_of_the_Technology_Sector_2025.pdf.

108 https://www3.weforum.org/docs/WEF_Technology_Policy_Responsible_Design_Flourishing_World_2024.pdf.

109 https://reports.weforum.org/docs/WEF_From_Minerals_to_Megawatts_2025.pdf.

Internet of Things (IoTs) and autonomous vehicles, typically contain nickel, manganese, cobalt or lithium, and iron.[110]

10.52 Critical raw materials are vulnerable natural resources, given they are typically found in only a small number of regions, are susceptible to geo-political issues and are finite natural resources.[111] In addition, they are often dangerous and costly to mine, and can take many years to be extracted.[112]

10.53 In one of the biggest indicators yet that we are at the precipice of the digital revolution, many jurisdictions have now taken active steps to protect those critical raw materials essential to Industry 4.0 technologies. For some of these raw materials their supply is limited and can only be found in limited regions globally, such as silicon and lithium, making them extremely valuable within the supply chain.[113]

UK

10.54 Under the Export Control (Amendment) Regulations 2024, the UK restricts the exportation of key semiconductor materials out of the UK without a specific licence.

EU

10.55 The EU implemented the Critical Raw Materials Act[114] in 2024. There are 34 critical raw materials protected under the Act, but this is subject to review in the future, so, as technologies develop it is likely that this list will evolve as well. There are also calls within the EU to promote a circular economy for critical raw materials, so that these can be extracted and then reused within the supply chain.[115]

10.56 In December 2025, the European Commission adopted its RESourcEU Action Plan,[116] which seeks to build on the Critical Raw Materials Act 2024 and creates a European Critical Raw Materials Centre tasked at stockpiling necessary resources for the EU and monitoring developments in new

110 Ibid.
111 Ibid.
112 Ibid.
113 https://www.europarl.europa.eu/RegData/etudes/BRIE/2023/739394/EPRS_BRI(2023)739394_EN.pdf.
114 Regulation (EU) 2024/1252.
115 https://www.europarl.europa.eu/RegData/etudes/BRIE/2024/766253/EPRS_BRI(2024)766253_EN.pdf.
116 https://single-market-economy.ec.europa.eu/document/download/01c448d6-dc93-40d7-9afe-4c2af448d00c_en.

raw materials.[117] In addition, the Plan also seeks to promote the recycling of critical raw materials.

CHINA

10.57 Most semiconductor chips are produced in China, Taiwan, South Korea and Japan, with the highest global producers being China, producing 24% of all semiconductor chips in the world.[118]

10.58 China restricts the export of key minerals used in the production of semiconductor chips, including gallium, antimony, germanium, tungsten, tellurium, indium, bismuth, and certain heavy rare earth minerals.[119] In addition, China has also implemented restrictions on the export of certain equipment that is used for processing rare earth materials.[120]

GLOBAL

10.59 Industry 4.0 and digitalisation cannot scale without resilience within the critical raw natural resources supply chain.[121] The Mineral Security Partnership is a diplomatic and financial initiative formed in 2022 to try and diversify the critical mineral supply chain, of which, amongst others, the USA, the EU, the UK, India, Japan and the Republic of Korea all participate.[122]

10.60 The World Economic Forum has also established the Future-Proofing Global Value Chain Initiative to raise awareness of the vulnerabilities of critical raw materials in the supply chain, as it considers that safeguarding these precious natural resources requires multistakeholder collaboration.[123]

UN

10.61 The equitable exploitation of critical raw materials, in line with the UN sustainability goals and commitments such as the Paris Agreement, is essential to ensure that countries that have these natural materials can benefit from their exploitation.[124] Accordingly, UNECE has drawn up a framework to deal with

117 Ibid.

118 https://reports.weforum.org/docs/WEF_From_Minerals_to_Megawatts_2025.pdf.

119 https://iea.blob.core.windows.net/assets/ef5e9b70-3374-4caa-ba9d-19c72253bfc4/GlobalCriticalMineralsOutlook2025.pdf.

120 https://single-market-economy.ec.europa.eu/document/download/01c448d6-dc93-40d7-9afe-4c2af448d00c_en.

121 https://reports.weforum.org/docs/WEF_From_Minerals_to_Megawatts_2025.pdf.

122 https://www.state.gov/minerals-security-partnership.

123 https://reports.weforum.org/docs/WEF_From_Minerals_to_Megawatts_2025.pdf.

124 https://unece.org/sites/default/files/2021-05/SG%20Policy%20Brief%20Extractives%20NOemb.pdf.

critical raw materials in line with the SDG,[125] which includes the UN Framework Classification for Resources (UNFC)[126] and the UN Resource Management System (UNRMS).[127]

NET-POSITIVE ARTIFICIAL INTELLIGENCE

10.62 Given the amount of energy that is used by AI systems, the World Economic Forum has produced a framework to create AI systems that are deliberately not detrimental to global energy consumption by design and calls on governments to utilise their framework to design systems with sustainability in mind.[128] It also promotes the need for education, collaboration and transparency, and believes that part of the issue is the current lack of consistent international regulations and standards.[129]

THE CIRCULAR ECONOMY

10.63 Experts warn that 'the world cannot meet its expanded renewable and electrification targets without a vastly more resilient and sustainable supply of critical minerals'.[130] As discussed above, Industry 4.0 is a big contributor to the depletion of a significant amount of critical raw materials including lithium and silicon. One way to try and mitigate this is by trying to move towards a circular economy.

10.64 The circular economy focuses on reusing waste, or increasing the continued use of materials, to try and regenerate the world and its natural resources. There is, however, currently a lack of a unified framework suitable for the move over to a circular economy.[131] There is a need for countries to invest not only in the systems, logistics and technology needed, but also to develop suitable regulations and policy.

10.65 Advancements in Industry 4.0 technologies, such as AI, can be used to speed up this transition, by providing key data to scale up the move to a circular economy.

125 https://unece.org/unece-and-sdgs/critical-raw-materials.

126 Which is aligned with SDG and Paris Agreement, and classifies all resources – https://unece.org/sustainable-energy/united-nations-framework-classification-resources-unfc.

127 A framework for resource management, it is principles-based – https://unece.org/sustainable-energy/unfc-and-sustainable-resource-management/unrms.

128 https://reports.weforum.org/docs/WEF_From_Paradox_to_Progress_A_Net_Positive_AI_Energy_Framework_2025.pdf.

129 Ibid.

130 https://www.weforum.org/stories/2026/01/circular-economy-clean-energy-supply-chain-critical-minerals/.

131 https://www.weforum.org/stories/2026/01/what-is-ai-driven-circular-economy/.

10.66 The EU has proposed the adoption of a Circular Economy Act which is intended to be adopted in 2026 as part of its Clean Industrial Deal. This will build on the following framework:

1. Regulation (EU) 2024/1781 of the European Parliament and of the Council of 13 June 2024;
2. Directive (EU) 2024/825 of the European Parliament and of the Council of 28 February 2024 amending Directives 2005/29/EC and 2011/83/EU;
3. Directive (EU) 2024/1799 of the European Parliament and of the Council of 13 June 2024;
4. Regulation (EU) 2017/2394 and Directives (EU) 2019/771 and (EU) 2020/1828;
5. Directive (EU) 2024/1785 of the European Parliament and of the Council of 24 April 2024;
6. Regulation (EU) 2025/40 of the European Parliament and of the Council of 19 December 2024;
7. Regulation (EU) 2024/1157 of the European Parliament and of the Council of 11 April 2024; and
8. revision to the Waste Electrical and Electronic Equipment Directive.

KEY TAKEAWAY POINTS

10.67 The key takeaway points in respect of environmental law and Industry 4.0 are:

- Industry 4.0, and its technology, can positively impact the environment, but can also present novel challenges. Laws and regulations need to keep pace with these to ensure that the digital revolution promotes nature, the environment and sustainability.
- The Government's revised Environmental Improvement Plan in 2025 promotes the use of emerging technologies for effective monitoring of environmental considerations. Many UK environmental initiatives, such as digital waste tracking and UK SHORE, promote the use of digital technologies.
- Data centres require specific consideration in the context of environmental law and Industry 4.0 given the significant water and energy consumption. The EU is establishing a rating system for data centres, who are now required to report on key consumption data.
- Industry 4.0 uses many critical raw materials within its processes. Active steps have been taken by many states to limit the export of these materials.
- Efforts are being taken to try and deploy Greentech, and create a circular economy, to drive forward economies but keep up with climate change commitments.

Chapter 11

Dispute resolution and jurisdictional issues in the industrial metaverse

'Law 4.0 is the inevitable next frontier for law as we navigate digitization, decentralization, the messy transition to clean energy, smart cities, ESG-compliant supply chains, and the coming metaverse. It is the thoughtful use of legal technologies to best help clients and society at large in sustainable development ... As clients, societies and countries march to the digital drummer, the legal community must keep pace.'[1]

James Cooper, Professor of Law and Director of International Legal Studies at California Western School of Law, San Diego & Kashyap Kompella, CFA, technology industry analyst and CEO of RPA2AI

11.1 Combining technologies such as advanced robotics, extended-reality (XR) interfaces, artificial intelligence (AI), next-generation communication networks and the Internet of Things (IoT), the industrial metaverse is where virtual and physical industrial worlds converge. Networked ecosystems enable seamless interaction between humans, machines and digital environments, allowing participants to collaborate and manage operations across borders. From digital twins that mirror real-world assets to cyber-physical systems that facilitate real-time operational control of industrial environments, this convergence offers immense promise for efficiency, safety and sustainability.

11.2 While fully persistent metaverse environments remain in their infancy, related industrial applications are already transforming practice. Airbus's Skywise aircraft monitoring platform,[2] Siemens's GenAI Copilot tools[3] and Shell's offshore oil and gas inspection systems[4] all illustrate how industrial processes can now be monitored, tested and optimised virtually within integrated digital ecosystems using predictive maintenance, defect detection and remote

1 J. Cooper and K Kompella, 'In a Digital World, Industry 4.0 Meets Law 4.0' (The Hill, 13 June 2022), https://thehill.com/opinion/judiciary/3520598-in-a-digital-world-industry-4-0-meets-law-4-0/.

2 Airbus, 'Skywise Core [X]' and 'Skywise Fleet Performance', https://aircraft.airbus.com/en/services/enhance/skywise-data-platform/skywise-core-x and https://aircraft.airbus.com/en/services/enhance/skywise-digital-solutions/skywise-fleet-performance.

3 K. Gallagher, 'Siemens at Hannover Messe 2025: Digital Manufacturing at the Forefront with AI, Digital Twin and Cloud Technologies', https://blogs.sw.siemens.com/nx-manufacturing/siemens-at-hannover-messe-2025-digital-manufacturing-at-the-forefront-with-ai-digital-twin-and-cloud-technologies.

4 M. Horn, 'How Shell Is Using XR and Digital Twins to Transform Deepwater Operations' (2025), https://innovateenergynow.com/resources/how-shell-is-using-xr-and-digital-twins-to-transform-deepwater-operations.

augmented-reality (AR) inspection capabilities. Similar convergence is emerging in other high-precision and high-risk domains including emergency services and healthcare, where metaverse and other immersive technologies are being used to train the likes of firefighters[5] and surgeons.[6]

11.3 Although adoption in the industrial metaverse remains selective and in part experimental, development is accelerating and the potential is vast. In 2024, the World Economic Forum estimated the value of the global industrial metaverse would grow to $100 billion by 2030, with 92% of US manufacturing executives in a 2023 survey claiming to already be experimenting with metaverse use cases.[7] The borderless and decentralised qualities that make this technology so powerful, however, also make it complex from a legal perspective.

QUESTIONS OF JURISDICTION

11.4 The industrial metaverse has the potential to significantly disrupt traditional assumptions about where conduct occurs and how legal authority attaches to it. Questions of jurisdiction generally presuppose identifiable actors, discrete events and conduct that can be readily attributed to a particular place and time. The activities that constitute participation in the industrial metaverse, however, may occur simultaneously across multiple jurisdictions and may be performed partly or wholly by autonomous systems. Where a case contains an aterritorial or omniterritorial element, rules of international jurisdiction become difficult to apply.[8]

11.5 Take, for example, a British manufacturer overseeing a virtual assembly line for electric-vehicle battery modules, hosted on a cloud server in Ireland and linked to IoT sensors monitoring cell-assembly equipment operating in Poland. Each component may be tied to different infrastructure providers, service agreements and terms of use, creating multiple and overlapping legal exposures. In such environments, disputes surrounding the performance of contracts, misuse of data or operating defects may arise in contexts where the notion of a single physical place of performance or harm becomes elusive, particularly if decentralised infrastructures are involved or if parties' interactions are mediated through avatars or algorithmic agents.

5 J. Oliveira and others, 'Exploring Immersive Multimodal Virtual Reality Training, Affective States, and Ecological Validity in Healthy Firefighters: Quasi-Experimental Study' (2024) 12 JMIR Serious Games e53683.

6 P. B. Lowry and others, 'Long Live the Metaverse: Identifying the Potential for Market Disruption and Future Research' (2025) Journal of Management Information Systems, 42(1).

7 World Economic Forum, 'Navigating the Industrial Metaverse: A Blueprint for Future Innovations' (March 2024), https://www3.weforum.org/docs/WEF_Navigating_the_Industrial_Metaverse_A_Blueprint_2024.pdf.

8 Law Commission, *Digital assets and (electronic) trade documents in private international law including Section 72 of the Bills of Exchange Act 1882* (Consultation Paper 273, 2025) para 3.105.

11.6 The use of smart contracts further intensifies this uncertainty. The term 'smart contract' was coined by computer scientist and legal scholar Nick Szabo[9] in the 1990s to refer to automated contractual arrangements. In recent years, the term has come to represent self-executing computer code that can perform obligations automatically when predefined conditions are met. While such automation can enhance trust and efficiency, it also raises difficult jurisdictional questions, such as where, legally speaking, formation and performance of a contract occur and how a forum might assert authority over it. As the Law Commission noted in its 2021 Advice to Government on smart legal contracts, a smart contract recorded solely in code is likely to be the most challenging context in which to apply the current rules and principles of contract formation.[10]

11.7 Machine-to-machine exchanges, now routine for supply-chain interactions such as delivery confirmations, inventory updates and payment instructions, further complicate this picture. When such exchanges represent the performance of a contractual obligation and occur across systems hosted in different jurisdictions, determining which country may hear any resulting dispute becomes considerably more complicated.

11.8 The increasing deployment of AI systems in industrial processes compounds the challenges. Machine-learning systems may autonomously determine when contractual triggers are satisfied or when other procedural events should be actioned. For example, an AI agent may initiate maintenance orders without human involvement when it detects what it perceives to be an anomaly in sensor data.

11.9 In a decentralised, automated industrial ecosystem, existing jurisdictional principles, including the CPR service-out gateways and proper-forum analysis under English law, together with comparative EU rules concerning domicile and the place of performance or harm,[11] may struggle to maintain coherence. Careful reconsideration of these doctrines may therefore be required.

QUESTIONS OF LAW

11.10 Just as the industrial metaverse complicates identification of the competent forum, it also challenges determination of the law that governs transnational relationships. Traditional conflict of laws analysis often relies on establishing a single governing law, ordinarily expressed through contractual choice or inferred from the place of characteristic performance. However, in metaverse environments, relationships are frequently layered across technical, contractual and regulatory boundaries.

9 Nick Szabo, 'Smart Contracts: Building Blocks for Digital Markets' (1996).

10 Law Commission, *Smart Legal Contracts: Advice to Government* (CP 563, 2021) para 7.21.

11 Regulation (EU) No 1215/2012 on jurisdiction and the recognition and enforcement of judgments in civil and commercial matters (recast) [2012] OJ L351/1 (Brussels I Recast).

11.11 A single transaction may incorporate multiple sets of terms: platform conditions imposed by the metaverse host; licensing agreements with software or hardware vendors; data-processing agreements with third-party providers; and industry-specific regulatory obligations. Each may specify a different governing law, or none at all. Even where a given contract designates a governing law, its execution may introduce other elements subject to other regimes, from data protection to export control. Overlaps and conflicts between these risk legal fragmentation.

11.12 Complicating matters further, the applicable law may even be influenced by choices made through code rather than human negotiation. A manufacturer's digital twin might interface automatically with multiple suppliers' inventory systems and logistics networks through standardised APIs[12] or smart contract templates. Each may incorporate its own governing law or implicit regulatory framework. In such configurations, the applicable law could be incidentally fixed by the operation of the technology itself, without human involvement or awareness, through processes that select where supplies are ordered from or which contractual templates execute. The task for courts and tribunals may therefore not simply be to identify a single governing law in the conventional sense, but to determine how the various layers of a transaction interact and whether code-based protocols can acquire binding legal force. The industrial metaverse thereby requires a re-examination of how far the traditional model of a territorially-anchored governing law can accommodate digital relationships.

QUESTIONS OF DISPUTE RESOLUTION

11.13 The borderless and decentralised nature of the industrial metaverse may affect not only the forum or seat of a dispute and choice of law, but also the mechanism by which it is resolved. Traditional approaches to resolving disputes generally depend on identifiable parties, clear procedural frameworks and a physical or institutional forum. Within digital and decentralised environments, these dependencies may be challenged.

11.14 In some contexts, smart contracts can themselves function as de facto dispute resolution or enforcement mechanisms. For example, in escrow arrangements, particularly those involving digital currencies, a self-executing smart contract can be coded to release payment when certain conditions are met (or missed), producing a practically final outcome without recourse to an external tribunal.

11.15 The Law Commission concluded in its 2021 Advice to Government that current legal principles apply to smart legal contracts in largely the same way as they do to traditional contracts and that there was no need for statutory reform.[13]

12 Application Programming Interface (API).
13 Law Commission, *Smart Legal Contracts: Advice to Government* (CP 563, 2021).

While such automation may, however, enhance efficiency and certainty and produce practical finality, it may also bypass conventional procedural safeguards, raising questions about consent, transparency and redress.

11.16 At the same time, some jurisdictions are experimenting with dispute-resolution fora that exist within the very environments this book considers. The Abu Dhabi Global Market (ADGM), for example, has created a mediation service in the metaverse,[14] enabling parties to meet in an immersive virtual space anchored to the ADGM's legal infrastructure. In Dubai, the Rental Disputes Center launched a Metaverse Litigation platform and an AI-driven Judicial Probe service with the aim of allowing litigants to file claims and receive rulings through digital, metaverse-based interfaces.[15]

11.17 These initiatives signal a practical move by some courts and jurisdictions toward a combination of traditional adjudication fora and automated or immersive digital environments. While they remain in their infancy and are limited in their scope, their creation demonstrates that dispute resolution mechanisms themselves are beginning to adapt and respond proactively to the metaverse, rather than waiting passively for it.

WHY THESE QUESTIONS MATTER

11.18 The credibility of any commercial ecosystem depends on the predictability of its dispute resolution framework. The industrial metaverse has enormous potential, though it will only flourish if participants can anticipate their rights, trust that their disputes will be fairly resolved and have confidence that outcomes will be effectively enforced. Without such, companies may be reluctant to engage across borders or to delegate key functions to autonomous systems.

11.19 Procedure, fora and mechanisms for dispute resolution must therefore accommodate the characteristics of this new industrial reality, unifying traditional safeguards with technological innovation. Accountability, jurisdiction and procedural justice must be reconstructed for a world where machines increasingly act as both participants in and objects of legal regulation, and where industrial processes, data flows and decision-making occur simultaneously across physical and virtual spaces, challenging established notions of territory and jurisdiction.

11.20 This chapter considers how jurisdictional principles, choice of law agreements and dispute resolution mechanisms apply to disputes arising within

14 Abu Dhabi Global Market, 'Abu Dhabi Global Market Launches Mediation in the Metaverse' (11 November 2022), https://www.adgm.com/media/announcements/abu-dhabi-global-market-launches-mediation-in-the-metaverse.

15 Dubai Land Department, 'The Rental Disputes Center Launches Metaverse Litigation and Activates the Judicial Probe Service' (2023), https://dubailand.gov.ae/en/news-media/the-rental-disputes-center-launches-metaverse-litigation-and-activates-the-judicial-probe-service/.

the industrial metaverse and where further development of the law may be needed. It has a particular focus on the law of England and Wales, although it offers comparative insights from elsewhere including the European Union.

11.21 The issues explored often fall within the field of private international law; that is, the body of rules that determine which country's courts have jurisdiction and which country's law applies when a dispute contains foreign elements. As will be seen, the industrial metaverse may undermine conventional assumptions of legal relationships being anchored to a territory, through the dispersal of activities across digital networks and decentralised systems with no clear physical locus.

JURISDICTION IN THE INDUSTRIAL METAVERSE

Re-examining the foundations

11.22 Jurisdiction in English and private international law traditionally rests on concepts of territorial connection and personal presence. The English courts have long recognised that physical presence, however brief, may ground jurisdiction.

11.23 In *Maharanee of Baroda v Wildenstein*,[16] the defendant's fleeting presence in England was held sufficient for service despite the substance of the dispute having no connection to the jurisdiction. Although the case predates the modern doctrine of *forum non conveniens* developed in *Spiliada Maritime Corp v Cansulex Ltd*,[17] it illustrates the degree to which the English courts have historically anchored the notion of jurisdiction to physical presence.

11.24 Today, the courts continue to assert authority through territorial jurisdiction, which generally (though not invariably) extends from the defendant's physical presence or conduct within the forum; through consent-based jurisdiction, such as a contractual choice of forum clause binding the parties; or through statutory or regulatory provisions. In the industrial metaverse, however, where activities can be performed entirely remotely or through autonomous systems, and where data flows and actions may lack a fixed geographical locus, concepts of territory and presence can quickly unravel.

11.25 The industrial metaverse is not the first intangible construct to strain territorial reasoning. Courts grappled with similar questions in the mid-20th century when considering the situs of company shares, finding in *R v Williams*[18] that these are situated in the location where the register of members is kept.[19]

16 [1972] 2 QB 283 (CA).
17 [1987] AC 460 (HL).
18 [1942] AC 541 (PC).
19 See also *New York Life Insurance Co v Public Trustee* [1924] 2 Ch 101, 109 (CA) concerning the situs of intangible debts.

11.26 Related difficulties have arisen in the context of cryptocurrency and virtual asset litigation, where the distributed and intangible character of such assets makes their territorial connection hard to define.

11.27 At an interlocutory stage in *Ion Science Ltd v Persons Unknown,*[20] the High Court held that there was at least a serious issue to be tried that the lex situs of a cryptoasset was 'the place where the person or company who owns it is domiciled', notwithstanding that the asset itself is recorded simultaneously on a distributed global ledger. In the later case of *LMN v Bitflyer*,[21] the High Court considered that there was a good arguable case that stolen cryptocurrencies were located in England and Wales at the time of a hack on the basis the claimant was 'resident and carries on its relevant business here', despite its servers being located in Romania. That judicial pragmatism has been matched by procedural reform, with the addition of a new gateway to the Civil Procedure Rules permitting service of claims outside of the jurisdiction where applicants seek disclosure of the true identity of a defendant or what has become of a claimant's property.[22] These developments illustrate a developing willingness to adapt jurisdictional principles to intangible phenomena that lack an obvious geographical anchor.

11.28 Operations within the industrial metaverse, however, push the boundaries even further. Industrial processes involving interlinked digital twins, IoT systems, AI-driven control systems and remote or avatar-mediated operators may act across an even more dispersed and overlapping technical substrate. A single manufacturing transaction might depend on cloud infrastructure hosted in multiple countries, blockchain nodes maintained on different continents and algorithmic decisions made autonomously by systems without a meaningful physical location. The result is a fragmented territorial nexus, which can complicate the task of identifying where conduct occurs and which court or legal system may properly assert authority.

11.29 For litigants and tribunals alike, the practical questions of who or what is present within the forum and where conduct occurs become increasingly difficult to answer.

11.30 The starting point for any action brought in the courts of England and Wales against a foreign defendant is governed by a number of different regimes and considerations. These include:

1. **International treaty obligations**. The Hague Convention on Choice of Court Agreements (2005), for example, requires the chosen court of a contracting state to hear disputes falling within an exclusive choice of court agreement, and requires non-chosen courts of other contracting states to suspend or dismiss competing proceedings, subject to limited exceptions. The Convention applied to the UK through EU membership from 1 October

20 (Unreported, Commercial Court, 21 December 2020).
21 [2022] EWHC 2954 (Comm).
22 CPR PD 6B, para 3.1(25).

2015, and the UK became independently bound following its accession to the Convention in its own right with effect from 1 January 2021. It governs many cross-border contracts incorporating exclusive jurisdiction clauses in favour of the courts of England and Wales, although non-exclusive and asymmetric clauses are generally regarded as falling outside its scope.[23]

2. **Party autonomy**. Under CPR rule 6.33(2B)(b) and (c), where a contract contains a term to the effect that the courts of England and Wales shall have jurisdiction over the relevant claim, proceedings may be served on a foreign defendant without the court's permission. There is no express requirement for the jurisdiction clause being relied upon to be exclusive.

3. **Common law jurisdiction and service-out gateways**. Where no treaty or jurisdiction term applies, common law rules may be used to establish whether proceedings can be served on a defendant outside the jurisdiction with the court's permission. A claimant must establish that there is a serious issue to be tried on the merits, that there is a good arguable case that the claim falls within one of the jurisdictional gateways in paragraph 3.1 of CPR Practice Direction 6B, and that England and Wales is the proper place in which to bring the claim. Applying the principles in *Spiliada*, this ordinarily requires England and Wales to clearly or distinctly be the appropriate forum for the trial. Even where it is not, the court may, however, exceptionally retain jurisdiction if justice requires it. For example, where a claimant would be deprived of substantial justice elsewhere.

4. **Sector-specific conventions and statutory regimes**. Certain categories of international dispute are governed by specialised instruments containing their own jurisdictional rules, such as the Convention on the Contract for the International Carriage of Goods by Road 1956[24] and the Warsaw and Montreal Conventions on international carriage by air.[25] These and other frameworks could, in principle, apply to disputes in the industrial metaverse that involve cross-border logistics or the operation of transport and supply-chain systems that interact through virtual environments because the underlying transport or carriage falls within their scope.

5. **Transitional European instruments**. Where proceedings were instituted before 11.00 pm on 31 December 2020 and therefore prior to the end of the UK-EU post-Brexit transition period, the European regime applies, including Brussels I Recast and the Lugano Convention.[26] Brussels I Recast ceased to apply to new proceedings at the end of the transition period, and the

23 T. Hartley and M. Dogauchi, *Explanatory Report on the Convention of 30 June 2005 on Choice of Court Agreements* (HCCH) paras 32, 105–106. The point is undecided in England and Wales: compare, obiter and under Brussels I Recast, *Etihad Airways Aviation Group PJSC v Flöther* [2020] EWCA Civ 1707, [2022] QB 303 and *Commerzbank AG v Liquimar Tankers Management Inc* [2017] EWHC 161 (Comm).

24 Article 31.

25 Articles 28 and 33, respectively.

26 Convention on jurisdiction and the enforcement of judgments in civil and commercial matters [2007] OJ L339/3 (Lugano Convention).

UK ceased to participate in the Lugano Convention. The UK's application to accede to the Lugano Convention in its own right has not received the support of the European Commission. The continuing relevance of these instruments to the UK is therefore principally transitional.

11.31 Working from the relevant starting point, the court will apply the facts before it to establish any connecting factors and determine the proper forum for a dispute. Within the industrial metaverse, however, this exercise becomes more complex, as the court may need to confront novel questions about what constitutes an agreement in code-based or decentralised transactions, where digital or hybrid acts legally occur, and how traditional connecting factors should be interpreted when physical and virtual operations are intertwined yet span jurisdictions.

11.32 Consider an energy infrastructure project involving an offshore wind farm physically located in Dutch territorial waters, jointly owned by English and Norwegian companies and operated by the English co-owner from England. Software developers employed by the Norwegian co-owner and based in Norway monitor and adjust the wind farm's digital twin, which is hosted on the English co-owner's servers in England. The twin is not merely a monitoring display; it sets the blade pitch, operating speeds and wind thresholds at which the physical turbines shut down. If a calculation error made by the Norwegian company leads to a misconfiguration of the digital twin resulting in damage to the physical turbines, where does the harmful act occur: Norway, England or the Netherlands? The distributed nature of the system means no one jurisdiction provides a wholly satisfactory anchor, with each plausibly asserting a connection.

11.33 In the absence of an applicable jurisdiction agreement between the co-owners requiring otherwise, the English operator may well prefer to sue the Norwegian co-owner in England on the basis that it operates the wind farm from England, the digital twin is hosted on its servers there, and litigating in the home forum carries obvious practical advantages and cost savings. In a decentralised industrial environment, organisational and virtual infrastructural anchors such as these may carry growing significance. The orthodox starting point, however, lies elsewhere. The miscalculation was made in Norway by the Norwegian company's employees, and the general rule under the 2007 Lugano Convention, which governed such claims prior to Brexit, allocates jurisdiction to the courts of the defendant's domicile. Norway would not, however, be the only candidate. In *Bier v Mines de Potasse d'Alsace*,[27] the Court of Justice established that 'the place where the harmful event occurred', which grounded special jurisdiction in tort under article 5(3) of the Brussels Convention and does so in identical terms under article 5(3) of the Lugano Convention, covers both the place of the event giving rise to the damage and the place where the damage occurs. Although the Lugano Convention no longer applies in the UK,[28] its rules are engaged by the

27 Case 21/76, EU:C:1976:166.

28 Save for proceedings instituted prior to the end of the UK-EU transition period at 11.00 pm on 31 December 2020.

defendant's domicile rather than the claimant's, and it continues to apply between the EU and Norway. A claim against the Norwegian co-owner might accordingly be brought by the English co-owner in the Dutch courts as the place where the physical harm to the wind turbines occurred, despite neither of the wind farm co-owners being domiciled there. That forum may hold practical attraction, as a Dutch judgment could be enforced directly against the Norwegian company's interest in the wind farm assets located there.

11.34 For the English operator wishing to sue at home, however, the question does not arise under the Lugano Convention, but under the tort gateway in paragraph 3.1(9) of CPR PD 6B instead. The limb at sub-paragraph (b) is engaged where damage results from an act committed within the jurisdiction. The English company might contend that the operative act causing the damage was the misconfiguration of the digital twin and that this occurred on servers in England.[29] Attributing events on a claimant's own infrastructure to a foreign defendant's conduct is not straightforward though. European authority, for example, has shown some reluctance to treat server location as the place of an event giving rise to damage.[30] The English tort gateway offers an alternative limb, however. Paragraph 3.1(9)(a) asks not where the defendant's harmful act was committed but where damage was sustained, and it is here that recent Supreme Court authority may offer the English operator a more promising route.

11.35 The scope of that alternative limb was considered in the UK Supreme Court's decisions in *Four Seasons Holdings Inc v Brownlie*[31] and, subsequently, *FS Cairo (Nile Plaza) LLC v Brownlie*.[32] Together these judgments illustrate an evolving approach to questions of harm in an increasingly transnational world. In the Court's later judgment, a majority adopted a broad interpretation of 'damage sustained'[33] for the tort service-out gateway. In consequence, in claims for personal injury and fatal accidents, at least, the gateway may be engaged where actionable harm, including continuing bodily effects and consequential financial loss, is sustained in England and Wales, notwithstanding that the wrongful act and initial injury occurred abroad. In this respect the English gateway is now broader than the European rule from which the *Bier* analysis derives.[34]

11.36 Although *Brownlie* arose in a different factual context, its reasoning is conceptually relevant to distributed industrial operations because it confirms that actionable damage resulting from a wrongful act may be sustained in more than

29 See *Ashton Investments Ltd v OJSC Russian Aluminium* [2006] EWHC 2545 (Comm) in which the claimant was held to have a good arguable case that unauthorised remote access from Russia to a London server was a tort committed in England.

30 See, for example, Case C-523/10 *Wintersteiger AG v Products 4U Sondermaschinenbau GmbH*, EU:C:2012:220.

31 [2017] UKSC 80, [2018] 1 WLR 192.

32 [2021] UKSC 45, [2022] AC 995.

33 CPR PD 6B, para 3.1(9)(a).

34 Compare Case C-220/88 *Dumez France SA v Hessische Landesbank*, EU:C:1990:8; Case C-364/93 *Marinari v Lloyds Bank plc*, EU:C:1995:289.

one country. However, whether the broader approach extends beyond claims for personal injury has yet to be authoritatively settled, and the courts have been more cautious where the loss is purely economic and consequential. The majority in *Brownlie* left undisturbed earlier authority under which financial loss merely felt at a claimant's English place of business would not, without more, engage the gateway.[35] The wind farm example sits on that line. The physical damage to the turbines occurred in the Netherlands, and what the English operator sustains in England is the financial consequence of damage suffered elsewhere, unless the corruption of the digital twin data on its English servers can itself be treated as damage. That question engages the contested status of data in English law.[36] The route may nevertheless be the more promising of the two limbs. It turns on characterisation of the harm rather than attribution of the act, and at the gateway stage the English operator need only show a good arguable case. This is a threshold at which the courts of England and Wales have proved willing to entertain novel characterisations of digital things.[37] While this point matters little to the liability of the Norwegian company, it may determine where liability can be tried.

11.37 *Brownlie* also illustrates the difficulties of localising legally significant events in cross-border transactions. In the 2017 proceedings, when addressing the place of formation of a contract concluded through instantaneous communications, Lord Sumption observed, obiter, that the exercise could present 'serious practical difficulties'. Those difficulties are intensified in the industrial metaverse, where digital systems and automated processes may cause harm in one state as a result of decisions, actions or data flows in one or more others.

11.38 Where a contractual choice of forum clause is operative, it will ordinarily bind the parties as an expression of party autonomy. Difficulties may arise, however, where such a clause is introduced or accepted automatically through the operation of digital contracting systems. In these circumstances, uncertainty may arise as to whether consent to the jurisdiction agreement can be attributed to the parties themselves, particularly where the clause is incorporated or accepted by software functioning in the course of automated performance rather than through an explicit act of assent. This issue is considered further in the section on 'Autonomous Agency' (at para **11.58**) which follows.

11.39 Overlapping jurisdictional claims illustrate how traditional doctrines struggle when applied to decentralised industrial systems, with parties potentially

35 *Erste Group Bank AG (London Branch) v JSC 'VMZ Red October'* [2015] EWCA Civ 379.

36 Electronic data has been held incapable of possession and thus of grounding proprietary remedies premised on tangibility: *Your Response Ltd v Datateam Business Media Ltd* [2014] EWCA Civ 281, [2015] QB 41. See also Property (Digital Assets etc) Act 2025, s 1, which confirms that a thing that is digital or electronic in nature may be the object of personal property rights, although it does not determine which digital things qualify. The Law Commission considers that digital files and records are unlikely to qualify in most cases: Law Commission, 'Digital Assets: Final Report' (Law Com No 412, 2023).

37 See the cryptoasset cases discussed at para **11.27** of this chapter.

facing litigation in parallel proceedings in different jurisdictions, raising practical concerns of inconsistent judgments and enforcement issues, quite aside from increased cost. These risks underscore the importance of contractual design (and careful pleading) where industrial systems straddle multiple legal systems. They also expose a deeper challenge: if actions and effects in the industrial metaverse are no longer tethered to territory, what does 'presence' or 'connection' mean for the purpose of asserting jurisdiction?

Algorithmic and digital presence

11.40 Traditional approaches to determining jurisdiction rely broadly on the idea of presence, such as a corporation doing business or maintaining a real and effective establishment within the forum. In England and Wales, the leading modern statement on this approach is found in *Adams v Cape Industries Plc*,[38] where the Court of Appeal observed that a foreign corporation is present if it has a fixed place of business in England and 'for more than a minimal period of time has carried on its own business from such premises by its servants or agents.'

11.41 The industrial metaverse unsettles these assumptions of presence by enabling persistent, cross-border, non-physical operations. Industrial platforms, digital twin environments and remote-monitoring interfaces allow companies to maintain an enduring commercial presence in one country, even when their infrastructure and personnel are in another. For example, a logistics system which is operated from a cloud platform abroad that coordinates outsourced transport, warehousing and data processing within the UK; or engineers or analysts supervising industrial processes through XR dashboards that engage in local economic activity in the UK without ever physically entering the jurisdiction.

11.42 Such phenomena echo debates on electronic presence in the early days of e-commerce, when courts grappled with whether a website's interactivity or targeting could amount to purposeful engagement with, or carrying on business within, the forum. The US decision in *Zippo Manufacturing Co v Zippo Dot Com*[39] famously proposed a sliding scale for questions of jurisdiction, with stronger degrees of 'interactivity' between a website and its users pointing to a company conducting business there. Albeit a simple proposition, and one that has played an important role in internet jurisdiction issues in the United States, the so-called 'Zippo' test has obvious limitations. The technical character of a website is an imperfect proxy for purposeful engagement with the forum. A site's features may be the same wherever it is viewed and therefore its interactivity may connect its operator to every jurisdiction at once and to none in particular, while even a wholly passive site may cause real harm in a given forum.

38 [1990] Ch 433 (CA).
39 952 F Supp 1119 (WD Pa 1997).

11.43 A different control, operating on the tort itself rather than the defendant's presence, appears in English law in *Jameel v Dow Jones & Co Inc*.[40] Publication of an internet article, hosted on servers in New Jersey, was taken to occur where it was downloaded and read. Only a handful of subscribers, however, had accessed the article in England, and the Court of Appeal struck out the claim as an abuse of process on the basis that no real and substantial tort had been committed in the jurisdiction. *Zippo* and *Jameel* arise in different doctrinal settings and apply different tests and standards, although they share a common insight. Bare digital contact with a territory may establish a relevant connecting factor, being purposeful engagement in one setting and publication in another, yet remain insufficient to justify the assumption or continuation of proceedings. Substance, targeting and local harm remain critical.

11.44 The reasoning in these early internet cases foreshadows the challenges of the industrial metaverse. Just as the earlier courts distinguished passive digital presence from substantial engagement, future courts will need to distinguish passive digital functions from active, sustained digital operations that amount to a commercial presence. In Industry 4.0, the question cannot merely be whether a company has infrastructure in England or Wales, but whether its systems operate with continuing effect here, by controlling assets, processing data or executing transactions integral to UK-based industrial activity.

11.45 Such analysis would effectively reframe 'presence' for jurisdictional purposes as algorithmic or digital. A business said to exert a constant digital footprint within a forum, such as through its automated systems, networked IoT infrastructure or large-scale processing of citizens' data, may then be found to be subject to the jurisdiction, despite its physical absence.

11.46 While such significant shifts are not yet recognised, some small movements toward such functional reframing are apparent in the acts of both the judicial and legislative branches of the EU. The European courts, for example, appear increasingly willing to shift their focus from the physical establishment of a non-domiciled defendant to the place where the relevant economic or operational activity is effectively carried out.

11.47 This approach is particularly evident in EU jurisprudence on cross-border data processing, such as in *Google Spain SL v Agencia Española de Protección de Datos*.[41] In *Google Spain*, the Court of Justice looked beyond the identity of the data controller and the location of its servers, both of which were said to be in the US, and asked instead, for the purposes of applying EU law, whether processing was carried out 'in the context of the activities' of an EU establishment.

40 [2005] EWCA Civ 75, [2005] QB 946.
41 Case C-131/12, EU:C:2014:317, [2014] QB 1022.

11.48 Small moves toward recognising functional or digital presence are also apparent in the EU's broader regulatory and fiscal frameworks. In its legislative-initiative resolution adopted on 16 December 2015, the European Parliament called on the Commission to propose a revised definition of 'permanent establishment' to capture significant digital presence where business activities are conducted remotely within the Union.[42] Similar principles underpin Council Directive (EU) 2021/514 (DAC7), which extends the EU's tax transparency regime to online and digital platforms.

11.49 The UK has introduced a comparable scheme, implementing the OECD's Model Rules for Reporting by Platform Operators through the Platform Operators (Due Diligence and Reporting Requirements) Regulations 2023. This regime requires digital platforms to identify and report sellers operating through them, effectively extending accountability to cross-border digital activity.

11.50 Although these measures concern regulatory and fiscal jurisdiction rather than the adjudicatory jurisdiction of civil courts, they illustrate a broader willingness to attach legal consequences to sustained digital or economic activity. This shift may in time influence how the courts approach questions of 'establishment' in the industrial metaverse. If a similar approach were adopted, an operation that maintains a continuous technical and commercial interface with assets or data in the UK or EU might, in principle, constitute a real and effective establishment for jurisdictional purposes, despite lacking human personnel or physical premises there.

11.51 Of course, extending jurisdiction on this basis may risk conflict with principles of comity and predictability, and changes would therefore need to be developed in a coordinated manner by governments to prevent over-expansive assertions of jurisdiction. However, the line distinguishing transient digital contact from enduring operational presence is already becoming more difficult to draw as industrial processes become embedded in globally distributed, data-driven infrastructures. The task of refining traditional notions of territorial connection may therefore fall to the courts and policymakers sooner than anticipated.

Uncertain presence

11.52 It is often said that 'where there is service, there is jurisdiction'.[43] Under the common law rules of England and Wales, valid service of the claim form is ordinarily the foundation of the court's jurisdiction. Where the location of one or more of the parties is uncertain, however, the courts have demonstrated flexibility in effecting service when asserting jurisdiction.

42 European Parliament resolution of 16 December 2015 with recommendations to the Commission on bringing transparency, coordination and convergence to corporate tax policies in the Union (2015/2010(INL)) [2017] OJ C399/74.

43 A. Briggs, *The Conflict of Laws* (4th edn, OUP, 2019).

11.53 In *D'Aloia v Persons Unknown*,[44] the High Court permitted service of proceedings via NFT airdrop to blockchain addresses associated with the defendants, recognising that service methods must evolve with technological realities. Similar pragmatism appeared in *Osbourne v Persons Unknown*,[45] where the Court again authorised service by NFT and email.

11.54 Service by Facebook Messenger, WhatsApp and other novel means has now become so prevalent that in *Tai Mo Shan Ltd v Persons Unknown*,[46] HHJ Pelling remarked that alternative service by NFT was 'in accordance with a growing body of authority permitting service by that alternative means in cryptocurrency frauds of this nature'.

11.55 Decisions such as these demonstrate a judicial willingness to adapt methods of service so as to achieve effective notice through technological channels where a defendant's physical location is indeterminate. In the industrial metaverse, this may acquire growing practical significance.

11.56 However, in *Tai Mo Shan*, HHJ Pelling noted an important potential limit to such developments: CPR rule 6.40(4) provides that nothing in paragraph (3) or any court order authorises or requires any person to do anything which is contrary to the law of the country where the claim form or other document is to be served. As HHJ Pelling observed, 'There is a potential risk therefore that such a person may be located in a country where it is contrary to the law of that country to serve process by means other than that authorised by the law of the country concerned.' While the judge considered such a risk to be rare, this possibility underscores the importance of parties mitigating the risk in the industrial metaverse by means of prior written agreement where possible.

11.57 In the industrial metaverse, greater formality for participation may be expected, reducing the risk of presence uncertainty; however, it remains conceivable that marketplaces or other transactional environments may emerge through which, for example, support services or ancillary functions may be provided, potentially on an anonymous basis, with suppliers identified only by untraceable usernames. In *Boonyaem v Persons Unknown*,[47] the High Court refused an application for summary judgment against certain crypto-fraudster defendants who the Court did not regard as identifiable persons. An earlier disclosure order had not succeeded in revealing the individuals within a particular group of perpetrators, and the Court therefore held that judgment could not properly be entered against them. That decision stands in contrast to *Mooij v Persons Unknown*,[48] in which the High Court granted summary judgment against an unidentified but sufficiently defined category of persons unknown following effective alternative service. The two authorities therefore diverge,

44 [2022] EWHC 1723 (Ch).
45 [2023] EWHC 39 (KB).
46 [2024] EWHC 1514 (Comm).
47 [2023] EWHC 3180 (Comm).
48 [2024] EWHC 814 (Comm).

although on either view anonymity does not itself preclude the commencement of proceedings or interim relief. The critical question is whether final judgment additionally requires the relevant defendants to be identifiable, or only that they be defined with sufficient precision and effectively served. In the industrial metaverse, English procedural rules may therefore permit jurisdiction to be asserted and interlocutory relief granted even where participants' names are unknown; however, final judgment and effective enforcement may face further obstacles.

Autonomous agency

11.58 While human acts in the industrial metaverse may present challenges, a defining feature of Industry 4.0 is the autonomous or semi-autonomous operation of AI systems within industrial processes. Such systems can detect anomalies, optimise production workflows and even initiate maintenance orders without direct human intervention. This autonomy raises two interrelated questions for jurisdictional purposes. First, can AI agents enter into binding contracts? Second, who is the 'actor' for jurisdictional attribution where AI is involved? These questions formed part of the broader problem of legal accountability for AI identified by the UK Government in its Study on the Impact of Artificial Intelligence on Product Safety (2021),[49] among others.

11.59 English law has long accepted that contracts may be formed by automated means. As early as *Thornton v Shoe Lane Parking Ltd*,[50] the Court of Appeal accepted that a contract could be formed by the operation of a machine without contemporaneous human involvement. Lord Denning MR observed that the car parking ticket machine concerned constituted an 'offer', which the customer accepted, demonstrating that mechanical or electronic contracting mechanisms can embody effective legal intention.

11.60 Building on this reasoning, the courts of England and Wales have since treated contracts formed through electronic systems as valid, provided these reflect a human principal's intention to be bound. In *Golden Ocean Group Ltd v Salgaocar Mining Industries Pvt Ltd*,[51] for example, the Court of Appeal confirmed that a contract identified from a sequence of negotiating emails could constitute an agreement in writing. This principle is also reflected domestically in the Electronic Commerce (EC Directive) Regulations 2002, which implement the EU E-Commerce Directive 2000/31/EC and recognise that contracts may be concluded by electronic means.

49 Office for Product Safety and Standards, *Study on the Impact of Artificial Intelligence on Product Safety* (2021), https://assets.publishing.service.gov.uk/media/628b58e3d3bf7f1f3aa5c13b/impact-of-ai-on-product-safety.pdf.

50 [1971] 2 QB 163 (CA).

51 [2012] EWCA Civ 265, [2012] 1 WLR 3674.

11.61 In *R (Software Solutions Partners Ltd) v HM Customs & Excise*,[52] the High Court accepted that an offer made by insurance software, without human intervention, was an 'automatic medium for contract formation'. This case informed, in part, the Law Commission's conclusion in its 2021 Advice to Government on smart contracts that the current legal framework in England and Wales is clearly able to facilitate and support the use of smart legal contracts, without the need for statutory law reform.[53] In each of the above cases, an automated system operated on only one side of the transaction. Even where the actor on both sides of the formation of a contract is non-human, the courts have however continued to analyse the resulting contractual situation as an ordinary contract concluded by, and attributable to, the humans or corporate parties who deployed the system. The Singapore Court of Appeal's decision in *Quoine Pte Ltd v B2C2 Ltd*,[54] while not binding in the UK, is frequently cited comparatively. The Court applied ordinary contract principles to its analysis of cryptocurrency trades executed by algorithms that were challenged on grounds of mistake, focusing its decision on whether the algorithms reflected their programmers' intentions.

11.62 The Singapore Court's findings in *Quoine* concerned deterministic algorithms operating according to rules fixed by their programmers, and therefore provide only a partial answer to more difficult questions raised by contemporary automated systems, including agentic AI and other adaptive systems. AI agents may plan and execute sequences of actions, interact with external tools or systems and pursue specified objectives with limited human supervision. Adaptive systems may also produce outputs or develop modes of operation that were not specifically anticipated by those who designed or deployed them. These capabilities complicate conventional notions of agency and legal attribution.

11.63 At present, none of the major legal systems considered by this chapter recognise AI as a bearer of legal personality for contractual purposes. In the United States, the Uniform Electronic Transactions Act (UETA), albeit drafted in 1999 with far simpler automated systems in mind, treats 'electronic agents' as mechanisms for effecting the intent of a natural person or legal entity. The position in the European Union is materially the same. The European Parliament briefly considered the creation of an 'electronic personhood' for sophisticated autonomous robots in order to facilitate the allocation of liability where no human could be clearly identified.[55] The concept was however widely rejected[56]

52 [2007] EWHC 971 (Admin).

53 Law Commission, *Smart Legal Contracts: Advice to Government* (CP 563, 2021) paras 1.26–1.28.

54 [2020] SGCA(I) 02.

55 European Parliament resolution of 16 February 2017 with recommendations to the Commission on Civil Law Rules on Robotics (2015/2103(INL)) [2018] OJ C252/239.

56 European Parliament, *European Civil Law Rules in Robotics* (Study, 2016), https://www.europarl.europa.eu/RegData/etudes/STUD/2016/571379/IPOL_STU(2016)571379_EN.pdf.

and found no replacement in the EU AI Act,[57] which instead continues to attach obligations to natural and legal persons.

11.64 The EU AI Act does not form part of the law of England and Wales. If an English court were required to determine the legal consequences of an act executed through AI, it would do so without an equivalent domestic statutory framework, and would have to apply existing principles of contract, agency, negligence, product liability and statutory responsibility to the natural or legal persons involved. In many cases, this is likely to involve attributing the legal consequences of the AI system's operation to the person or entity deploying or benefiting from it. A sector-specific example of this attribution is evident in the Automated Vehicles Act 2024, which establishes a framework for the safe deployment of self-driving vehicles in Great Britain.

11.65 Once the Act is fully implemented, every authorised automated vehicle will have an 'authorised self-driving entity' responsible for its behaviour while self-driving, typically the manufacturer or software operator. The automated system is not treated as a legal person or agent, but as a product whose use and outcomes are legally attributed to its human or corporate developer, operator or insurer. This legislative model illustrates a policy of locating responsibility in identified human or corporate actors, rather than in the automated system itself.

11.66 Transposed by analogy to the industrial metaverse, this model suggests that, even where automated systems exceed what was initially anticipated, jurisdictional connection should nonetheless attach to the person or entity that exercises effective control or derives benefit from the automated process. Such an approach would ensure that those harmed can pursue redress and would prevent the autonomy of the system from creating a gap in legal responsibility, even where the causative act was executed by code.

Reconceptualising jurisdiction

11.67 The industrial metaverse challenges the concept of jurisdiction as a singular territorial attachment, recasting it as a multidimensional construct encompassing human actors, autonomous agents, technological infrastructures and economic influence. Traditional private international law reasoning presupposes that conduct can be localised and attributed to identifiable legal persons. Industrial metaverse activity may however operate through distributed digital networks in which decision-making, execution and data storage are fragmented across multiple actors and states.

11.68 Faced with these challenges, substantial changes to jurisdictional doctrine may be perceived as necessary. Jurisdictional overreach, however,

57 Regulation (EU) No 2024/1689 laying down harmonised rules on artificial intelligence [2024] OJ L, 2024/1689 (EU AI Act).

presents its own set of issues and could compromise the willingness of the courts to enforce judgments obtained outside the jurisdiction. The question is therefore not whether territoriality should be abandoned when considering jurisdiction. Rather, it is how it should adapt and be re-layered to reflect the different forms of presence and connection that may arise in the industrial metaverse, where and when appropriate.

11.69 Despite repeated predictions of the death of geography in cyberspace,[58] territoriality remains the organising principle of jurisdiction, albeit the premise is increasingly strained by technological development. Courts across several jurisdictions have already confronted tensions analogous to those which may arise in Industry 4.0. For example, in *Berezovsky v Michaels*[59] the English courts treated publication as occurring wherever the material was read, an approach subsequently extended to online publication, which was held in *King v Lewis*[60] and *Richardson v Schwarzenegger*[61] to occur in any jurisdiction where material was downloaded.

11.70 In *Dow Jones v Gutnick*,[62] the High Court of Australia adopted a similar approach. The CJEU's approach in *eDate Advertising GmbH v X and Olivier Martinez and Robert Martinez v MGN Limited*[63] developed these principles further, by allowing claimants to bring proceedings either in the courts of the publisher's establishment or those of the claimant's centre of interests, or alternatively in each Member State in which the online content was accessible for the damage caused in that state. This approach recognises that in networked environments, multiple locations may share a connection to the dispute.

11.71 These cases illustrate the durability and the elasticity of territorial reasoning, with the law adapting questions of jurisdiction to the realities of diffuse activity. Consistent with broader currents in the literature on internet jurisdiction,[64] however, courts confronting the industrial metaverse may need to layer questions of jurisdiction with additional forms of presence and connection. These might include the following, offered as possible lines of development rather than statements of current law, several of which would require extension of, or departure from, existing authority:

1. **Human presence or connection**. Traditional domicile, residence and establishment remain the anchor for personal and corporate accountability, and even in decentralised systems, someone often designs, deploys or benefits from the infrastructure such that human presence can be located.

58 D. Johnson and D. Post, 'Law and Borders: The Rise of Law in Cyberspace' (1996) 48 Stanford Law Review 1367.

59 [2000] 1 WLR 1004 (HL).

60 [2004] EWCA Civ 1329.

61 [2004] EWHC 2422 (QB).

62 [2002] HCA 56,

63 Joined Cases C-509/09 and C-161/10, EU:C:2011:685.

64 Dan Jerker B. Svantesson, 'A New Jurisprudential Framework for Jurisdiction: Beyond the Harvard Draft' (2015) 109 AJIL Unbound 69.

The question of whether a decentralised collective is capable of being sued has already arisen. In *CFTC v Ooki DAO*,[65] the US District Court for the Northern District of California held that a decentralised autonomous organisation was a voluntary group of people united by mutual consent for a common purpose and without a formal charter, and as such was an unincorporated association amenable to suit, permitting service through the DAO's own online help chat and discussion forum. The case illustrates that the human substrate of an ostensibly autonomous system can remain legally reachable. Precisely how human presence is established may need to adapt for the industrial metaverse; however, its substantial utility in establishing jurisdiction will remain important.

2. **Infrastructural presence or connection**. As industrial processes increasingly depend on globally distributed network infrastructures, data centres and sensors, these may need to be considered as creating a territorial anchor. Existing authority points the other way, cautioning against treating the location of servers as a sufficient territorial anchor.[66] Industrial infrastructure however differs in kind from passive hosting. Sensors and actuators embedded in local operations do not merely record activity within a territory, they perform it. In an industrial metaverse context, courts may therefore need to regard the maintenance of infrastructure that enables or supports industrial activity as establishing sufficient connection for jurisdictional purposes, even if the operating entity is itself outside the territory.

3. **Digital presence or connection**. Persistent algorithmic or data operations within a territory present a new reality in which digital activity might be said to constitute a form of 'establishment' in the jurisdiction. Such an approach might draw by analogy on the *Somafer SA v Saar-Ferngas AG*[67] conception of a branch or establishment as a centre of operations manifesting itself with sufficient permanency as an extension of the parent body. When considering digital non-physical infrastructures, existing authority holds that the mere accessibility of a website within a jurisdiction does not amount to an establishment existing there.[68] Where an industrial platform however consistently processes local data, interacts with local devices or provides services to local enterprises, the analogy with a place of business becomes materially closer than mere accessibility. Courts may therefore come to recognise a digital establishment where a platform's operations within the territory exhibit the permanence and business function that *Somafer* requires of a physical one.

4. **Proprietary presence or connection**. The location of assets within the territory has long supplied a jurisdictional anchor, and paragraph 3.1(11)

65 *Commodity Futures Trading Commission v Ooki DAO*, No 3:22-cv-05416-WHO (N.D. Cal., 20 December 2022).

66 Case C-523/10 *Wintersteiger AG v Products 4U Sondermaschinenbau GmbH*, EU:C:2012:220.

67 Case 33/78, EU:C:1978:205.

68 Case C-191/15 *Verein für Konsumenteninformation v Amazon EU Sàrl*, EU:C:2016:612.

of CPR PD 6B provides a gateway where the subject matter of the claim relates wholly or principally to property within the jurisdiction. In the industrial metaverse, the significance of this connection is likely to grow rather than diminish, but difficult questions arise as to where an intangible asset is located and whether it is property at all. As discussed earlier in this chapter, the courts have proved willing to recognise certain cryptoassets as property[69] and attribute situs to them by reference to the residence or domicile of their owner, notwithstanding that the asset itself subsists on a distributed global ledger. Comparable questions will arise for the assets native to industrial virtual environments, including digital twins, sensor data streams and virtual inventories. Some may fail the threshold question of proprietary status altogether, being closer to pure information than to the digital things the courts and Parliament have recognised. For those that do qualify, however, the situs-attribution reasoning developed for cryptoassets could be extended with the location of an industrial digital asset perhaps fixed by reference to its owner's residence, the operational centre of the system in which it functions or the physical assets to which it is tethered, allowing the property gateway to operate in virtual environments as it does in physical ones.

5. **Functional presence or connection**. Recognising significant operational effects in a territory as a form of functional connection would align with the effect-based doctrines found elsewhere in the law, such as the 'targeting' principle in EU data protection law and the 'minimum contacts' analysis found in US jurisprudence.[70] A defendant that purposefully directs digital or automated industrial activity towards a state, deploying systems that predictably affect assets or operations there, should expect to answer for it before that forum's courts.

6. **Economic presence or connection**. Where digital operations are directed toward a particular market, the resulting economic activity may be considered to supply a jurisdictional nexus. This approach is already visible in areas of tax reform, including the UK's digital services tax, which remains in force at the time of writing and taxes certain revenues of search engines, social media services and online marketplaces deriving value from UK users, including where the relevant company is non-resident. Where cross-border Industry 4.0 systems, though technically located abroad, create or derive substantial economic value within a domestic market, this might suffice for the purpose of jurisdiction.

11.72 These different layers are not discrete or freestanding tests. They could assist courts and policymakers however in calibrating jurisdiction flexibly for the industrial metaverse. Greater attention might therefore be given to where a

69 This position has now received statutory confirmation. Section 1 of the Property (Digital Assets etc) Act 2025 provides that a thing, including a thing that is digital or electronic in nature, is not prevented from being the object of personal property rights merely because it is neither a thing in possession nor a thing in action.

70 *International Shoe Co v Washington*, 326 US 310 (1945).

business is effectively operated or targeted and where its economic or operational effects are felt, rather than the place of its incorporation or physical establishment.

11.73 The proposed approach has analogies in regulatory law which looks beyond physical territorial presence to allocate responsibility. Data protection regimes such as the General Data Protection Regulation, for example, reach controllers and processors outside the Union where their processing relates to offering goods or services to individuals within it or to monitoring their behaviour there.[71]

11.74 It would still be necessary to ensure that jurisdiction was properly founded in any particular case, given the likely heightened importance of cross-border recognition and enforcement of judgments in the industrial metaverse. A court asked to recognise or enforce a foreign judgment will apply the relevant treaty, statutory or common law regime, and recognition will commonly depend on whether the originating court exercised jurisdiction on a basis accepted under that regime. Any expansion of jurisdictional principles in response to the industrial metaverse will need to be appropriate and sufficiently predictable if resulting judgments are to be recognised and enforced abroad. Despite these concerns, however, an incremental reconceptualisation of jurisdictional principles may be needed if the industrial metaverse is to deliver a commercially viable ecosystem.

Applicable law in the industrial metaverse

11.75 Party autonomy, manifested through an express choice of governing law, is a cornerstone of modern conflict-of-laws doctrine.[72] In the industrial metaverse, however, commercial relationships are often layered across technical, contractual and jurisdictional boundaries that may make a single, clear governing law difficult to identify.

11.76 Industrial metaverse ecosystems are likely to involve interoperability and data-sharing arrangements between manufacturers, software vendors and infrastructure providers. These may comprise a cloud-service contract governed by one law, a licensing agreement for a digital twin governed by another, and sensor or analytics-service terms subject to a third.

11.77 When disputes arise, for example, over data quality or the consequences of an automated shutdown, courts must identify which governing law applies across this stack of interrelated obligations. Before the courts of England and Wales, the governing law of each contract is determined under the assimilated

71 Regulation (EU) No 2016/679 on the protection of natural persons with regard to the processing of personal data [2016] OJ L119/1 (GDPR), art 3(2).

72 Regulation (EC) No 593/2008 on the law applicable to contractual obligations [2008] OJ L177/6 (Rome I).

Rome I Regulation.[73] Where the parties have made a valid choice of law, that choice is given effect. In its absence, article 4 designates the applicable law through a cascade of rules turning principally on the type of contract and the habitual residence of the party effecting the characteristic performance, subject to displacement where the contract is manifestly more closely connected with another country.[74]

11.78 These rules operate contract by contract. Rome I designates a governing law for each bilateral relationship in isolation; it contains no mechanism for subjecting a multi-party ecosystem to a single law. In the industrial metaverse, that architecture matters, as participants may interact through standardised interfaces or platform terms that evolve dynamically, without negotiation or conscious agreement on governing law. The article 4 default rules, rather than deliberate party choice, may then apply. The result, even before blockchain, automation or AI add further complexity, is that a system experienced by its participants as unified may be parcelled out among several systems of law.

11.79 Consider an English vehicle manufacturer developing components through a shared digital twin platform. The platform is operated by a cloud services provider with its central administration in Germany; the manufacturer uploads aerodynamic models and simulation data to it; and a supplier with its central administration in India manufactures the components to the designs held on the platform. All parties perceive the digital twin environment as a single, integrated industrial workspace. Legally, however, it sits atop a stack of distinct bilateral contracts, each capable of attracting its own governing law.

11.80 At the base layer, the platform service agreement between the English manufacturer and the German cloud provider would ordinarily be characterised as a contract for the provision of services. Before an English court, and in the absence of an express choice of law, article 4(1)(b) of Rome I designates the law of the service provider's habitual residence, that being German law, unless the contract is manifestly more closely connected with another country, as per article 4(3).[75]

11.81 At the supply layer, and assuming the component manufacturing agreement between the English manufacturer and the supplier in India is properly characterised as a contract for the sale of goods, article 4(1)(a) of Rome I would ordinarily point to the law of the seller's habitual residence, namely Indian law, again subject to the manifestly more closely connected exception under

73 Rome I and Rome II were retained in UK law (now, as amended, 'assimilated law') by the European Union (Withdrawal) Act 2018, as amended by the Law Applicable to Contractual Obligations and Non-Contractual Obligations (Amendment etc.) (EU Exit) Regulations 2019, SI 2019/834.

74 Rome I, arts 3 (choice of law) and 4 (applicable law)

75 The analysis would be substantively the same before the courts of an EU Member State applying the EU Regulation, as the relevant provisions are materially identical to those of the assimilated Rome I.

article 4(3). It is immaterial that India is neither an EU Member State nor a party to any Rome instrument; article 2 gives the Regulation universal application.

11.82 Now assume that simulation data corrupted by the German cloud service causes a manufacturing defect in India, and, once the components are integrated into vehicles at the manufacturer's English plant, physical damage and production losses in England, prompting a product recall. The resulting disputes could engage three distinct systems of law:

1. German law in relation to the allegedly defective data service contract;
2. Indian law in relation to the manufacturing obligations; and
3. English law in relation to non-contractual claims for the direct damage sustained in England and Wales.[76]

11.83 No single governing law may apply to the overall digital twin ecosystem, nor would a court be likely to seek to impose one. Instead, it would generally be expected to identify the legally distinct contractual and non-contractual claims and determine the law applicable to each relationship or issue by reference to its characteristics and closest connection. The outcome is a mosaic of governing laws regulating what the participants perceive as one seamless, integrated industrial environment.

11.84 In the industrial metaverse, even routine cross-border data flows can generate overlapping legal regimes, forcing courts to identify not only where performance occurs, but which contractual layer governs the contested obligation.

11.85 A related, but increasingly relevant, issue arises from platform-imposed terms. Industrial metaverse participants often access shared environments via software-as-a-service licences or IoT dashboards, whose terms of use purport to designate a particular governing law. These terms may not be individually negotiated, though may form the default framework for participation.

11.86 Under English law, incorporation by reference is valid only where the referenced terms are accessible and brought to the other party's attention. Classic authorities include *Interfoto*,[77] which requires prominent notice of unusual or onerous terms, and *Thornton v Shoe Lane Parking Ltd*[78] which prevents terms being introduced after contract formation. The same principles apply in digital contracting environments, where industrial users may assent to terms through online enrolment or API registration, without ever reading the legal provisions. The situation is analogous to the early jurisprudence on click-wrap versus browse-wrap agreements. Agreements are generally considered enforceable

76 Under article 4(1) of assimilated Rome II, the law applicable to a non-contractual obligation is, as a general rule, that of the country in which the damage occurs, irrespective of the country of the event giving rise to it.
77 *Interfoto Picture Library Ltd v Stiletto Visual Programmes Ltd* [1989] QB 433 (CA).
78 [1971] 2 QB 163 (CA).

where assent is explicit, though of questionable enforceability where consent is passive or ambiguous. In more recent online cases such as *Parker-Grennan v Camelot UK Lotteries Limited*,[79] the Court of Appeal upheld the incorporation of terms where the user flow gave sufficient, timely notice, while in *Andrew Green v Petfre (Gibraltar) Ltd (t/a Betfred)*,[80] exclusion terms failed where presentation was convoluted or unclear.

11.87 A related concern is that the operation of technology may, without contemporaneous human involvement or awareness, select the counterparty, contractual template or platform terms from which the applicable law is subsequently determined. In *Quoine Pte Ltd v B2C2 Ltd*,[81] the Singapore Court treated transactions executed by deterministic algorithms as attributable to the parties who deployed them, where the systems operated according to parameters fixed by their programmers. This was so notwithstanding that no human had reviewed or approved the individual transactions at the time they were executed.

11.88 When validly incorporated, platform-imposed terms may offer predictability and reduce negotiation costs in the industrial metaverse. They may also however relocate the locus of consent from the contracting parties to the platform architects and programmers. This raises questions about incorporation, the validity of consent and the allocation of contractual risk where key terms result from system design rather than negotiated intention.

Dispute resolution

11.89 The resolution of disputes within the industrial metaverse must operate across a landscape that is both technically complex and legally fragmented. Activities occur simultaneously across jurisdictions and may involve actors who never meet, obligations and agreements that exist only in code and transactions that are executed by machine rather than human hands.

11.90 In his 2022 lecture on 'The Future for Dispute Resolution: Horizon Scanning',[82] Master of the Rolls Sir Geoffrey Vos presented his view of the next 20 years in civil litigation, observing that 'The smart systems that already drive our online digital justice system will, of course, become much smarter'. Sir Geoffrey also repeated, in his speech, his view that integrated (alternative) dispute resolution processes can and should be driven by AI, although he questioned how far parties and the public would be willing to trust machine-driven dispute resolution processes.

79 [2024] EWCA Civ 185.
80 [2021] EWHC 842 (QB).
81 [2020] SGCA(I) 02.
82 Sir Geoffrey Vos MR, 'The Future for Dispute Resolution: Horizon Scanning' (Sir Brian Neill Lecture, Society for Computers and Law, 17 March 2022), https://www.judiciary.uk/wp-content/uploads/2022/03/MR-to-SCL-Sir-Brain-Neill-Lecture-2022-The-Future-for-Dispute-Resolution-Horizon-Scannings-.pdf.

11.91 Whether Sir Geoffrey's fuller predictions for the future of the justice system come to pass, it is clear that traditional models of adjudication will need to adapt to reflect the pace and structure of Industry 4.0 disputes.

Litigation

11.92 Litigation remains the foundation of legal accountability, providing authoritative judgments, precedent and the coercive power of the state. For disputes however arising within the industrial metaverse, the traditional strengths of litigation may also reveal its limits. The cross-border, data-intensive, technologically advanced and often automated nature of industrial metaverse operations brings three particular tensions into focus: first, the practical difficulties of enforcing judgments across jurisdictions; second, the competing imperatives of open justice and commercial confidentiality; and third, the challenge of procedural adaptation to digital evidence and distributed parties.

11.93 *Adams v Cape Industries Plc*[83] illustrates the practical limits when it comes to the cross-border enforcement of court judgments. The US claimants had obtained a substantial judgment in Texas against an English company. When enforcement was sought in England, however, the Court of Appeal held that the judgment was not enforceable because the company had neither been 'present' within the jurisdiction of the Texan court nor submitted to it. The case remains a powerful reminder that a judgment valid in its state of origin may nevertheless be denied recognition where the originating court's jurisdiction does not satisfy the enforcing state's rules of international competence. This risk is particularly relevant to Industry 4.0, where assets and operations may be distributed across multiple jurisdictions.

11.94 As between the UK and Europe, cross-border enforcement was facilitated by the European regime, latterly Brussels I Recast. That regime ceased to apply to the UK at the end of the Brexit transition period, save for the recognition and enforcement of judgments given in proceedings instituted before the end of the transition period. While the UK has applied to accede to the Lugano Convention, the European Commission has declined to support its application. Two instruments of the Hague Conference on Private International Law have therefore assumed increased importance.

11.95 The Hague Choice of Court Convention 2005, to which the UK acceded independently on 1 January 2021, provides that where parties have an exclusive jurisdiction clause in favour of the courts of a contracting state, judgments of those courts must be recognised and enforced by others. It thereby provides a treaty-based mechanism for cross-border enforcement that closely parallels,

83 [1990] Ch 433 (CA).

for litigation, the function that the New York Convention 1958[84] performs for arbitration. The EU, Singapore, Mexico and Switzerland are among its current contracting parties.[85] However, the Convention is confined to exclusive clauses and civil or commercial matters, leaving significant areas of industrial activity outside its scope.

11.96 The more recent Hague Judgments Convention 2019, which entered into force for the UK on 1 July 2025, extends that protection beyond exclusive choice-of-court agreements. It provides for the recognition and enforcement of civil and commercial judgments more broadly, including those based on non-exclusive clauses or certain tort claims, subject to defined exceptions. Although its geographic reach is not yet as wide as the New York Convention, its adoption marks a significant step towards a more predictable enforcement regime for litigants operating across decentralised industrial ecosystems. For a UK claimant whose counterparty lacks assets in the jurisdiction, these frameworks may determine whether a judgment is an enforceable instrument or merely declaratory.

11.97 Nonetheless, substantial gaps remain. Important trading states with heavy digital infrastructure or data-processing presence, such as the United States, China and several Asia-Pacific economies, are not presently bound by either Convention in their relations with the UK. Consequently, English judgments may still face uncertainty. Arbitration, with its far greater enforcement network under the New York Convention, retains a comparative advantage in this respect.

11.98 A second tension arises from the public nature of court proceedings. English civil procedure is founded on the principle of open justice, enshrined in CPR rule 39.2 and given enduring expression by Lord Hewart CJ's dictum in *R v Sussex Justices, ex parte McCarthy*,[86] that 'not only must justice be done; it must also be seen to be done'. The presumption of publicity serves democratic accountability, ensuring that the administration of justice occurs in the public eye.

11.99 For industrial metaverse disputes, open justice may present a genuine dilemma. Many such disputes will engage with sensitive technical materials, such as proprietary algorithms, control data or digital twin models representing critical infrastructure. Public disclosure of that material could expose valuable intellectual property or even safety-critical information. Courts may manage those risks through measures such as private hearings for specific evidence and the restricted publication of some judgments. Complete secrecy and wholly closed hearings nevertheless remain exceptional.

11.100 When it comes to procedure, procedural law in England and Wales has already evolved toward digitisation, which may assist industrial metaverse

84 Convention on the Recognition and Enforcement of Foreign Arbitral Awards (New York, 1958).

85 HCCH, 'Status Table: Convention of 30 June 2005 on Choice of Court Agreements', https://www.hcch.net/en/instruments/conventions/status-table/?cid=98.

86 [1924] 1 KB 256.

disputes where participants, data and infrastructure are more likely to be geographically dispersed and evidence is more likely to be stored digitally. For example, the Civil Procedure Rules permit electronic service, online filing and remote hearings. Together with initiatives such as the HMCTS Reform Programme, these point towards an ever-more digitised civil justice system. The Online Procedure Rule Committee, established under the Judicial Review and Courts Act 2022, has now made the first Online Procedure Rules. The Online Procedure (Rules and Practice Directions) Rules 2026 come into force on 7 September 2026 and will initially apply to specified possession proceedings. They represent the first implementation of a unified procedural framework for specified online civil, family and tribunal proceedings. These developments signal an institutional commitment to a 'digital by default' justice infrastructure.

11.101 Litigation will continue to play a vital role in shaping the legal landscape of the industrial metaverse, as it is within the courts that the principles of jurisdiction, attribution, consent and liability for automated conduct will be tested and articulated. The parties however will need to approach it with a clear understanding of its limitations. The enforcement of judgments remains patchwork and procedural transparency may sit uneasily with industrial confidentiality. Where these constraints are unacceptable, arbitration or technologically embedded dispute resolution mechanisms may provide more suitable alternatives. Nonetheless, litigation's role as the authoritative, precedent-setting mechanism will ensure it remains central to the development of law in Industry 4.0.

Arbitration

11.102 Arbitration has long served as a leading forum for the resolution of transnational commercial disputes, valued for its flexibility, confidentiality and enforceability under the Convention on the Recognition and Enforcement of Foreign Arbitral Awards 1958 (the New York Convention). These characteristics make it particularly apt for industrial metaverse disputes, which often involve parties from multiple jurisdictions and sensitive data. The cornerstone of international arbitration remains the New York Convention, to which over 170 states are now parties. It requires contracting states to recognise written arbitration agreements and to enforce arbitral awards subject only to narrow exceptions, such as incapacity, procedural irregularity or violation of public policy. Few international instruments in private law have achieved such breadth or practical reliability.

11.103 From a metaverse perspective, this global enforceability is significant. Where industrial processes, data and participants are dispersed across borders, it may be unpredictable at the outset where assets will ultimately be located or where an award may need to be enforced. Reflecting on the cross-border wind farm example provided earlier in this chapter, it may be that a defendant's assets are not even located in the territory where they operate, and that enforcement may therefore need to occur in a third country. The New York Convention provides a network of legal interoperability for cross-border enforcement that national court judgments, even under the Hague Conventions, cannot yet replicate.

11.104 For this reason, arbitration clauses remain a principal means by which commercial parties might mitigate the enforcement uncertainty inherent in the distributed operations of Industry 4.0. A well-drafted arbitration agreement can create a pathway for enforceable outcomes and reduce some of the territorial complexities that the industrial metaverse introduces. That benefit however may be undermined where interdependent contracts, such as those involving platform operators, cloud providers, software developers, sensor suppliers, manufacturers and logistics providers, do not contain coordinated dispute resolution provisions. Joinder or consolidation will ordinarily depend on consent, compatible arbitration agreements and the applicable institutional or procedural rules.

11.105 For arbitrations commenced on or after 1 August 2025, the statutory framework for arbitrations seated in England and Wales has been modernised by the Arbitration Act 2025, which amended the Arbitration Act 1996. Among its reforms, the Act clarifies the law governing the arbitration agreement. Unless the parties expressly agree that a particular law applies to that agreement specifically, it is governed by the law of the arbitral seat, and a choice of law for the wider contract does not, without more, amount to such an express choice.[87] The rule has particular value for technologically layered transactions. Suppose, for example, that a components manufacturer runs its production line through an industrial metaverse platform licensed under a contract governed by Californian law, and acquires the sensor-equipped machinery that feeds data to that platform under a supply contract governed by South Korean law, each contract providing for London-seated arbitration. Despite those differing governing laws, both arbitration agreements are now governed by English law as the law of the seat. The validity, scope and effect of each arbitration agreement, including whether it reaches claims in tort, are accordingly measured against a single law, rather than varying with the governing law of each host contract.

11.106 The 2025 Act also strengthens the procedural adaptability of arbitrations seated in England and Wales. It gives tribunals an express power to make an award on a summary basis upon the application of a party where a claim or issue has no real prospect of succeeding,[88] reinforces the effectiveness of emergency-arbitrator procedures[89] and clarifies the courts' powers to grant relief in support of arbitration, including against third parties.[90] These reforms may prove valuable in industrial metaverse disputes, where urgent intervention, efficient disposal and access to evidence or assets held by infrastructure providers may be particularly important.

87 Arbitration Act 1996, s 6A, inserted by Arbitration Act 2025, s 1.
88 Arbitration Act 1996, s 39A, inserted by Arbitration Act 2025, s 7.
89 Arbitration Act 1996, s 41A, inserted by Arbitration Act 2025, s 8, with consequential amendments to ss 41, 42, 44, 82 and 83.
90 Arbitration Act 1996, s 44, as amended by Arbitration Act 2025, s 9.

11.107 Confidentiality is another of arbitration's defining characteristics. Unlike civil court proceedings, which are public by default, arbitral hearings are ordinarily private and awards are typically not published. Under English law, an obligation of confidentiality is generally implied in relation to the proceedings, evidence and award, as in *Ali Shipping Corporation v Shipyard Trogir*,[91] where the Court of Appeal recognised an implied obligation of confidentiality arising from the private nature of arbitration. The scope of confidentiality obligations however remains subject to recognised exceptions, including consent, court order, reasonable necessity for the protection of a party's legal rights and the interests of justice.

11.108 For industrial metaverse disputes, confidentiality serves both commercial and technical imperatives. The evidence in such cases may include proprietary source code, process algorithms or confidential operational datasets. Arbitration offers a means of adjudication that can preserve secrecy over these materials while still providing a binding and enforceable resolution. In practice, of course, parties should not rely solely on the implied obligation. Express confidentiality clauses are advisable.

11.109 A further strength of arbitration lies in its capacity to accommodate technological change without legislative intervention. The modern rules of major arbitral institutions have already evolved to permit fully digital procedures. The London Court of International Arbitration (LCIA) Rules 2020, for example, provide that all written communications shall be delivered electronically unless otherwise directed,[92] explicitly authorise remote or hybrid hearings[93] and allow for electronic signatures of awards.[94] Similarly, the International Chamber of Commerce (ICC) Arbitration Rules 2026, which entered into force on 1 June 2026, confirm that hearings may be held 'in hybrid form or by videoconference, teleconference or other form of electronic communication',[95] that written communications with the Secretariat are ordinarily to be made electronically[96] and that awards may be signed electronically.[97] The World Intellectual Property Organization (WIPO) Arbitration and Mediation Centre, which specialises in technology and intellectual property disputes, has gone further, developing online case management and hearing facilities.[98] US dispute resolution provider JAMS has also published specialised rules and model clauses addressing AI,[99] smart contract and digital asset[100] disputes. Such procedural flexibility makes

91 [1999] 1 WLR 314 (CA).
92 LCIA Arbitration Rules 2020, art 4.2.
93 LCIA Arbitration Rules 2020, art 19.2.
94 LCIA Arbitration Rules 2020, art 26.2.
95 ICC Arbitration Rules 2026, art 27(1).
96 ICC Arbitration Rules 2026, art 3.
97 ICC Arbitration Rules 2026, art 38(1).
98 World Intellectual Property Organization, 'WIPO eADR', https://www.wipo.int/amc/en/eadr/wipoeadr/.
99 JAMS, 'Dispute Resolution in the AI Age: The New JAMS AI Rules' (2025), https://www.jamsadr.com/blog/2025/dispute-resolution-in-the-ai-age-the-new-jams-ai-rules.
100 JAMS, 'Smart Contract and Blockchain Disputes', https://www.jamsadr.com/smartcontracts.

arbitration inherently compatible with disputes connected to the industrial metaverse. Arbitration's emphasis on procedural autonomy also permits parties to tailor their proceedings to a technological context. Arbitral rules rarely constrain how evidence may be presented, allowing for innovations such as interactive data visualisation and expert walkthroughs of virtual environments. This capacity for bespoke procedure may prove crucial in industrial metaverse cases, where there may be vast quantities of machine-generated evidence, or where the conduct complained of must be reconstructed from AI outputs or in a virtual setting.

11.110 While arbitration is adaptable, its legitimacy depends on the impartiality and independence of the tribunal. The UK Supreme Court's decision in *Halliburton Company v Chubb Bermuda Insurance Ltd*[101] confirmed the duty of an arbitrator to disclose circumstances that might reasonably give rise to justifiable doubts as to impartiality, especially where overlapping appointments may create an appearance of bias. The Arbitration Act 2025 has since placed the disclosure duty on a statutory footing.[102] It applies to relevant circumstances of which a prospective or appointed arbitrator is aware or ought reasonably to be aware. In the context of industrial metaverse disputes, where a limited pool of technical experts may serve repeatedly as arbitrators, the principle is likely to take on additional significance, and the parties should expect robust disclosure of prior engagements within the same technological or factual ecosystem.

11.111 At the same time, arbitration's system of party appointment enables the constitution of a tribunal with subject-matter expertise that may be difficult to replicate in generalist courts. In disputes concerning digital twins, autonomous control systems or machine-learning processes, the ability to appoint arbitrators with engineering, data science or sector-specific experience may improve the efficiency and quality of decision-making and assist the tribunal in evaluating competing expert evidence.

11.112 Arbitration offers a procedural architecture that aligns closely with the structural characteristics of the industrial metaverse. Although legally anchored to a seat and governed by institutional or ad hoc procedure, it remains sufficiently flexible to accommodate cross-border parties, complex digital evidence and technological change. Its broad enforceability through the New York Convention addresses one of the most intractable challenges of digital industrial operations: the uncertainty of cross-border recognition and enforcement and therefore the extent of a court's reach. In addition, its procedural autonomy accommodates the presentation of complex digital evidence and the use of emerging technologies in case management. Where supported by law, the parties' agreement or applicable institutional rules, obligations of confidentiality may also safeguard the proprietary and operational data that are likely to lie at the heart of many metaverse disputes. Arbitration is therefore a mechanism that participants in the industrial metaverse would be well-advised to consider.

101 [2020] UKSC 48, [2021] AC 1083.
102 Arbitration Act 1996, s 23A, inserted by Arbitration Act 2025, s 2.

Online and autonomous dispute resolution

11.113 The digital transformation of commerce has long been accompanied by efforts to deliver equally digital forms of justice. What began as a pragmatic response to the transactional scale of e-commerce has, over three decades, evolved into a more ambitious project: the automation of adjudication itself. In the industrial metaverse, where transactions are coded, data may be decentralised and performance executed without human intervention, dispute resolution too may become embedded in technological systems.

11.114 Online Dispute Resolution (ODR) emerged in the 1990s alongside the rise of internet commerce. Early models were largely administrative, with web-based interfaces for negotiation and mediation designed to handle high volumes of consumer claims. The non-binding UNCITRAL Technical Notes on ODR (2016) provide a major international reference point for this field, defining ODR as 'a mechanism for resolving disputes through the use of electronic communications and other information and communication technology'.[103] The Notes emphasise accessibility, transparency, fairness and accountability as the essential safeguards of legitimacy, while recognising that technological processes can enhance speed and efficiency in cross-border contexts where jurisdictional diversity would otherwise frustrate resolution.

11.115 In the three decades since its emergence, the scope of ODR has widened. Some jurisdictions are even experimenting with immersive online dispute resolution environments. The ADGM has established a Mediation in the Metaverse service, providing a virtual space anchored to the ADGM's legal infrastructure, within which mediations can take place via avatars in a three-dimensional environment.[104] In Dubai, the Rental Disputes Center has launched a Metaverse Litigation platform alongside separate AI-enabled services including a Judicial Probe Service,[105] designed to permit filing, hearing and even judgment issuance within a digital interface. Their significance lies not in the novelty of the environments, but in the attempt to integrate immersive digital spaces into formal procedural frameworks. Each forum remains that of a recognised jurisdiction, applying its substantive and procedural law; however, its interface with the parties is through digital immersion. For industrial metaverse disputes, where the disputed conduct may itself have occurred within virtual environments,

103 UNCITRAL, Technical Notes on Online Dispute Resolution (2016) para 24, https://uncitral.un.org/sites/uncitral.un.org/files/media-documents/uncitral/en/v1700382_english_technical_notes_on_odr.pdf.

104 Abu Dhabi Global Market, 'Abu Dhabi Global Market Launches Mediation in the Metaverse' (11 November 2022), https://www.adgm.com/media/announcements/abu-dhabi-global-market-launches-mediation-in-the-metaverse.

105 Dubai Land Department, 'The Rental Disputes Center Launches Metaverse Litigation and Activates the Judicial Probe Service' (2023), https://dubailand.gov.ae/en/news-media/the-rental-disputes-center-launches-metaverse-litigation-and-activates-the-judicial-probe-service/.

such hybridity may be more than symbolic, helping to ensure that adjudication remains accessible, efficient and contextually relevant.

11.116 Whereas early ODR platforms mirrored traditional processes in digital forms, later systems have sought to integrate technology into the adjudicative logic itself. For example, automated negotiation tools incorporating AI[106] have blurred the distinction between human procedure and machine process. In the industrial metaverse, where obligations may be defined and executed by code, ODR may no longer sit outside the transaction but within it. A contract, its performance and the dispute mechanism could all potentially operate through the same digital infrastructure.

11.117 This shift gives rise to a new category of autonomous dispute resolution, where automated processes may implement pre-programmed consequences that affect the parties' practical rights through the operation of code. The technical foundations of this development lie in the use of smart contracts, where self-executing code performs obligations when pre-programmed conditions are met. In industrial contexts, smart contracts may automatically release payments upon confirmation of delivery or allocate costs when a system failure occurs, for example.

11.118 The novel feature of such disputes is that the same code that performs the contract may also execute its enforcement. An autonomous system could, in principle, reallocate digital assets or record rights on a distributed ledger and thereby produce and enforce a practically final outcome without recourse to any external adjudicator. Such mechanisms blur the distinction between performance and enforcement, however, and raise questions concerning the remedies available for error or fraud. The procedural safeguards that characterise judicial oversight, such as appeal, review or stay of execution, have no natural counterpart in code.

11.119 The UK Jurisdiction Taskforce's Digital Dispute Resolution Rules (DDRR),[107] published in 2021, attempt to mediate this tension. They recognise that parties to a smart contract may agree to have disputes resolved by a tribunal capable of implementing its decision directly on-chain using a private key. However, the Rules preserve the parties' ability to anchor that process to a legally recognisable form of adjudication. By default, this is by means of the decision taking effect as an arbitral award capable of recognition under the Arbitration Act 1996.[108] In this way, the on-chain process remains referable to a forum that the legal system of England and Wales will recognise and whose outcomes can be supervised or enforced through ordinary legal mechanisms.

106 ODR.com, 'Ethics in Online Dispute Resolution: Balancing Technology and Human Judgment' (2025), https://odr.com/ethics-in-online-dispute-resolution-balancing-technology-and-human-judgment/.

107 UK Jurisdiction Taskforce (UKJT), Digital Dispute Resolution Rules (2021), https://lawtechuk.io/ukjt/digital-dispute-resolution-rules/.

108 As amended by the Arbitration Act 2025.

11.120 In autonomous dispute resolution systems, adherence to the fundamentals of procedural fairness, including principles commonly associated with natural justice, becomes a question of design. An algorithmic decision-making process intended to produce a legally enforceable adjudicative outcome must be auditable, transparent and explainable to the parties it affects. The growing body of regulation surrounding artificial intelligence, notably the EU AI Act, reinforces these principles, classifying certain AI systems intended for the administration of justice as 'high risk'[109] and requiring robust human oversight, traceability and accountability.[110] Even though the Act does not form part of the law of England and Wales, its approach reflects a broader international consensus that, while automation may assist adjudication, it cannot yet replace the function of human judgement.

11.121 The jurisprudential rationale for this is clear. Legitimate decision-making requires evaluative judgement, the exercise of discretion where appropriate, procedural fairness, reasoned justification and an identifiable legal actor responsible for the outcome. Automated computation may assist with several of those functions but, for now, human agency remains at the heart of the decision-making process.

11.122 Online and autonomous dispute resolution methods illustrate the tension between technological determinism and legal oversight. Although the Law Commission's 2025 discussion paper 'Artificial Intelligence and the Law'[111] considered the 'perhaps radical' possibility of granting AI systems some form of legal personality as one potential response to accountability gaps, it made no proposal for reform. For the time being, a credible ODR system must retain an identifiable person or institution responsible for the process, with digital platforms facilitating procedural efficiency and algorithms aiding analysis. Where smart contracts implement awards, this should be under human supervision.

11.123 The UNCITRAL Technical Notes and UKJT Rules illustrate how those requirements can be embedded in the design of dispute resolution processes. Both place technology within an agreed framework governing participation, procedure and outcome, rather than treating automation as an independent source of adjudicative authority. Applied in this way, ODR may improve the speed, efficiency and effectiveness of dispute resolution in the industrial metaverse without displacing due process, human oversight or legal responsibility.

109 Art 6(2) and Annex III, para 8(a).

110 Arts 9, 12–14, 16 and 26.

111 Law Commission, *Artificial Intelligence and the Law: A Discussion Paper* (2025), https://lawcom.gov.uk/publication/artificial-intelligence-and-the-law-a-discussion-paper/.

HYBRID JUSTICE IN THE INDUSTRIAL METAVERSE

11.124 Jurisdiction in the industrial metaverse cannot always be analysed by reference to a single place of activity or physical presence. As the preceding discussion has shown, industrial operations increasingly unfold through distributed systems, data and decision-making processes that span multiple borders. While English law continues to anchor jurisdiction in established rules of service, consent and the connecting factors prescribed by statute, treaty and common law, the factual matrix to which these rules are applied is becoming increasingly complex. Digital operations, automated decision-making, data location and control over technological infrastructure may all become relevant when determining whether a connecting factor required by an applicable jurisdictional rule is present in a particular case. In future, sustained technological or functional engagement with a jurisdiction may therefore acquire greater significance alongside traditional geographical connections.

11.125 Against this backdrop, the mechanisms of dispute resolution are themselves diversifying. Litigation and arbitration remain the principal forms of enforceable adjudication. However, they increasingly coexist with online procedure and automated systems of dispute management. The emergence of hybrid procedures, whether arbitral platforms operating through immersive interfaces or smart contracts executing tribunal decisions within digital infrastructures, demonstrates a gradual convergence between procedural law and technological process. The UKJT's Digital Dispute Resolution Rules exemplify this synthesis: automation that operates within, rather than outside, a recognised adjudicative framework.

11.126 The resulting landscape is one of plurality and convergence. Traditional courts and arbitral tribunals will continue to provide the authoritative means by which rights are declared and enforced; however, they need to function alongside technologically enabled systems that deliver speed and new efficiencies for users. The challenge for law is not to abandon its territorial and procedural foundations. Instead, it needs to extend them to accommodate new forms of digital presence and new methods of procedural engagement, without eroding accountability or the rule of law.

11.127 In this sense, the industrial metaverse does not herald the displacement of legal authority. Rather, it represents its evolution. Hybrid justice, anchored in human adjudication, augmented by automation, offers a framework through which Industry 4.0 can be effectively governed.

11.128 Participants must recognise, however, that in decentralised, data-driven environments, jurisdictional certainty cannot be assumed: it must be engineered. Thoughtful contractual design, anchoring legal relationships to identifiable fora, governing laws and dispute resolution procedures, will remain one of the most effective safeguards against the uncertainty that the industrial metaverse and its innovations are already starting to bring.

KEY TAKEAWAY POINTS

11.129 The key takeaway points in respect of dispute resolution and jurisdictional issues in the industrial metaverse are:

- Identify territorial anchors at the outset. Participants in the industrial metaverse should map where parties, infrastructure, data, assets, contractual performance and potential harm are located, recognising that distributed systems may create connections with several jurisdictions.
- Address jurisdictional uncertainty contractually. Governing law, jurisdiction and dispute resolution provisions should be coordinated across interdependent platform, cloud, software, data, manufacturing and other supply agreements.
- Allocate responsibility for automated systems clearly. Participants should identify in advance who bears the risk of erroneous data, autonomous decisions, system failures and unintended transactions or behaviour.
- Choose the dispute resolution mechanism deliberately. Litigation offers authoritative precedent and the coercive power of the state, while arbitration may offer stronger cross-border enforceability, confidentiality and procedural flexibility.
- Keep automated dispute resolution within a recognised legal framework. Technology may assist with procedure and the implementation of a resolution, though automated outcomes should remain subject to effective human oversight and meaningful routes for review or challenge.

Chapter 12

The future of work in the industrial metaverse

'Every industrial revolution brings along a learning revolution.'

Alexander De Croo[1]

12.1 The industrial metaverse, Industry 4.0 and the digital revolution is revolutionising the way of work. The advancements in emerging technologies are expected to fundamentally change not only the types of roles that we will see being performed by human workers, but also the way of working and the workplace. This, however, is largely to be expected in any industrial revolution, where seismic changes to work and employment have historically occurred. The changes we are already starting to see are yet more evidence of our progression into the digital revolution of Industry 4.0. It is vital that not only laws and regulations are updated to deal with this new landscape, but also processes and policies accurate reflect these changes, new expectations and opportunities.

12.2 Whilst technology may initially displace some staff, this is not necessarily going to be the case in the long run.[2] There may, however, still be some form of unrest initially whilst we experience the initial ramifications of these changes,[3] but this is not expected to continue forever, and in fact we expect that we will see a rise in new roles and new jobs as has happened in previous industrial revolutions. For example, Amazon's use of robotics within its fulfilment centres means that there is a reduced need for heavy lifting by humans, which in turn prevents injuries, but humans are still needed alongside the robots including as 'floor monitors' and engineers.[4]

12.3 The skills required in the workplace are changing as a result of the digital revolution, which is likely to initially result in a shortage of talent, and it is therefore very important to ensure a good work culture within the

1 https://www.weforum.org/stories/2018/01/universal-right-to-learn/.

2 It is estimated that the digital revolution (to include a move towards a green economy) will displace around 92 million jobs but will create 170 million new jobs by 2030, https://reports.weforum.org/docs/WEF_Four_Futures_for_Jobs_in_the_New_Economy_AI_and_Talent_in_2030_2025.pdf.

3 Steven R. Smith (2023), 'The Fourth Industrial Revolution and Legal Education', 39 GA ST U L REV 337, available at http://readingroom.law.gsu.edu/gsulr/vol39/iss2/9.

4 https://www.aboutamazon.com/stories/amazon-robotics-autonomous-robot-proteus-warehouse-packages.

workplace is achieved, and staff are suitably upskilled.[5] As discussed further in **Chapter 16**, education will also need to adapt to the industrial revolution to meet the new demands of the workplace. The ramification of any changes to education is going to take time to have an impact in the workplace, and therefore employers will need to be mindful that they educate their current staff on new technologies and the new skills required for Industry 4.0 and the digital industrial revolution. Under the UNESCO artificial intelligence (AI) ethical standards it is recommended that member states conduct impact assessments of AI on the workforce now, and also ensure that the education being provided is suitable for the future workforce, including teaching relevant skills for the new landscape, and promoting collaborations between the state, academics and industry to ensure that its society has relevant skills.[6] Member states should also ensure that they put in place provisions to deal with vulnerable workers who lose their role because of automation.[7]

12.4 Steps must be taken now to deal with the foreseeable upcoming changes to the world of work, the workplace and the new roles that are expected to come about due to the digital revolution, including upskilling workers, incentivising work in new industries, and having suitable education and training in place.[8] One serious area of consideration is the impact of automation on the common law relationship of mutuality of obligations as between employees and employers. This is the obligations that the employer will pay the employee and that the employee will work. Where the work becomes increasingly automated there are questions over the impact of this on the personal service element of the obligation.[9]

FUTURE OF JOBS

12.5 The World Economic Forum, has established the Global Future Council on Jobs and Frontier Technologies, and in January 2025 published its report on the future of jobs.[10] Emerging technologies such as AI and automation are expected to have a significant impact on jobs and job roles for the next five years; however, 'these technological advances … are…[also]… converging with a broader array of challenges, including economic volatility, geoeconomic realignments, environmental challenges and evolving societal expectations.'[11]

5 https://www3.weforum.org/docs/WEF_Impact_of_the_Fourth_Industrial_Revolution_on_Supply_Chains_.pdf.

6 2021 UNESCO AI ethical standards Standard 116, https://unesdoc.unesco.org/ark:/48223/pf0000381137.

7 2021 UNESCO AI ethical standards Standard 118, https://unesdoc.unesco.org/ark:/48223/pf0000381137.

8 https://reports.weforum.org/docs/WEF_Global_Risks_Report_2026.pdf.

9 https://researchbriefings.files.parliament.uk/documents/CBP-9817/CBP-9817.pdf.

10 https://reports.weforum.org/docs/WEF_Future_of_Jobs_Report_2025.pdf.

11 Ibid.

12.6 Some roles will diminish entirely, whilst new roles will come into existence to deal with issues and opportunities presented by these new technologies. The report predicts that by 2030, 39% of the existing 2025 skills that are being used by workers will change; however, this is actually lower than the changes in other skills over recent years from 2020.[12] This may be because we are already starting to see some of the impact of the changes in industry that have been caused by the emerging technologies of Industry 4.0. The biggest trend driving the changes in business is the broadening digital access and digitalisation, which in turn is impacting employment and job roles.[13] Employers considered that out of all those emerging technologies it is AI which is by far having the greatest impact.[14] This was followed by robotics and autonomous systems, but it was felt that this smaller than anticipated impact may be because the use of robotics is predominantly only found in a few countries being China, Japan, the Republic of Korea, Germany and the USA.[15]

12.7 Roles which are expected to grow within Industry 4.0 include big data specialists, FinTech engineers, AI and machine learning experts, robotics engineers, blockchain developers, security management specialists, autonomous vehicle specialists and renewable energy engineers.[16] It is expected that by 2030, AI will create 11 million jobs, but robotics and autonomous systems will replace around 5 million job.[17] Industry 4.0 technologies are also expected to have a significant impact on the world's largest jobs of agriculture, manufacturing and construction, each of which are discussed later in this book.[18]

12.8 As a result of the digital revolution, there will be a change in core skills required for the workplace between 2025 and 2030.[19] As shown in Figure 12.1,[20] technological key skills such as AI, and being proficient at big data and technological literacy, are all considered to be of fundamental importance by 2030, whilst precision and manual dexterity will become out of focus skills.[21]

12 Ibid.
13 Ibid.
14 Ibid.
15 Ibid.
16 Ibid.
17 Ibid.
18 https://reports.weforum.org/docs/WEF_Jobs_of_Tomorrow_Technology_and_the_Future_of_the_Worlds_Largest_Workforces_2025.pdf.
19 https://reports.weforum.org/docs/WEF_Future_of_Jobs_Report_2025.pdf.
20 Ibid.
21 Ibid.

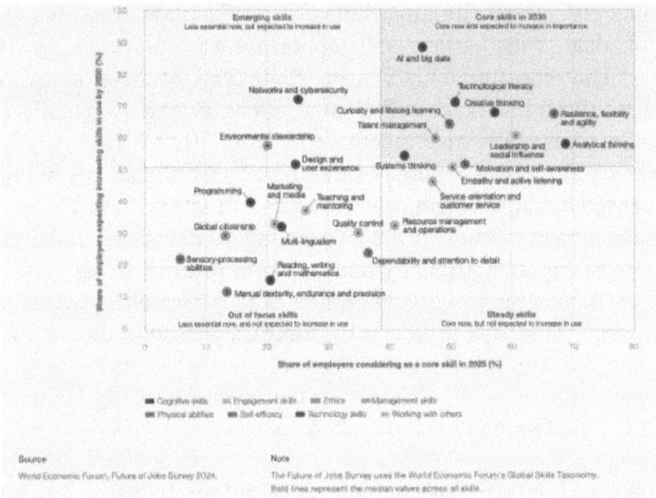

Source: World Economic Forum, Future of Jobs Survey 2025, https://reports.weforum.org/docs/WEF_Future_of_Jobs_Report_2025.pdf. Reproduced with the kind permission of the World Economic Forum. © World Economic Forum.

Figure 12.1 Future key skills

12.9 Skills needed by front line workers in industry will also change as a result of Industry 4.0, which may in turn reduce productivity and result in a shortage of talent; a skills gap between manual work to digital work within industry; a change in the needs of workers, which includes a need for greater flexibility; too much burden on supervisors who then are unable to dedicate sufficient time to helping staff; and a lack of reward whether in monetary compensation or other ways of compensating staff.[22]

12.10 Between 2025 and 2030, technological changes will significantly change jobs, and it is vital for staff to adapt to the emerging technologies and employers to upskill workers.[23] In fact, the World Economic Forum consider that 86% of businesses expect AI to transform their business by 2030 and one of the most important strategies for the workplace therefore to adapt is the upskilling of staff, especially with the use of autonomation and emerging technologies.[24] Businesses need to start preparing now for the seismic changes anticipated by AI on the workforce.[25]

12.11 Whilst many consider that the turning point was the release of ChatGPT 3.5 in November 2022, generative AI models are still not able to replace all

22 https://reports.weforum.org/docs/WEF_Putting_Talent_at_the_Centre_An_Evolving_Imperative_for_Manufacturing_2025.pdf.
23 https://reports.weforum.org/docs/WEF_Future_of_Jobs_Report_2025.pdf.
24 Ibid.
25 https://reports.weforum.org/docs/WEF_Four_Futures_for_Jobs_in_the_New_Economy_AI_and_Talent_in_2030_2025.pdf.

human skills that are needed in the workplace, including those of empathy, creative thinking, teaching, mentoring and environmental stewardship.[26]

12.12 The European Parliament resolution of 12 February 2019[27] considers the impact of AI and robotics on jobs. It highlights that roles will change, but that there are also many positives that will arise with these changes to the workplace and job roles including a reduction in dangerous and hazardous job roles. Focus, as we move into Industry 4.0, therefore should be on training staff in new areas of work, as there are still job opportunities within the new landscape. It is important that employers act now to address removing existing barriers to entry in these new roles and in new areas of expertise.

12.13 Finally, some of the innovations of Industry 4.0 can in fact help to plug gaps where there are shortages of workers or where there is expected to be a gap in the future; whether this is because of the cost of training, certain jobs will become unattractive or because the traditional human-workforce cannot keep pace with the growing need. For example, there is a shortage of lorry drivers globally and the rise of autonomous freight vehicles may actually help to alleviate this.[28]

WORKING IN INDUSTRY 4.0

12.14 Industry 4.0 will change HR and the way that staff and people are managed.[29] As a result new strategies are needed to manage people within businesses, especially where technology is rapidly evolving and presenting unique challenges as a result. The World Economic Forum coin the phrase 'HR 4.0' to describe this new way of delivering HR and even believe that there are likely to be new roles in HR following the fourth industrial revolution such as 'Head of Reinvention and Reskilling', 'Digital HR Lead', 'Bot Monitor' and 'Chief Learning Officer'.[30]

12.15 The types of leaders who will excel in Industry 4.0 will prioritise social impact issues; be those who are focused on data-driven outcomes; innovators who are prepared to disrupt the status quo; and are vested in championing talent within their organisation.[31]

12.16 There will be a need for new policies and procedures as part of the changes on jobs and employment generally in Industry 4.0. This needs to be able to reflect the changes brought about due to the new innovations, to help

26 https://reports.weforum.org/docs/WEF_Future_of_Jobs_Report_2025.pdf.
27 On a comprehensive industrial policy on artificial intelligence and robotics (2018/2088 (INI).
28 https://researchbriefings.files.parliament.uk/documents/POST-PB-0062/POST-PB-0062.pdf.
29 https://www3.weforum.org/docs/WEF_NES_Whitepaper_HR4.0.pdf.
30 Ibid.
31 https://www.weforum.org/stories/2019/01/these-four-leadership-styles-are-key-to-success-in-the-fourth-industrial-revolution/.

employees transition to the new ways of working and deal with the use and integration of the new technologies. HR teams will need to manage the transition to digitalisation and the challenges faced by the staff as a result of this carefully, especially where there are jobs which are at risk of being replaced or significantly changed whether immediately or in the near future. One way of approaching this is by focusing on creating a suitable culture within the workplace to ease this transition and foster an environment where staff want to upskill or change their role and working practices. It is expected that we will see a focus on valuing human interactions and relationships as the landscape becomes increasingly digital.

12.17 Interestingly, notwithstanding the seismic changes anticipated by the technological revolution, it is expected, however, that we will see a move towards putting employees, and employee culture at the centre of a business, with the belief that to maximise the transformation of businesses with new technology it will become vital to invest in the retention of staff as it is 'people, rather than technology ...[which]... remain the true heart of industry'.[32] Staff cannot be treated in the same way as machines, therefore employers need to show that they appreciate that staff cannot be standardised, and that there should be investments made in the distinctiveness of staff and in their stability through improvements being made that will increase their loyalty to the business, with a view to long term talent retention.[33]

12.18 Creating a good culture in the workplace for staff and upskilling workers is necessary for digital transformation for Industry 4.0 since 'as we navigate an era of rapid technological advancements and supply chain disruptions, our approach to talent must evolve in tandem'.[34] Unilever and Haier both seek to promote suitable career paths and progression for operatives within their manufacturing facilities, whether by creating new roles, or using AI technologies themselves to create individualised career paths for people, recognising the importance of providing flexibility and other incentives desired by Gen Z workers, and upskilling workers, including using XR technologies and other innovations for training.[35]

12.19 Industry 4.0 will also bring about new job roles. Such roles include data stewards[36] and a meta-operator.[37] A meta-operator is someone participating in the industrial metaverse via XR, and expected to monitor and interact with others within the industrial metaverse; effectively supervising operations virtually having entered the industrial metaverse via VR headsets, or smart-glasses, and acting as 'the operator's gateway to the Industrial Metaverse', monitoring the

32 https://reports.weforum.org/docs/WEF_Putting_Talent_at_the_Centre_An_Evolving_Imperative_for_Manufacturing_ 2025.pdf.

33 Ibid.

34 https://reports.weforum.org/docs/WEF_Empowering_Frontlines_2025.pdf.

35 Ibid.

36 https://www.turing.ac.uk/sites/default/files/2023-05/turing_asg_whitepaper_digitaltwins.pdf.

37 https://ieeexplore.ieee.org/document/10596039.

digital space, as well as checking in-on and controlling the Internet of Things (IoT) sensors.[38]

MANAGEMENT OF STAFF IN THE INDUSTRIAL METAVERSE

12.20 Whilst AI is not the only emerging technology in Industry 4.0, it is certainly one of the driving forces. The advent of the fourth industrial revolution reminds us of the need to ensure that there is only responsible AI use within the workplace, especially when it comes to monitoring staff, and decision making, and that there needs to be suitable laws and regulations to govern and protect this.[39] The TUC warns that 'new technologies should not cause a loss of transparency and accountability, nor a loss of human interaction leading to an increase in alienation'.[40]

12.21 Technology continues to advance and we now have the widespread availability of low-cost wearable devices, such as smart glasses, which can easily be used to monitor staff in the workplace and form the basis of decision making by organisations. Many staff are concerned about the impact of emerging technologies on the workplace and do not trust it; the idea of trust therefore needs to be addressed from the outset with full and proper transparency.[41]

12.22 There are serious concerns that the use of emerging technologies within the workplace will contribute to an 'always on' culture, which in turn has a negative impact on the mental health of the workforce and will erode the common law principles of mutuality of obligation, personal service, and trust and confidence.[42] Other concerns about the use of AI in the workplace includes the risk of discrimination; the fact that there is no existing right of employees to specifically know about the use of AI being deployed in the workplace and its impact on them; the impact on privacy under Article 8 ECHR; data protection concerns; a lack of safeguards around the protection against unfair dismissal when using AI systems; and serious questions around the impact of automation on the employment relationship.[43]

12.23 The TUC has expressed its desire to use collective bargaining powers to try and protect workers from AI in the workplace, setting out five areas which it considers are the 'red line' for use of AI in the workplace, namely: (1) if it is used for high-risk decisions then the staff should know this and understand what is being done; (2) AI should not be discriminatory; (3) staff should be involved in decisions about the use of AI in the workplace; (4) any use of AI in the workplace

38 Ibid.
39 https://www.tuc.org.uk/sites/default/files/Technology_Managing_People_2021_Report_AW_0.pdf.
40 Ibid.
41 Ibid.
42 Ibid.
43 Ibid.

should be transparent; and (5) staff should know how the system works so that they can decide whether it is reasonable, lawful, and not discriminatory.[44] In addition, the TUC considers that employers should be obliged to keep a register of AI being used in the workplace, that there should be the new right against detrimental treatment caused by inaccurate data being processed, and where relevant, an employer should have to prove that they have not discriminated the employee by the use of any AI system.[45]

12.24 Concerns were raised by the All-Party Parliamentary Group on the Future of Work about the negative impact of AI and automation on the workforce, such as its use for surveillance and monitoring, and confirmed that people are nervous about the lack of transparency with AI and automation, and accordingly the law needs to hold AI to account so that there is a focus only on responsible innovation.[46] Where AI is being deployed to make employment decisions, effective steps should be taken to understand and assess the presence, and impact, of any bias in data contained within the AI system being used.

TRAINING

12.25 Upskilling and training are vital aspects of the digital revolution. It is important as part of the innovation process to look at what is needed to be able to train a suitable workforce to deploy the technology, whether this is in a smart factory, or in finance utilising emerging technologies. There should be a suitable curriculum developed which addresses the different technologies, which should be developed through a collaboration between industry and education providers.[47] There is the need for staff to be able to interact with machines, as well as use virtual reality, digital twins, AI and 3D printing; staff should also be able to competently deal with technology, data analytics and cyber security.[48] Immersive technology is an important method of training staff, which reduces costs and has been shown to improve training without the need to use the manufacturing facility and equipment itself.[49]

44 Ibid.
45 Ibid.
46 https://uploads-ssl.webflow.com/5f57d40eb1c2ef22d8a8ca7e/62459a045de6afc1d9973bf4_The%20New%20Frontier%20-%20Artificial%20Intelligence%20at%20Work%5B4%5D.pdf.
47 https://hub.unido.org/sites/default/files/publications/UNIDO%20-%20Guidelines%20for%20the%20establishment%20of%20a%20Smart%20Factory%20Lab_Automotive%20Sector_Final.pdf.
48 Ibid.
49 https://reports.weforum.org/docs/WEF_Putting_Talent_at_the_Centre_An_Evolving_Imperative_for_Manufacturing_2025.pdf.

12.26 The acute need for upskilling staff has been acknowledged by the EU who, under Article 4 of the EU AI Act,[50] specifically deals with the need to make AI literacy available to all staff as we move into Industry 4.0:

> 'Providers and deployers of AI systems shall take measures to ensure, to their best extent, a sufficient level of AI literacy of their staff and other persons dealing with the operation and use of AI systems on their behalf, taking into account their technical knowledge, experience, education and training and the context the AI systems are to be used in, and considering the persons or groups of persons on whom the AI systems are to be used.'

12.27 This is monitored in the EU by the National Market Surveillance Authorities, which introduces the AI Skills Academy and European Digital Innovation Hubs.

HEALTH AND SAFETY

12.28 Health and safety considerations will change as a result of the development of Industry 4.0 technologies. In many cases, this will be beneficial, as adaptions have been sought to try and aid human workers through the deployment of these different technologies. For example, Hyundai and Kia have developed the 'X-ble Shoulder' which is a robotic wearable being used by Korean Air to reduce the need for overhead work by its maintenance staff, which historically resulted injuries and strains.[51] These types of wearables are also set to be deployed within the construction industry, shipbuilding industry and agricultural industry. The robotic shoulder is designed to reduce the load on the shoulder joint by 60% and on the deltoid muscles by 30%.[52] The robot is accredited under ISO 13482:2014 for personal care robots, which demonstrates the importance of international standards in this field.

12.29 Thought has to be had, however, to the potential risks associated with the introduction of various new technologies into the workplace. Often the risks are overlooked in favour of the advancements brought about by the technology. The Civil Law Rules on Robotics warns that 'the development of robotics and

50 Regulation (EU) 2024/1689 of the European Parliament and of the Council of 13 June 2024 laying down harmonised rules on artificial intelligence and amending Regulations (EC) No 300/2008, (EU) No 167/2013, (EU) No 168/2013, (EU) 2018/858, (EU) 2018/1139 and (EU) 2019/2144 and Directives 2014/90/EU, (EU) 2016/797 and (EU) 2020/1828 (Artificial Intelligence Act).

51 https://www.hyundai.com/worldwide/en/newsroom/detail/hyundai-motor-and-kia%25E2%2580%2599s-robotics-lab-delivers-first-%25E2%2580%2598x-ble-shoulder%25E2%2580%2599-wearable-robot-to-korean-air-0000000982?utm_source=superhuman&utm_medium=newsletter&utm_campaign=robotics-special-robots-ride-the-subway&_bhlid=8b6a526008e25efff42473dec925b0df587ddc88.

52 https://www.hyundai.com/worldwide/en/newsroom/detail/hyundai-motor-and-kia%25E2%2580%2599s-robotics-lab-delivers-first-%25E2%2580%2598x-ble-shoulder%25E2%2580%2599-wearable-robot-to-korean-air-0000000982?utm_source=superhuman&utm_medium=newsletter&utm_campaign=robotics-special-robots-ride-the-subway&_bhlid=8b6a526008e25efff42473dec925b0df587ddc88.

AI will definitely influence the landscape of the workplace what may create new liability concerns and eliminate others; whereas the legal responsibility need to be clarified from both business sight model, as well as the workers design pattern, in case emergencies or problems occur'.[53]

12.30 As discussed in **Chapters 5** and **6**, the Health and Safety at Work etc Act 1974 will continue to apply, and where lifting is being done it will fall under the Lifting and Operations and Lifting Equipment Regulations 1998. It is imperative that an up-to-date risk assessment is carried out which fully appreciates the risks associated with the new technology being deployed.

EQUALITY, BIAS AND DISCRIMINATION

12.31 It is important to note that an AI system, including its algorithm and training data will be considered as a 'provision, criterion or practice' under section 19(1) of the Equality Act 2010 and capable of causing indirect discrimination.[54] This is because of the risk of biased data being used as training data within the system, inadvertently resulting in this same bias then being used within the decision making process. There is the risk of gender discrepancies with the use of AI within the workplace, and in particular such issues can present in the use of automation within the recruitment process itself.[55] AI systems are reliant on the integrity of their data. It is important that effective steps are taken to understand what a software provider is doing to reduce, mitigate or address bias within their data and system. Procurement teams should undertake comprehensive due diligence on the tool and seek contractual protection to mitigate their risks of liability in such circumstances.

12.32 In certain circumstances it is felt, however, that the use of emerging technologies, within the workplace, such as robotics and exoskeletons, can actually be used to bring about a more inclusive workplace, and can drive an increase in women in the workforce.[56] Policy-makers should ensure that suitable steps are taken to encourage the upskilling of all workers within the business, including disabled workers, ethnic minorities and female members of staff, and take active steps to ensure that they are properly positioned in leadership roles within organisations as well.[57] Employers and policy makers should also take active steps to address parity in recruitment in innovative technology roles.[58]

53 European Parliament resolution of 16 February 2017 with recommendations to the Commission (2015/2103(INL)).

54 https://www.tuc.org.uk/sites/default/files/Technology_Managing_People_2021_Report_AW_0.pdf.

55 https://reports.weforum.org/docs/WEF_Gender_Parity_in_the_Intelligent_Age_2025.pdf.

56 Ibid.

57 Ibid.

58 Ibid.

MODERN SLAVERY

12.33 Emerging technologies of Industry 4.0, such as federated AI systems, are already being utilised to try and combat the global issues of forced labour. The Global Data Partnership Against Forced Labour has been established by the World Economic Forum to create an infrastructure to record and share data internationally to support compliance with legislation such as the Modern Slavery Act 2015.[59] This demonstrates the positive benefits of Industry 4.0.

KEY TAKEAWAY POINTS

12.34 The key takeaway points in respect of the Future of Work in the industrial metaverse are:

- Changes to the world of work, and the workplace are some of the most significant changes which will come about as a result of the digital industrial revolution. Historically, this has been witnessed in every industrial revolution, and the move to Industry 4.0 is not going to be any different. We expect to see a change in desirable skills for workers as part of the digital revolution, which includes the ability to work with the new emerging technologies themselves, but also to demonstrate some of the more fundamental human skills such as empathy and emotional intelligence.
- Jobs and job roles will change in Industry 4.0. This will require HR teams, and those working within employment law and commercial law, to adapt to the new landscape. We expect to initially see a rise in redundancies as staff are replaced with these technologies, but also the opportunities for upskilling and redeployment into new roles, which will come about due to the new technologies (including those overseeing or monitoring the output of the technology).
- Upskilling is key. Employers need to ensure that its workforce is ready and able to work in the new landscape.
- There are positive impacts related to the use of emerging technologies on the health and safety of the workplace; however, suitable risk assessments, and measures have to be adopted to protect against harm that may be caused by some technology, such as autonomous robots.
- There is the risk of discrimination and bias through the use of some technologies, such as AI. Care needs to be taken when using this technology for decision making without the workplace.

59 https://reports.weforum.org/docs/WEF_Harnessing_Data_and_Intelligence_for_Collective_Advantage_2026.pdf.

Chapter 13

Agriculture, food production and the industrial metaverse

'Deep tech offers agriculture the critical breakthrough it urgently needs. By integrating AI, remote sensing and data science, we can transform fragmented farming systems into resilient, productive and climate-smart ecosystems. These innovations empower farmers, financial institutions, agribusinesses, governments and development agencies with real-time intelligence, reduce inefficiencies across the value chain'.[1]

Krishna Kumar, Chief Executive Officer, Cropin Technologies

13.1 The agricultural metaverse is seeking to revolutionise farming and agriculture. What is termed 'smart farming solutions' by some,[2] precision agriculture,[3] and Agriculture 4.0 by others,[4] sees the use of emerging technologies in farming, and a move towards more targeted decision-making.

13.2 Smart farming is already seeing the following technologies transform agriculture:[5]

1. generative artificial intelligence (AI), such as personalised farming advice;
2. robotics and drones;
3. computer vision, in areas where pictures can be used to identify concerns such as crop detection, pest identification, weed identification. Computer vision may also be embedded within robots or drones or autonomous vehicles used on the farm;
4. edge internet of things, allowing autonomous systems on a farm such as for fertilising the soil;
5. satellites, which means greater connectivity for the farms especially in more remote areas; and means systems such as autonomous systems can be utilised; and
6. genome editing[6] and nanotechnology.

1 https://reports.weforum.org/docs/WEF_Shaping_the_Deep_Tech_Revolution_in_Agriculture_2025.pdf.
2 https://capsulesight.com/metaverse/real-examples-and-use-cases-of-metaverse-in-agriculture/.
3 https://epthinktank.eu/2017/12/01/precision-agriculture-legal-social-and-ethical-considerations/.
4 https://www.oliverwyman.com/content/dam/oliver-wyman/v2/publications/2021/apr/agriculture-4-0-the-future-of-farming-technology.pdf.
5 https://reports.weforum.org/docs/WEF_Shaping_the_Deep_Tech_Revolution_in_Agriculture_2025.pdf.
6 Clustered regularly interspaced short palindromic repeats (CRISR).

13.3 Just like industry generally, Industry 4.0 is revolutionising agriculture. We are already seeing the benefits of higher production rates, better crops, a reduction in the impact of climate change and cost efficiencies.[7] Smart farming is expected to be worth $12.9 billion by 2027[8] and $24.09 billion by 2030.[9] In the EU, over €200 million has been awarded from the Horizon 2020 grants alone for the digitalisation of agriculture.[10] We are also seeing changes in food itself through the use of emerging technology; one such example is with 3D printing technology, using 'printed' matter made out of algae and alternative meats, to create new forms of food.[11]

13.4 Experts call on the use of Agriculture 4.0 to achieve the UN Sustainable Development Goals (SDGs) by 2030, through the effective targeting of resources and the use of precision farming to reduce global poverty;[12] however, others caution that it may actually widen the digital divide given the costs associated with the technology, which acts as a barrier to adoption for many developing nations.[13]

13.5 There are a number of benefits of Industry 4.0 in agriculture, including assisting farmers with decision making and decision mapping to maximise resources and minimise costs, improving the welfare of animals through increased real-time monitoring, improving the working conditions of workers through the use of technology, and improving transparency in the supply chain.[14] Some of the risks, however, include the need for increased upskilling of workers in this area, the increasing digital divide, the high costs associated with this technology, the risks around privacy, sharing data and the interoperability failings which still exist.[15]

13.6 There is, however, currently a low adoption rate globally of deep tech within agriculture. In order to combat this an innovative ecosystem should be created. Change is needed generally given the serious issues currently facing agriculture including climate change, global conflicts, increasing populations, and a depletion of natural resources.[16] One of the main barriers of entry for Industry 4.0 into farms generally is that farms are not the same standardised environment as a manufacturing plant. They are typically someone's home, and the costs associated with the transition tend to be significant, especially when compared to the produce being farmed.

7 https://www.agmatix.com/blog/the-role-of-industry-4-0-in-agriculture/.
8 https://pmc.ncbi.nlm.nih.gov/articles/PMC10000125/.
9 https://www.agmatix.com/blog/innovation-and-developmemt-in-agritech/.
10 https://digital-strategy.ec.europa.eu/en/policies/digitalisation-agriculture-horizon-2020.
11 https://www.oliverwyman.com/content/dam/oliver-wyman/v2/publications/2021/apr/agriculture-4-0-the-future-of-farming-technology.pdf.
12 Ibid.
13 https://digital-strategy.ec.europa.eu/en/policies/digitalisation-agriculture.
14 Ibid.
15 Ibid.
16 https://reports.weforum.org/docs/WEF_Shaping_the_Deep_Tech_Revolution_in_Agriculture_2025.pdf.

13.7 The largest growing job role globally in the next five years is considered to be the farmworker.[17] This is likely to be related to the transition to sustainability and a move to protect against climate change. Any digital revolution in farming therefore needs to have sustainability and climate protection at its heart.[18]

13.8 There are numerous ethical and legal implications in smart farming which need to be addressed.[19] These include the lack of control over the technology; safety concerns; being able to identify where liability sits; privacy; the digital divide and challenges with access to infrastructure; the balance between traditional farming techniques and modernisation through digitalisation; and the cost of moving towards digitalisation in farming, which requires upfront investment in expensive equipment, especially where costs are already stretched in farming generally.[20]

13.9 Whilst some policy-makers, like the EU, have started to try to consider and address some of these challenges, much more is still required. In its Investment and Innovation blueprint for growth policy document, the National Farmers' Union calls for a suitable regulatory framework which enables innovation but still provides some certainty to the sector.[21]

REGULATION

13.10 There remains a distinct lack of regulation on smart farming, and especially the use of devices in animal husbandry.[22] Experts call on governments to ensure that there are suitable regulations to ensure that good food safety standards are maintained, as well as providing suitable financial incentives, fostering collaborations and investing in education within these fields.[23] Environmental considerations, and the benefit of Industry 4.0 on issues such as sustainability and climate change are addressed in **Chapter 10**.

13.11 There is the need for sufficient agricultural policy and regulation to address the changes being brought about by Industry 4.0, as there are numerous concerns, including those specifically around data privacy, as well as highly regulated areas such as genome editing and nanotechnologies.[24] Any regulation

17 https://www.weforum.org/publications/the-future-of-jobs-report-2025/.
18 https://www.oliverwyman.com/content/dam/oliver-wyman/v2/publications/2021/apr/agriculture-4-0-the-future-of-farming-technology.pdf.
19 https://epthinktank.eu/2017/12/01/precision-agriculture-legal-social-and-ethical-considerations/.
20 https://www.europarl.europa.eu/RegData/etudes/STUD/2017/603207/EPRS_STU(2017)603207_EN.pdf.
21 https://www.nfuonline.com/media/rmtnbuzz/investment-and-innovation.pdf.
22 https://pmc.ncbi.nlm.nih.gov/articles/PMC10000125/.
23 https://www.oliverwyman.com/content/dam/oliver-wyman/v2/publications/2021/apr/agriculture-4-0-the-future-of-farming-technology.pdf.
24 https://reports.weforum.org/docs/WEF_Shaping_the_Deep_Tech_Revolution_in_Agriculture_2025.pdf.

should be agile, encourage openness and promote the use of sandboxes, develop regulatory pathways and use other incentives to reduce both the risks and perceived risks.[25] There should also be active involvement from insurers from an early stage to consider issues around liability. They suggest the benefit from sandboxing in this space, as well as promoting commercial benefits to incentivise adoption such as research and development grants and subsidies.[26]

13.12 The UN also calls on policymakers globally to address the regulation of FoodTech, considering that there should be effective governance in place which prioritises the promotion of knowledge sharing and collaboration, promotes education, invests in the infrastructure and has local government support.[27]

13.13 The EU is heavily investing in the digitalisation of agriculture.[28] In its 2017 study, the European Parliamentary Research Services considered the legal, social and ethical issues associated with precision agriculture, caused primarily by the rapid digitalisation of the sector, and the need to avoid losing sight of environmental considerations and responsible farming techniques that respect nature and biodiversity.[29]

GLOBAL POLICY

13.14 The World Economic Forum released its insight report in November 2025 titled 'Shaping the Deep-Tech Revolution in Agriculture'.[30] The report is the output of the Agriculture Innovation initiative, which was established in 2021, and considered the revolution to farming that is being caused by deep tech such as in AI, biotechnology and satellites. Deep tech can help address five upcoming areas of challenge: (1) the change in the workforce and the reality that there are less people wanting to work in agriculture; (2) climate change; (3) the reduction in natural resources; (4) more demand for food; and (5) geopolitical concerns which directly impact on agriculture, such as war.[31]

Data

13.15 Data is a fundamental consideration, and commodity, in agritech. It has led to initiatives within the EU such as the Common European Agricultural Data

25 Ibid.
26 Ibid.
27 https://unhabitat.org/sites/default/files/2026/01/activating_food-tech_ecosystems_in_intermediary_cities_for_sustainable_food_security.pdf.
28 https://digital-strategy.ec.europa.eu/en/policies/digitalisation-agriculture.
29 https://www.europarl.europa.eu/RegData/etudes/STUD/2017/603207/EPRS_STU(2017)603207_EN.pdf.
30 https://reports.weforum.org/docs/WEF_Shaping_the_Deep_Tech_Revolution_in_Agriculture_2025.pdf.
31 Ibid.

Space and the EU code of conduct on agricultural data sharing by contractual agreement. The National Farmers' Union, however, raise serious concerns on the inequity of power between farmers and tech giants, and the significant risks associated with data sharing in farming.[32] With this in mind, the EU Data Act,[33] considers that commercial performance data from a farm gathered from the collection of data from the Internet of Things (IoT) devices should not be used within commercial negotiations with users. The Common European Agricultural Data Space, a project funded by the EU, is creating a decentralised platform for sharing data in the agricultural space based on the Data Act and Data Governance Act.[34]

13.16 Data is collected from a variety of different sources in agritech; from IoT sensors, to drones, and contains a mix of personal data, sensitive data and confidential trade secrets. The data collected may be used for a variety of different reasons, from informing decision making to regulatory monitoring and compliance. Some of the data may not be readily identifiable as personal data where it is images, for example, which may inadvertently include people on the farm.[35] Privacy notices and data protection policies need to be updated to ensure that these accurately reflect the use of this technology on the farm.

13.17 In many cases farms serve not only an industrial purpose, but also tend to be family homes. This makes them rather unique when considering the issue of data collection through Industry 4.0 technologies. The issue of data collection from farming environments therefore raises serious article 8 Human Rights Act 1998 considerations – being the right to respect for private and family life. As set out above, there is a significant risk of occupiers, visitors and workers having their privacy infringed as a result the enhanced and frontier technology being used.

AGRICULTURAL DATA SHARING BY CONTRACTUAL AGREEMENT

13.18 The EU Code of Conduct on Agricultural Data Sharing By Contractual Agreement sets out voluntary guidelines on the use and exchange of data within digital farming. This is important given the value in the proper flow of data within this space, and its impact on areas such as data protection and intellectual property rights.[36] Farmers tend to be reluctant to share their data with other

32 https://www.nfuonline.com/media/rmtnbuzz/investment-and-innovation.pdf.

33 Regulation (EU) 2023/2854 of the European Parliament and of the Council of 13 December 2023 on harmonised rules on fair access to and use of data and amending Regulation (EU) 2017/2394 and Directive (EU) 2020/1828.

34 https://agridataspace-csa.eu/wp-content/uploads/2024/09/AGRIDATA-SPACE-FINAL-BROCHURE.pdf.

35 https://www.europarl.europa.eu/RegData/etudes/STUD/2017/603207/EPRS_STU(2017)603207_EN.pdf.

36 https://croplifeeurope.eu/wp-content/uploads/2021/03/EU_Code_of_conduct_on_agricultural_data_sharing_by_contractual_agreement_2020_ENGLISH.pdf.

competing farms given its commercial importance and sensitivity. In many cases, much of this data is a farm's trade secrets or at the very least should be treated as confidential. Without this data, and its sharing, however, agritech largely fails at the first hurdle. The reluctance of users to share sensitive commercial data, however, could be addressed by effective contracts which cover key areas as are addressed under the code of conduct.[37]

13.19 The Code of Conduct uses the term 'agri-chain operator', to mean the person who owns or controls the data, typically the farmer from the farm in which the data originates, and who should be compensated for the use of the data.[38] Noting, however, that proper contracts should still be put in place to determine the different rights to use the different types of data, and whatever controls are necessary for the different varying degrees of sensitive data. It calls upon parties to set out clear parameters in respect of the use of data, and how this can be collected, shared and processed.[39] It suggests that consent via a suitable contract should be established from the farmer from where the data originated, the purpose for which this data can be used, how it can be shared and for what reason.[40] The data should also be suitably encrypted, with clear security requirements and the contract should contain clear terms around liability and intellectual property rights.[41]

FOOD SAFETY AND INDUSTRY 4.0

13.20 Industry 4.0 shows great potential in advancing food safety given the ability to track multiple data sets across a variety of different steps of the growing and food sale process, which in turn gives people greater insights and learnings on the food they eat.[42]

13.21 Whilst the potential for innovation in the food standards arena is predicted, the Food Standards Agency (FSA) Science Council does however raise concerns over the issues these innovations face in trying to raise sufficient funding for products and ideas to be properly realised.[43]

UK

13.22 In the UK, food safety is governed by the Food Safety Act 1990 and The Food Safety and Hygiene (England) Regulations 2013, both of which pre-

37 Ibid.
38 Ibid.
39 Ibid.
40 Ibid.
41 Ibid.
42 https://www.europarl.europa.eu/RegData/etudes/STUD/2017/603207/EPRS_STU(2017)603207_EN.pdf.
43 https://www.food.gov.uk/print/pdf/node/17691.

date the rise of Industry 4.0 technologies in agriculture. The Food Safety Act 1990 puts the responsibility on the human actors concerned with the production of food.[44] As systems evolve at pace, some thought has to be had as to whether this remains relevant and where blame will lie when emerging technology is deployed within the food supply chain and something detrimental happens. The current position of the FSA is that responsibility lies with the human actors, and that suitable policies and governance is needed to ensure the correct use and implementation of technology.[45] Where traditional food producers seek to implement emerging technology techniques, caution must be exercised to ensure that contractual accountability is afforded to the technology provider, especially where it is clear that regulators are going to pursue the users of technology.

13.23 The FSA regulates food safety in England. The FSA Science Council, is an expert committee of the FSA and has undertaken a number of different studies on the impact of emerging technologies on food safety in recent years. There is still, however, a lack of a relevant legal framework and standards in this area for the emerging technologies we are experiencing as we move ever closer to Industry 4.0 and beyond.[46] The FSA Science Council has identified that the FSA is lacking in horizon scanning for new risks and opportunities, that technological developments will impact on food safety and that there is a gap in policy and regulation in this space.[47] Whilst it is felt that the FSA is in a good position to deal with keeping food safe in the digital revolution, it does as a minimum need to establish data standards.[48]

13.24 In October 2025, the FSA Science Council reported on the use of AI on food safety.[49] It raised concerns over issues of bias, trust and transparency where AI systems are used, but highlighted, as discussed below at para **13.26**, that there are benefits of using AI in respect of food safety. Legal concerns in respect of the use of AI in food safety include those around privacy and protection of trade secrets; and there are ethical considerations about how to establish trust in the system when using AI.[50] It concludes that 'the Food Standards Agency (FSA) has a responsibility to ensure that innovation does not undermine consumer protection, regulatory oversight, or public confidence' and that there is the strong need for suitable governance and guidance.[51] Any use of AI within food needs to be properly monitored by a human in the loop. Whilst there are concerns around the lack of relevant legal frameworks and standards on the use of AI in respect of food safety, the FSA does not feel that there is currently the need to update

44 https://science-council.food.gov.uk/Introduction1.
45 Ibid.
46 Ibid.
47 https://webarchive.nationalarchives.gov.uk/ukgwa/20200803142353/https://science-council.food.gov.uk/science-council-subgroups/science-council-working-group-on-food-system-risks-and-horizon-scanning.
48 https://science-council.food.gov.uk/sites/default/files/2020-08/finrepscwgondatausageanddigtech.pdf.
49 https://science-council.food.gov.uk/Introduction1.
50 Ibid.
51 Ibid.

food safety regulations specifically to deal with AI.[52] It does, however, call for effective sandboxing for the safe adoption of AI in the food sector.[53]

13.25 The FSA Science Council goes on to make the following recommendations: (1) calling for suitable guidance to be published for the use of AI within the food industry; (2) the monitoring of AI use; (3) the development of industry standards; (4) the feeling that the FSA should collaborate with other regulators to design a suitable regulatory framework; and (5) more research must be undertaken in this field.[54]

13.26 There are many benefits of using AI within food safety, including its use in monitoring safety and hygiene requirements, identifying and monitoring outbreaks and contaminations and carrying out real-time continuous surveillance.[55] Over time AI can supplement, or even replace, food inspectors; however, caution does need to be exercised in respect of this to ensure that adequate safeguards are put in place to protect public health, and retain public trust in the oversight of food standards.[56]

GENETICALLY MODIFIED FOODS AND NOVEL FOODS

13.27 Genetically modified (GMO) food in Great Britain fall under Regulation (EU) 1829/2003 plus assimilated law.[57] This requires that GMO food, and any products derived from the same, must be first authorised by the Food Standards Authority and listed on a GMO register. Due largely to the ethical issues associated with GMOs, even as we move further through this industrial revolution, we are not seeing an uptake in GMOs. That is not to say that we are not seeing a revolution in foods and alternative production methods and food stuff.

13.28 Novel food[58] is subject to the retained EU Regulation 2015/2283 in Great Britain. This requires the registration of the food through the FSA and being listed on the Register of Novel Foods, which contains any restrictions and terms upon which the authorised food can be sold.[59] It is for the applicant to demonstrate that the food is not a novel food. GMO food which is already subject to other regulations[60] falls outside of this regulation.

52 Ibid.
53 Ibid.
54 Ibid.
55 Ibid.
56 Ibid.
57 Being Regulation (EC) 641/2004 and Regulation (EU) 503/2013.
58 Which are foods without a history of consumption prior to 15 May 1997, including those subject to new processes.
59 https://www.food.gov.uk/business-guidance/regulated-products/novel-foods-guidance#:~:text=terms%20of%20authorisation.-,Assimilated%20Regulation%20(EU)%202015%2F2283%20(Opens%20in%20a,set%20out%20in%20the%20register
60 Such as Regulation (EC) 1829/2003.

13.29 This regulation does recognise the importance of innovations in food and food production, and its impact on the environment, food security and benefit for consumers.[61] It seeks to provide an agile framework that can adapt as the technologies themselves advance[62] and novel food production processes evolve.[63]

EU

13.30 Foodstuff is regulated in the EU under the EU General Food Law Regulation.[64] This regulation pre-dates the rise of Industry 4.0, despite the adoption of the 2018 transparency and sustainability revisions in 2018[65] and therefore does not provide for the radical advancements seen in the industry. It is necessary for regulators to keep a firm eye on the developments in this space.

PEST CONTROL

13.31 Pest control and crop protection are key areas of concern in agriculture, and are not immune from transformation as a result of the digital revolution. Precision farming, is being used to try and reduce the vast need for herbicides, fungicides and insecticides and to combat climate change concerns.[66] Computer vision (a form of AI), robotics, and genome editing of crops are being touted as innovative crop protection solutions.[67] In the UK, there is a raft of legislation that deals with pest control, which those revolutionising this sector through digitalisation will need to take into account including the Prevention of Damage by Pests Act 1949, the Health and Safety at Work etc. Act 1974, the Wildlife and Countryside Act 1981, the Animal Welfare Act 2006 and the Environmental Protection Act 1990.

13.32 The Saudi Arabian Centre for the Fourth Industrial Revolution considered a case study on the management of red palm weevil in 2025 known as the RPW Infestation Solutions Project.[68] As part of the project, the Centre also looked to create governance and regulation for the initiative. This is to

61 Recitals paragraph (29) of Regulation (EU) 2015/2283.
62 Recitals paragraph (8) of Regulation (EU) 2015/2283.
63 Recitals paragraph (9) of Regulation (EU) 2015/2283.
64 Regulation (EU) 178/2002.
65 Regulation (EU) 2019/1381 of the European Parliament and of the Council of 20 June 2019 on the transparency and sustainability of the EU risk assessment in the food chain and amending Regulations (EC) No 178/2002, (EC) No 1829/2003, (EC) No 1831/2003, (EC) No 2065/2003, (EC) No 1935/2004, (EC) No 1331/2008, (EC) No 1107/2009, (EU) 2015/2283 and Directive 2001/18/EC.
66 https://www.europarl.europa.eu/RegData/etudes/STUD/2021/656330/EPRS_STU(2021)656330_EN.pdf.
67 Ibid.
68 https://www.c4irsaudiarabia.org/docs/RPW%20Infestation%20Solutions_Technical%20Report.pdf.

balance safeguarding agriculture against innovation. The Centre looked at the underlying framework needed to encourage farmer's engagement with agritech and considered that policy and regulation must be promoted via public-private partnerships (PPP) and through authorisations and permits, such as licensing requirements for drones and the use of PPP partnerships, such as the IBM partnership in India. One of the concerns with regulation, however, is ensuring that it is up-to-date given the rapid pace of change.

13.33 It is vital, however, that trust is encouraged in the system to ensure its proper adoption. The European Parliament has considered the adoption of emerging technology in respect of pest control in detail, highlighting that farmers will often seek to utilise the most cost-effective solution, and that it is therefore necessary to balance this objective with the Common Agricultural Policy objectives and the need to promote fair trade in this space.[69]

ANIMAL WELFARE AND INDUSTRY 4.0

13.34 Animal welfare is governed in the UK under the Animal Welfare Act 2006. The Animal Health and Welfare Pathway sets out expectations in respect of animal health and welfare, and now do offer grants for farmers which can be used directly towards purchasing technology.[70]

13.35 Smart farming, or precision livestock farming, involves the use of cameras, onsite sensors and wearable devices, and many farmers do consider that it does help with animal welfare and health, helps predict health concerns and disease outbreaks. Precision farming can help animal welfare through real-time monitoring on the farm, and by having greater insights into the livestock and wider external data to use for decision making.[71] Concerns have, however, been expressed over the costs associated with this technology given the uncertain economic climate which has faced farmers in the UK generally for the last decade or more.[72]

13.36 Some consider, however, that the use of precision farming can have a detrimental impact on animal health and welfare, by reducing contact with people and therefore making animals more fearful towards them.[73] Some believe that precision farming could reduce the standard of care as farmers may start to see the animals more like devices and there may be issues caused by less human

69 https://www.europarl.europa.eu/RegData/etudes/STUD/2021/656330/EPRS_STU(2021)656330_EN.pdf.

70 https://www.gov.uk/government/publications/animal-health-and-welfare-pathway/animal-health-and-welfare-pathway.

71 https://www.biology.ox.ac.uk/article/smart-farming-artificial-intelligence-how-can-we-ensure-animal-welfare-is-a-priority.

72 https://www.appg-agscience.org.uk/_files/ugd/f77b24_81df3d4c0e84414d9ed35859e1889520.pdf.

73 Ibid.

interactions with their animals.[74] Finally, there is also still a lack of quantitative data on the impact of these devices and sensors on the animals and in their environment.[75]

13.37 The British Veterinary Association recommends that where farms use emerging technologies or innovations, this should not be at a cost to animal welfare or human observation and expertise. It does however welcome innovations which measure health and welfare of livestock such as those being used within dairy farming which automate milking and can monitor numerous data outputs and present these to farmers via mobile applications, and 3D camera systems in pig farming to identify tail biting.[76]

13.38 The British Veterinary Association expressed its concerns of genome editing of agricultural animals, which is permitted in theory under the Genetic Technology (Precision Breeding) Act 2023, because of the risk of it causing poor welfare concerns for animals who are byproducts of these experiments and a reduction in animal welfare standard generally since animals will be more robust.[77] Notably genome editing of animals is, however, not currently permitted under the Genetic Technology (Precision Breeding) Regulations 2025.

AI IN AGRICULTURE

13.39 Digital twin technology and AI is already being deployed in agriculture due to the significant time and cost saving that it creates, as well as insights and opportunities. For example, AI is being used within agriculture for: weather forecasting; to assist in seed sowing and crop planning; for crop health management and soil health management; to explore soil nutrients through soil analysis; to gain insights for fertiliser use; to predict pest infestations by using previous data to predict outbreaks and encouraging farmers to report and record outbreaks and for market forecasting; and looking at pricing and demand, through smart marketplaces which record volume of crops, pricing and also facilitate sales using both real-time and historical data, and other data such as weather data.[78]

13.40 Digital twin technology is also now being adopted within agriculture to increase yield and production, one such example is the University of Florida

74 J. Schillings and R. Bennett (2021), 'Exploring the potential of Precision Livestock Farming technologies to help address farm animal welfare', Frontiers in Animal Science, https://centaur.reading.ac.uk/97469/9/fanim-02-639678.pdf.

75 https://pmc.ncbi.nlm.nih.gov/articles/PMC10000125/.

76 https://www.bva.co.uk/media/1181/bva-position-on-uk-sustainable-animal-agriculture-full.pdf

77 https://www.bva.co.uk/media/6120/241008-finalbva-policy-position-gene-editing.pdf.

78 World Economic Form insight (August 2025), 'Future Farming in India', https://reports.weforum.org/docs/WEF_Future_Farming_in_India_A_Playbook_for_Scaling_Artificial_Intelligence_in_Agriculture_2025.pdf.

Institute of Food and Agricultural Sciences digital twin, which is being used for strawberry fields, and saw a 92% accuracy in the detection of fruit with a very low margin of error.[79] In addition, NASA has created the 'Agricultural Digital Twin', which uses NASA sensors to identify where crops would yield the best results, and enables farmers to use this information to make informed decisions for their farms.[80]

13.41 In 2025, the World Economic Forum published 'A Playbook for Scaling Artificial Intelligence in Agriculture'.[81] The playbook, aimed at policymakers, considers that there is the need for governments to support the uptake of AI in farming by encouraging inclusive scalable use, and having clear policies and support available. The IMPACT AI framework should be used for AI in agriculture[82] to achieve 'AI for all'.[83] The principles of the IMPACT AI framework are to (1) Enable; (2) Create; and (3) Deliver. There should always be a clear and transparent infrastructure, public safety must be paramount and all system should be created with the 'do no harm' principle at the forefront. Further all regulations should be risk-based, governments should encourage AI ecosystems; and the governments should be the catalyst for innovation in the AI in agriculture space.

13.42 The European Parliament explored the idea of AI in the agricultural sector in 2023 given the vast amount of data already being collected, or that could be collected, within the agricultural setting, which can help gain insights and knowledge that can be fed back into the food production process.[84] It considers that the key questions to cover in any AI in agriculture policy are:[85]

1. What is expected by each of the different stakeholders?
2. What should be the risks and liabilities for the software providers?
3. How can you regulate these databases?
4. How can you protect workers?
5. How can you ensure that farmers are able to change software or systems and not be beholden to specific systems?
6. How can you encourage uptake of this technology?

79 https://reports.weforum.org/docs/WEF_Shaping_the_Deep_Tech_Revolution_in_Agriculture_2025.pdf.

80 https://esto.nasa.gov/nasa-agricultural-digital-twin-will-help-farmers-improve-crop-yield-forecasts/.

81 World Economic Form insight (n 78).

82 The Inclusive Multistakeholder Pathway for the Accelerated Convergence of AI Technologies (IMPACT AI) Framework.

83 World Economic Form insight (n 78).

84 https://www.europarl.europa.eu/RegData/etudes/STUD/2023/734711/EPRS_STU(2023)734711_EN.pdf.

85 Ibid.

7. How can you protect smaller farms, especially when dealing with large technology providers?
8. How are high risks such as health concerns in humans, and to the environment factored in?

BIO-TECHNOLOGY

13.43 It is not only traditional digital technologies that are powering the industrial changes in Industry 4.0. We are also experiencing other technological innovations, such as those in biotechnology and nanotechnology. Biotech innovations include synthetic biology, fermentation technologies and bio-processing technologies.[86] These advances are all equally as important technologies for Industry 4.0 and the industrial metaverse as those digital technologies of AI and virtual reality. In fact, in many cases, the only way in which biotechnology and nanotechnology have been able to advance is because of advances in these other technologies, making what was previously impossible, possible. As with any industrial revolution, it is the coming together of multiple different factors, and one of the key areas impacted is agriculture and food, given its vital importance to our lives.

13.44 There is, however, a general lack of confidence and fear that many have in biotechnology and nanotechnology, especially in agriculture and relating to foodstuff, and there is therefore the need to focus on regulation, financing, education and incentivisation of biotechnologies.[87]

13.45 The World Economic Forum Bioeconomy Initiative has established a practical framework for the regulation and adoption of biotechnology, highlighting that effective, clear and transparent regulations are needed, which utilise the skills of technical scientific experts, to help to propel the uptake of this technology.[88] Suitable test beds should be established to test the technologies such as the EU Test Farms programme.[89] Any regulation has to be agile and able to react to different developments in the technology; this is an area where there is a lack of existing regulations, the field is extremely broad and does not neatly fit into traditional areas of regulation.[90] The UK's Regulatory Innovation Office is seen by many as a positive development in the regulation of innovative technologies such as biotech.

86 https://reports.weforum.org/docs/WEF_Next_Generation_Bio_Innovation_2025.pdf.

87 https://reports.weforum.org/docs/WEF_From_Policy_to_Practice_Actionable_Recommendations_for_a_Commercial_Bioeconomy_2025.pdf.

88 Ibid.

89 Ibid.

90 https://reports.weforum.org/docs/WEF_From_Policy_to_Practice_Actionable_Recommendations_for_a_Commercial_Bioeconomy_2025.pdf.

GENOME EDITING

13.46 Genome editing is where a crop's DNA is edited precisely to create a desirable outcome. The most commonly used system is CRISPR.[91]

13.47 Genome editing in crops is now governed by the Genetic Technology (Precision Breeding) Act 2003 and the Genetic Technology (Precision Breeding) Regulations 2025 in England. The Genetic Technology (Precision Breeding) Act 2003 covers plants and animals[92] where 'modern biotechnology' has been deployed but the results of which could have occurred naturally or from traditional techniques and the genetic changes have to be stable.[93] The regime is more streamlined than it was previously, to enable innovation, but still retains strict regulations for GMOs.[94] This sees a departure in England from the EU European Court of Justice 2018 decision (as discussed below at para **13.51**), which has also been modified in the EU.[95]

13.48 The Genetic Technology (Precision Breeding) Regulations 2025 covers plants only at this time.[96] It is important that the plants meet the qualifying criteria under the regulations and that it is not inadvertently a GMO instead, which has separate enhanced requirements as discussed earlier in the chapter. Under the Regulations, the Department for Environment, Food and Rural Affairs (DEFRA) has to be notified before starting any trial and there are strict requirements on how the plants are dealt with during this stage.[97]

13.49 The FSA oversees any genome edited food entering the food chain as discussed above, and it is expected that genome edited plants could be sold in England as early as 2026.

13.50 Finally, it is important to note that the Genetic Technology (Precision Breeding) Act 2003 and the Genetic Technology (Precision Breeding) Regulations 2025 do not apply to any of the devolved nations of the UK, and therefore, at least for now, we will see a difference between England, Scotland, Wales and Northern Ireland on this position.

91 The CRISPR-Cas was developed by Jennifer Doundna and Emmanuele Charpentier who won the Nobel Prize for Chemistry for the device in 2020.

92 Other than humans and human embryo which are excluded.

93 https://www.gov.uk/government/publications/acre-guidance-on-producing-precision-bred-plants/acre-guidance-on-producing-precision-bred-plantsv.

94 https://www.gov.uk/government/news/genetic-technology-act-key-tool-for-uk-food-security.

95 https://researchbriefings.files.parliament.uk/documents/POST-PN-0663/POST-PN-0663.pdf.

96 Section 2 definition of '"precisions bred organism" means precision bred plant'.

97 https://www.gov.uk/government/publications/precision-bred-plants-releasing-and-marketing/releasing-precision-bred-plants-into-the-environment.

13.51 In the EU, genome edited crops did until summer 2026 all just fall under the GMO legislation as a result of a 2018 case.[98] EU GMO legislation is, and remains, extremely administrative and there has only been a very limited number of organisations which have sought to comply with this regime. The EU has however now changed the way in which it will regulate genome editing and new genomic techniques under Regulation 2026/1388 of 17 June 2026 by introducing new regulations distinguishing between category 1 and category 2 plants. Category 2 plants would still have to comply with GMO rules, whilst category 1 plants now have their own regime.[99] Much of the new procedures and requirements, however, will not come into effect until 2028.[100]

The Rapporteur has said of the new regulations:

> 'This is a historic victory for Europe's farmers and Europe's future. By approving the use of NGTs, we have chosen innovation, competitiveness, and food security. European farmers have long been calling for access to these modern breeding tools, to help them develop crops that are more resilient and less dependent on pesticides. By making these safe, science-based breeding technologies available, Parliament is delivering for European farmers, safeguarding our food security, and building a more competitive and innovative Europe.'[101]

13.52 The complicating factor between traditional genetic modification and genome editing, is that with genome editing it is very difficult to identify a crop which has been edited once it leaves the laboratory as it can be confused easily with naturally occurring phenomena, which presents a regulatory challenge.[102] It is possible to patent the genome edited plant in the EU, as a plant variety right, but any application has to confirm that the method is not 'essentially natural'.[103] Given the size and scale of players in this market, it is expected that many varieties will be patented and intellectual property licences will be required to exploit such variety and to utilise the CRISPR-Cas crops.[104] The new genomic technique regulations in the EU see compulsory requirements for disclosing all patents

98 Directive 2001/18/EC, Regulation (EC) 1829/2003, Directive 2015/412, Regulation (EC) 1830/2003, Directive 2009/41/EC, this is as a result of case C-528/16 which sets wide parameters for the designation of GMO foods where there is mutagenesis.

99 https://www.consilium.europa.eu/en/policies/new-genomic-techniques-for-plant-breeding/.

100 Article 29 of Regulation (EU) 2026/1388 of the European Parliament and of the Council of 17 June 2026 on plants obtained by certain new genomic techniques and their products, and amending Regulation (EU) 2017/625.

101 https://www.europarl.europa.eu/news/en/press-room/20260611IPR45215/new-genomic-techniques-for-plants-to-boost-innovation-in-sustainable-agriculture.

102 https://www.europarl.europa.eu/RegData/etudes/IDAN/2022/690194/EPRS_IDA(2022)690194_EN.pdf.

103 Ibid.

104 Ibid.

(and pending patents) owned by that organisation, which will be contained on a public database.[105] Transparency is a key part of the new regulations.[106]

ALTERNATIVE PROTEINS

13.53 The World Economic Forum foresees a 50% projected increase in the global consumption of meat by 2050.[107] There is a big driver for changes to food choices as we embrace Industry 4.0, in part due to climate change and the need to adapt to meet an increased population and changing weather conditions. Alternative proteins are now being explored and used to re-create meat. This may be using plants, animal cells, fungi or fermentation. This market is expected to be worth in the region of $570 billion by 2030.[108]

13.54 Given the nature of this innovation, it is vital that the food is safe, but there is also the need to balance regulation against the innovation in this space given the underlying and fundamental need for this. We are already seeing country-led initiatives to explore the use of this technology and its regulation.[109] The role of the government in respect of the alternative protein field is significant as developments in this space will be through collaborations between government regulators and private facilities, bringing together a mix of government resources and industry experience and innovation.

13.55 There is the need for an agile, clear and efficient regulatory systems in this space that give trust to consumers and ensure that there are suitable structures and standards in place. Lessons should be taken from Israel, Singapore and the United States of America in respect of their regulation in this space.[110]

KEY TAKEAWAY POINTS

13.56 The key takeaway points in respect of agriculture, food production and the industrial metaverse are:

- Smart farming, otherwise known as precision agriculture/ precision farming, is not limited only to digital technologies, but technological innovations which include alternative foods, biotechnology and nanotechnology.

105 https://www.consilium.europa.eu/en/press/press-releases/2025/12/04/new-genomic-techniques-council-and-parliament-strike-deal-to-boost-the-competitiveness-and-sustainability-of-our-food-systems/.

106 https://www.europarl.europa.eu/news/en/press-room/20260611IPR45215/new-genomic-techniques-for-plants-to-boost-innovation-in-sustainable-agriculture.

107 https://www3.weforum.org/docs/WEF_Protein_Diversification_2024.pdf.

108 Ibid.

109 Ibid.

110 https://www3.weforum.org/docs/WEF_Protein_Diversification_2024.pdf.

- Data is of fundamental importance in smart farming. Recognising this the EU has established the Common European Agricultural Data Space and the EU code of conduct on agricultural data sharing by contractual agreement.
- Food safety is of paramount concern. Its regulation in the UK falls under legislation which is over 35 years old, predating any form of the seismic advances in innovations we are now experiencing. The FSA has released guidance on the use of AI in the food supply chain, raising concerns over bias and discrimination, but believes that it can be used not least by the regulators to monitor providers.
- GMOs have never taken off in the UK, most likely due to the ethical issues associated with them. Novel foods, however, fall under retained EU regulation, and require registration on a Register of Novel Foods.
- Emerging technologies are being used for pest control, including forms of AI and computer vision. It is vital that there are effective regulations to cover their use to avoid harms and risks to wildlife.
- Animal welfare is paramount, and emerging technologies need to ensure that this is not negatively impacted through the use of these technologies, but instead used for good and to promote self and responsible animal husbandry.
- Genome editing is governed by the Genetic Technology (Precision Breeding) Act 2003 and the Genetic Technology (Precision Breeding) Regulations 2025 in England.
- Whilst alternative proteins are seen as positive for sustainability, it is vital that these are safe, and that innovation is balanced against risks to foodstuff for human consumption or entering the human foodchain.

Chapter 14

The industrial metaverse, healthcare and the pharmaceutical industry

'Healthcare in combination with the metaverse truly has the potential to make the world a better place and create value in an innovative way.'[1]

Wolter Jalink, Head of Technology Transformation, EY Switzerland

14.1 The healthcare industry is also being revolutionised as part of Industry 4.0, and medicine is a key use of the industrial metaverse.[2] Emerging technologies are being used for training, as well as to test prototypes of medical devices, to maintain medical equipment remotely, to undertake collaborative research, and digital twins are being deployed in many different iterations; from virtual hospitals to virtual replicas of different organs and the body. In 2020, surgeons even started using augmented reality to perform surgery on patients.[3]

14.2 One key aspect of the digital revolution in healthcare is a move towards personalised medicine.[4] This is the ability to deliver effective medicine, and treatment, specific to the individual, ideally as proactive preventative measures, and predicting harms and risks. With rising populations, rising diseases and rising mental health illnesses, there are significant opportunities to use emerging technologies to disrupt the existing status quo in medicine.[5] For example, countries such as Abu Dhabi are now creating a smart healthcare system through an 'intelligent health system' to create a data rich personalised healthcare system, and as a result they are seeing faster care being delivered, earlier detection rates, reduced healthcare costs and improved societal health overall.[6]

14.3 There are however, many regulatory and legal issues which impact on the pace of adoption of digitalisation within the health sectors. This includes

1 https://www.ey.com/en_ch/insights/technology/how-can-life-sciences-and-healthcare-thrive-in-the-metaverse.
2 https://www.iec.ch/basecamp/industrial-metaverse.
3 https://www.hopkinsmedicine.org/news/articles/2021/02/johns-hopkins-performs-its-first-augmented-reality-surgeries-in-patients.
4 Personalised medicine is being promoted by NHS England as being transformative in respect of the delivery of the 'four Ps':
   1. **P**rediction and Prevention of disease
   2. More **P**recise diagnoses
   3. **P**ersonalised and targeted interventions
   4. A more **P**articipatory role for patients"
   https://www.england.nhs.uk/healthcare-science/personalisedmedicine/.
5 https://reports.weforum.org/docs/WEF_A_New_Era_for_Digital_Health_2026.pdf.
6 Ibid.

the general concerns with the 'black box' effect of these technologies, and the fear caused by the unknown inner complexities of how these systems actually work. The general view is that healthcare regulators will adopt a conservative and risk adverse position in this area. In all cases patient health and wellbeing must be prioritised, as well as the fundamental preservation of data protection principles. There are also many other legal considerations around liability, risk and insurance within the sector, and the need for clarity and trust in the system.

14.4 There is currently a lack of internationally harmonised standards and frameworks within the industry, and it would be beneficial to encourage the safe adoption of emerging technologies within the sector, through coordinated efforts of innovators, clinicians, and policy-makers.[7] Artificial intelligence (AI) has made significant progress within the healthcare industry, but there are still significant regulatory gaps and a distinct lack of consistent training on AI and other digital technologies.[8] Professor Powis, the NHS England Medical Director reminds us that:

> 'Innovation and technological advancement is not, and should never be seen as, an end in itself. While in the operating theatres of the future we might be reaching for the lasers instead of the scalpel, or welcoming artificially intelligent robots as members of our teams, the recipient of these new types of care and treatment – the patient – will remain very much human'.[9]

INNOVATION

14.5 The industrial metaverse has significant opportunities for the healthcare sector. We are already starting to see a convergence of emerging technologies such as AI, augmented reality, and blockchain being utilised together within the sector. There are calls, however, for much wider changes across the entire industry rather than just isolated piecemeal adoption of discrete pieces of emerging technology from hospital trust to hospital trust.[10] Instead, there is the call for wider systematic change to the healthcare system fuelled by industry 4.0 technologies. As above, Abu Dhabi has undertaken a seismic change to its health infrastructure, which has revolutionised its healthcare system, moving completely over to a digital system, using a multitude of different emerging technologies, including a full digital twin of the healthcare system supported by an agile regulatory framework, to deal with issues such as privacy and other safeguards. The Abu Dhabi system is being touted as a playbook for innovating healthcare in Industry 4.0.[11]

7 J. Rodriguez-Manzano et al (2024), 'Innovative diagnostic technologies: navigating regulatory frameworks through advances, challenges, and future prospects', The Lancet Digital Health, 6(12): E934–E943.

8 https://iris.who.int/server/api/core/bitstreams/d2913ae3-c8e0-4a46-b6ff-b4b121e936f4/content.

9 https://futureofsurgery.rcseng.ac.uk/report/Future%20of%20Surgery%20Report.pdf.

10 https://reports.weforum.org/docs/WEF_A_New_Era_for_Digital_Health_2026.pdf.

11 Ibid.

14.6 Whilst this technology all still remains at the early stages, it is important that the future of medicine is not overlooked. In doing so, however, it brings with it complex legal and ethical challenges, which need to be addressed to ensure that patients retain trust within the system and in the delivery of medicine. This includes proper training for those working within the system, as well as giving them the necessary confidence to work and experiment in this evolving sector. The Royal College of Surgeons of England feel that it is very important that trainees learn about the new innovations in healthcare, and that these updates should be contained both within the training curriculum for new medics, but should also be offered as ongoing continuous training for existing practitioners.[12]

LIABILITY

14.7 The changes being brought about by the introduction of personalised medicine through digital twins, and other uses of autonomous technology and emerging technologies, need us to rethink the traditional basis for liability within the medical setting.[13] This depends on the extent and degree of the incorporation of the technology within the actual decision-making, diagnosis and treatment process. As the landscape changes, however, these questions will come to the forefront, especially in medical negligence where the exposure to risk and catastrophe are magnified. In addition, those dealing with liability will have to navigate a significant amount of data from multiple different sources, given in most emerging technologies data will be collected in real-time.

14.8 In its legal statement on liability for AI harms the UK Jurisdiction Taskforce specifically considered the non-delegable vicarious duty imposed on NHS trusts in respect of its patients, as well as medical negligence in general.[14] The statement is discussed in more detail in **Chapter 16**; however, it does note that in general the common law is well placed to be able to deal with issues concerning liability arising from AI, including those relating to negligence, where the Taskforce believes that the same legal test will still apply. Using the example of a radiologist using AI to analyse scans, it considers that the AI should be treated as a tool in the same way as any piece of equipment, and therefore under the radiologists control and responsibility.

14.9 Some commentators have considered the extent to which the patient themselves should assume any responsibility where they are part of the digital twin, and point out that it is fundamental to a well running healthcare system to maintain the trusted regard held for doctors, and to ensure that their views are properly heard in amongst the data.[15] Finally, it will be vital for full disclosure to

12 https://futureofsurgery.rcseng.ac.uk/report/Future%20of%20Surgery%20Report.pdf.

13 M. Teller (2021), 'Legal aspects related to digital twin', Philos Trans A Math Phys Eng Sci, 379(2207): 20210023, https://doi.org/10.1098/rsta.2021.0023.

14 The UK Jurisdiction Taskforce, 'Legal Statement on liability for AI harms' (July 2026), https://lawtechuk.io/ukjt/liability-for-ai-harms-under-the-private-law-of-england-and-wales/.

15 Ibid.

patients of the use of emerging technologies to enable them to provide informed consent.

HEALTH DATA

14.10 Data is intrinsically linked to Industry 4.0, as it is the fuel for the digital revolution. This is recognised by the EU, who has established the European Health Data Space (EHDS) under Regulation (EU) 2025/327. The regulation provides guardrails for the safeguarding of digital health records, and their use within the health system. This is largely a precursor to pave the way for complete digitalisation of the healthcare sector. The regulation provides for data portability and the right for users to be able to manage their own health records, as well as healthcare providers. It permits the effective exchange of health data within the EU, and the ability of citizens to have full transparency over their records. This includes the ability to restrict access to certain data, such as sexual health or specific procedures, from certain healthcare professionals. The regulation clearly signals that health data belongs to the patient, and that they should be empowered to use that themselves for their treatment.

14.11 The regulation does, however, also provide for the secondary uses of the electronic health data, such as for innovation purposes and for personalised medicine.[16] This means that health data can be used as part of specific datasets, for example, to train AI systems. The regulation encourages the effective collection and use of health data for innovation and public policy initiatives. The data is, however, safeguarded through the regulation which balances the data subject's rights as against the opportunities for the use of the data.[17]

14.12 The EHDS is transformational in its approach to health data and its use within the Industry 4.0 landscape. The EHDS is a clear indication of Industry 4.0 and the digital transformation of medicine.[18]

14.13 The Sudlow Review,[19] considered the idea of health data in the UK in the context of the digital revolution and Industry 4.0. It concluded that the UK is currently not taking proper advantage of health data as part of the critical infrastructure because of inefficacies but, that in order to change this, investment is needed in the infrastructure as well as implementing streamlined procedures and strategic partnerships.[20]

16 European Health Data Space (EHDS) under Regulation (EU) 2025/327, recital (1).

17 https://health.ec.europa.eu/ehealth-digital-health-and-care/reuse-health-data_en.

18 https://health.ec.europa.eu/ehealth-digital-health-and-care/artificial-intelligence-healthcare_en.

19 Also known as the 'Uniting the UK's Health Data: A Huge Opportunity for Society: a review of the UK health data landscape commissioned by the Chief Medical Officer for England, the UK National Statistician and NHS England's National Director for Transformation' report.

20 https://zenodo.org/records/13353747.

14.14 The report highlights that proper safeguards are needed to protect the integrity and confidentiality of health data, but that this data is necessary for the technological changes needed to improve the NHS. The use of health data to fuel innovations in the NHS was called upon in Lord Darzi 's recent NHS review, in which he recommends the establishment of a National Health Data Service, similar to the National Data Library.[21]

CYBER-SECURITY IN HEALTHCARE

14.15 With the increased digitalisation of healthcare there is a greater risk of cybersecurity attacks.[22] This was seen first-hand in 2017 with the 'WannaCry' attack. Cybersecurity is a fundamental concern in healthcare now, even before we are fully emerged in Industry 4.0, and it requires constant real-time monitoring and detection. The Cyber Security and Resilience Bill will take steps to try and protect healthcare infrastructure.

14.16 In the EU the European Commission has launched an action plan on 'cybersecurity of hospital and healthcare providers',[23] having noted that the EU's healthcare system was the most attacked industry infrastructure in the EU by cybercriminals. This is expected to increase as we move through more and more forms of digitalisation in the healthcare sector and, with increased digitalisation the impact of such attacks will detrimentally impact patient health and will even cause death.[24]

14.17 The EU Commission calls on the use of the European Digital Identity Wallets, which are being implemented across the EU, to try and help mitigate the cybersecurity concerns in this sector.

BIAS AND DISCRIMINATION IN HEALTHTECH

14.18 Given the prominence of data within Industry 4.0, there is always a risk of bias where these emerging technologies are deployed. This is an incredibly sensitive issue, especially in the context of health and social care, where many steps have been taken in real-life to try and eradicate historical bias.

21 Ibid.

22 O. Freyer, K. Rajput, M. Ostermann, S. Gilbert and S. Ghafur (2026), 'Are we heading towards a cybersecurity crisis in health care and are actions needed?', The Lancet Digital Health, 8(1): 100946.

23 https://digital-strategy.ec.europa.eu/en/library/european-action-plan-cybersecurity-hospitals-and-healthcare-providers

24 Communication from the Commission to the European Parliament, the Council, the European Economic and Social Committee and the Committee of the Regions: European action plan on the cybersecurity of hospitals and healthcare providers, Brussels, 15.1.2025, COM(2025).

14.19 In 2024, the Government published its independent report on bias in medical devices, which had been commissioned to consider whether there was evidence of gender, race or ethnicity bias in the design of medical devices.[25] The report considered AI-enabled devices, amongst other types of devices, and their propensity to replicate historical bias; especially when used in diagnosis and screening.[26] The report called for the establishment of a specific taskforce to explore the impact of health equity on emerging technologies and their adoption within healthcare.[27] The report also looked ahead at issues of bias in respect of wearables and other digital devices.[28]

14.20 Eight recommendations were made in the report to try and prevent bias in AI-assisted medical devices being: (1) developers should involve a diverse group of people in the design stage of the devices and use a recognised framework such as the NHS England engagement framework; (2) there should be comprehensive training for all stakeholders in the process to understand the concerns in respect of bias and how this can be mitigated; (3) there should be transparent disclosure throughout the research and development of the products, including with regulators implementing reporting requirements on these indices; (4) there should be collaboration between all stakeholders in the development of the devices throughout its lifecycle to coordinate best practices and adoption of the MHRA Principles for Good Machine Learning Practice for Medical Device Development as discussed below at para **14.32**; (5) suitable guidance should be provided by regulators as a long-term guide on the development of devices in this new era; (6) the NHS must uphold its own standards to influence other stakeholders; (7) diversity and inclusion should be prioritised in research; and (8) an expert led panel should be established to assess and monitor AI and equity.[29]

ARTIFICIAL INTELLIGENCE

14.21 AI is revolutionising healthcare; however, concerns have been expressed that current regulations do not suitability cover its use, and this needs to be updated urgently.[30] The use of AI in the health and medical field has to balance the opportunities presented by the innovations against the need to protect patients, both in terms of their health and wellbeing, and their privacy and personal data.[31] One issue with the regulation of AI in healthcare generally is that most regulations are not properly set up to deal with the agile nature of AI.[32] Traditionally, regulation in the healthcare sector has been relatively slow.

25 https://assets.publishing.service.gov.uk/media/65e89e9e62ff48001a87b2d8/equity-in-medical-devices-independent-review-report-web-accessible.pdf.
26 Ibid.
27 Ibid.
28 Ibid.
29 https://assets.publishing.service.gov.uk/media/65e89e9e62ff48001a87b2d8/equity-in-medical-devices-independent-review-report-web-accessible.pdf.
30 https://reports.weforum.org/docs/WEF_Earning_Trust_for_AI_in_Health_2025.pdf.
31 Ibid.
32 (2025), 'Rapid generative AI rollout in health care', The Lancet Digital Health, 7(8): 100909.

14.22 The World Health Organisation has cautioned that currently there is uncertainty in respect of liability, risk and compliance in the medical use of AI since the technology is developing much faster than regulations can keep pace.[33] Furthermore, regulations remain inconsistent generally, and there is a lack of consistent ethical guidelines and rules on the secondary use of health data for public benefits.[34]

14.23 In fact, despite the EU AI Act,[35] the World Health Organisation found in November 2025 that legal uncertainty was the most reported barrier to the adoption of AI in healthcare in the European region and to address this called on the effective use of regulatory sandboxes, the need for alignment of AI with ethical standards, the need to decide which healthcare responsibilities should be dealt with by the state and which can be delegated to private corporations, as well as the use of transparent private public partnerships (PPPs).[36] The World Economic Forum identify three key considerations for dealing with AI in healthcare: (1) those involved in healthcare need to be upskilled on AI and its use in respect of medicine and health;(2) there need to be suitable regulations and laws in place which protect the public and ensures that there are high safety standards in place; and (3) that PPPs should be effectively utilised.[37]

14.24 Just as there is no universal consensus on how AI itself should be regulated, there is certainly no universal view on the regulation of AI within healthcare and medicine. For some uses it will be governed by existing frameworks, which present unique difficulties that emerging harms may not be adequately covered nor contemplated when the policies and laws were prepared.

THE UK

14.25 In the UK, medical AI systems are regulated by the Medicines and Healthcare Products Regulatory Agency (MHRA) under the Medical Devices Regulations 2002. The MHRA established the Regulation of AI in Healthcare (the National Commission) in September 2025 in order to make recommendations on suitable regulatory frameworks on AI in healthcare.[38] Proposals are under way for updates on the regulation of medical devices using AI, which must balance

33 https://iris.who.int/server/api/core/bitstreams/d2913ae3-c8e0-4a46-b6ff-b4b121e936f4/content.

34 Ibid.

35 Regulation (EU) 2024/1689 of the European Parliament and of the Council of 13 June 2024 laying down harmonised rules on artificial intelligence and amending Regulations (EC) No 300/2008, (EU) No 167/2013, (EU) No 168/2013, (EU) 2018/858, (EU) 2018/1139 and (EU) 2019/2144 and Directives 2014/90/EU, (EU) 2016/797 and (EU) 2020/1828 (Artificial Intelligence Act).

36 https://iris.who.int/server/api/core/bitstreams/d2913ae3-c8e0-4a46-b6ff-b4b121e936f4/content.

37 https://reports.weforum.org/docs/WEF_Earning_Trust_for_AI_in_Health_2025.pdf.

38 https://www.gov.uk/government/groups/national-commission-into-the-regulation-of-ai-in-healthcare.

innovation and patient safety,[39] and as part of which they put out a call for evidence and requested feedback on existing rules and stakeholders' concerns.[40]

14.26 The National Commission is aiming to try and address questions such as:

1. Where does liability sit? Is it with the medical practitioner or the software developer?[41]
2. What steps can be implemented to ensure patients are safe and can be confident to utilise the innovations?[42]
3. How do we effectively horizon scan in this landscape so that new emerging technologies and risks can be effectively identified?[43]
4. How can patient feedback and experiences be factored into the regulation of AI in healthcare?[44]
5. How can the Patient Safety Principles around transparency and accountability be properly and meaningfully incorporated into the regulation of AI in healthcare?[45]

14.27 The Chair of the National Commission, Professor Alastair Denniston considers that 'the future of AI in healthcare will not be defined by machines, but by the values we bring to their use' and that the three core principles should be factored into the regulation of AI in healthcare being (1) patient safety: the most fundamental objective is patient safety, but it needs to be recognised that this does not mean 100% guaranteed safety, since there has to be acceptance that some element of risk is proportionate to the potential benefits in medicine; (2) without delay: where the technology will help patients this should be implemented as swiftly as possible, since delays to beneficial treatments will cause harm; and (3) effective regulation: there needs to be a clear and transparent regulatory framework to encourage trust in the systems being deployed.[46]

14.28 The Medicines and Medical Devices Act 2021 does permit changes to the governance of medical devices. In June 2022, the UK Government responded to consultations about the future of regulating medical devices. In its hope to be world-leading in medical device innovation, it noted the need to remain agile but

39 https://assets.publishing.service.gov.uk/media/69257c789fd433badebc30fe/Summary_minutes_first_meeting_of_National_Commission.pdf.

40 https://www.gov.uk/government/calls-for-evidence/regulation-of-ai-in-healthcare.

41 https://www.ourhealthpartnership.com/2025/10/23/blog-between-innovation-and-integrity-reflections-from-the-national-commission-on-ai-in-healthcare/.

42 https://www.ourhealthpartnership.com/2025/10/23/blog-between-innovation-and-integrity-reflections-from-the-national-commission-on-ai-in-healthcare/.

43 https://www.health.org.uk/features-and-opinion/blogs/ai-in-health-care-staying-ahead-of-the-issues.

44 https://www.gov.uk/government/news/professor-henrietta-hughes-putting-patient-safety-at-the-heart-of-regulatory-innovation.

45 Ibid.

46 https://www.gov.uk/government/news/professor-alastair-denniston-the-future-regulation-of-ai-in-healthcare.

that this needs to be balanced against patient safety, which is always paramount.[47] As part of the consultation, software as a medical device (SaMD), including AI as a medical device (ALaMD), were specifically considered. It was acknowledged that the significant technological developments in this area have come about after the 2002 regulations came into force and therefore the regulations do not have any specific provisions which specifically address this area. It concludes that, on the whole, it is just updated guidance which is required rather than extensive regulatory reform[48] with the key considerations being: (1) the implementation of effective cyber security measures as part of any SaMD; (2) the protection of patient data; and (3) aligned standards.[49]

14.29 The Medical Devices (Post-market Surveillance Requirements) (Amendment) (Great Britain) Regulations 2024 do, however, slightly amend the Medical Devices Regulations 2002. Whilst the regulations largely remain unaffected, the new regulations introduce new reporting requirements for SaMD on the market, including for indirect harm such as misdiagnosis from poor results of the software, malfunctioning devices and interfaces.[50] There is also considered the need for the creation of new industry standards to properly deal with ALaMD (AI as a medical device).[51]

In its 2024 White Paper on the impact of AI on the regulation of medical products, the MHRA confirmed its commitment to the Government-wide 'pro-innovation' stance. It introduces the MHRA's AI-Airlock sandbox; promotes international collaboration and harmonisation through the International Medical Devices Regulators Forum (IMDRF); promotes compliance with ISO/IEC TR 24027:2021; makes a commitment to a risk-based/proportionality approach to the regulation of AlaMD; and is developing a specific data strategy.[52]

The MHRA reminds developers that the regulations also cover data sets and the continual monitoring of AI products once on the market.[53]

47 https://assets.publishing.service.gov.uk/government/uploads/system/uploads/attachment_data/file/1085333/Government_response_to_consultation_on_the_future_regulation_of_medical_devices_in_the_United_Kingdom.pdf.
48 Ibid.
49 Ibid.
50 https://www.gov.uk/government/publications/reporting-adverse-incidents-involving-software-as-a-medical-device-under-the-vigilance-system/guidance-for-manufacturers-on-reporting-adverse-incidents-involving-software-as-a-medical-device-under-the-vigilance-system.
51 https://www.gov.uk/government/publications/software-and-ai-as-a-medical-device-change-programme/software-and-ai-as-a-medical-device-change-programme-roadmap#introduction.
52 https://assets.publishing.service.gov.uk/media/662fce1e9e82181baa98a988/MHRA_Impact-of-AI-on-the-regulation-of-medical-products.pdf.
53 Ibid.

14.30 Finally, the MHRA has established the Software and AI as a Medical Device Change Programme to try and ensure that technological advances in medical devices remain suitably governed.[54]

GOOD MACHINE LEARNING PRACTICE

14.31 Together with the US Food and Drug Administration (FDA) and Health Canada, the MHRA has agreed 10 guiding principles for the development of good machine learning for medical devices. This demonstrates a co-ordinated cross-border effort in this space given the impact that these medical devices have across multiple jurisdictions.

14.32 The guiding principles are: (1) the use of multi-disciplinary experts throughout the produce lifecycle; (2) the use of good software practices, including in the engineering and security of the products; (3) the reduction of bias by proper representative samples of data utilised; (4) the use of independent training data and test data; (5) the use of the best available data sets; (6) the model should be designed for the intended purpose of the device; (7) there must be a 'human in the loop' (8) there is suitable and accurate tests developed for the device (9) users are made clear of key information such as the use of the product, data, use of data and limitations; and (10) there is effective monitoring of the use of the devices.[55]

NHS

14.33 The NHS has established an internal AI team which confirms that it:

> 'aims to lead the NHS in harnessing AI innovations to deploy them in an ethical, efficient, and responsible manner that delivers enhanced health outcomes and system efficiencies, while upholding transparency, trust, and patient safety … [its]… mission is to embed responsible, ethical and sustainable AI into NHS services to improve patient care, optimise resources, and empower NHS staff.'[56]

14.34 Part of the initiative was to establish the STANDING Together partnership,[57] which was established in 2021 to explore ethical considerations in AI in healthcare, including reviewing risks of bias and inequalities.[58]

54 https://www.gov.uk/government/publications/software-and-ai-as-a-medical-device-change-programme/software-and-ai-as-a-medical-device-change-programme-roadmap#introduction.

55 https://www.gov.uk/government/publications/good-machine-learning-practice-for-medical-device-development-guiding-principles/good-machine-learning-practice-for-medical-device-development-guiding-principles.

56 https://digital.nhs.uk/services/ai-knowledge-repository.

57 STANdards for data Diversity, Inclusivity, & Generalisability.

58 https://www.datadiversity.org/recommendations.

NICE EVIDENCE STANDARDS FRAMEWORK

14.35 The NICE evidence standards framework (ESF) was created by the National Institute for Health and Care Excellence (NICE), NHS England, Public Health England and MedCity for digital health technologies, and was updated in 2022 to include AI.[59] The standards are a benchmark for safety, and include the requirements for appropriate marking under UKCA or CE Marks, regulation by the Care Quality Commission, compliance with the Data Protection Act 2018 and UK GDPR, and fulfilment of industry ISO/BS standards. In addition, the digital technology has to be proven as being credible to medical professionals, not biased, have good professional oversights and good data processes.[60]

THE EU

14.36 The European Commission in its consideration of the use of AI in healthcare believes that there is the need to balance innovation against safeguarding patients.[61]

14.37 In the EU, the EU Artificial Intelligence Act[62] will cover the use of AI within healthcare, and it is likely most of these systems will be classified as high risk. AI systems may also be covered under the Product Liability Directive,[63] the Medical Device Regulation,[64] the *In Vitro* Diagnostic Medical Devices Regulation,[65] the Health Technology Assessment Regulation[66] and European Health Data Space.[67]

DIGITAL MENTAL HEALTH

14.38 The MHRA governs digital mental health technologies (DMHTs). This is where the product is an SaMD for mental health services, and is intended to be used for medical purposes and the functionality is complex, rather than a simple non-complex device. There can, however, become a gap in the regulation where

59 https://www.nice.org.uk/corporate/ecd7.

60 https://www.nice.org.uk/corporate/ecd7/chapter/how-to-meet-the-standards.

61 European Commission: Directorate-General for Health and Food Safety, PwC, EEIG and Open Evidence, Study on the deployment of AI in healthcare – Final report, Publications Office of the European Union, 2025, https://data.europa.eu/doi/10.2875/2169577.

62 Regulation (EU) 2024/1689.

63 Regulation (EU) 2024/2853.

64 Regulation (EU) 2017/745.

65 Regulation (EU) 2017/746.

66 Regulation (EU) 2021/2282.

67 Regulation (EU) 2025/327.

the technology is not considered to be a medical device, instead a lifestyle device, which can be confusing in the context of digital mental health devices.[68]

14.39 In January 2026, as part of an ongoing effort and collaboration with other organisations such as NHS England and Mind, the MHRA published guidance for mental health technology.[69] This resulted from an ongoing partnership between the MHRA and NICE, funded by Wellcome, and which has been tasked to look at the regulation and governance of mental health technologies, both direct to consumer and for use by medical practitioners.

HEALTH AND CLIMATE CHANGE

14.40 Climate change and health are intrinsically linked. The impact of climate change is already being seen in increased health crises, whether this is from global warming, more detrimental insects such as mosquitos or increased extreme weather events. The World Economic Forum calls on innovators to help solve this issue[70] and believes that it will be Industry 4.0 technologies which will help drive this change, predicting that using technology could reduce the impact of climate related issues on health by 3.6% by 2050.[71] It also considers that climate data should be tracked against health as well to manage this issue effectively, that there is the need for more harmonised international policies and regulations,[72] and that innovations should be designed as 'climate resilient', which should include both new drugs and infrastructure.

EMERGING TECHNOLOGY FOR TRAINING

14.41 The emerging technologies of Industry 4.0 provide a significant opportunity for training in medicine and healthcare. Virtual reality and augmented reality present a significant opportunity for training, as do digital twins; meaning that trainee surgeons no longer have to wait now for a patient requiring a specific operation to be able to practice a procedure and to analyse the outcome.[73] AI, either within a metaverse environment or on its own, is being used in various ways within medical education; from personalising learning to simulating 'virtual patients' that trainee care providers can practice on as part of their training.[74]

68 G. Hopkin et al (2025), 'Building robust, proportionate, and timely approaches to regulation and evaluation of digital mental health technologies', The Lancet Digital Health, 7(1): E89–93, https://www.thelancet.com/journals/landig/article/PIIS2589-7500(24)00215-2/fulltext.

69 https://www.gov.uk/government/news/mhra-issues-new-guidance-for-people-using-mental-health-apps-and-technologies

70 https://reports.weforum.org/docs/WEF_Healthcare_in_a_Changing_Climate_2025.pdf.

71 Ibid.

72 Including on both the regulation and approval of drugs, as well as data protection regulations.

73 L. Asciak et al (2025), 'Digital twin assisted surgery, concept, opportunities, and challenges', NPJ Digital Medicine, https://www.nature.com/articles/s41746-024-01413-0.

74 Y. Ning et al (2025), 'How can artificial intelligence transform the training of medical students and physicians', The Lancet Digital Health, 7(10): 100900.

14.42 There are, however, still concerns with the use of AI within medical education, including its current unreliability, the issue of bias, privacy concerns. It is still important that human teachers remain actively involved monitoring the training being provided.[75]

DIGITAL TWINS IN HEALTHCARE

14.43 Digital twins are being adopted in healthcare as a form of personalised medicine. These use data obtained from a specific patient through sensors[76] and create a 'patient-in-silico', with continuous real-time data updates.[77] Digital twins have been used to assist in surgery, and even to create a complete 'Digital Human Twin'.[78]

14.44 With the adoption of a 'personal digital twin' comes many legal considerations including those deeply rooted in human rights and data privacy, as well as intellectual property rights and medical liability.[79] In most cases, the digital twin will be considered a medical device requiring regulation by the MHRA; however, given the novelty of this technology, there are inherent risks in respect of its regulation, especially for use in surgical interventions.[80] It is essential that there is a suitable legal framework and grounding in place, as medicine and the use cases for digital twins evolve.[81]

14.45 Digital twins in healthcare for example present more complex challenges than in industry generally, since the data is typically sensitive data based on the human actor involved, so are more complex to acquire, calibrate and track. There are also numerous ethical considerations concerning the use of digital twins in medicine, including the extent to which patients can properly consent to the extraction and use of their sensitive and confidential data.[82]

14.46 With the increased use of digital twins we will start to see new types of specialists becoming involved in medical treatment, such as data analysists and cyber-security experts, and a 'stepping back' by other professionals where technology means that their intervention, such as surgeons, may not be necessary in some aspects of the pre-treatment, treatment and post-treatment work; and other health professionals could be utilised instead.[83] Further complexities arise where the digital twins are used as part of a wider procedure, perhaps as part of the

75 Ibid.
76 Termed 'Internet of Medical Things' or IoMT.
77 C. Sadée et al (2025), 'Medical digital twins: enabling precision medicine and medical artificial intelligence', The Lancet Digital Health, 7(7): 100864.
78 Asciak et al (n 73).
79 Teller (n 13).
80 Asciak et al (n 73).
81 Teller (n 13).
82 Asciak et al (n 73).
83 https://futureofsurgery.rcseng.ac.uk/report/Future%20of%20Surgery%20Report.pdf.

exploratory or preparatory work prior to surgery, or to train autonomous robotics by 'closing the loop' or be combined with AI as post-operative monitoring.[84] This has an impact on liability, and therefore it is essential to ensure that it is clear who is responsible for what within the process.

14.47 Concerns have been raised previously by the Royal College of Surgeons of England that surgical innovations typically have less trial data or evidence than new drug testing, and that steps therefore need to be taken to strengthen the pathways for the introductions of these types of innovations, which should be trialled and tested on a case-by-case basis, in collaboration between regulators, such as the MHRA, and professional bodies such as the Royal College of Surgeons, centrally registered, and monitored via patient tracking and with longer term tracking via searchable databases.[85]

DRONES AND AUTONOMOUS VEHICLES

14.48 Drones and autonomous vehicles are being used for medical logistics, such as transporting medicines, blood and even organs. The World Economic Forum has been looking at how drones can help with medical logistics for some time. In 2021, it explored the use of drones for medical logistics in Rwanda and Ghana.[86] Further, it undertook a case study in Saudi Arabia, with the involvement of the Saudi Ministry of Health, using drones to transport blood during Hajj in June to July 2023.[87] This study showed how drones could assist with medical logistics and facilitate more responsiveness, especially at times of high demand and events including for the 2034 FIFA World Cup.[88]

PHARMACY

14.49 The digital revolution taking hold in the life sciences and the pharmaceutical industry is termed 'Pharma 4.0™',[89] which in 2017 was trade marked by the international Society for Pharmaceutical Engineers (ISPE).[90] Standards organisations such as the ISPE are looking to produce an effective standards framework for Phara 4.0.

84 Asciak et al (n 73).

85 https://futureofsurgery.rcseng.ac.uk/report/Future%20of%20Surgery%20Report.pdf.

86 https://www.weforum.org/stories/2021/06/how-drones-in-cities-can-help-distribute-medical-supplies/.

87 https://reports.weforum.org/docs/WEF_Deployment_Pathways_Advanced_Air_Mobility_2025.pdf.

88 Ibid.

89 https://ispe.org/initiatives/pharma-4.0

90 https://pharmasource.global/content/pharma-4-0-definition-benefits-and-how-to-implement-effectively/.

14.50 The Industry 4.0 technologies are being used to revolutionise the pharmaceutical industry, but are also being used for regulatory oversight and continuous monitoring.[91] The pharmaceutical industry is using smart factories to improve efficiencies, as well as sustainability.[92] Important considerations, however, are having to be had as to whether existing facilities are upgraded to smart facilities or whether new facilities are created.[93]

14.51 The Royal Pharmaceutical Society has confirmed that it supports the use of AI in the pharmacy sector provided this is done responsibly, with the involvement of pharmacists, that there are suitable governance and standards implemented and its use is done in accordance with the law and regulation.[94]

ROBOTS

14.52 Robotic technology can revolutionise health and social care, but there are ethical and legal considerations including human rights issues of autonomy, consent and privacy, data protection, the need for trust in medical professionals and bias.[95] Care robots, especially those used for vulnerable patients, can gain trust in a similar manner to real-life caregivers and therefore it is important to implement a suitable regulatory and ethical framework to safeguard privacy, confidentiality, and autonomy.[96]

14.53 As with other autonomous systems, questions also arise as to liability where personal care robots are used within the healthcare industry. There remain gaps in the regulation and laws concerning robots use within medical and healthcare settings, which was highlighted by the European Commission when considering the use of robotic exoskeletons.[97] In its resolution of 16 February 2017 concerning civil law rules on robotics,[98] the European Parliament calls on both personal care robots and AI to be designed to protect 'dignity, autonomy and self-determination' and it has created a Charter on Robotics which is annexed to the resolution.[99] The resolution does consider the idea as to where the liability of a robot should sit, which depends on the degree of autonomy of the robot, noting that currently liability sits with the human operator;[100] however, the

91 Ibid.
92 https://www.deloitte.com/us/en/Industries/life-sciences-health-care/blogs/health-care/smart-manufacturing-digital-supply-chains-may-help-pharma-boost-value.html.
93 https://www.pharmamanufacturing.com/production/article/33014823/pharmas-smart-factory-future-is-now.
94 https://www.rpharms.com/recognition/all-our-campaigns/policy-a-z/ai.
95 https://researchbriefings.files.parliament.uk/documents/POST-PN-0591/POST-PN-0591.pdf.
96 Valarie K. Blake (2020), 'Regulating care robots', Temple Law Review, 92(3): 551–594.
97 https://cordis.europa.eu/article/id/447687-laying-down-the-rules-for-safer-wearable-robots.
98 European Parliament resolution of 16 February 2017 with recommendation to the Commission on Civil Law Rules on Robotics (2015/2103) (INL) C252/239.
99 Ibid, Introduction (o).
100 European Parliament resolution of 16 February 2017 with recommendation to the Commission on Civil Law Rules on Robotics (2015/2103) (AD).

EU Parliament feels that current legislation needs adapting for certainty as the technology evolves.

14.54 Humans should not be fully replaced in caregiving.[101] The EU Parliament highlights that: health professionals must receive suitable education and training on medical robots;[102] suitable testing must be carried out on medical robotics;[103] ethics teams should be present in hospitals using robotics to repair or assist the functioning of damaged organs;[104] the suggestion that independent entities be created to deal with the maintenance and repair of the software;[105] consideration is needed about what happens if the system is 'hacked', especially if this is within the human body.[106] It also stressed the need for equity of access to the innovations.[107]

14.55 International standard ISO 13482:2014, set to be replaced in due course by ISO/CD 13482, is the benchmarking EU harmonised international technical standards on personal care robots, but does not cover robots as medical devices. Experts warn that whilst progressive, this regulation still causes a legal and ethical gap for devices designed for personal care, such as lower-limb exoskeletons, since the standard fails to comprehensively cover areas of risk other than physical risk with these devices, such as privacy, sustainability, gender differences, and network security concerns.[108]

KEY TAKEAWAY POINTS

14.56 The key takeaway points in respect of the industrial metaverse, healthcare and the pharmaceutical industry are:

- There are many digital innovations now revolutionising the medical sector. It is vital that these are properly regulated, with key legal safeguards around privacy, confidential information, and protection against harm.

101 Section 32 European Parliament resolution of 16 February 2017 with recommendation to the Commission on Civil Law Rules on Robotics (2015/2103).
102 Section 33 European Parliament resolution of 16 February 2017 with recommendation to the Commission on Civil Law Rules on Robotics (2015/2103).
103 Section 35 European Parliament resolution of 16 February 2017 with recommendation to the Commission on Civil Law Rules on Robotics (2015/2103).
104 Section 36 European Parliament resolution of 16 February 2017 with recommendation to the Commission on Civil Law Rules on Robotics (2015/2103).
105 Section 38 European Parliament resolution of 16 February 2017 with recommendation to the Commission on Civil Law Rules on Robotics (2015/2103).
106 Section 39 European Parliament resolution of 16 February 2017 with recommendation to the Commission on Civil Law Rules on Robotics (2015/2103).
107 Section 40 European Parliament resolution of 16 February 2017 with recommendation to the Commission on Civil Law Rules on Robotics (2015/2103).
108 E. Fosch-Villaronga et al (2023), 'How can ISO 13482:2014 account for the ethical and social considerations of robotic exoskeletons?', Technology in Society, 75: 102387.

- Ethics must not be sacrificed as we embark on the digital revolution. These include considerations around autonomy and consent.
- There is a distinction between the use of new technology for medical purposes or to assist with selfcare; regulatory lines should not be blurred and sufficient safeguards should be installed to properly categorise any product.
- Health data is a big issue. Steps are being taken to permit secondary uses of this data, such as to train AI systems; however, strict guardrails are needed to protect against harm and to avoid embedding historical bias within the systems.
- Like most sectors AI is revolutionising the healthcare sector. There is a need for international standards and expectations to avoid, amongst other harms, a widening digital divide.
- The National Commission has been established to advise the MHRA on AI regulation in healthcare.
- Changes to the Medical Devices (Post-market Surveillance Requirements) (Amendment) (Great Britain) Regulations 2024 deal with reporting requirements for software medical devices and cover indirect harms from poor results.
- The Good Machine Learning Practice principles are the efforts of a joint US-UK-Canda collaboration to establish guiding best practice principles for AI medical devices.

Chapter 15

Construction, smart cities and the industrial metaverse

'Cities are the solution-makers and testbeds of the future. Only by creating a joint trust-based framework can we realize the full potential of smart city technologies for the benefit of all mankind in the future.'[1]

Jan Vapaavuori, Mayor of Helsinki (2017–2021), Finland

15.1 The industrial metaverse is transforming the construction industry. From entire smart cities, connecting buildings, and digital infrastructure 'citiverses', to the use of virtual reality on building sites reducing site inspection times by 97%;[2] we are already seeing the digital revolution impact the design, build and construction industries. The way that buildings are being built is changing, but so too is the underlying energy, water, road networks and other infrastructure. For example, the Kawakami Dam in Mie Prefecture, Japan was built autonomously, using robotics such as remote-controlled cranes, resulting in reduced health and safety risks and a reduction in construction costs.[3] Changes are being made throughout the entire construction process, from the design stage, through completion, sale and asset management. For example, the Republic of Georgia has already started to move its whole land register onto the blockchain;[4] and digital twins are being used by asset managers, giving them real-time data in respect of a building without needing to inspect the physical site[5] and providing efficiency in identifying defects.[6]

15.2 We are at a pivotal time to embrace the technology, but we also need to ensure that laws, regulations and contracts are also reconsidered in light of these technologies to ensure that these remain relevant and fit for purpose in the Industry 4.0 landscape.

15.3 This chapter explores the use of Industry 4.0 technologies both within city infrastructure, and as part of individual building projects. There are many benefits of these technologies including being able to identify faults quicker and more cost effectively, vast safety improvements and a positive impact on the

1 https://www.weforum.org/impact/smart-cities-governance-alliance/.
2 https://assets.publishing.service.gov.uk/media/613b7b7fd3bf7f05b5a902db/IPA_TIP_Roadmap_to_2030_v6__1_.pdf.
3 https://www.water.go.jp/honsya/honsya/english/topics/2020/200707_kawakami.html.
4 https://unhabitat.org/sites/default/files/2022/06/playbook5_infrastructure_and_security.pdf.
5 https://www.uctoday.com/immersive-workplace-xr-tech/it-leadership-interview-inside-the-smart-building-revolution-digital-twins-at-work/.
6 Ibid.

environment. Yet there are also serious concerns around the impact on human rights, data protection and cyber security, as well as practical challenges such as interoperability and costs.[7] As with other real-life areas, which see the mix of traditional industry and emerging technologies, there is a need to clearly ascertain where liability sits if something goes wrong, whether this is part of a connected structure or smart city, or within a building project. It is important that the division of risk and liability is set out clearly within the building contracts and other contracts. As part of this discussion, it is vital that specialist insurers are brought into any project at the outset to ensure that all aspects of the project are comprehensively covered given the novel risks presented by embedding smart infrastructure into both individual buildings, complexes, and wider towns, cities and metropolises.

15.4 Finally, there is the need to address ethical issues relating to smart cities[8] and there is still a distinct lack of harmonised rules and regulations in this field, which, given the significant risks and huge sums involved should be rectified without delay.

CITIES AND INFRASTRUCTURE

Smart cities

15.5 Smart cities, sometimes called 'connected places' or 'future cities'[9] use the different emerging technologies of Industry 4.0 to reimagine urban infrastructure. This includes using technology to gain insights, learning and monitor issues such as waste management, housing and planning. The pinnacle of a smart city being the digital twin, of a building, infrastructure or even the entire municipality.

15.6 There are many opportunities and benefits associated with digital twins of cities. There is an acute need, however, for these to be properly regulated, with effective governance in place to protect against issues concerning privacy, data, cyber-security and intellectual property rights. We are already seeing digital twins in practice in Dublin, Rotterdam and Milan amongst others.[10]

15.7 The Alan Turing Institute is involved in the MX3D project,[11] which is a collaboration implementing digital twin technology into a 3D printed steel bridge in the Netherlands. This enables real-time monitoring of the use and condition of the bridge, using over 100 sensors, and which is being tested as a new method of bridge-building. To address privacy concerns in respect of the deployment of

7 https://build-up.ec.europa.eu/en/resources-and-tools/articles/overview-article-digital-transformation-built-environment-and-0.
8 https://unhabitat.org/sites/default/files/2024/12/un_smart_city_outlook.pdf.
9 https://researchbriefings.files.parliament.uk/documents/POST-PN-0656/POST-PN-0656.pdf.
10 https://eurocities.eu/latest/helping-cities-make-better-decisions-with-digital-twins/.
11 https://www.turing.ac.uk/about-us/impact/bridging-gap-between-physical-and-digital.

videos on the bridge the technology converts the bridge users into stick figures before it is analysed.

15.8 The Tallinn-Helsinki Dynamic Green Information Mode, known as the 'GreenTwins' is a project which includes plants and vegetation within the digital twins for Helsinki and Tallinn, and which can assess the changes to the vegetation caused by the changing seasons.[12]

15.9 Smart cities present unique challenges. The collection of an abundance of real-time data, such as via sensors located on public infrastructure like traffic lights or on public buildings, and its ongoing monitoring, present both legal and ethical challenges. There are concerns across the world about the lack of governance and policies in respect of smart cities, which have failed to keep pace with innovations.[13] In fact, a lack of governance, or a lack of comprehensive and effective governance in respect of smart cities is a reoccurring theme, and is an area which must be addressed.[14]

15.10 There is an acute need, for regulation and comprehensive laws on smart cities, at both a national and local level to catch up in this area, with the World Economic Forum cautioning that a lack of proper governance of smart cities presents a significant risk and calls for global rules for effective frameworks in this area,[15]. The UN has confirmed that only 36% of cities currently have artificial intelligence (AI) guidelines in place.[16]

Smart infrastructure

15.11 Coined by CSIS, the idea of 'smart infrastructure' is utilising emerging technologies with real-life infrastructure in order to assess and monitor infrastructure, where the data itself can become an asset and improve construction and construction techniques, asset management and building management.[17] There has, however been slow adoption of smart infrastructure in the UK, perhaps due to the existing building regulatory constraints, costs associated with the technology, the need to abide by strict timeframes in construction, the hype surrounding these technologies, lack of training and specifications; however, perhaps a call for collaboration between the different sectors of the built community can bring this into fruition.[18]

12 https://finestcentre.eu/project-pilot/greentwins/.
13 https://www3.weforum.org/docs/WEF_Governing_Smart_Cities_Use_Cases_for_Urban_Transformation_2023.pdf.
14 https://eurocities.eu/latest/helping-cities-make-better-decisions-with-digital-twins/.
15 https://www.weforum.org/impact/smart-cities-governance-alliance/.
16 https://unhabitat.org/sites/default/files/2025/02/international_guidelines_on_people_centred_smart_cities_10.02.25_shared.pdf.
17 https://www-smartinfrastructure.eng.cam.ac.uk/files/smart_infrastructure_bau_-_discussion_paper_-_final.pdf.
18 Ibid.

Amenities

15.12 Just as the buildings needs to be smart, so too does it amenities and infrastructure. Water-Boost is a World Economic Forum initiative in conjunction with Imperial College.[19] Many different emerging technologies have been used to try and deal with the issue of water supply, such as digital twins, AI and decentralised systems; however, dealing with the issue of water scarcity requires more than just innovation – it requires the infrastructure to allow for innovation to flourish, suitable policies, regulations, governance and infrastructures.[20]

15.13 The Digital Roads Prosperity Partnership is a University of Cambridge, National Highways, Costain Group and Didimi initiative, which is running until 2027 exploring the digitalisation of the road networks such as the use of digital twins, smart materials such as nanotechnologies and robotics within the road infrastructure.[21]

15.14 The industrial metaverse can be used for infrastructures such as roads, water and electricity. Digital twins can map out these infrastructures, with a view to enhancing these systems and reduce costs. The systems can be monitored remotely in real-time and where necessary action can be focused. Using augmented reality and smart glasses the systems can be mapped out and then monitored using digital twins and predictive maintenance.[22]

Governance of smart cities

15.15 It is imperative that smart cities have suitable governance in place which clearly sets out expectations, and sets standards to enable the public authorities to comply with their public law requirements. Globally, there is still a lack of policies, and ethical guidelines,[23] for the governance of smart cities, with the focus principally only being on data protection regulation in isolation.[24]

15.16 There is still a distinct lack of coordination between different policymakers in respect of the governance of smart cities.[25] Parliament, however, noted in its briefing that one complicating factor is that smart cities straddle different government departments, making it harder to create and then implement harmonised guidance on smart cities.[26]

19 https://reports.weforum.org/docs/WEF_Water_BOOST_Enabling_Innovation_for_Future_Ready_Cities_2025.pdf.
20 Ibid.
21 https://drf.eng.cam.ac.uk/digital-roads-prosperity-partnership.
22 https://www.iec.ch/basecamp/industrial-metaverse.
23 https://www3.weforum.org/docs/WEF_State_of_the_Connected_World_2023_Edition.pdf.
24 https://www3.weforum.org/docs/WEF_Governing_Smart_Cities_2021.pdf.
25 https://unhabitat.org/sites/default/files/2024/12/un_smart_city_outlook.pdf.
26 https://researchbriefings.files.parliament.uk/documents/POST-PN-0656/POST-PN-0656.pdf.

15.17 Where local councils are adopting smart systems within their cityscape infrastructure governance can be adapted to suit local requirements;[27] however, it is important that clear rules and powers are established for local authorities to ensure that citizens have transparency over their power and the ability to hold them to account if this is exceeded. The lack of certainty in respect of local authorities' powers over smart cities causes risk of harm to citizens. The OECD cautions that the use of AI within urban infrastructures is not a simple 'plug-and-play solution', instead there is the vital need for adaptive governance suitable for the use case being deployed.[28]

15.18 The central issues of governance of smart cities are (1) inclusiveness; (2) security (3) being clear and transparent (4) being interoperable; and (5) being sustainable.[29] It is also important that suitable ethical standards are adopted in respect of data and that there are legal protections in place in respect of personal data.[30] Effective data governance frameworks must promote autonomy, consent and inclusion, and must respects the core values of society, have suitable security, promotes data sovereignty and be trusted.[31]

15.19 Furthermore, it is important that standards and governance of smart cities, once adopted, are properly enforced otherwise this will cause serious failures,[32] discontent, and a lack of trust in the systems.

Steps forward

15.20 In 2019, the G20, in collaboration with the World Economic Forum established the Global Smart Cities Alliance. The Alliance has completed a number of important projects, such as the Smart Cities Policy Benchmarking Tool, which enables cities to self-assess their compliance and propose an action plan. The Alliance has developed seven model policies for governing smart cities, including those on open data, sustainability, cyber-security and privacy.[33]

15.21 In addition, some steps have been taken to try and address the idea of emerging technologies at a local authority level in the UK. For example, in 2023 London adopted its voluntary Emerging Technology Charter[34] which is an

27 https://unhabitat.org/sites/default/files/2022/06/wcr_2022.pdf.

28 https://www.oecd.org/content/dam/oecd/en/about/programmes/cfe/the-oecd-programme-on-smart-cities-and-inclusive-growth/Issues-Note-AI-for-advancing-smart-cities.pdf.

29 https://www.c4irsaudiarabia.org/project-details/smart-cities/a0sTG0000001SNFYA2.

30 https://unhabitat.org/sites/default/files/2026/02/digital_metropolis.pdf.

31 https://unhabitat.org/sites/default/files/2022/06/playbook5_infrastructure_and_security.pdf.

32 https://www.oecd.org/content/dam/oecd/en/about/programmes/cfe/the-oecd-programme-on-smart-cities-and-inclusive-growth/Issues-Note-AI-for-advancing-smart-cities.pdf.

33 https://www3.weforum.org/docs/WEF_Governing_Smart_Cities_Use_Cases_for_Urban_Transformation_2023.pdf.

34 https://www.london.gov.uk/publications/emerging-technology-charter-london#emerging-technology-charter-for-london-146697-title.

agile policy setting out the four principles for utilising technology in London, which are:

1. Principle 1 that London should be open and transparent about what is being used;
2. Principle 2 that diversity and human rights should be respected;
3. Principle 3 that personal data should be protected, with the systems embodying privacy by design; and
4. Principle 4 that that any system must be sustainable

'The built environment as a system of system'[35]

15.22 The vision for the built environment to 2030 is a collaboration between many key stakeholders including the Royal Institute of British Architects, the Health and Safety Executive, the National Digital Twin Programme, the University of Cambridge's Cambridge Centre for Smart Infrastructure and Construction (CSIS), which seeks to connect existing systems through digitalisation and view each different system, the building, nature and cyber-physical as connected using Industry 4.0 technologies of AI, digital twins and the Internet of Things (IoT).[36]

15.23 The vision calls for a shared strategy and policy. The Infrastructure and Projects Authority reported its Transforming Infrastructure Performance roadmap to 2030 to the Cabinet Office and HM Treasury in 2021. Its focus was on the use of data from the system and digitalisation, with 'digital-by-default' infrastructure and called for effective policies, using the UN Sustainable Development Goals (SDGs) as a basis for the desired societal outcomes, together with technology to increase productivity but also address climate change concerns through a flexible roadmap.[37]

15.24 The report calls on the effective use of digital twins in the built community, utilising and leveraging data about all aspects of the community, and suggesting the National Digital Twin Programme Information Management Framework and Gemini Principles, as discussed in **Chapter 4**, be utilised.[38]

35 https://www.visionforbuiltenvironment.com/wp-content/uploads/2023/06/Vision_090621.pdf.

36 Ibid.

37 https://assets.publishing.service.gov.uk/media/613b7b7fd3bf7f05b5a902db/IPA_TIP_Roadmap_to_2030_v6__1_.pdf.

38 Ibid.

UN-Habitat International Guidelines on People-centred Smart Cities

15.25 The UN-Habitat has developed International Guidelines on People-centred Smart Cities. These are voluntary standards for the design of national and local regulations and policies for smart cities, which were published in 2025.[39] These standards were mandated under United Nations Habitat Assembly of the United Nations Human Settlements Programme resolution HSP/HA.2/RES1, and requested by 193 countries.[40] This recognises the very real impact of smart cities on people and the need for the development of governance around the ethical use of emerging technology such as AI. They also show the need to implement suitable safeguards around privacy, cybersecurity measures, as well as provide suitable training and education.

15.26 The standards highlight the legal and regulatory gaps in transitioning to smart cities, and provide a framework for policymakers looking to implement smart city regulations. At the centre of all regulations must be that the city is human-centric, designed for its citizens, and the technology may be a driving force but not the purpose. The aim is for 'urban innovation… [that] … enhances the quality of life for all residents while addressing broader societal and environmental challenges'.[41] The UN-Habitat calls on the need to employ staff for the new roles which are being created and skills needed to oversee the changes to the system, as well as implement suitable infrastructure with effective cyber-security and protection against discrimination and bias.

15.27 The framework, as set out in Figure 15.1 divides the standards into eight themes, with the core principles being:

1. Equity: There should be shared prosperity for everyone. To achieve this there needs to be proper legal frameworks implemented which promotes inclusivity and, the proper allocation of resources and incentives.
2. Environmental sustainability: climate change, nature and the environment are key factors, which can be achieved through suitable infrastructure and disaster plans with the development of proper standards and regulations which promote positive environmental sustainability impact, with eco-friendly designs being promoted through incentives, procurement processes and investment.
3. Community engagement: it is imperative that the community are invested in the project through meaningful participation, transparency, active dialogues and collaboration. This can be achieved through regulatory guidelines.

39 https://unhabitat.org/international-guidelines-on-people-centred-smart-cities.
40 As noted in the General Assembly Resolution 77/211 of 15 December 2022 on 'the right to privacy in the digital age'.
41 https://unhabitat.org/sites/default/files/2025/02/international_guidelines_on_people_centred_smart_cities_10.02.25_shared.pdf.

4. Protection of human rights: this is important for the development of any smart city. This should be monitored with effective due diligence and steps taken to mitigate inequalities and the digital divide. This requires effective legislation to promote inclusivity and protect citizens, especially in respect of personal data and other issues caused by digitalisation including bias.

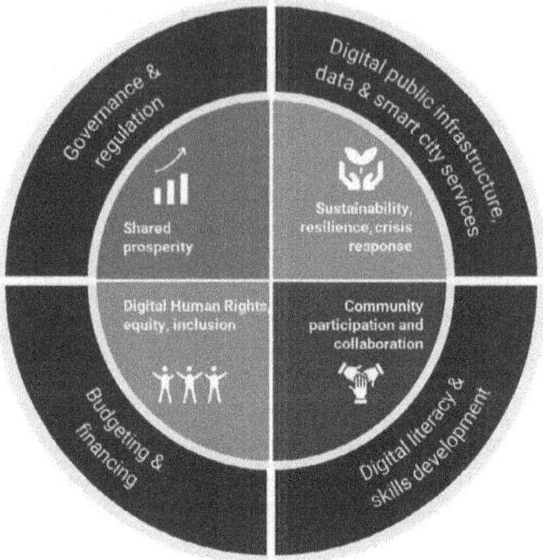

Source: UN-Habitat, 'A step-by-step guide for a "people-centred smart city strategy" (December 2025).[42] Reproduced with the kind permission of the UN-Habitat.

Figure 15.1 UN-Habitat International guidelines on People-centred Smart Cities standards framework

15.28 The UN does, however, recommend a flexible type of governance for smart cities, so to remain agile and respond to evolving technologies and applications[43] and considers that there are five connected phases to building a 'people centred' smart city. The first stage is laying the foundations, which require garnering public engagement; the second stage is assessing the readiness for the smart city, looking at the various stakeholders and assessing them; the third stage is developing the plan, including developing governance, procurement processes and establishing the policy frameworks; the fourth stage is implementing the smart city through initially piloting the operations and then building out the infrastructure and training staff; and the final stage is ongoing monitoring of the system by implementing regular feedback loops.[44]

42 https://unhabitat.org/sites/default/files/2025/02/international_guidelines_on_people_centred_smart_cities_10.02.25_shared.pdf.

43 https://unhabitat.org/sites/default/files/2026/02/digital_metropolis.pdf.

44 https://unhabitat.org/sites/default/files/2025/12/unitac_a_step_by_step_guide_for_a_people_centred_smart_city_strategy. pdf.

Artificial intelligence

15.29 There is an urgent need to establish governance of AI for cities. This requires the promotion of responsible AI use and the need to protect citizens in respect of their privacy, their human rights; and eliminate discrimination, bias, inequality and misinformation, by prioritising ethics, regulation, and recognising the different stakeholders and their different interests.[45]

15.30 There is a distinct lack of suitable AI governance within cities and at localised city-level, and a skills gap generally in respect of the use, understanding and deployment of AI.[46] There is the need for a detailed AI strategy which can be used to create the governance framework, supported by policies and a legislative framework which upholds ethics and societal values and helps mitigate the risks associated with AI within the city environment and with smart cities.[47]

Human rights

15.31 A key consideration of smart cities, and the digitalisation of urban environments, is human rights. These must be protected and smart cities must have the following foundations:

1. 'Equality, equity and inclusion;
2. Freedom, autonomy;
3. Privacy, safety, security and protection;
4. Community participation and public engagement;
5. Transparency and accountability;
6. Public goods, open infrastructure, and local public service provision'.[48]

15.32 There is a serious concern in respect of the digital divide in the move to smart infrastructure, cautioning that this divide is not only between nations but can also exist between different regions and also within communities.[49] The UN Sustainability Development Goals seek to embed human rights into cities generally; Goal 11 requires that smart cities be 'inclusive, safe, resilient and sustainable'.

45 https://unhabitat.org/sites/default/files/2025/11/global_assessment_of_responsible_ai_in_cities_24112025.pdf.
46 Ibid.
47 Ibid.
48 https://unhabitat.org/sites/default/files/2022/11/digital_rights_guide_web_version_14112022.pdf.
49 https://unhabitat.org/sites/default/files/2025/02/international_guidelines_on_people_centred_smart_cities_10.02.25_shared. pdf.

15.33 The UN-Habitat suggests tools to incorporate human rights into smart cities including having suitable data protection policies, implementing and installing proper inclusion, having transparency over decision-making decisions, allocating sufficient resources, allowing citizens to have control over their data and suitable education and protecting privacy as a fundamental human right with effective security and privacy by design.[50] Further it is vital that smart cities are designed to be sustainable and equitable, focused on protecting privacy, being accessible, being secure, being fair and equitable, having open standards, and with a view not to perpetuate existing inequalities and instead to focus on improving the lives of people given the risks that smart cities present to human rights and discrimination, and calls on aligning the design and implementation of smart cities infrastructure with SDGs goals, as discussed above at para **15.32**.[51]

15.34 Typically, smart cities use some form of surveillance and monitoring, usually in real-time and using facial recognition technologies, which presents challenges around privacy and bias. There are also significant issues concerning the digital divide, and where access to key resources and infrastructure may be impacted or limited as a result of the lack of access to the information. Misinformation is a serious issue for cities embracing Industry 4.0.[52] When selecting AI systems for use within smart cities procurement teams need to carry out extensive bias due diligence and audits on the data utilised within the system.

15.35 Eurocities is an initiative of over 200 European counties, which seeks to place the protection of human rights led by cities at the heart of the digital revolution, and call for both harmonised EU policies, and local rules and policies[53] with trust and transparency at its core.[54]

Discrimination and inclusive design

15.36 It is vital that smart cities are designed as accessible, and inclusive. In the UK, the Equality Act 2010 will apply. Smart cities should not be prohibitive for older people, nor those with disabilities.[55] Further innovation should not discriminate those that live in rural areas nor those that are unable to access the technology.[56]

50 https://unhabitat.org/sites/default/files/2022/11/digital_rights_guide_web_version_14112022.pdf.
51 https://unhabitat.org/sites/default/files/2022/06/playbook5_infrastructure_and_security.pdf.
52 https://eurocities.eu/latest/cities-step-up-to-rebuild-trust-in-the-digital-age/.
53 https://eurocities.eu/latest/eurocities-digital-forum-places-digital-rights-at-the-heart-of-cities/.
54 https://eurocities.eu/latest/cities-step-up-to-rebuild-trust-in-the-digital-age/.
55 https://www3.weforum.org/docs/WEF_ICT_Accessibility_Model_Policy_2023.pdf.
56 https://researchbriefings.files.parliament.uk/documents/POST-PN-0656/POST-PN-0656.pdf.

15.37 The Global Smart Cities Alliance has created the model Accessible ICT public procurement policy that cities can adopt.[57] It stipulates that the objective is to ensure that ICT maintained or provided by the city is accessible to everyone equally, and therefore smart cities should be designed intentionally with this in mind and that stakeholders should receive sufficient training and awareness of the importance of this objective.[58]

Privacy and data in smart cities

15.38 Privacy is one of the key concerns in respect of smart cities, yet globally many cities adopting smart technology fail to carry out privacy impact assessments[59] and many experience difficulties in trying to enforce data protection principles.[60]

15.39 Data fuels the digital revolution, and this is no different in respect of smart cities and connected infrastructure. There remains, however, a distinct lack of global legal frameworks on dealing with the exchange and sharing of data within smart cities, and this needs to be addressed as a priority principally in the areas of privacy, security, accountability, interoperability and data integrity.[61] Complicating factors in smart cities also arise in the mix of public and private organisations collecting data[62] and the problems of technological silos and concerns around intellectual property rights and trade secrets.[63] 'Private sector data' and 'public sector data' should be separated out, and there is the need to balance safeguarding individuals and business rights around privacy, trade secrets, intellectual property rights, against national security.[64] Trusted platforms and decentralised distributed ledgers such as blockchain should be used.[65]

15.40 Finally, it is important for cities to adopt AI data governance frameworks which deal with transparency, ethics, data protection and citizens' rights in respect of their data, as well as how training AI models use the data and security.[66]

57 https://www3.weforum.org/docs/WEF_ICT_Accessibility_Model_Policy_2023.pdf.
58 Ibid.
59 https://www3.weforum.org/docs/WEF_Governing_Smart_Cities_Use_Cases_for_Urban_Transformation_2023.pdf.
60 https://unhabitat.org/sites/default/files/2024/12/un_smart_city_outlook.pdf.
61 https://www3.weforum.org/docs/WEF_Unlocking_Shared_Value_Smart_City_Data_2022.pdf.
62 https://researchbriefings.files.parliament.uk/documents/POST-PN-0656/POST-PN-0656.pdf.
63 https://www3.weforum.org/docs/WEF_Unlocking_Shared_Value_Smart_City_Data_2022.pdf.
64 Ibid.
65 Ibid.
66 https://www.oecd.org/content/dam/oecd/en/about/programmes/cfe/the-oecd-programme-on-smart-cities-and-inclusive-growth/Issues-Note-AI-for-advancing-smart-cities.pdf.

Planning

15.41 The way in which people now think about properties, towns and cities has fundamentally changed because of the impact of emerging technologies such as smart buildings and use of AI.[67]

15.42 Towns and cities need to be built with technology in mind, especially the changing and evolution of technologies to ensure that these are sufficiently resilient. Infrastructure must be designed with cybersecurity in mind. This means that town planners need to be aware of the vital importance of protecting smart infrastructure and cities from cyber-threats.

15.43 The real-time data of smart cities is important for town planners as this can be used to continually improve the infrastructure. Some cities are already using dashboard controls and technology that can be used to improve sustainability and to improve well-being.

15.44 The UN New Urban Agenda was adopted under Resolution 71/256 of General Assembly on 23 December 2016[68] and looks at the way that cities are 'planned, designed, financed, developed, governed and managed'[69] and affirms the SDGs.[70]

15.45 The UN launched its Agenda to Action in 2025 as part of its monitoring of the New Urban Agenda. The UN New Urban Agenda[71] also makes a commitment to adopting smart cities that use the opportunities of the digital revolution for sustainability and economic growth,[72] and promotes the need to have equality for all, including accessibility to those with disabilities.[73]

15.46 The UN has also established the United Nations Innovation Technology Accelerator for Cities (UNITAC), which is based in Hamburg, and seeks to use the SDGs as a driver to trial and develop urban innovative solutions as a sandbox for new prototypes,[74] such as using AI to map settlements.[75]

67 World Economic Forum (2024), 'Reimagining Real Estate: A Framework for the Future' in collaboration with the C.H. Chen Institute for Global Real Estate Finance New York University Stern School of Business, https://reports.weforum.org/docs/WEF_Reimagining_Real_Estate_2024.pdf.

68 https://www.un.org/en/development/desa/population/migration/generalassembly/docs/globalcompact/A_RES_71_256.pdf.

69 Regulation 5.

70 Regulation 9.

71 UN General Assembly Resolution 71/256 adopted on 23 December 2016.

72 Article 66.

73 Article 36.

74 https://unitac.un.org/en.

75 https://unitac.un.org/en/BEAM_impact.

15.47 The UN-Habitat calls on planning laws to be adapted to deal with the use of emerging technologies, in particular the use of spatial technology and XR.[76] Its GeoAI Toolkit for urban planners acts as a blueprint for town planners in the advent of Industry 4.0, trying to balance buildings, infrastructure, administration and amenities in this landscape by using innovative tools such as geospatial AI which can assist with identifying and classifying land use, managing green spaces, monitoring infrastructure such as traffic systems, water management, waste management, and utilities such as hospitals.[77] It does, however, caution against the risk of 'black box' GeoAI where the data used to train the models may contain unknown bias.[78]

CONSTRUCTION

> 'Buildings are increasingly becoming more than just physical structures; they are evolving into smart, interconnected environments that use digital technologies to enhance functionality, efficiency and occupant experience ... This increasing reliance on digital infrastructure introduces a new set of risks that require careful management.'
>
> Paul Bagust, Principal Head of Professional Practice,
> Royal Institute of Chartered Surveyors[79]

Construction 4.0

15.48 The construction industry is set to be worth US$16.11 trillion by 2030, and will include a shift to smart construction or Construction 4.0.[80] The key Industry 4.0 technologies being adopted within the construction industry include Building Information Modelling (BIM), IoT, drones, 3D scanning, digital twins, AI, robotics, and XR.[81] The Institute of Chartered Engineers considers that these technologies are the future for engineering.[82] The Royal Institution of Chartered Surveyors (RICS) has looked at the use of smart contracts for building contract, which can record base costs and take into consideration fluctuations in price increases automatically and also have payments made automatically on

76 https://unhabitat.org/sites/default/files/2026/01/hlp_tool_series_vol_ii.pdf.
77 https://unhabitat.org/sites/default/files/2025/12/ai_for_spatial_mapping_and_analysis.pdf.
78 Ibid.
79 https://www.rics.org/content/dam/ricsglobal/documents/standards/Digital-risks-in-buildings-1st-edition.pdf.
80 https://build-up.ec.europa.eu/en/news-and-events/news/smart-construction-powers-global-growth.
81 https://build-up.ec.europa.eu/en/resources-and-tools/articles/overview-article-digital-transformation-built-environment-and-0.
82 https://www.ice.org.uk/news-views-insights/inside-infrastructure/types-of-digital-technology-shaping-engineering.

completion of agreed stages of work,[83] and also promotes the use of data-driven technologies such as AI by quantity surveyors to benchmark data.[84]

15.49 There are many environmental benefits of adopting Construction 4.0 methods, and the future of construction is in using existing products and materials, as part of the circular economy.[85] This is anticipated to reduce carbon emissions by 2050 by 75%.[86]

15.50 Construction 4.0 is promoted in the EU due to its positive environmental and sustainability impact, with 16 member states actively promoting the digitalisation of the construction section.[87] The EU published its Transition Pathway for Construction in 2023. The Pathway fits into the Digital Decade and the wider updated EU Industrial Strategy, under which the EU is preparing for the digital revolution of Industry 4.0. It is anticipated that the digitalisation of non-residential construction will save up to €1 trillion globally a year.[88]

15.51 There are, however, challenges with using technology such as digital twins in construction due to the lacking uniform standards, defective privacy standards, risks with accuracy, lack of integration and the significant costs involved.[89] In addition, there are serious security concerns that smart buildings could become the subject of cyber-attacks and be targeted to obtain sensitive or confidential information.[90] Further there is still a knowledge gap in respect of the risks associated with the digitalisation of the construction industry, the complexities caused by the fact that not all buildings are the same, with lots of different stakeholders and suppliers, the costs when something goes wrong with the real-life building assets in the construction sector and the need to coordinate the approach with multiple insurers.[91]

15.52 Given the fundamental changes to the industry caused by Industry 4.0, it is imperative that standards and codes of conduct are updated to reflect the same.[92]

83 https://www.rics.org/news-insights/wbef/a-smart-way-forward-for-construction-contracts.

84 RICS World Built Environment Forum (June 2023), 'Role and importance of data and technology in quantity surveying and cost management practice', https://glodon-en2021.oss-ap-southeast-1.aliyuncs.com/uploads/public/64a/391/5c2/64a3915c2fe2b944227127.pdf.

85 https://www.weforum.org/stories/2025/09/circular-economy-built-environment-future/.

86 https://www3.weforum.org/docs/White_paper_Circular_Economy_in_Cities_report_2018.pdf.

87 https://build-up.ec.europa.eu/en/resources-and-tools/articles/overview-article-digital-transformation-built-environment-and-0.

88 Ibid.

89 https://www.ube.ac.uk/whats-happening/articles/digital-twins/.

90 https://www.rics.org/content/dam/ricsglobal/documents/standards/Digital-risks-in-buildings-1st-edition.pdf.

91 Ibid.

92 Ibid.

Contracting

15.53 Care and attention is needed when a construction project is either utilising smart methods or incorporating emerging technology, whether this is a full digital twin or a connected infrastructure or a smart building. The Construction Playbook,[93] which deals with public procurements of public projects considers the idea of embedded emerging technology such as digital twins.

15.54 The guidance is from 2022, and there have been considerable advances in the technologies since this date; however, it does seek to promote the use of the Gemini Principles (discussed in **Chapter 4**) and the need to implement good standardised data information and security procedures.[94] Key aspects around liability and data must be clearly set out in any contracts. There are also intellectual property law considerations, which need to be reflected, and which diverge from traditional design and construction services since construction companies who invest significantly into this new technology will want to protect its intellectual property rights as will software providers.

15.55 The Royal Institute of Chartered Surveyors released practice information on digital risks in buildings in June 2025, which calls for the need to map out the different technology systems within a building to understand where liability and responsibility should reside,[95] as well as where these overlap, and to record where vulnerabilities exist such as unsupported software.[96] Further, it cautions that there is risk to the value of a building where it is not ready for the digital revolution, and that commercially, tenants will avoid properties which have not been sufficiently modernised.[97]

15.56 Going further, the Royal Institute of Chartered Surveyors cautions that given the pace of the changes, and the fundamental shifts as a result, construction contracts need to be checked to ensure that these remain relevant, especially to ascertain who may be responsible on a practical and legal basis where there be an issue arising in respect of the smart system. These issues are often overlooked as falling outside of the construction contract negotiations and are wrongly assumed to automatically fall under existing insurance policies.[98]

93 https://assets.publishing.service.gov.uk/media/6312222de90e075880923330/14.116_CO_Construction_Playbook_Web.pdf.

94 Ibid.

95 Which is not always straightforward.

96 https://www.rics.org/content/dam/ricsglobal/documents/standards/Digital-risks-in-buildings-1st-edition.pdf.

97 Ibid.

98 Ibid.

JCT

15.57 In his 2020 address at the JCT Povey Lecture, Doctor Damien Buie of Laing O'Rourke considered that standard contractual terms are limiting a move towards the adoption of emerging technologies in the construction field. He highlighted in particular restrictive provisions around the definition of 'confidential information', the desire of clients to own intellectual property outputs which limits the ability to use this data within emerging technologies such as AI and digital twins, payment terms which prioritise on-site work as opposed to work done offsite, and non-agile change management procedures which is not aligned to smart systems which provide real-time data that can be utilised to drive outcomes.[99]

BIM

15.58 In its 2020 publication on the digitalisation of the construction industry, RICS considered Building Information Modelling (BIM), and how it has been impacted by Industry 4.0. This is because the idea of BIM is itself a dynamic concept, provided this is done in accordance with industry standards BS EN ISO 19650 on information management.[100] BIM is technologically agnostic, and can be utilised with AI and XR technologies.[101]

Design

15.59 XR technology can be used in urban design and architecture to achieve the UN SDGs.[102] For example, people can use mixed reality to visualise redevelopments that are being proposed, and be inclusive in its approach, be transparent and engage local communities in their participation.[103]

Digital twins in construction

15.60 There are opportunities for the construction industry to utilise digital twins to provide continuity between each stage of the construction life cycle.[104] The digital twin will effectively become the trusted blue-print, preserving data from pre-build, throughout the build and different trades, to practical completion

99 http://corporate.jctltd.co.uk/wp-content/uploads/2020/11/JCT-Povey-Lecture-2020-Damien-Buie-FINALWEB.pdf.
100 https://www.rics.org/content/dam/ricsglobal/documents/standards/The-future-of-BIM_April-2023.pdf.
101 Ibid.
102 https://unhabitat.org/sites/default/files/2019/06/mixed_reality_2019_0.pdf.
103 Ibid.
104 https://www.digitaltwinconsortium.org/2021/01/the-impact-of-digital-twins-on-smart-buildings/.

and into the buildings use. Further digital twins can help with construction project budgeting and allocation of resources,[105] as well as safety on site and effective site handovers.[106]

15.61 Digital twins are touted as a good tool to try and mitigate some of the record-keeping issues identified at the Grenfell Tower inquiry. RICS promotes the benefits of their use from the outset of a construction project, from its initial design and then construction, especially in the context of the 'golden thread'.[107]

15.62 Digital twins in civil engineering generally can be used to achieve the UN SGDs, which include being able to assess factors impacting health, wellbeing and sustainability, including air quality, water and waste.[108]

15.63 It is not only new construction projects that can utilise digital twin technology, since digital twin technology is being retrofitted to existing infrastructure such as at Pollok Country Park in Glasgow where the plans anticipate a 34% reduction in carbon and forms part of the 2030 net zero carbon initiative.[109]

UK Building Safety Act 2022

15.64 There is now the need for the presence of a 'Golden Thread of information'[110] as part of information management on certain building projects involving higher-risk buildings under the Building Safety Act 2022.[111] The prescribed standards for such records are set out under regulation 7 of the Higher-Risk Buildings (Management of Safety Risks etc) (England) Regulations 2023 and include the need for such records to be accurate,[112] accessible as soon as reasonably practicable[113] and secure.[114]

15.65 The use of effective data within the infrastructure of constructions can help fulfil this requirement[115] and the use of digital twin technology can assist with the fulfilment of this.

105 https://www.ube.ac.uk/whats-happening/articles/digital-twins/.
106 https://www.rics.org/content/dam/ricsglobal/documents/research/digital-twins-from-design-to-handover-of-constructed-assets.pdf.
107 Ibid.
108 https://www.ice.org.uk/news-views-insights/inside-infrastructure/digital-twins-transforming-construction-industry.
109 https://www.iesve.com/pollok-country-park.
110 https://builduk.org/wp-content/uploads/2025/07/Golden-Thread-An-Overview.pdf.
111 Section 88.
112 Regulation 7(1)(b).
113 Regulation 7(1)(d).
114 Regulation 7(1)(e).
115 https://www-smartinfrastructure.eng.cam.ac.uk/files/smart_infrastructure_bau_-_discussion_paper_-_final.pdf.

Modern methods of construction

15.66 The term 'modern methods of construction' refers to construction methods which are considered to be quicker than traditional style building methods. Modern methods of construction, or MMC often uses technology within the construction process.[116] The cross industry working group on MMC defined it as 'a range of approaches which spans offsite, near site and onsite pre-manufacturing, process improvements and technology applications'[117] and includes additive manufacturing, drones, wearables, robots, XR and exoskeletons.[118]

15.67 MMC is synonymous with smart construction, although has also been associated with a number of negative connotations over the years, mostly linked with funding affordable low-quality housing. The use of MMC is often done off-site, which does have an impact on JCT and traditional building contracts where the assumption is that a bulk of the building work is done on site. Care is needed to ensure that building contracts accurate reflect any MMC utilised within the design and build stages.

3D printing and construction

15.68 3D printing or additive construction is expected to be worth US$680 million by 2030.[119] It has significant benefits within the construction industry, from helping to create parts of a structure to tooling using a range of materials including concrete, plastic and metal.[120] It is quick, flexible, low risk, cost effective and sustainable but there are concerns around the lack of regulation and guidelines on its use within the construction industry.[121]

15.69 One use of 3D printing has been to create low-cost housing solutions, such as the Building for Humanity Scheme in Lancashire which is using 3D printing to build houses for the homeless and low-income families.[122] 3D printing has been used to print facades using concrete, but there are still concerns around quality with the emerging technology.[123] ISO/ASTM standard 52939:2023 concerns additive manufacturing for construction.

116 https://www.weforum.org/stories/2025/09/how-modern-methods-of-construction-support-the-sdgs/.
117 https://lordslibrary.parliament.uk/modern-methods-of-construction-in-the-housing-industry/.
118 Ibid.
119 https://unhabitat.org/sites/default/files/2019/06/mixed_reality_2019_0.pdf.
120 Ibid.
121 https://www.cemexventures.com/3d-printing-in-construction/.
122 https://www.ribaj.com/intelligence/could-3d-printing-boost-housing-supply/.
123 https://www.ube.ac.uk/whats-happening/articles/3d-printing-construction/.

AI in construction and intelligent buildings

15.70 AI has considerable opportunity in helping to manage construction projects, from managing project costs and the supply chain, to managing the whole project.[124] There is, however, currently a lower-than-expected uptake within the construction industry, which could be due to lack of information or skills gap, or currently under-developed or achieving systems.[125] The lack of standards and regulations in this area, however, are not helping with mainstream adoption and the lack of certainty.[126]

15.71 RICS does caution that construction firms do need to recognise, and exploit, the potential that AI has in revolutionising safety, regulatory compliance and sustainability, but that it is vital to have in place suitable company policies to cover AI use.[127]

15.72 RICS released the first edition of its responsible use of AI in surveying practice, which is effective from 9 March 2026, as professional standards in respect of the use of AI by surveyors. The purpose of which is to balance the beneficial use of AI when used responsibly against its risk, and mitigation of these risks.[128] The standards promote the inclusion of a 'surveyor-in-the-loop', as well as effective policies, training, protection of data, the use of a written risk assessment, risk register updated quarterly, written registers of AI use and the documenting of the different liabilities of the people involved.[129]

Drones in construction

15.73 It is estimated that by 2030 there will be 76,000 drones being used within the construction industry for a multitude of purposes including surveying and inspections.[130] There are a number of benefits of using unmanned aerial vehicles within the construction industry, including the reduction in safety risks, speed, the ability to reach hard to reach areas, ability to obtain other data such as heat.[131] In addition, the drones can be used to extract data, and even be used to create

124 https://www.rics.org/news-insights/artificial-intelligence-in-construction-report.
125 Ibid.
126 Ibid.
127 https://www.rics.org/news-insights/artificial-intelligence-in-construction-report.
128 https://www.rics.org/content/dam/ricsglobal/documents/standards/Responsible-use-of-artificial-intelligence-in-surveying-practice_September-2025.pdf.
129 Ibid.
130 https://www.rics.org/content/dam/ricsglobal/documents/standards/The-future-of-BIM_April-2023.pdf.
131 https://www.ricsfirms.com/residential/moving-home/surveys/how-have-drones-impacted-building-surveying/.

digital twins.[132] There are, however, also risks around privacy, health and safety and cyber-attacks.[133]

Data

15.74 As in all sectors, data is vital in respect of the digitalisation of the construction sector; however, this data historically has been lacking and fragmented which has led to inefficiencies and higher costs in this sector.[134] As a result, the EU has introduced the idea of a Buildings Digital Logbook framework. This is a digital repository for key data in respect of a building, with the overall goal of promoting transparency and access to building data for interested stakeholders.

15.75 In the EU, the framework for Buildings Digital Logbook is important for the revised Energy Performance of Building's Directive.[135] We can expect to see licences and permits to become increasingly digital, which in turn will encourage greater uptake in digitalisation within the build environment.

Health and safety

15.76 Many of the emerging technologies of Industry 4.0 present opportunities to improve the health and safety of construction workers. One such opportunity is the use of wearable devices, such as exoskeletons which support the workers body in different ways as they carry out construction work, including helping with lifting and carrying heavy items, as well as wearables which can monitor compliance with safety standards and requirements.[136]

15.77 Concerns have been raised, however, that the use of these technologies may impact on the autonomy of the workers.[137] Further, the sensors will collect significant volumes of personal data, so it is imperative that proper provisions and safeguards are implemented.

132 Ibid.

133 https://www.rics.org/content/dam/ricsglobal/documents/to-be-sorted/drones-applications-and-compliance-for-surveyors-rics.pdf.

134 European Commission (2020), 'Definition of the Digital Building Logbook', https://op.europa.eu/en/publication-detail/-/publication/cacf9ee6-06ba-11eb-a511-01aa75ed71a1/language-en.

135 https://build-up.ec.europa.eu/en/resources-and-tools/articles/overview-article-digital-transformation-built-environment-and-0.

136 https://build-up.ec.europa.eu/en/resources-and-tools/articles/human-centric-innovation-and-skills-safety-construction.

137 Ibid.

Training

15.78 There is an acute need for proper upskilling of construction professionals in the skills needed for the industry post-digitalisation.[138] The EU in its 'Developing Digital Competency in the Built Environment' calls on the need to urgently ensure that those working in the construction sector are upskilled on digital skills.[139] In the EU there are initiatives already established to try and encourage training and upskilling of construction workers, including the Renovation Wave and Resilience and Recovery Facility.[140]

15.79 The Construction Leadership Council recognised the need to deliver the skills needed for the digitalisation of the industry, including new uses of off-site methods and embedded technologies since clients have an expectation that their constructions projects will include modern methods and be technologically advance (even if this is not necessarily expressly discussed nor they will not necessary be aware of these options and instead will rely on their contractors to advise and to innovate).[141] It further considers that there needs to be standard training and qualifications for upskilling and training workers on the use of emerging technologies in the construction sector and embracing innovation.[142]

15.80 There is likely to be the need for new roles such as data analysts within the sector[143] and RICS acknowledges that the role of chartered surveyors will change as a result of the digitalisation, but feels that this may increase diversity within the built environment industry.[144]

Data centres

15.81 Brief consideration is needed in respect of the building of data centres, given their importance in powering the digital revolution and are vital infrastructure for Industry 4.0 and the industrial metaverse. In the UK it is estimated that by 2035 data centres will generate an additional £44 billion for the UK economy, generate £9.7 billion in tax and generate 40,200 more jobs.[145]

138 https://build-up.ec.europa.eu/en/resources-and-tools/articles/overview-article-digital-transformation-built-environment-and-0.
139 https://build-up.ec.europa.eu/en/resources-and-tools/publications/developing-digital-competency-built-environment.
140 https://build-up.ec.europa.eu/en/resources-and-tools/articles/overview-article-digital-transformation-built-environment-and-0.
141 https://www.constructionleadershipcouncil.co.uk/wp-content/uploads/2021/03/B06322_CLC_SkillsPlan_v27.pdf.
142 Ibid.
143 https://www.rics.org/content/dam/ricsglobal/documents/standards/The-future-of-BIM_April-2023.pdf.
144 https://www.rics.org/news-insights/wbef/how-can-the-construction-workforce-benefit-from-industry-four-point-zero.
145 https://www.techuk.org/resource/techuk-report-foundations-for-the-future-how-data-centres-can-supercharge-uk-economic-growth.html.

In Spring 2026, there was over 500 data centres in the UK, with the majority of these in London[146] and the growth of data centres in the UK is being promoted by the Government.[147]

15.82 In themselves data centres are not separately regulated. They were, however, designated as Critical National Infrastructure in 2024 under the Network and Information System (NIS) Regulations 2018. Under this regulation they will be regulated by Ofcom. Concern also has to be had to climate change considerations such as the climate change levy, energy targets under the Climate Change Agreement, compliance with the UK GDPR and data protection regulations, and cyber security concerns as designated operators of essential services. The Climate Neutral Data Centre Pact is a voluntary initiative committing to environmental targets concerning principally energy use and water consumption.[148]

15.83 Data centres present a significant risk of being attacked or services being disrupted, whether physically being damaged, staff targeted or the supply chains infiltrated, or risks of cyber-attack. In 2022, the National Cyber Security Centre and the Centre for the Protection of National Infrastructure published guidance for data centres, which has been split into guidance for owners and guidance for users.[149] The guidance works from the starting position that you should expect that at one stage the data centre will be breached, and works back from that point. It advises looking at steps to try and mitigate the risk through effective risk assessment, protecting against foreign direct investment from hostile countries, suitable design,[150] effective building management systems, limiting the release of sensitive information publicly,[151] site security, suitable staff screening, monitoring and training, early detection and proper responses.[152]

15.84 There are also favourable planning regulations for data centres. The National Planning Policy Framework requires local authorities to consider the need for data centres when considering planning applications and there are fast-track planning routes for new AI data centres.[153] In addition, data centres are able to make an application under section 35 of the Planning Act 2008 using the descriptions under the Infrastructure Planning (Business or Commercial Projects) Regulations 2013 as an 'industrial process or processes' and 'research and development of products or processes'. Once in force, the draft statutory instrument Infrastructure Planning (Business or Commercial Projects)

146 https://www.datacentermap.com/united-kingdom/.

147 https://researchbriefings.files.parliament.uk/documents/CBP-10315/CBP-10315.pdf.

148 Ibid.

149 https://www.npsa.gov.uk/system-information-security/data-centre-security.

150 Considering the 'Build It Secure' guidance from the National Protective Security Authority (NPSA).

151 Such as not releasing sensitive information on planning portals but working with planning officials early to mitigate this risk.

152 https://www.npsa.gov.uk/system/files/documents/NPSA%20Data%20Centre%20Security%20-%20Guidance%20for%20Owners.pdf.

153 https://commonslibrary.parliament.uk/research-briefings/cbp-10315/.

(Amendment) Regulations 2026 will see data centres expressly permitted under section 35 of the Planning Act 2008.[154] In addition, the Government is currently considering further reform in respect of the delays data centres are experiencing in connecting to the National Grid, despite the reforms in November 2023 in the Connections Action Plan.[155]

KEY TAKEAWAY POINTS

15.85 The key takeaway points in respect of construction, smart cities and the industrial metaverse are:

- Smart cities present a number of legal considerations around privacy, human rights, transparency, discrimination and bias.
- There is a need for effective regulation of smart cities.
- The Global Smart Cities Alliance has developed model governance policies.
- The Infrastructure and Projects Authority's Transforming Infrastructure Performance roadmap to 2030 calls for 'digital-by-default' infrastructure with effective policies using the UN SDGs.
- The UN-Habitat has developed voluntary International Guidelines on People-centred Smart Cities.
- Effective contracting is essential in Construction 4.0. Existing frameworks such as the JCT contract present issues for both digital technology and MMC.
- Digital twin technology can help with establishing the 'Golden Thread of information' for higher-risk buildings under the Building Safety Act 2022.
- RICs has published its standards on the responsible use of AI in surveying practice, which is effective from 9 March 2026.
- Data centres have been designated as Critical National Infrastructure in 2024 under the Network and Information System (NIS) Regulations 2018. The National Cyber Security Centre and the Centre for the Protection of National Infrastructure have published guidance for data centres and their cybersecurity risks.
- Data centres have favourable planning regulations given their importance.

154 https://questions-statements.parliament.uk/written-statements/detail/2025-10-15/hcws966.
155 https://researchbriefings.files.parliament.uk/documents/CBP-10315/CBP-10315.pdf.

Chapter 16

Emerging legal challenges in Industry 4.0, legal strategies and the future of industry

> *'The Industrial Metaverse will be a place where we innovate at the speed of software. It will offer enormous potential to transform our economies and industries.'*
>
> Roland Busch, President and CEO of Siemens AG[1]

16.1 We are in the midst of an industrial revolution, and the technology is literally rewriting almost every aspect of life, work and society. If lawyers are going to be able to advise their clients, they need to understand the world that they are living and working in. Lawyers will need to do some of the 'heavy-lifting' as we transition into the fourth industrial revolution, to balance the benefits of these changes against the risks they present.[2]

16.2 We are now all staring down the barrel of quantum computing, which will completely revolutionise the way that everything works. It can quite literally break the internet as we know it. We have already seen a paradigm shift in the way that the internet works and is being used. It is not just lawyers of the future that need to be familiar with these technologies; it is the lawyers of here and now. These technologies are not futuristic sci-fi but, in some form or other these technologies are already being developed and deployed. We already have smart factories, smart hospitals, autonomous logistics, smart cities, and precision farming. If we learn nothing from the rate at which generative artificial intelligence (AI) has been adopted across industry, it is that the pace of adoption is rapid and will leave you behind if you let it.

16.3 Lawyers need to be able to understand the underlying technologies of Industry 4.0 to be able to advise their clients, understand the legal issues, and to be able to present materials in court.[3] There is currently a disconnect between how the technologists explain these technologies and what lawyers need to understand to be able to safeguard their clients, understand the legal

1 https://www.siemens.com/global/en/company/digital-transformation/industrial-metaverse.html.

2 Steven R. Smith (2023), 'The Fourth Industrial Revolution and Legal Education', GA ST U L REV, 39: 337 available at http://readingroom.law.gsu.edu/gsulr/vol39/iss2/9.

3 M.C. Buiten, L.A. Dennis and M. Schwammberger (2023), 'A Vision on What Explanations of Autonomous Systems are of Interest to Lawyers', paper presented at 2023 IEEE 31st International Requirements Engineering Conference Workshops (REW), 332–336, https://doi.org/10.1109/REW57809.2023.00062.

issues, interpret the legal position and present cases to court.[4] Lawyers, need to be able to understand and explain the system and how it works; the cause of any harm; and what the users understood in terms of the system.[5] No area of law can escape the technological revolution. All lawyers need to understand how these technologies are specifically impacting their area of law, and their clients.

16.4 Not only is the digital revolution pushing metaphorical frontiers, it is also pushing real-life frontiers through the modern space race lining up between Big Tech billionaires, Elon Musk with SpaceX, and Jeff Bezos with Blue Origin. The technological capabilities to achieve the innovations in space exploration are powered by the emerging technologies of Industry 4.0.

EDUCATION

16.5 Education needs to change to meet the needs of Industry 4.0, but the emerging technologies of Industry 4.0 can also revolutionise education.[6] The current education system is not suitable for preparing the future workforce for the changes that are being brought about, and will come about, as a result of the digital revolution.[7]

16.6 In order to take advantage of the benefits of the emerging technologies of Industry 4.0, it is vital to transform education so that students learn about the importance of data, and learn the relevant skills necessary for the new digital landscape.[8] There is also the risk that the digital divide will continue to expand.[9] Education systems need to evolve to reflect the changes brought about by the industrial revolution, and meet the demand for skills in big data, AI and cyber-security.[10]

16.7 It is important for governments to invest properly in the resources necessary for the education system to be able to teach these new skills. It may also be necessary to rethink the way in which education is delivered to accommodate the agility of emerging technology. There is the need for innovative learning, such as learning within virtual environments such as through 'digital sandboxes' or 'virtual labs', and the need for consideration about how skills can be assessed and benchmarked, which is likely to be a move towards practical based assessment.[11]

4 Ibid.
5 Ibid.
6 https://initiatives.weforum.org/reskilling-revolution/education-4-0.
7 https://reports.weforum.org/docs/WEF_New_Economy_Skills_2025.pdf.
8 Studies report that this is currently costing the economy £23 billion in growth opportunities, https://reports.weforum.org/docs/WEF_New_Economy_Skills_2025.pdf.
9 https://reports.weforum.org/docs/WEF_New_Economy_Skills_2025.pdf.
10 Ibid.
11 Ibid.

16.8 There is currently a skills gap[12] and there is the need for suitable investment to prepare people properly for the future workplace.[13] Standardised recognised relevant accreditations are needed across work and education and the need for 'a workforce that is fluent in AI, data and digital skills to deploy new technologies effectively'.[14]

16.9 Education across the board is needed, from primary education, all the way through to workplace education and upskilling. It is vital that this is addressed urgently to ensure that society is able to effectively embrace the digital revolution.

LEGAL EDUCATION

16.10 Legal education also needs to evolve to meet the demands of Industry 4.0 and beyond. Changes in the delivery and extent of legal education generally can be tracked alongside the main industrial revolutions.[15]

16.11 Given the advances in technology there will be a need for an increase sophistication in legal services.[16] We are already starting to see this with the shift in societal use of generative AI. This, however, is only part of the story. Generative AI is only one tiny sub-section of AI, there is much more to come. There are also many more inter-linked technologies in addition to AI needed to power the fourth industrial revolution, such as the Internet of Things (IOTs), which collect a vast amount of indiscriminate data, both personal and corporate, including highly sensitive trade secrets and proprietary data. Students need to develop core competencies, including the ability to analyse, make reasoned judgments, be ethical, emotionally intelligent and problem-solvers, whilst understanding global and cultural considerations, but as we embrace Industry 4.0 some of the traditional drafting skills may not be as fundamental.[17]

LAW FIRMS IN THE INDUSTRIAL METAVERSE

16.12 Law firms are not immune to the digital revolution. There are many different risks and opportunities with the emergence of these innovative technologies. We are already seeing the changes being brought about by lawyers' use of AI within their practices.

16.13 It is vital that law firms invest in upskilling their staff now to be able to adapt and embrace the digital revolution. This is not only about how to use the

12 Ibid.
13 Ibid.
14 Ibid.
15 Smith (n 2).
16 Smith (n 2).
17 Smith (n 2).

different technologies, but also to understand the real risks and challenges that they present not only on clients and their industries, but also on legal practice. We are already seeing clear warnings from the courts around the misuse of AI within legal practice, with reminders from the courts in various cases now[18] that use of AI can be a breach of regulatory obligations, may be a contempt of court and a breach of data protection regulations. The latest cases call for self-reporting to both regulators and the Information Commissioner's Office especially where free, commercial level, non-protected open-source AI is being used. In the USA, the courts have determined that client attorney privilege does not apply to AI generated documents.[19]

16.14 It is essential that law firms keep pace with technological changes and implement effective policies and procedures which protect their clients. Staff should be effectively supervised and it is essential that proper training is provided and insurance is in place. Considerations around the issue of confidentiality and privilege must be protected as we see the new emergence of these revolutionary technologies. Whilst we are starting to learn the lessons associated with AI, there are also risks and issues around other technologies. For example, the use of virtual reality and the metaverse to hold client conferences or court hearing presents issues around knowing who you are speaking with and verification of identity; the issue of quantum computing puts at risk safeguards and encryptions around sensitive data; the continuous monitoring of real-time data from IoTs can represent a security issue and leakage of confidential information; and use of deep fake technologies cast doubt even on who you may be liaising with and the providence of evidence.

16.15 Finally, it is important to keep abreast of the changes to key developments which may affect you across your whole career. This includes desires for judicial appointment, given the Judicial Appointments Commission has now announced that it will permit some limited use of AI within applications to the judiciary; however should such use fall within one of their prohibited uses then you will run the risk of exclusion from future office and even being referred to the regulator.[20] The messaging is very clear, the use of AI in a way which impacts on your integrity as a legal professional contravenes professional obligations and is likely to result in regulatory consequences.

LEGAL PRACTICE IN INDUSTRY 4.0

16.16 The Law Society has issued guidance for the responsible use of generative AI within legal practice. The Law Society highlights that the key

18 Such as in *UK and R (on the application of Munir) v Secretary of State for the Home Department* [2026] UKUT 00081 (IAC) and *R (on the application of Ayinde) v The London Borough of Haringey and Hamad Al-Haroun v Qatar National Bank QPSC and QNB Capital LLC* [2025] EWHC 1383.

19 *United States v Heppner* (2026) 25 Cr 503.

20 https://judicialappointments.gov.uk/corp-publication/the-jacs-artificial-intelligence-guidance/.

risks of the technology include intellectual property concerns, data protection issues, cybersecurity risks, concerns around the systems training on your data, bias, accuracy and reputational risk.[21] The Solicitors Regulation Authority has cautioned:

> 'We do … seek to create an environment within which firms can confidently take advantage of any technologies that will help them to deliver improved services to the public. At the same time, we work to ensure that public protection is maintained during the development and deployment of any new advance'.[22]

16.17 In July 2026, the UK Jurisdiction Taskforce, chaired by Sir Geoffrey Vos MR, considered liability for AI harms. Under this statement it explored the idea of professional negligence in the context of AI, which is relevant especially in the context of lawyers, who owe duties to their clients to act with reasonable skill and care.[23] The statement[24] highlights that: (1) the standard of 'reasonable skill and care' evolves as society evolves – therefore the use of AI (or non-use) today may be appropriate, but lawyers need to keep abreast of the changing standards of the profession; (2) effective due diligence must be conducted on any AI system to be deployed; (3) lawyers must understand the nature of the AI system being used – which doesn't necessarily require being a technical expert on the system, but at least knowing how it works. This is not necessarily straight-forward given the 'black box' effect, and the general misunderstandings concerning AI systems; (4) lawyers should be transparent about their use of AI to clients, although this alone is not sufficient to discharge their duty; (5) lawyers should be aware of the risk of breaching confidentiality through their use of AI; (6) the AI system must have been properly tested; and (7) there must be suitable human oversight.

16.18 Regard must also be had to the impact of technology on a lawyer's obligations to court and in dealing with court documents. In February 2026, the Civil Justice Council released its interim report and consultation on the use of AI for preparing court documents.[25] The report acknowledges that 'legal practice is changing as a result of these new and powerful tools'[26] but reminds practitioners of their regulatory obligations not to mislead the court. The proposals seek to attribute responsibility to the lawyer for documents where there is an identifiable lawyer with oversight of the document, for example, skeleton arguments and statements of case. With witness statements, the proposal flags the importance of these being in the words of the witness and these principles do seem at odds with the use of AI.

21 https://www.lawsociety.org.uk/topics/ai-and-lawtech/generative-ai-the-essentials.

22 https://www.sra.org.uk/sra/research-publications/artificial-intelligence-legal-market/.

23 The UK Jurisdiction Taskforce, 'Legal Statement on liability for AI harms' (July 2026), https://lawtechuk.io/ukjt/liability-for-ai-harms-under-the-private-law-of-england-and-wales/.

24 Ibid.

25 https://www.judiciary.uk/related-offices-and-bodies/advisory-bodies/cjc/current-work/use-of-ai-in-preparing-court-documents/.

26 Ibid.

16.19 In May 2026, the Law Society[27] responded to the Civil Justice Council's consultation, discussed at para **16.18** above, and called 'for urgent new guidance from the SRA and HMCTS'.[28] The Bar Council in its response also calls for new rules and policies.[29]

GOVERNANCE IN THE NEW INDUSTRIAL AGE

16.20 Just as the legal system and education system must react to the digital revolution, so must government itself. The UK Government's 'Blueprint for modern digital' sets the stage for these reforms and to deal with the changes caused by AI, and digitalisation.[30] The blueprint highlights that there is the need to prioritise making seismic changes in government and across public services to deal with digitalisation, including upskilling staff, changes to processes, policies and infrastructure, and that this all needs to be properly funded.[31]

16.21 To deal with 'a future where "digital" is not an add-on, an optional extra, or something that's outsourced: it is embedded. It is structural. And it is permanent',[32] the blueprint is a vision which establishes six priorities: (1) public sectors should be joined up; (2) use AI for good; (3) invest in the digital and data infrastructures; (4) focus on upskilling staff and leaders; (5) provide proper funding for innovation; and (6) implement transparency in respect of data.[33]

16.22 The Government has established the Government Digital Service (GDS), which is part of the Department for Science, Innovation and Technology. The GDS states that it 'is responsible for setting, leading and delivering the vision for a modern digital government'[34] by, amongst other functions, setting the Government's digital agenda and promoting AI for public good. It acknowledges that with regards to AI:

> 'Business-as-usual is not an option. Instead, government will need to be prepared to absorb some risk in the context of uncertainty. This will require a whole of government commitment, with senior and visible leadership and a relentless focus on driving progress. This is no small task. Nevertheless, the benefits are likely to be transformational, not just to support economic growth, but to people's lives across the whole of the UK'.[35]

27 Law Society, 'The Use of AI for Preparing Court Documents – Law Society response', 12 May 2026.
28 Ibid.
29 https://www.barcouncil.org.uk/static/bbb74182-4859-4a76-85b1e4b729b84489/Bar-Council-response-to-the-CJC-consultation-on-AI.pdf.
30 https://assets.publishing.service.gov.uk/media/678f6665f4ff8740d978864c/a-blueprint-for-modern-digital-government-web-optimised.pdf.
31 Ibid.
32 Ibid.
33 Ibid.
34 https://www.gov.uk/government/organisations/government-digital-service/about.
35 https://www.gov.uk/government/publications/ai-opportunities-action-plan/ai-opportunities-action-plan.

NEW RISKS

16.23 Whilst the adverse outcome of emerging technologies currently accounting for less than 1% of the current global risk, the risk of AI ranks in fifth place for long-term risks over the next 10 years, with misinformation in fourth place and cyber insecurities in eighth place.[36] The risk with AI, however, is one of the biggest changes in perceived risks between now and the next 10 years.[37] The risks from these technologies are increasing in the background, but are largely being unchecked.[38] These risks include the risks on jobs, the risk on skills,[39] and the misuse of the technology.[40] Whilst the risks of frontier technologies are considered as relatively lower risks over the next 10 years, being in 25th place, and supply chain disruptions in 26th place, this may be more reflective of the other global risks of extreme weather and the impacts of climate change ranking in the top half of the list for this period. Technological risks are still considered to be a higher risk over the next 10 years than today, and also present as perceived higher risks for those over 30 years old, rather than those of the younger generations.[41]

16.24 It is important to note, however, that industry 4.0 also impacts on defence, and the changes in international warfare. The Global Combat Air Programme is one such example of Industry 4.0, digitalising the defence sector in a collaboration between the UK, Japan and Italy. It utilises the digital supply chain and 'intelligent factories'.[42]Therefore, whilst the risks associated with frontier technologies in industry may be perceived as a lower risk for society over the next 10 years, the threats of unrest and international wars is considered a high risk.[43] The risk of wars, tensions and trade deals over critical raw materials, which are synonymous with Industry 4.0, the use of drones within international conflict disrupting critical infrastructure and water shortages, in parts caused by the drain on these resources as result of Industry 4.0 are all increasing.[44]

QUANTUM COMPUTING

16.25 Quantum computing is an emerging short-term and long-term global risk.[45] The rise of quantum technology will change the technological landscape, whilst organisations scramble to mitigate the risks and opportunities presented

36 https://reports.weforum.org/docs/WEF_Global_Risks_Report_2026.pdf.
37 Ibid.
38 Ibid.
39 And whether we will see a decline in our ability to perform tasks taken over by AI.
40 https://reports.weforum.org/docs/WEF_Global_Risks_Report_2026.pdf.
41 Ibid.
42 https://www.baesystems.com/en-uk/product/global-combat-air-programme.
43 Ibid.
44 Ibid.
45 https://reports.weforum.org/docs/WEF_Global_Risks_Report_2026.pdf.

by this technology (which includes the ability to 'crack' blockchain) as currently only 5% of organisations have suitable encryption in place for quantum.[46]

16.26 Benefits of quantum technology, however, include its use within health and medicine, such as for drug discoveries and precision medical diagnosis.[47] It will be fundamental for regulators and policy-makers to set clear ethical guidelines and laws on the use of quantum as early as possible, without which there is uncertainty for adopters which is likely to delay adoption given the seismic risks it presents.[48]

16.27 The Government published its National Quantum Strategy in 2023.[49] Under this strategy the UK is aiming to become a quantum-fuelled economy by 2033, and to do this, the goal is to help support quantum businesses and create an ecosystem which is conducive for growing innovative quantum businesses. The strategy stresses the importance of collaboration, which is one of the fundamental linchpins of Industry 4.0 generally itself, and a necessity to be able to lead on the regulation of quantum. The Government[50] again intends to focus on establishing national and international standards, but still respecting the need for any regulations to be agile and flexible.

16.28 In 2024, the Department for Science, Innovation and Technology published its paper on addressing those points raised by the Regulatory Horizons Council regarding regulating quantum.[51] It recognises that regulation is necessary for dealing with emerging technologies, but this again has to be balanced against fostering innovation. It was felt that it was still too early to look to legislate quantum technology, but that it is important that a close eye is kept on this emerging field to ensure that it is regulated at the most appropriate time.[52] The Government highlights that it needs to work with industry to ensure that regulating quantum is dealt with in a timely manner, and that the Digital Regulation Cooperation Forum should assist with this. In addition, international standards should be developed to set benchmarks for the technology.

16.29 The World Economic Forum published 'Governance Principles on Quantum Computing' in 2022.[53] It recognises that whilst it may be a new and advanced form of technology, some of the key principles are shared with traditional issues found in computing generally. The principles are split into

46 Ibid.
47 https://reports.weforum.org/docs/WEF_Quantum_Technologies_Strategic_Imperatives_for_Health_and_Healthcare_Leaders_2025.pdf.
48 Ibid.
49 https://assets.publishing.service.gov.uk/media/6411a602e90e0776996a4ade/national_quantum_strategy.pdf
50 Ibid.
51 https://www.gov.uk/government/publications/regulating-quantum-technology-applications-government-response-to-recommendations-made-by-the-regulatory-horizons-council/regulating-quantum-technology-applications-government-response-to-the-rhc.
52 Ibid.
53 https://www.weforum.org/publications/quantum-computing-governance-principles/.

seven core value and nine themes. Each theme is underpinned by the core values. The themes are identified as:

1. transformation;
2. widescale infrastructure access;
3. a collaborative and open approach to the technology;
4. responsible engagement and raising awareness of the technology;
5. a skilled work-force who are able to deal with quantum;
6. secure systems;
7. privacy;
8. promotion of standards; and
9. sustainability.

16.30 The seven core values are:

1. quantum computing should be used for good;
2. all stakeholders should be accountable for ensuring that the systems are not intentionally misused;
3. quantum should be inclusive;
4. quantum systems should be fair and equitable;
5. quantum should not put humans at the risk of harm;
6. systems should be accessible; and
7. transparency by stakeholders of the systems purpose and intent.

INDUSTRY 5.0 AND BEYOND

16.31 It is hard to try and draw any distinct lines between Industry 4.0 and Industry 5.0. It is, however, widely considered that the key features of Industry 5.0 will just be an evolution of Industry 4.0 but with an increased focus on sustainability and 'social fairness'.[54]

16.32 Either way, what is true, however, is that technologies continue to improve and evolve; and will continue to do so. Their evolution has a direct impact on society, and what was previously either technologically impossible or prohibitive because of its cost is now being opened up and accessible to many more people.

54 https://ieeexplore.ieee.org/document/10596039?denied=.

16.33 What we do know now, however, is that no one should be left behind in this industrial revolution. The digital divide, whatever the reason, is a fundamental concern and active steps must be taken to address this before this widens.[55]

16.34 It is in our hands to help shape the future. We are living through a significant industrial revolution, which will impact on all aspects of life. The law is reactive and must at some point react to these changes; this may be at a pace slower than hoped, but whether through legislation, case law or regulatory guidance and oversight we will see new harms have to be addressed, we will eventually settle on an accepted principle over where fault and liability should sit and what are normal practices and expectation within the new industrial landscape. Until then we have history and legal principles to help guide us.

KEY TAKEAWAY POINTS

16.35 The key takeaway points in respect of the emerging legal challenges in Industry 4.0, legal strategies and the future of industry are:

- Legal practice is being impacted by the digital revolution. Care needs to be taken to understand the impact of these emerging technologies not only on clients and the law, but on the practice of law itself.
- Education, and legal education must adapt to the industrial metaverse. Those skills that cannot be replaced by technology must be honed, and preserved. We must train our future workforce to be able to thrive in the new digital landscape, and upskill existing members so that no one is left behind.
- The Government itself must adapt to Industry 4.0 and the changes in society.
- Quantum computing has the propensity to change everything. This technology can literally break the internet as we know it. Everyone needs to start to prepare for these changes, through investment in technology, effective policies and good horizon scanning.
- Emerging technologies, and their continued evolution, present a significant ongoing risk to society and it is imperative that effective governance is implemented.

55 https://www.un.org/en/un75/impact-digital-technologies.

Index

[*all references are to paragraph number*]